"Finally, here is an authoritative, extensively documented book on what is *really* going on with terrorism today, and how it affects the decisions which national leaders make. It's about time we had this information in the public domain."

—Gregory Copley
Defense & Foreign Affairs **Strategic Policy**

D1311176

TARGET AMERICA & THE WEST

Terrorism Today

by
Yossef Bodansky

S.P.i.
BOOKS
A division of Shapolsky Publishers, Inc.

Target America

S.P.I. BOOKS
A division of Shapolsky Publishers, Inc.

Copyright © 1993 by Yossef Bodansky

Printed outside the U.S. under the title *Target, the West*

ISBN 1-56171-269-8

For any additional information, contact:

S.P.I. BOOKS/Shapolsky Publishers, Inc.
136 West 22nd Street
New York, NY 10011
212/633-2022 / FAX 212/633-2123

Manuscript edited in part by Marc Cohen
Manufactured in the United States of America

10 9 8 7 6 5 4 3 2 1

To Lena, for making this book possible.

CONTENTS

INTRODUCTION
by Congressman Bill McCollum

The World Trade Center bombing has brought into sharp and dramatic focus what a select group of experts have been warning for years: that the United States is a prime target for terrorism by militant Islamist fundamentalists.

Although claiming to represent the true spirit of Islam, the militant fundamentalists are, in fact, a small and radical minority of Muslims. It is because of their extreme violence, not their numbers, that they constitute such a threat to all religions whether they be Muslims, Christians, Jews, Budhists and Hindus alike. One of the primary objectives of the Islamists is to prevent, at all costs, the modernization, liberalization and development of the Muslim world. Indeed, several Islamic countries are daily victims of Islamist terrorism. Their populations are repeatedly subjected to terror and violence in an effort to prevent them from practicing and realizing the true spirit of Islam, that of moderation and compassion.

Nevertheless, the World Trade Center tragedy must not be dismissed as an isolated incident committed by ''fringe'' elements. Rather, the attack must be seen as part of a wide-ranging Islamist low-intensity war that is aimed at destroying the values of peace and freedom which we all hold dear.

In order to effectively battle this type of warfare, we must first strive to understand which terrorist networks exist in America, how they operate and how they are funded. Additionally, we must examine whether countries such as Iran, Sudan and Syria are acting as sponsors of terrorist cells operating all over the world, including, now, in the United States.

Only by shining the bright light of truth on the links between terrorist acts committed in America and any possible state-sponsored terrorism will we as a nation be able to stop these acts at their source.

In the aftermath of the Cold War's conventional war threat, I believe such an in-depth critical examination of terrorist warfare is now in the vital national security interests of the United States of America.

In this regard, I know of no finer expert capable of unraveling and explaining the intricacies of U.S. and foreign terrorism than Yossef Bodansky. For more than four years, Yossef Bodansky has been Director of the House Republican Task Force on Terrorism and Unconventional Warfare, of which I am the Chairman. Mr. Bodansky's often controversial research reports have proved to be, unfortunately, all too accurate in predicting and assessing terrorist activities and threats against America and its allies. The Task Force on Terrorism has been an independent voice in alerting the U.S. Government to these threats. The Task Force has exposed numerous state-sponsored terrorist operations, including the counterfeiting of U.S. dollars by Iran and Syria and a vast range of worldwide terrorist activities.

This is why I believe it is vital that all Americans read Mr. Bodansky's book *Target America*, and become familiar with the nature of the terrorist threat and who is behind it. Mr. Bodansky's painstaking, diligent research illuminates the normally dark and obscure world of terrorism. It is only by publicly exposing this threat to America and through educating our citizens that we can stop the terrorists from carrying out their nefarious plans and protect our freedoms.

Bill McCollum (R.FL),
United States House of Representatives
Washington, D.C.
April, 1993

AUTHOR'S PREFACE

The explosion that shook the World Trade Center, and the rest of America, was only the beginning. The bombing in New York and the few terrorist operations that preceded it, (most of which had been interpreted as crimes), are but a prelude to an escalation in Islamist terrorism in the United States and Canada.

Islamist terrorism has embarked on a Holy War — *Jihad* — against the West, especially the United States, which is being waged primarily through international terrorism. Unlike past terrorist campaigns, the forthcoming *Jihad* will be waged on American soil, as well as in other political theaters throughout the world.

In assessing the extent of the terrorist threat facing the US, it should be emphasised that Islamist international terrorism is state controlled. The terrorist sponsoring states, led by Iran, Syria, and Sudan, consider international terrorism an indispensable instrument of state policy. They are determined to gain through the use of terrorism what they could not have achieved through any conventional means of diplomacy and international relations.

At present, the leaders in Tehran, Damascus, and Khartoum, are convinced that they must prevent, virtually at all cost, the emergence of a post-Cold War world order in which the US is the sole super-power and western democratic values dominate. The terrorist controlling states are determined to prevail in this fateful confrontation. The escalation of the terrorist campaign is their main weapon against the United States. Therefore, no effort and expense are being spared. This, of course, has a direct bearing on the intensity and magnitude of Islamist terror-ism in the US.

That Islamist terrorism operates in the US should not have come as a shock or surprise. The bombing of the World Trade Center was been a logical step in the unfolding of the grand strategy of the leaders of the Islamist trend, mainly in Tehran, Damascus, and Khartoum. This strategy has been in the mak-ing for several years, its objectives clearly stated. Ultimately, the implementation was only a question of time.

As of the summer of 1989, and even more so since the Gulf Crisis, a relatively obscure international network of the *HizbAllah* terorrists under tight Iranian and Syrian control have actively prepared for an escalatory surge of operations against the West, and specifically against America and Ameri-cans, including attacks inside the United States. In June 1989, Sayyid Hasan Nasrallah, a senior *HizbAllah* commander, an-nounced the launching of a "real war against the United States." Intense preparations for implementing this declara-tion of war took place over the next two years, and were even intensified in the aftermath of the Gulf Crisis.

In early 1992, there was a major leap forward in the Islamists' preparations for a terrorist campaign. The Armed Islamic Movement, popularly known as "the International Legion of Islam," was consolidated from among the ranks of the Muslim Brotherhood worldwide with their world center in Khartoum, Sudan. The leading terrorists are known as 'Af-ghans,' having been trained with the *mujahideen* in Pakistan, and, for some, having also fought in Afghanistan.

A joint elite force of the Islamist internal terrorism was established by Iran last summer from among the very best terrorists and networks of both the *HizbAllah* and the Armed Islamic Movement [AIM]. It is already poised to strike on behalf of the leaders in Tehran, Damascus, and Khartoum. Indeed, since the fall of 1992, there has been a marked escala-tion in Islamist terrorism, subversion and violence in such diverse countries as India, Pakistan, Israel, Egypt, Jordan, Algeria, Nigeria, Somalia, and many others. Despite the seemingly different circumstances and conditions of these incidents, they are not isolated cases that just happened simultaneously. In fact, they were the first incidents in the escalation in the Islamist *Jihad* against the Judeo-Christian world order.

The climax of this struggle will be a spate of terrorism throughout the West, and especially in the United States. Thus, the bombing of the World Trade Center was among the very first incidents signalling the beginning of the decisive phase of the Islamists' *Jihad*, when they take on America.

The magnitude of the threat should not be underestimated. Toward this end, the terrorist controlling states and their proteges have prepared for this escalation for several years. Consequently, highly professional and proficient Islamist terrorist cells and networks, already in place in the United States and Canada as well as in Western Europe are ready for such an escalation. These, the *HizbAllah* operational center in Lebanon, and the AIM operational centers in Sudan, Pakistan, and Afghanistan, are being reinforced by supplies and expert terrorists arriving from Iran, Syria and many other Islamic countries. An instrument of state policy, the *HizbAllah*-AIM terrorist system and its networks now await orders from Tehran before launching their next operations.

The Islamist terrorist, such as the *HizbAllah*'s, is popularly associated with odd individuals doing crazy things such as the smiling suicide driver crashing into the US Marines barracks in Beirut, the taking and holding of Western hostages, or a stern-faced Sheikh Fadlallah admonishing and threatening the West. The *HizbAllah*'s main hideaway and bastion in Beirut seems to be a place made possible only by the chaos and insanity of the Lebanese civil war. Indeed, *HizbAllah* terrorists are commonly known in French as "the lunatics of *Allah*."

The reality is very different. The *HizbAllah* is actually the cover name for a highly professional and well organized system of state-controlled international terrorism. Iran and Syria organized and continue to control these terrorists in order to affect world politics through irregular means when no other conventional process can deliver results. As such, the *HizbAllah*, directly and through its sub-entities known as Islamic Jihad and other obscure names, provides both Tehran and Damascus with vital services. Little wonder, therefore, that both tightly control the *HizbAllah*, and that the so-called "lunatics of *Allah*" are actually well disciplined, well- organized instruments of state-sponsored special operations.

This sophisticated terrorist system has been markedly expanded and reinforced in the 1990s with the consolidation of an Islamist regime in Khartoum, and, subsequently, the transformation of the Sudan into a bastion of terrorist sponsor-ship. Moreover, the decline of the war in Afghanistan enabled scores of 'Afghans' to redirect their attention and zeal to other Islamist causes, from Kashmir to Bosnia-Herzegovina, from Algeria to the United States and Canada. Sudan is thus rapidly transforming itself into an Iranian fiefdom and a major terrorist sponsoring state.

Islamist terrorism, in all its radicalism, extremism, and apparant lunacy, is actually controlled, sponsored, and supported by calculating states. This book is their real story.

Islamist terrorism is on the rise, reflecting the commitment of the controlling states to escalate their confrontation with the West, and expressing the growing despair, agitation, and rage of the Third World's masses. Contrary to popular impressions, it is far from declining. Such things as Iran's economic moderation under Hashemi-Rafsanjani, Syria's desire to get closer to the West in the aftermath of the collapse of the USSR, the failure of the terrorist campaign promised by Saddam Hussein, and the release of the last American and British hostages in Beirut in the fall of 1991 are often cited as an indication of the decline of militant Islam.

However, these are all instruments and means used by Iran,

Syria, and their allies to further their own interests and policies, rather than the essence of the strategic objectives that brought these states to use terrorism in the first palce. Thus, what the West sees as "little victories," such as the release of the hostages, are for both the controlling states and the Islamists techniques and means that outlived their usefulness. Once one method is exhausted, the terrorist masters and the perpetrators shift to other means and methods as needed.

An instrument of the grand strategy of Iran, Syria, Sudan, and their allies, Islamist terrorism has been activated in its current form to accomplish certain strategic objectives, most of which are still unrealized. For example, a distinct and frequently declared objective of the *HizbAllah* has been the eviction of the US, both as a political-military power and as the symbol of Western and Judeo-Christian values, from the Islamic World, and especially the Near East.

In the wake of the Gulf Crisis, Tehran, Damascus, and Khartoum are more committed to these objectives than ever before, considering the US prominence and presence a threat to their very existence. Therefore, they currently need drastic measures, such as international terrorism, even more than in the 1980s to develop irregular forms of confrontation to evict the US from the region and defeat it. Having witnessed what the US did to Iraq, the Islamist states would avoid direct confrontation with the US, putting even more emphasis on the seemingly deniable and indirect form of warfare — international terrorism.

Therefore, for as long as radical states, especially Muslim, feel threatened by the West, and as long as the disparity in both popular appeal and actual power between the Third World and the West continues to increase, there will be a distinct role for international terrorism in the radicals' political culture.

As for the perpetrators, the terrorists themselves, they are devout Islamists who genuinely believe in the Islamist cause and are wholly committed to furthering it. Islam is fatalistic and everything is ultimately determined by *Allah*. The Islamist terrorists KNOW that their objective will ultimately be realized through *Allah*'s Will. The belief in this inevitability can be compared to the belief in miracles. It is a profound commitment of the individual that is not affected by one's own temporary setbacks or the logic of others.

The terrorists of the *HizbAllah* and AIM are motivated by rage and the desire for revenge. Looking at the world around them, they are fully aware that only a cataclysmic event would change it in their favor, and that such an eventuality is highly unlikely. Therefore, in their desperation and fury, the Islamists are drawn into taking revenge against the Western world that has created such adverse conditions, furthering what they perceive to be the cause of Islam just a little bit in the process.

In the wake of the Gulf War, Arabs feel shamed and humiliated, and this is gradually being transformed into rage. Moreover, the Iranian warnings, throughout the 1980s, of the US hostility toward Arabs and Muslims were "confirmed" in the Gulf War by the fury of the air campaign and the magnitude of the damage. Consequently, a growing number of volunteers join the ranks of these who are eager and ready to kill and die for the Islamists' cause.

The Islamist awakening is the spearhead of a surge in the Third World where fundamental changes are occurring. The most important factor there is the emergence of radicalized, often Westernized (and often corrupt), local elites and a widespread popular sentiment for a return to original tribal, religious, or ethnic self-identities. A younger generation seeks to attain traditionalist goals using the most radical means and methods. In the dynamics of these indigenous trends lie the roots of another wave of terrorism aimed against the West, the agent of change, and especially against its pre-eminent symbol, America. This frustration and rage in the Third World combines with that of the Islamists to feed into the resurgence of international terrorism. But it cannot, and does not, do so unaided.

In analyzing Islamist terrorism, and most other Third World revolutionary and terrorist movements, a distinction should be made between the source of emotional commitments and the source of capabilities. In the Middle East, the socio-political process commonly called modernization brought about upheaval in society, confusion, exploitation and manipulation, leading ultimately to the agitation of individuals and a revolutionary reawakening of the masses. However, revolutionary zeal cannot automatically translate into effective militant, terrorist, or freedom fighter capabilities. Irrespective of one's commitment or dedication, individuals, especially in the Third World, lack virtually all the preconditions for a successful armed movement: from conspiratorial knowledge to technical aptitude, to the availability of weapons and explosives as well as funds.

It takes highly specialized expertise and immense assets to make an armed movement from a group of incited and despairing individuals. The coming together of several components constitute the key to an *effective* terrorist or revolutionary movement. An ideology that mobilizes masses and especially a young elite eager for both fighting and sacrifices is crucial. The young perpetrators must be guided by an older, mature leadership that personifies the ideology in whose name they kill and die. However, successful operations cannot be conducted without comprehensive conspiratorial and military knowledge as well as access to funds, weapons and explosives.

Finally, not a single irregular armed movement can survive, let alone operate, but for supporting states. Without safe havens and support a terrorist movement cannot function effectively in the modern world. The crucial significance of expertise and funds that only states can provide ultimately transforms any terrorist movement, irrespective of its original ideological characterization, into a state controlled entity. In the case of Islamist terrorism, the subservience of the *HizbAllah* to Iran and Syria, both practically and ideologically, is complete. The same can be said about the total control Iran and Sudan exercise over the myriad forces of AIM throughout the world.

Currently, international terrorism is characterized by extremely daring operations carried out by a what appear to be a fragmented myriad of groups — some long-standing and well-known, others new and unknown — acting in the name of indigenous and/or global causes. There is a growing use of organizational names that point to the members' ostensible ideological thrust rather than to their organizational identity and character. But this seemingly chaotic diversity of causes and perpetrators in fact conceals a tightly-bonded international terrorism system, visible in the growing convergence of their terminology.

The common element that cements all these diverse groups and causes, influencing them to the point of affecting their ideological conceptions of themselves, is the state control and support system without which international terrorism would not be possible. Without the technical and professional expertise provided by the controlling states, these scattered bands of would-be terrorists from dozens of remote and often backward corners of the world would not have been able to express their rage in spectacular operations in the heart of the world's most advanced countries.

Most young terrorists come from those segments of Third World societies that choose to withdraw into traditionalism at the expense of modern technical aptitude. They claim to act on behalf of the downtrodden and oppressed. Yet their overseas operations demonstrate mastery of complex technologies and sophisticated techniques as well as access to virtually unlimited funds. In fact, there exists a sophisticated, well-heeled and multi-layered system of states which, for their own varied reasons, facilitate, control, and support the vast network of organizations of all kinds which carry out international terrorist activities.

This fact must be emphatically understood: none of the rage of the Third World, and especially the Muslim World, could have been transformed into the sophisticated and lethal extremist violence the West is currently facing had it not been for the comprehensive support and funding provided to international terrorism by Iran, Syria, Sudan, and a myriad of allies and proxies. And despite the much-heralded recent changes in Eastern Europe and the Soviet Union, the death of Khomeini and the hope for more "moderate" successors such as Hashemi-Rafsanjani, Assad's apparent rallying to the US-sponsored peace process, the relative silence of Qaddafi and other seeming changes, behind the scenes these activities have not ceased. On the contrary, as noted above, preparations are now well underway to escalate the terrorist struggle and bring the battle to American soil.

Thus, during the 1980s, Iran and Syria brought the state control, sponsoring, and support of international terrorism to new heights. For ideological reasons, Iran first concentrated on Shi'ite terrorism, the *HizbAllah*, which is now in the forefront of Islamist terrorism. Syria has a long tradition of sponsoring radicals, primarily Palestinians, and providing them with high-levels of expertise. In Sudan, Iran accomplished a comparable feat with the Armed Islamic Movement within a remarkable short time.

Since the early 1980s, and even more so since the early 1990s, as a major component of the strategic alliance between Iran, Syria and Sudan, their respective terrorist systems have been unified, expanded, and consolidated into the world's most lethal system of international terrorism. Their declared primary objective is the US. This book is their story.

The objective of this book is to acquaint the reader with the Islamist terrorist system in the US, Canada, and the West as a whole. In order to fully comprehend the terrorist threat and capabilities in America, and the West, one should first understand the Islamist international terrorist system and the state control mechanism. The reader should also come to know some of the leaders of Islamist terrorism who rose to power and prominence while in the Middle East or Western Europe but now play a central role in sponsoring terrorism in the US. Only when one realizes where the Islamist terrorists are coming from, can one grasp the extent of their commitment and assess their capabilities.

The book is structured to lead the reader through these challenging and relatively unknown subjects.

The book starts with the basics. It defines what the Islamist terrorist system is. Islamist terrorism began expanding in the aftermath of Khomeini's rise to power. The *HizbAllah* was established and nurtured after the Iranian revolution, emerging as a major instrument of Tehran's export of the Revolution policy. The *HizbAllah* is uniquely important because it is the prototype of the current Islamist terrorist system. Moreover, its first achievements in Beirut in the early 1980s are still looked upon by the terrorist leaders as a proof of the effectiveness of terrorism as an instrument of state policy. The principles of car bomb making, as detonated in New York, are still based on lessons learned in Beirut.

The book then studies the mature Islamist terrorist system built by states during the 1980s, initially around the *HizbAllah* as the core. It is important to understand the motives of the Islamist terrorists, essentially the extent of their hatred for the US and the West, the extent of their determination to deliver death and destruction. The book looks at where the terrorists came from both in the Middle East and the hubs of the Muslim World. The background continues with a discussion of the ideology that mobilizes the Islamist terrorists, a key issue for an ideologically-religiously driven terrorist group that is as yet largely misunderstood. The book then provides a detailed survey of the Islamists' training infrastructure, especially in Iran, a survey that points out what the terrorists can actually do.

It is a study of their command and control system, of where it is run from and who makes the decisions, pointing out who gives the orders to deliver strikes against the West. The consolidation of the international terrorist system and the organization of joint operations are then explained.

The book then concentrates on the emergence and consolidation of the international Islamist terrorist capabilities in and against the West, including the US, that now threaten America. The Gulf Crisis was a major trauma for the Muslim World from which it is yet to emerge. Moreover, it was in the context of that crisis that the concept of using terrorism to punish the West was reaffirmed. Understanding why the anticipated terrorist campaign did not materialize is important to understanding of why the next campaign already works. Major improvements in the Islamist terrorist system have been incorporated in the aftermath of the Gulf War, directly affecting its effectiveness. Specific decisions on terrorist strategy were made in terrorist conferences in Tehran, especially in late 1991.

The subject next addressed is the emergence of the new Armed Islamist Movement and its integration into the state controlled Islamist system. The rise of Sudan and the terrorist training capabilities there are closely examined. Also studied is the consolidation of the leadership of Islamist terrorism derived from organizations affiliated with the Muslim Brotherhood. The role and importance of Sheikh Umar Abd-al-Rahman can be be understood in the context of this leadership. The rise of the 'Afghans' and their integration into the Islamist terrorist system is then explained. As shall be seen below, the 'Afghans' now provide some of the most dangerous terrorists on American soil. The book then surveys the latest developments and improvements in the terrorist training system, and shows what new systems are currently available for terrorists to use in the West.

The development of Islamist terrorism in Western Europe is most important for understanding of the terrorist threat in the

US and Canada. It is in Europe that the Islamist terrorist learned to operate in the sophisticated urban environment. The organization of the networks now pitted against the US was carefully studied and tested 'in action' in Europe before the lessons were implemented across the Atlantic. This book surveys the development of the Islamist terrorist networks in Europe. It provides detailed description and analysis of several terrorist operations, with attention paid to the lessons derived and implemented in America. The evolution of the organization, command and control mechanisms of the Islamist terrorist networks in Western Europe is looked into in detail because the same process is now being implemented in the US and Canada. Similarly, the Islamists' manipulation and subversion of the Muslim emigre communities in Western Europe is examined. Finally, the beginning and evolution of the Iranian secret assassination wars in western Europe, with the first shots of the American campaign already fired, are described in great detail.

With this knowledge of the background, the reader can fully realize the magnitude of the terrorist threat in the United States and Canada. The book first surveys the initial build-up of terrorist infrastructure in the US during the early 1980s and explains why, with so much terrorism in Europe and the Middle East, the US was largely spared. The Islamist takeover and reinforcement of the terrorist system in the US and Canada is then explained. Meanwhile, the terrorist controlling states embarked on a series of 'back door operations,' establishing relations with Latin American groups, ranging from terrorist organizations to drug lords. These relationships are being utilized against the US.

The Iranian-led strategy for an Islamist terrorist struggle against the US is then described in detail. The various types of terrorist networks and systems already operating in the US and Canada are then studied in great detail. The role of Sheikh Abd-al-Rahman in the terrorist machination is explained. Several terrorist operations in the United States, some largely unknown, others headline-grabbing, are described and reconstructed in great detail. They are presented in the context of their role in the overall evolution of Islamist terrorist capabilities in America, and the on-going shift into a major terrorist campaign.

Once the current terrorist preparations in Iran, Syria and Sudan, as well as the process of terrorist build-up in Western Europe, are compared with the state of the Islamist terrorist infrastructure in the US, it becomes self-evident that the Islamist terrorist system in America is already undergoing a major reinforcement that will lead into a major escalation in terrorism. The explosion in the World Trade Center in New York was, therefore, only the beginning.

Since this is such a dramatic and little-known subject, a note on sources and methodology may be useful:

This book is based on material researched and prepared for a far larger book also to be published by Shapolsky Publishers, which will be a definitive study of the entire Islamist terrorist system world wide, in the Middle East and Africa, as well as Europe and the United States.

The text is thoroughly source-noted. Whenever possible, published material is identified.

Ultimately, the book is based for the most part on extensive indigenous material, including a private collection of several thousand Middle Eastern, Iranian, Russian and European books, manuals and articles. In addition, the author draws on a unique private collection of primary sources developed over nearly two decades of intensive research. These include extensive interviews and communications with numerous emigres, defectors and otherwise involved individuals from Iran, Afghanistan, Pakistan, the Middle East, several countries of sub-Saharan Africa, Latin America, the former USSR, and Europe, plus original publications, documents and reports from these and other areas.

This wide range of sources constitutes a unique data base

for expert analysis regarding the conduct of terrorism, subversion, intervention and other involvement, combat operations and power projection capabilities, and other aspects of this problem.

I have been studying subversion, terrorism and unconventional warfare in the Third World for some twenty years. Over such a period one has the opportunity to absorb an extensive amount of material through reading and personal discussions. Ultimately, opinions and conclusions are formulated on the basis of protracted exposure to the topic in question in addition to the mere accumulation of data over such a long period.

Finally, the opinions expressed in this book are mine, and do not necessarily reflect the views of the members of the Republican Task Force on Terrorism and Unconventional Warfare, the U.S. Congress, or any other branch of the United States Government.

Yossef Bodansky,
Washington D.C.
May 1993

N.B. In order to preserve the spirit of the original text, all translations were made as precisely as possible. Excerpted text and quotes may, therefore, contain unaltered idioms and other specific and colloquial usages that may appear inappropriate. This linguistic roughness was maintained intentionally; it should not reflect poorly on the translator's facility with English or the fluidity of the original text.

CHAPTER 1

RADICAL ISLAM AGAINST THE U.S.

The Muslim World is at a historical crossroads. It has embarked on a fateful global *Jihad* (Holy War) against the West and its Judeo-Christian values. America is its primary target.

> We are at war. And our battle has only just begun. Our first victory will be one tract of land somewhere in the world that is under the complete rule of Islam. . . . Islam is moving across the earth . . . Nothing can stop it from spreading in Europe and America.[1]

These prophetic observations, made in the late 1970s by Sheikh Abd al-Qadir as-Sufi ad-Darqawi, a leading Islamic thinker in the United Kingdom, succinctly defined the Islamists' quandary. To their way of thinking the crisis of Islam they perceive will only be resolved through a violent confrontation with the West, particularly America, in which international terrorism will be the main weapon. There can be no compromise in this *Jihad* because, they argue, Islam cannot co-exist with the prevailing world order dominated by Judeo-Christian values.

The leading Iraqi Shi'ite scholar Ayatollah Muhammad Baqir al-Sadr emphasized that the contemporary world as shaped by the West — "others" he calls them — is unacceptable to Islam. It is incumbent upon the Muslim faithful to embark upon a fateful confrontation.

"The world as it is today is how others have shaped it," he explained. "We have two choices: either to accept it with submission, which means letting Islam die, or to destroy it, so that we can construct the world as Islam requires."[2]

Since the early 1980s, numerous terrorist acts have been committed throughout the Middle East, Western Europe and the United States in the name of this Islamist *Jihad*. These have not been the crazy deeds of a few ardent followers. Rather, they stem from the fundamentalist Islamists' analysis of the state of the world. Moreover, the terrorists themselves could not have operated in the West without their control by, and assistance from, terrorist-sponsoring states, of which Iran and Syria are the most dangerous.

BEGINNINGS

A simmering throughout the Muslim world reached its boiling point after the Ayatollah Khomeini came to power in Iran in February 1979. He delivered a potent message to the masses: that it was commendable and legitimate to aspire to return to Islam's roots and to reject the West. The new Iranian Constitution emphasized the pan-Islamic character of the Revolution. It stated that "all Muslims" constitute a "single nation"(*Ummah*) and that the regime was obliged "to devote unending efforts" to realize "the unity-oneness of the Islamic nation."[3] In this cataclysm there emerged an alternate reality for Muslims, the possibility that the *Ummah* could actually be achieved in the contemporary world. Since Islam does not recognize boundaries or statehood, for Tehran the export of the Islamic Revolution throughout the Muslim World was an internal problem of the *Ummah*. Iranian leaders openly stated that "Iran will export its revolution to all Islamic countries."[4]

There was no doubt in Tehran that America would resist the spread of the Islamic Revolution. Nevertheless, Khomeini was insistent upon Iran leading a global Islamic Revolution. On January 14, 1980, he presented his perception of the state of the world to a group of 120 Pakistani Army officers on a pilgrimage to the Iranian holy city of Qom: "We are at war against infidels. Take this message with you — I ask all Islamic nations, all Muslims, all Islamic armies and all heads of Islamic states to join the holy war. There are many enemies to be killed or destroyed. *Jihad* must triumph."[5]

By then, Iran was already implementing this *Jihad* by holding 52 Americans hostage, most of whom had been captured in the November 4, 1979 storming of the U.S. embassy in Tehran. Iranian agents and operatives were actively involved in inciting scores of riots and rebellions throughout the sheikdoms and emirates of the Persian Gulf. Tehran was offering substantial help to virtually any Islamic armed movement engaged in violence against Western or pro-Western targets.

Moreover, the Khomeini regime considered its involvement in revolutionary struggles abroad not only obligatory but vital to its very existence. Khomeini emphasized Iran's commitment to the spread of the Islamic Revolution in his New Year message on March 21, 1980:

> We must strive to export our revolution throughout the world, and must abandon all idea of not doing so, for not only does Islam refuse to recognize any difference between Muslim countries, it is the champion of all oppressed people. Moreover, all the powers are intent on destroying us, and if we remain surrounded in a closed circle, we shall certainly be defeated. We must make plain our stance toward the powers and the superpowers and demonstrate to them that, despite the arduous problems that burden us, our attitude to the world is dictated by our beliefs.[6]

The Shi'ites of Iran and Lebanon saw themselves as the vanguard of this struggle, launching an all-out *Jihad* to destroy the existing world order and political culture through international terrorism. From the very beginning, international terrorism was considered a legitimate instrument in Islam's war against the West. The Pakistani Brigadier S.M. Malik explained that the Koranic way of war is "infinitely supreme to and more effective'' than any other form of warfare because ''in Islam a war is fought for the cause of *Allah*'' and, therefore, all means and forms are justified and righteous. Terrorism, Malik argued, is the essence of the Islamic strategy for war:

> Terror struck into the hearts of the enemies is not only a means, it is the end in itself. Once a condition of terror into the opponent's heart is obtained hardly anything is left to be achieved. It is the point where the means and the end meet and merge. Terror is not a means of imposing decision upon the enemy; it is the decision we wish to impose upon him.[7]

Moreover, such a terroristic *Jihad*, explained Sheikh Mortaza Motahari, is the essence of Islam:

> Islam is the religion of agitation, revolution, blood, liberation and martyrdom.[8]

Thus, a relentless campaign of international terrorism, led by the Shi'ite clergy, was to be Iran's primary instrument in spreading a global Islamic revolution. Dedicated militant Islamic organizations would carry the message of Khomeini's Islam the world over. However, Iran lacked clandestine capabilities, and the first terrorist actions in this campaign were carried out in Western Europe with the help of, or even by, other organizations in the name of Iran.

Simultaneously, Tehran began a thorough effort to establish and consolidate a system of terrorist training, support and command and control for world-wide operations. The terrorist infrastructure that already existed in Lebanon, and Iran's own national military system, would serve as the foundation of the new Islamic revolutionary movement. Iran tried at first to build this system on its own but realized that, at least initially, it had to have the close cooperation of its allies. Tehran was determined, however, to take over virtually every anti-imperialist, revolutionary and terrorist movement in the world that emphasized Muslim and radical Third World values.

The Islamic Republic moved quickly to institutionalize its support for world revolution. In mid-1979 Tehran established "the Department for Islamic Liberation Organizations" dedicated to the export of the Islamic Revolution. The department came under the command of Muhammad Montazeri (a.k.a. Ayatollah Ringo because of his violent temper and his aggressive behavior), a veteran of clandestine activities and terrorist training. As one of his first activities, Montazeri travelled to Damascus and Beirut in December 1979 to confer with Syrian intelligence and military commanders as well as several Palestinian leaders, including Yassir Arafat, on the escalation of terrorist operations. On January 2, 1980 Montazeri called a press conference in Beirut to announce Iran's intention to send "volunteers" to fight Israel from Lebanon and to support a world liberation struggle.

(Montazeri was killed on June 28, 1981, in an explosion in Tehran.[9])

In the summer of 1980, Ayatollah Khomeini ordered a small group of trusted radical aids to formulate a terrorist policy and to organize an elite strike force enlisting the participation of the most dedicated Shi'ite militants and terrorists. Ayatollah Hussein Ali Montazeri, Khomeini's designated successor and Muhammad Montazeri's father, was nominated to oversee the organization of Iran's terrorist empire. This move alone demonstrated how important and central international terrorism is for Tehran. Ultimately, Hojat ol-Islam Ali Akbar Hashemi-Rafsanjani would take over control of Iran's international terrorist campaign as part of his bid for supreme power in Tehran.[10]

The practical organization and consolidation of Iran's international terrorist capabilities was entrusted to a committee under the command of Hojat-ol-Islam Fazl-Allah Mahalati, a former student of Khomeini, known as "the uncorruptible."[11] In the 1970s, Mahalati ran a terrorist training school in South

Yemen where he was assisted by East German and Bulgarian experts and trainers.[12] In Tehran, Mahalati was aided by two veteran professionals: Mustafa Chamran, the "father" of Islamic terrorism in North America, and Ali-Akbar Mohtashemi who, as Iran's ambassador to Damascus, would play a crucial role in establishing the Lebanese terrorist group *HizbAllah* and in conducting terrorist actions against U.S. targets. (Both Chamran and Mahalati were killed in air crashes during the Iran-Iraq War, in 1981 and 1985 respectively, and it would be up to Mohtashemi to complete the organization of Iran's impressive global terrorist system.)

Mahalati brought in two operatives experienced in international terrorism: Muhammad Montazeri, who had close ties to Syria and Lebanon, and Ayatollah Ali-Akbar Natiq-Nuri, who was close to Libya and knew Qaddafi himself. Mahalati also asked three Afghan Islamic militants and veterans of terrorist training in Lebanon, Jalaluddin Farsi, Hussein Forqani and Abdul-Karim Akhlaqi, to abandon their anti-Soviet *Jihad* in favor of an anti-American one.[13] Meanwhile, Javad Mansuri, a founder and the first commander of the Iranian Revolutionary Guard, was nominated in November 1980 as Deputy Foreign Minister in charge of "revolution exportation affairs" whose essence was "to transform every Iranian embassy abroad into an intelligence center and a base for exporting the revolution."[14]

By now, key members of the Iranian leadership already had very close relations with the Palestinian terrorist movement, especially the organizations sponsored by Syria and based in Lebanon. Among the many Iranians who received military and terrorist training from the Palestinians in Lebanon, mainly in Rashidiyah and Baalbaak, were several leaders of the Islamic Republic.[15,16]

Since 1973, militant supporters of Khomeini had had access to facilities near the as-Sayda Zaynab camp, not far from Damascus, which was used as the most important forward base in support of the Islamic Revolutionary movement.[17] With Syria's help, by the mid-1970s Lebanon became a cornerstone of the movement that would ultimately overthrow the Shah's government and install Khomeini in Tehran.[18] Many Iranian militants were trained in this area. *Harakat Amal*, the first Shi'ite militia in Leabanon, considered "moderate" when compared to the *HizbAllah*, was also running a network smuggling weapons and personnel into Iran since the mid-1970s. Lebanese Shi'ite militants took an active part in the Iranian Revolution, especially in the purging of the SAVAK, the Shah's secret police force.[19]

The training of Iranians in Palestinian camps in Lebanon increased significantly in the mid-1970s.[20] Altogether, the Palestinians and their Arab supporting states provided the Iranian revolution with a sizable force. In early 1979 Yassir Arafat and Hani al-Hassan claimed that the PLO had trained and equipped with AK-47s and other types of weapons "more than ten thousand anti-Shah guerrillas" in Lebanon.[21] The Iranians acknowledged that 6,000 troops of the *Pasdaran*, the Islamic Revolutionary Guards Corps (IRGC) of Iran, were trained in Lebanon before the revolution.[22] Arafat claimed that Iranians trained by *al-Fatah*, the main military wing of the Palestine Liberation Organization (PLO), were responsible for the fires and the "greatest sabotage" in Tehran and other cities during the revolution.[23] Similarly, Bassam Abu-Sharief explained that the PFLP (the Popular Front for the Liberation of Palestine, a left-wing radical terrorist organization under the command of George Habash, sponsored by Syria) trained Iranian revolutionaries "in everything from propaganda to the use of weapons."[24] In late 1979, Ahmad Jibril pointed out that "we (the PFLP-GC — the Popular Front for the Liberation of Palestine-General Command, a left-wing radical terrorist organization under Jibril's command, an extremist group that broke with the PFLP, sponsored by Syria and Iran) have been in touch with Iranian activists since 1970. We have trained tens of

their leaders, giving them arms and experience."[25]   Jibril
attributes the close cooperation between the PFLP-GC and
Tehran to the legacy of this cooperation in the struggle against
the Shah.[26]

It soon became clear Iran would need the cooperation of
Libya and Syria to establish its international terrorist system.
Mahalati, Muhammad Montazeri and Natiq-Nuri held lengthy
discussions in Damascus and Tripoli in order to establish
lasting and intimate working relations at the highest levels of
government. Ayatollah Montazeri determined that the Shi'ite
character of the Islamic Revolution should not prevent close
cooperation with messianic Sunnis like Qaddafi, pro-Soviets
like Assad, as well as the participation of revolutionary Christians such as George Ibrahim Abdallah and his LARF (Lebanese Armed Revolutionary Faction, a Syrian-dominated and
Iranian sponsored small elite terrorist group that operated in
Western Europe during the early 1980s) or Varoudjian
Garabedjian and his ASALA (the Armenian Secret Army for
the Liberation of Armenia, a left-wing radical terrorist organization, sponsored by Syria and Iran), as long as they were
supported directly by Iran and Syria. Consequently, a Grand
Alliance of Terrorists was formulated by Iran in mid-1981.
"The Supreme Council of the Islamic Revolution" was founded
in Tehran in September and assigned "to coordinate terrorist
actions in the Near East and Europe" under Sayyid Mehdi
Hashemi.

Earlier, on February 11, 1981 the second anniversary of the
Islamic Revolution, Khomeini inaugurated the first international training camp of his embryonic terrorist empire. It was a
largely symbolic gesture aimed at emphasizing the oneness
and continuity of the two Islamic revolutions — the one that
brought Khomeini to power and the global Islamic Revolution,
or the export of the Iranian revolution).[27] Within a short time,
Iran would control a terrorist training infrastructure second
only to the USSR's.

Meanwhile, to gain access to expertise of states sponsoring

terrorism, Iran became a part of the emerging alliance of the world's radicals which would form the foundation of the new system of international terrorism. This group succeeded the alliance of progressive movements and terrorist organizations consolidated in the Baddawi conference in 1972. It was at this conference, held in the Baddawi refugee camp in Lebanon in May of 1972, that left-wing international terrorism was institutionalized. George Habbash chaired the conference. Participants included Palestinian commanders and representatives of various terrorist organizations from Europe and the Third World, as well as representatives from the Soviet and several Arab intelligence services.

A major aspect of the new system was the coordination of activities of the leading terrorist organizations and supporting states. Tehran had become convinced that it was crucial to cooperate with other radical states, irrespective of their ideological character, in order to intensify and improve its anti-U.S. campaign.

The origins of the current state-support system can be traced to The International Conference of the World Center for Resistance of Imperialism, Zionism, Racism, Reaction and Fascism organized by the Soviets and their allies in Tripoli, Libya, in mid-June 1982. Representatives from 240 organizations in 80 countries took part in this gathering. An executive committee was established by Libya, Iran, Syria, Cuba and Benin. (Soon afterwards, Benin was replaced by North Korea.) The head of the Cuban delegation was Manuel Piniero Losada, the head of the DGI's *Departmento de America* (the DGI Cuban Intelligence Service), which is essentially KGB-controlled.[28] The Cubans led a unified delegation of Central American revolutionaries and left a clear message among the leadership of the international terrorist movement. In preparation for, and during, the conference the Cubans clearly demonstrated their tight control over the other Central American and Caribbean Basin movements.[29]

In a subsequent speech in which he discussed the conference, Qaddafi praised all those revolutionaries "who are going to follow the Vietnamese and Nicaraguan precedents and destroy the bases of U.S. Fascism."[30]

Thus, Cuba, North Korea, Syria, Libya and Iran emerged from the Tripoli conference as the leading states actively supporting a world-wide terrorist struggle against the United States.[31] However, it was in Iran, the relative newcomer, that a training system which would revolutionize the capabilities of terrorists world-wide soon emerged.

THE TRAINING INFRASTRUCTURE

The terrorist training establishment in Iran is unique. Its objective is to transform zealots into terrorist machines. The Iranian terrorist experts concluded that only highly professional experts would be able to carry out lethal strikes against choice targets, especially in the U.S., Canada and Western Europe. The primary goal of the training camps became the selection of the most suitable candidates and transforming aspiring terrorists into professional operatives.

The Manzarieh camp in northern Tehran was Iran's first major terrorist training camp. The site was selected by Khomeini himself.[32] The lessons accumulated there helped shape the entire Iranian training system. The camp was opened in February 1981 under the command of Sheikh Abbas Golru, who had been a member of the Syrian controlled *al-Saiqa*, a Palestinian terrorist organization, in 1973-75. However, Golru had been not an operative but rather an expert in forging documents, and thus proved unsuitable for his responsibility. Although Mustafa Chamran was also directly involved in organizing the training program, he had failed to determine specific objectives by the time he died in an air crash. Consequently, the initial training program was confused, shifting between emphasis on basic military skills and ideological indoctrination. Initially, there were 175 hand-picked trainees in Manzarieh, including foreigners. Fewer than 150 of them graduated on 30 July 1981.[33]

Tehran realized that it would need the assistance of expert terrorists. Soon after he took office as chief of VEVAK (the Ministry of Intelligence and Internal Security), Ayatollah Muhammad Muhammadi-Reyshahri made the contacting of various radical Islamic terrorist movements in the Near East, and the pursuit of Iranian enemies in the West, priorities of the Ministry.[34] Soon afterwards, Golru was replaced by Nasser Kohladuz, a graduate of terrorist training by the Palestinians in Lebanon and a combat veteran with the IRGC (the Islamic Revolutionary Guards Corps of Iran, a.k.a. the *Pasadaran*). Kohladuz opened the Manzarieh camp to expert trainers from North Korea, Syria and radical Palestinian groups. The North Koreans sent 3 commando experts and a translator. The Syrians sent 9 officers from Rif'at Assad's security and commando forces. A large number of Palestinians were invited on the basis of personal knowledge of former Iranian trainees and colleagues.[35] Iranian experts also visited "commando and paratroop schools" in Libya in 1983 to study training techniques and preparedness methods.[36] A cadre of IRGC experts remained in Libya to acquire expertise in the terrorist training camps, taking part in instructing African recruits in assassination, sabotage and terrorist techniques.[37]

Meanwhile, in early 1982, the foreign experts were joined by some 300 Farsi-speaking KGB officers operating in Iranian uniforms. Their objective was to help the VEVAK "to exploit the Islamic Revolution to create chaos in the Arab world."[38] The relationship with the USSR was further strengthened when Tehran nominated Reyshahri, Mahalati, and Mussavi-Khoiniha (attorney general of the Islamic Republic) to a high level committee charged with maintaining close and continued relations with the KGB-GRU (the KGB was the Soviet Intelligence Service; the GRU was the Soviet Military Intelligence). Sessions were devoted to drawing up common strategies of intelligence, terrorism and subversion. All three Iranians had been trained by the Soviets and radical Palestinians. They were therefore known to the KGB and were inclined to expand cooperation with the USSR.[39]

During the organization of the training system in the early 1980s, Iran continued to train Muslim terrorists. Thousands of militants underwent "intensive training" in Iran.[40] Those from Middle East countries received three to six months of training in fighting and subversion.[41] By 1985 Hojat-ol-Islam Fazl-Allah Mahalati had 15-18 operational terrorist training centers and schools where recruits received commando training and intense indoctrination.

Thousands of Muslim youths from all over the world were centrally processed and then dispatched to training camps all over Iran. There was specialized training for suicide operations.[42] There was specialized training for female terrorists at the Beheshita camp in Karaj, west of Tehran, at which some 300 women, including American and Irish citizens, were taught under the command of Zahra Rahnevard, Mir-Hussein Mussavi's wife.[43] According to Cpt. Hamid Zomorrod, a defector from Iran, the Iranian terrorist training system prepared some 3,000 individuals for terrorist operations between 1981 and 1985. Many thousands of lower level terrorists were trained for operations on the Iran-Iraq front, in Iraq, in Lebanon and to support missions for the higher level terrorists.[44]

The Manzarieh Park camp in Tehran remained the largest and most diverse school, with some 900-1,000 "students" enrolled at any given time. The camp included training facilities for the "suicide unit." Since 1983, the camp has been under the command of Muhammad Shamkani. Arab terrorists, mainly from Iraq and the Persian Gulf sheikdoms and emirates, are provided military and paramilitary skills.[45] The trainees for suicide operations are given extensive Islamic indoctrination extolling the merits of death and martyrdom in the name of Khomeini's pan-Islamic revolution. They are exposed to long lectures and Qoranic readings on cassettes. The trainees must be psychologically conditioned before they are exposed to actual terrorist training.[46] At the end of the training, having passed rigorous examinations, the terrorists receive diplomas signed by Khomeini.

Sophisticated training installations with foreign experts then prepare the most devoted candidates for suicide operations. The primary center for the development of suicide techniques and the training of operatives was at the Marvdasht camp near Persepolis. Col. Ali Vesseghi of SAVAMA (the Iranian Intelligence Service, subordinated in the mid-1980s to the Ministry of Intelligence and Internal Security, VEVAK, and made responsible only for internal security, leaders' security, and fighting enemies of the regime) who served there until the spring of 1983, reported that the camp was manned by expert trainers from East Germany, Bulgaria, North Korea and Vietnam. The East Germans and the Bulgarians were responsible for the development of bombs, explosive charges and diversified detonators, as well as for preparing the technicians who would assemble the bombs on-site prior to the sabotage operation. The North Koreans and the Vietnamese turned their trainees "into death volunteers thanks to brain washing."[48]

Training techniques were developed in the early 1980s on prisoners condemned to death. According to Col. Vesseghi, the development phase concluded with a test in which one prisoner, who was brainwashed over the course of a month, drove a truck loaded with explosives through a complex course and crashed it head on into a brick wall. In a subsequent experiment, two prisoners drove their truck bombs straight into each other despite an explicit briefing to avoid a collision. "They now had proof," Vesseghi recounted, "that a well-trained kamikaze could no longer be stopped in his mission, even by his own teachers."

The volunteer trainees were present during these tests and demonstrations. "Far from being horrified by what they saw, my students in terrorism were fascinated, thrilled by this new form of human sacrifice. They also wanted one day to give their lives for the Imam," concluded Col. Vesseghi. The training of the first group of volunteers from Iran and Lebanon started soon afterwards. They would not have to wait long for their operations in Beirut.[49]

Hushang Morteza'i, an experienced Iranian pilot, served as a flight instructor for the IRGC until 1983. He described another form of suicide bombings in which pilots crashed Pilatus PC-7 aircraft loaded with explosives into major targets and died like martyrs. The training of suicide pilots started in Busher air base in Iran in the early 1980s, with some 80 Pilatus PC-7 aircraft purchased from Switzerland. But the Iranian *Pasdaran* pilots were inexperienced, and several fatally crashed during low-altitude flying. Three aircraft crashed in fledgling operational sorties against Iraq. Therefore, Tehran decided to send experienced pilots, including Hushang Morteza'i, to the Won San air base in North Korea, where they would "be trained under the supervision of Korean instructors, known for their kamikaze flights" for one year.

In the mid-1980s, some of Iran's PC-7 suicide planes were ready for operations, based at the Dowshan Tappeh air base near Tehran. Their targets were the palaces of heads of state of the Gulf states. The pilots of this suicide squadron were graduates of the North Korean training program. *Pasdaran* pilots, who trained on PC-7s for suicide missions, were also based in the *Shahid* Chamran air base in Bushehr. Additional suicide pilots trained in North Korea were sent to Lebanon, where their intended targets were part of the U.S. 6th Fleet. By 1983, the IRGC suicide squadrons also included 25 Cessna TurboJets [sic], some 15 Falcon Jets and a few DC-3s.[50]

Among the highly specialized terrorist training facilities were some dedicated to narrow purposes. The training camp in Bandar Abbas prepared for irregular naval warfare such as ship-mining and underwater sabotage. The camp in Isfahan trained experts in the handling of sophisticated and unique explosives as well as advanced bomb-making techniques.[51] A highly specialized suicide training camp, staffed by Vietnamese and North Korean experts, was located in the Ghayour-Ali base near Ahwaz. Volunteers there are brainwashed and trained to become human bombs in Western cities. They are taught to carry on their persons diversified explosives ranging from suitcase-bombs, with 10-15 kilograms of explosives aimed at railroads and other forms of public transportation, to small charges of less than 1 kg of explosives concealed in their coats, to be exploded in the middle of crowded shopping centers and streets.[52]

For the disruption of aerial traffic in the West, from airport attacks to hijacking, Iran maintained two major installations for terrorist training. The first installation was established in Wakilabad near Mashhad. The entire Western-built airport was given over to the terrorist training program. The latest Western airport equipment was purchased and transferred to the training facility. Iran Air maintained a Boeing 707 and a Boeing 727 jet in the airport, and could send a Boeing 747 for special classes. There were several former Iran Air and Iranian Air Force pilots among the staff and students, including some who were trained in the United States.

According to a former trainee in Wakilabad, one of the exercises included having an Islamic *Jihad* detachment seize (or hijack) a transport aircraft. Then, trained air crews from among the terrorists would crash the airliner with its passengers into a selected objective. Other exercises included the storming of terminals and parked aircraft for the capture of hostages and the inflicting of massive casualties.

The second installation was established in mid-1983 in the Shiraz airport. This academy provided students with a program of overall intelligence and sabotage training. For this training, Iran Air contributed an A300 Airbus, which was parked at the airport, so that the trainees could practice the storming and hijacking of real airplanes. The trainees also conducted exercises on the airport facilities.[53] Graduates of these schools took part in all the major hijackings during the 1980s.

One of the main objectives of the Iranian terrorist system was to launch daring operations in the West, especially in the United States. The Iranians and their allies were fully aware that such operations would require a comprehensive support system in place. Therefore, in the early 1980s, Tehran made active preparations for, and put special emphasis on, the long-term penetration and all over the world to achieve an operation capability.

A former Iranian intelligence official explained that thousands of secret agents were sent to settle as long-term plants, called submarines by the Iranians, in many American, European, Asian, and African cities. Many of these submarines were dispatched as students, workers, diplomats, employees of air, shipping, and transport agencies, etc. Nearly all of them are citizens of Muslim nations from Indonesia to Saudi Arabia, Muslims from Africa and Muslims from Argentina who are legal residents in their target countries. They are taught to seek citizenship of their new countries, if possible.[54]

The installing of submarines in the West was Tehran's ultimate priority. In several West European countries they were disguised as refugees and political asylum seekers. After initial success in Europe, the Iranians unleashed a "flood of refugees and escapees" from many Arab and Muslim countries to several West European countries, the United States, Canada, and Australia. These groups of submarines had undergone especially rigorous training and preparation before they were sent to the West, so that they could retain their loyalty to the Islamist cause despite the constant exposure to the high quality of life in the West, and especially the temptations of liberalism and secularity.[55]

A few of the first graduates of these training camps were captured by security authorities almost immediately. For example, the saboteurs captured in Morocco in the summer of 1983 were Moroccan Muslims who had received terrorist training in Iran in preparations for their sabotage tasks.[56] However, available data from defectors suggest that only a very small fraction of the deployed submarines were actually captured. The vast majority made it safely to their destinations where they are still waiting for further instructions to strike.

For example, a Lebanese Shi'ite in his early 20s, a former member of Islamic *Jihad* who received asylum in Denmark, provided data on his training for terrorist support tasks. His class in Iran had some 1,000 students from numerous countries. They were prepared meticulously to state their claim for political asylum convincingly so they would be in a position to get permanent residence papers, thus freeing them from the surveillance that existed for diplomats and officials. Subsequently, these submarines would disappear in the urban centers of America and Europe.[57] Moreover, in France, young progressive activists, veteran supporters of the Palestinian terrorist movement, continued to provide some services, possibly including weapons trafficking. They demonstrated active support for progressive movements and helped the absorption of Iranian-trained "refugees" from the Third World.[58]

FIRST BLOOD

Iran devoted the early 1980s to the establishment of a professional and comprehensive terrorist infrastructure. Expert terrorists were trained and a comprehensive support system was established. However, it was in Lebanon that the terrorist system sponsored by Iran, popularly known as the *HizbAllah* or *Islamic Jihad*, was first consolidated and proven in action against the U.S. The lessons of the success of the *HizbAllah* terrorist operations in Beirut served as a major lesson for preparing terrorist operations in the primary target countries, most notably the U.S.

Back in 1979-80, immediately after the Iranian revolution, many Lebanese Shi'ite clerics began travelling to Tehran where one of the first tasks of the SAVAMA was to recruit the most loyalist Shi'ite fighters in the Lebanese civil war and the Palestinian terrorist organizations. Tehran also convinced Sheikh Fadlallah, the most senior cleric in Lebanon (more on him below), to turn his 500 or so students and followers into the core of a future militant organization that would become the

HizbAllah.[59]

Meanwhile, the clashes in southern Lebanon intensified and several Shi'ite villages suffered from Israeli retaliations against Palestinian shelling.[60] In late 1981, Tehran began accelerating the build-up of terrorist capabilities in the Middle East in order to cope with the building tension between the Palestinian organizations, Syria and Israel. Anticipating a major escalation in the Middle East fighting, Syria and Iran began the construction of a military infrastructure to support terrorist operations in and from Lebanon. For example, in the spring of 1980 there were 170 Iranians in the Hamouriyah camp near Damascus alone.[61] In early 1982, the Iranian Revolutionary Guard Corps established their first major military base outside Iran in Zabadani in Syria.[62] Zabadani would become the main rear area deployment site for Iranians and Iran-trained terrorists for the entire Middle East.

On June 6, 1982, Israeli forces crossed the border into Lebanon and began a campaign that would ultimately destroy the bulk of the PLO-dominated terrorist infrastructure then existing in Lebanon. Iran immediately dispatched some 5,000 *Pasdaran* to Lebanon via Damascus in order "to assist the inhabitants of Lebanon" in their fight against Israel. Iranian Ambassador Ruhani emphasized that this deployment took place at the request of President Sarkis.[63] Some 1,000 of these *Pasdaran* joined the Syrian defenses in the Shouf mountains and fought quite well, if for a brief period.[64] The Syrian Armed Forces established a forward base for the IRGC in Yanta in the Biqaa.[65] After the fighting was over, some 500 Iranian fighters remained in Lebanon, establishing a "cultural unit" of the Revolutionary Guards.[66] Many Palestinian and Lebanese terrorists who survived the fighting rapidly regrouped in the Biqaa under the protection and control of the Syrian forces. Several organizations, from Abu Nidal's to the Libyans, to the Iranian *Pasdaran* and the Lebanese *Amal*, built camps in the Baalbak area.[67] In September 1982, Nayif Hawatimah declared the Biqaa the hub for the rejuvenation of the struggle against

Israel and the U.S. that would be conducted with Syrian support.[68]

The Shi'ites and their allies were supplied by an airlift from Iran via Damascus. Because of the large amounts of money and weapons they controlled, the Iranians became the core of a new terrorist system.[69] In November 1982, Tehran and Damascus moved to further increase their influence over the Palestinian forces in Lebanon. Muhammad Sheikh ol-Islam and Mohtashemi, senior Iranian officials, held high-level meetings in Damascus where "the sensitive issues of the region were reviewed"[70] in order to escalate the "joint struggle against imperialism and Zionism."[71] Sheikh ol-Islam then proceeded with follow-up negotiations in Libya, Algeria, the PDRY (People's Democratic Republic of Yemen, a.k.a. South Yemen) and the UAE (United Arab Emirates),[72] all but the last, centers of Palestinian terrorism.

The unfolding political crisis in Lebanon hastened the further radicalization of the Shi'ite terrorist movement. Influenced by the *Pasdaran*, commanders and activists rebelled against the Amal leadership.[73] It was not by accident that the three principal leaders of the "rebellion" — Sheikh Sayyid Ibrahim al-Amin, Hojjat ol-Islam Hussein Mussawi and Sheikh Raghib Harb — had just returned from consultations with Ayatollah Mahalati in Tehran. They would emerge as the leaders of the *HizbAllah*.[74] Meanwhile, the *Pasdaran* "continuously fanaticized the terrorists" gathering in the Baalbak area.[75] Iranian funds were used to recruit and sustain some 20% of *Harakat Amal*'s fighters and commanders, as well as Fadlallah's 500 students, who constituted the core of the fledgling *HizbAllah*.[76] The message of Islamic agitation spread all over Lebanon. A growing number of fighters and detachments left their organizations and began moving to the Iranian-controlled part of the Biqaa.

Those arriving in Baalbak included well-organized and combat-proven units. Most important was the Mughaniyah militia. It was under the command of Imad Mughaniyah (born

1952), till then an *al-Fatah* officer who had fought in southern Lebanon in 1982.[77] He also received specialized training under Mahmud al-Natur (Abu-Tayib) and served with Force 17, the PLO's elite intelligence and security unit.[78] Dissatisfied with the PLO's lack of fighting spirit, Imad Mughaniyah established a 150-man strong force, all of whom were Shi'ites from southern Lebanon. This force was under the oversight of Sheikh Ahmed Mahmud Mughaniyah, the leading cleric of the clan who had studied in Najaf while Khomeini was there. When the *Pasdaran* arrived in Lebanon, Sheikh Mughaniyah arranged an affiliation with the Iran-dominated *HizbAllah* and brought in the forces of Imad Mughaniyah.[79] In 1983, Imad Mughaniyah would be involved in the bombing of U.S. and French facilities as part of Hussein Mussawi's Islamic Amal organization.[80]

In November 1982, the Iranians consolidated their hold in the Biqaa with the active support of the Syrian military.[81] Hussein al-Mussawi and Subhi al-Tufayli immediately announced the establishment of an organization "directly connected with the Syrian command" and began recruiting local Shi'ites to the "Iranian Revolutionary Guards and *HizbAllah*." The recruitment announcement explained that these movements would be "working for the establishment of an Islamic republic in Lebanon and for spreading the Islamic Revolution to all Arab states."[82] In Tehran, Ali Khamenei applauded the attack and vowed that the *Pasdaran* would remain in Lebanon "for as long as Iran would think it necessary."[83] As of late 1982, entire *Pasdaran* units were arriving at the Biqaa through Syria.[84] They immediately began training the Shi'ite fighters of Sheikh Ibrahim al-Amin.[85] From the Biqaa, the Iranians moved into Beirut, establishing their own zones of influence. Syria actively supported the *Pasdaran* entry because it saw in the terrorist operations revenge for the defeat of 1982 when Israel, defending its northern border, invaded Lebanon in "Operation Peace for Galilee".[86]

Meanwhile, the continued radicalization of the Lebanese

Shi'ite population resulted in the sudden emergence of a myriad of small armed groups, usually gathered around religious and military personalities. Once the base area in the Baalbak was secured, Sheikh Fadlallah used his religious and moral authority, as well as control over the vast supplies of funds and weapons from Iran, to organize 13 Islamic terrorist movements (11 Shi'ite and 2 Sunni) into a confederation called *HizbAllah*. He tailored *HizbAllah* after the upper echelons of the Iranian leadership where a supreme religious authority is in command, though without any formal title, and all decisions are reached by a council of leading religious, military and financial leaders.[87] Among the key *HizbAllah* leaders were Mahdi Shams ad-Din, Muhammad Hussein Fadlallah, Sa'id Sha'ban, Subhi al-Tufayli, Ibrahim al-Amin, Muhammad Yassir Fanash, the brothers Muhammad Hussein Mussawi, Haydar Mussawi, and Abbas Mussawi, Na'im Qassin, Muhammad Ra'ad, Hajj Hussein Khalin and Hassan Nasrallah.[88] *HizbAllah* blossomed in the Biqaa through the summer of 1983 with the infusion of Iranian Revolutionary Guards and massive assistance from Iran and Syria.[89] Ultimately, it would take yet another year for the structure of the *HizbAllah* to stabilize in a practical form but, in mid-1982, the die was already cast.

The Shi'ite terrorist establishment as organized in *HizbAllah* could not have reached its current position without the leadership of Sheikh Sayyid Muhammad Hussein Fadlallah. Fadlallah was born in 1943-44 in Najaf, Iraq, to a family originating in south Lebanon. He studied in Najaf under Muhsin al-Hakim and Abu al-Qasim al-Kho'i who ordained him. He maintains very close relations with Tehran. Fadlallah rose to prominence only after the Iranian Revolution. Like Khomeini, he envisions the establishment of a pan-Arab pan-Islamic state as the only viable solution to the Palestinian problem. Fadlallah defines himself as the "ideological nucleus only" of *HizbAllah* who provides "inspiration to believers," and denies that he is the "leader of *HizbAllah*." Yet he has been involved in sectarian violence in Lebanon since 1975 and inspired the bombing of U.S., French and Israeli objectives in 1982. He is brilliant, and his two books, *Islam and the Concept of Power* and *Dialogue in the Koran*, are important foundations of militant Shi'ism. Like Khomeini, Fadlallah refuses any official title, although his authority is unquestionable. His statements in sermons and religious decrees are in essence political incitements concealed as religious preaching. Fadlallah provides the Islamic legitimization for the *HizbAllah* terrorist attacks:

> The weak peoples lack the technology and lethal weapons available to the United States and European countries. Therefore, they must fight with the means available to them. Why is it that what Muslims do in self-defense is seen as terror?! As oppressed peoples, we are entitled to consider all unconventional means to combat these tyrants. We see no terror in what weak Muslims are doing in the world with the primitive, unconventional means at their disposal. This is a legitimate war.[90]

With the increase of the *HizbAllah* and *Pasdaran* forces in Lebanon and Syria, Tehran and Damascus further institutionalized their cooperation and coordination. Ali Akbar Mohtashemi, now Iran's Ambassador to Damascus, was to oversee all the Iranian supported operations as well as the financing and supply of specialized weapons, mainly from Bulgaria. Syrian military intelligence under Gen. Ali Dubbah was to provide all the professional services and expertise.[91] Gen. Ali Dubbah maintained extremely close relations with the KGB and was considered "the Soviet Union's man in Syria."[92] He saw to it that KGB experts directed, assisted and supported the Lebanese network from the safety of the as-Sayda Zaynab camp near Damascus. This camp had been used by Syrian intelligence for special operations concerning Iran since the 1970s and, after the Iranian Revolution, was nominally under the responsibility of Mohtashemi as a final training and dispatch point for Shi'ite terrorists for major operations overseas.[93]

The first real opportunity to test the Syrian-Iranian terrorist system in Lebanon came in early 1983. The KGB and Syrian intelligence learned of intensified U.S. intelligence and political activities at the U.S. Embassy in Beirut. April 18, 1983, seemed to be a most opportune day. R.C. Ames, the CIA's top Middle East and South Asia expert, and three of his deputies, Mr. Mead, the CIA Beirut station chief, and four other CIA officers were planning to convene in the Embassy building along with a major agent Ames had inserted into the PLO. Seventeen young Lebanese, then being trained to steal a Soviet SA-5 missile just supplied to Syria, were also to be in the Embassy on that day. Moreover, senior U.S. diplomats Philip Habib and Morris Draper, then mediating an Israeli-Lebanese peace treaty, were also expected at the Embassy that day for consultations.[94] It was decided to hit all of these targets by blowing up the American Embassy in Beirut.

Syria, the USSR and the PLO had strong motives to hit the U.S. on that day. Iran, ever eager to strike at 'the Great Satan', joined in and Rafiq-Dust, in Tehran, ordered Ambassador Mohtashemi to deliver $25,000 as operational expenses.[95] Hussein Mussawi, representing *HizbAllah*, was to provide diversified services in Beirut. The coordination of the operation also involved Abu-al-Haul, the former head of PLO's intelligence who was determined to get the CIA agent, and Khalil al-Wazir (Abu-Jihad), the head of the PLO's military arm. Abu-Jihad suggested giving the operation an ''Iranian character,'' and Hussein Mussawi enthusiastically endorsed it. The operation itself was planned by Lt. Col. Abdul Diab of the Syrian military intelligence. Sami Mahmud al-Hajji, an Egyptian-born KGB agent who had been trained for five years in the USSR and later served with Syrian military intelligence, was put in charge of the operation in Beirut.[96] Hasan Salih Harb, another Egyptian, and Muhamad Najif Jabir, a Palestinian, were two of al-Hajji's chief assistants in Beirut.[97]

Fully aware of the significance of the forthcoming strike,

the Syrians and their allies began preparing for the expected retaliation and retribution. On March 25, with the operation nearing, a delegation of Soviet, Iranian and Libyan experts inspected the military-terrorist facilities in the Biqaa while the local Syrian forces were put on alert.[98] In early April, reinforcements of Palestinian terrorists were rushed to the Biqaa,[99] soon followed by major Syrian forces including tank units[100] and 2 Iranian battalions.[101] The military preparations peaked on April 18.[102] By the time the build-up was completed the number of Iranian reinforcements reached 1,500. Libyan volunteers were also deployed. The Syrians added tanks and heavy artillery.[103] Meanwhile, Ali Akbar Velayati, the Iranian foreign minister, arrived in Damascus on April 12 and immediately met with Hafiz al-Assad and other senior Syrian officials as well as Mohtashemi.[104] The leaders and senior commanders of the DPLF and the PFLP-GC also arrived in Damascus.[105] (The DFLP is the Democratic Front for the Liberation of Palestine, a left-wing radical terrorist organization under the command of Nayif Hawatima, sponsored by Syria and Iran. The DFLP is an extremist split off of the PFLP that enjoyed special close relations with the KGB in the 1970s and 1980s. The PFLP-GC is identified earlier in this chapter.) Khalil al-Wazir arrived at the PLO's headquarters in the Biqaa on the 17th.[106]

In Beirut, the Syrians were running the operation with a team of seven operatives and agents. Al-Hajji recruited a major Syrian agent, Ahmad, who kept him up-to-date on the schedules of the American VIPs. He also rented an apartment overlooking the U.S. embassy and carefully studied the building and the routines. Another Syrian agent was a 30-year-old Druze driver of the Embassy.[107] Other assets of Syrian military intelligence were involved in data collection and in the design and construction of the bomb and its specific placement in the van.[108] The driver delivered the Embassy's black GMC van with diplomatic plates. Shi'ite technicians under Mussawi's control installed 150 kgs of Hexogene explosives inside special compartments in the modified van under Syrian supervision.[109]

A Syrian intelligence officer arrived in Beirut especially to wire the explosives.[110]

The original plan called for a suicide driver to ram the van into the Embassy building. Earlier, in March 1983, Sheikh Raghib Harb signed *fatwa*s for suicide drivers.[111] However, on the eve of the operation, al-Hajji was reluctant to gamble on the determination of the Shi'ite volunteer and therefore asked the Druze driver to park the van near the U.S. Embassy wall. Unbeknownst to the driver, al-Hajji intended to activate the bomb with a remote-control detonator, thus knowingly sacrificing both the driver and Ahmad.[112] As a rule, the Soviets supervised the design and construction of bombs for Lebanon. They also tightly control specialized key items such as remote-control detonators.

This applied in the assassination of Bashir Gemayel on September 14, 1982. "The detonator was a highly sophisticated Japanese device designed to set off the explosion from a distance of several miles away. According to Lebanese intelligence sources, the device was supplied by or through Bulgaria, which often acted on behalf of the Soviets in such matters."[113] Paul Ariss of Bashir's personal intelligence staff believes that "the Syrians and the Soviets" killed Bashir. "The detonator was a sure sign," Ariss said. "Only the Soviets could have supplied that."[114] Therefore, even if the USSR had not been involved in preparations for the bombing of the U.S. Embassy, the Soviets would have learned about the operation when the Syrian military intelligence made a request for a highly specialized detonator.

Sometime on April 17th, al-Hajji and the Syrians confirmed the whereabouts of all their intended targets, especially that all would converge on the U.S. Embassy on the morning of the 18th, and immediately activated their strike plan. As planned, the black GMC van drove into the Embassy on 18 April 1983. At exactly 1:05 PM the van blew up. The powerful explosion brought down a wing of the seven story building. At least 63 people were killed, including 17 Americans. Among the dead were all the targeted CIA personnel. Habib and Draper were not in the building.[115] With a single car bomb, the conspirators succeeded in "wiping out the top level of U.S. intelligence in Lebanon."[116] Ten minutes later a caller to credit for the bombing, called the Dawn Operation, in the name of *al-Jihad al-Islami*. A caller to *Al-Liwa* stated that the bombing was "part of the Iranian revolution's campaign against imperialist targets throughout the world." The style of the announcement pointed to an extremist Shi'ite group like Mussawi's Islamic Amal.[117] Damascus was impressed with the outcome and increased its tacit support for the Iranian-supported terrorism.[118]

It was clear from the beginning that the bombing of the U.S. Embassy was not an isolated incident. After the bombing, the Islamic Jihad warned that it would "keep striking at any imperialist presence in Lebanon, including the multinational force."[119] Nevertheless, Tehran was stunned by the success and lingering effect of the bombing in Beirut. Ali-Akbar Hashemi-Rafsanjani, Ali Velayati and Muhsin Rafiq-Dust, the leading troika who were in charge of relations and cooperation with foreign intelligence services and terrorist organizations, decided on a major operation that would expel the foreign peacekeeping force from Lebanon.[120] Sheikh Fadlallah explained that, "Our aim is to expel the aggressive forces of the United States and other so-called multinational forces including the Zionists."[121] Syria threatened that because of U.S. activities in Lebanon, "Arab vengeance against the United States has become deep-rooted, and the interests that Reagan claims he is fighting for will be destroyed by the Arab masses to avenge the blood of their martyrs and sons and defend their Arabism and pan-Arab soil." Damascus added that the "U.S. plot makes Syria party to the forces that face the U.S. concentrations against it," and that Syria "has one alternative only: to fight like all peoples who, armed with right, emerge victorious over their enemies."[122]

Mustafa Talas warned that "the American threats in Lebanon will not deter us from our struggle to reply to any aggression to which our forces are exposed,'' and that Syria ''will not hesitate in adopting a decision to ensure the defense of the Syrian Arab region.''[123]

Indeed, actual preparations for the next major strike started in September 1983. This time, Iran would have a central role in the operation. Indeed, Muhsin Rafiq-Dust would ultimately admit that ''Both the high explosives and the ideology which in one blast sent to hell 400 officers, NCOs, and soldiers at the Marines headquarters were provided by Iran.''[124]

The operational coordination was conducted from the Iranian Embassy in Damascus. Ali Akbar Mohtashemi was the project manager. He was assisted by the military attache, Ahromi Zadeh, who coordinated activities between Baalbak and Zabadani. Sayyid Ahmad al-Fihri, Khomeini's personal representative to Damascus, acted as an auditor for Tehran.[125] The Syrians were responsible for the technical aspects of the operations because only they and their allies had the intelligence assets and the technical expertise to determine the requirements and design the bombs.[126] Lt. Col. Abdul Diab of Syrian Military Intelligence remained in charge of the Syrian component. He was assisted by *Al-Saiqa* commanders Ahmad al-Hallak and Bilal Hassan in Beirut. He also used former PLO commanders now with Abu-Mussa, Ahmad Kaddoura, one Oumaya who was responsible for security in Abu-Mussa's organization, and Nablan al-Shaykh, a former security chief in the PLO known as Abu-Kifah (who may also have participated in the U.S. Embassy bombing).[127] The *Pasdaran* commander in the Biqaa, known only as Abu-Muslih, was in charge of coordinating the Shi'ite activities there.[128] Islamic Amal of Hussein al-Mussawi fronted for the operation and provided support services.[129] Spiritual guidance and oversight was given by Sheikh Fadlallah, then identified as the leader of the Iranian *ad-Da'wah* Party.[130]

Lt. Col. Abdul Diab went immediately to Beirut to supervise the preparations for the operations. The Syrians and their Palestinian agents studied carefully the U.S. and French compounds. An important question was how to get past the guards and into the buildings. For the U.S. barracks, the Syrians decided on a truck identical to the several trucks delivering cargo to the Beirut airport that used to pass routinely in front of the Marines barracks. For the French barracks they would use a small truck like the one supplying vegetables to the French headquarters. The operational phase was entrusted to the hands of Hussein Mussawi and the *HizbAllah*. He lead the underground support organization in Beirut's Shi'ite suburbs. Abu Haydar Mussawi, a cousin of Hussein Mussawi, arrived in Beirut to find the trucks. Wafic Safa delivered the two tons of special explosives to the experts who would install the bombs. One of the bomb makers was Ibrahim Akil. (In 1986 he would operate in Paris). Hasan Hamiz cashed a $50,000 check in the Iranian Embassy in Damascus and delivered the money to Beirut. In early October, Lt. Col. Abdul Diab was still in Beirut to supervise the work of Abu Haydar Mussawi. Abu Kifah was with him looking at operational security.[131]

The design of the truck proved a complex challenge. A sophisticated mixture of explosives had to be used, and it was imperative to place them with great accuracy in order to achieve the enhanced blast effect. High quality Hexogene and plastic explosive PTN (Pentaerythritol TetraNitrate, a type of high explosive) were shipped from Bulgaria and delivered via Damascus. This was Mohtashemi's usual method.[132] Apparently, the experts supervising the preparations in Beirut were not satisfied with the quality of the work done on the trucks. Therefore, at least one specially modified truck was delivered from Tehran via Damascus. The truck was brought to Brital, already a center of Syrian intelligence and the *HizbAllah* where cars stolen in Beirut were modified for intelligence operations, and where three Syrian intelligence officers and *Hizbollahi* from the Tumays clan booby-trapped the cars.[133] The Mercedes truck used for the Marines barracks came from an assembly plant in Iran.[134]

The bombs used were composite-shaped charges built to

have directed-enhanced blast so that their impact on the buildings above them was maximal. The bomb used against the Marines barracks consisted of 300 kilograms of Hexogene reinforced by PTN. The bomb used against French headquarters consisted of 75 kilograms of Hexogene with PTN.[135]

In early October, the suicide drivers were brought to Syria from the Marvdasht Camp near Tehran. They adopted the title "Martyr": Martyr Talabkaran for the French headquarters and Martyr Chubtarasha for the Marines barracks. Both had been especially trained and brainwashed for the operation by the Vietnamese and North Korean experts in Marvdasht.[136] In Syria, they were provided with advance professional training such as Beirut-style driving, avoiding obstacles, how to crash their vehicles into the buildings and other unique and specialized aspects of their intended mission. The training took place in the Assayda Zaynab camp near Damascus under Bulgarian and East German experts.[137] The drivers were then taken to the terrorist and sabotage training camp run by Syrian intelligence officers under the cover of the Islamic Mission Scouts (*Kashshaf ar-Risalah al-Islamiyah*) in An-Nabih Chit in the Biqaa, where they waited for the operation.[138]

Preparations were nearly complete by mid-October. Hussein Mussawi travelled to Tehran on October 13-15 to personally report the progress and status of the impending operation.[139] Meanwhile, the Iranian Embassy in Beirut was the center of field activities.[140] Iranian and Syrian intelligence officers met in the Iranian Embassy in Beirut around October 13 to survey the progress of the preparations.[141] Beirut was awash with rumors of an impending terrorist event. On October 17, *Al-Markazuyya* warned of terrorist attacks being organized by Syrian agents in Beirut.[142]

Hussein Shaykh-ol-Islam Zadi had arrived in Damascus in mid-October.[143] A graduate of the Patrice Lumumba University, he was then "in charge of exporting the revolution."[144] (The Patrice Lumumba University was a KGB-run university in Moscow that was used to train terrorists, intelligence opera-

tives and "loyal" Third World leaders.) On the 16th, Shaykh-
ol-Islam met with Hafiz al-Assad to go over the details and
implications of the impending operation. The Syrians also
ensured the Soviets of their active support. Assad authorized
the activation of the operation under the cover of Hussein al-
Mussawi's Islamic Jihad.[145] He then made some low-key inspection visits to Lebanon in a black Mercedes.[146] On the 19th
he met with Hussein al-Mussawi and Abu-Mulish and received their opinion about the impending operation.[147] The
final reexamination of the operation and the go-ahead decision
took place in meetings on October 21 and 22, 1983, in the
Iranian Embassy in Damascus. These meetings were chaired
by Ali Akbar Mohtashemi, the Iranian ambassador and project
manager, and included Shaykh-ol-Islam, Ahromi Zadeh, Sayyid
Ahmad al-Fikri, Lt. Col. Abdul Diab, Nablan al-Sheikh and a
few other Syrians and Palestinians. It is not clear whether
Hussein Mussawi or any representative of the *HizbAllah* took
part in these final meetings. Although Shaykh-ol-Islam was
expected to stay until October 25-26, he left suddenly for Iran
on the 22nd.[148]

Beirut was notified of the go-ahead decision on the 22nd.[149]
Early that morning, three senior commanders of Abu-Mussa,
led by Habib Siyam, a former senior commander in Beirut, and
a small detachment inspected the route between the Biqaa and
West Beirut, arriving in Burj al-Barajinah at 10:00 AM. They
brought with them PFLP-GC sabotage experts to support the
Shi'ites in case of a sudden problem. Habib Siyam coordinated
the opening and securing of the road between Sawafar and ash-
Shuwayft with Walid Junblatt's forces (also known as Jumblatt,
he is the leader of the Druze forces in Lebanon). This coordination and road-securing operation was conducted with the full
knowledge of the Soviet advisers operating in the area.[150] By
then, some 120 Soviet experts were permanently deployed in
the Biqaa and Jabal Lubnan, all the way to the Beirut suburbs,
providing assistance and guidance in all aspects of the fighting
against the multinational forces stationed in Beirut. At least 50

Soviet officers were present in the area where the Syrian-*HizbAllah* trucks were to pass.[151] Then, once the road to Beirut was secured, the two trucks, the dismantled explosive charges, the detonators, and the experts were brought to Beirut in several shipments. The car-bombs were dismantled prior to the shipment for safety reasons. They arrived in al-Fakihani and were reassembled for the operation by the Syrian experts assisted by Ahmad Jibril's men and Mussawi's *Hizbollahi*.[152]

That night, the two drivers were taken from the Biqaa to the house of Sheikh Muhammad Hussein Fadlallah, who "gave his blessings" and assured them of a place in heaven for their sacrifice.[153] The next morning they woke up an hour before the operation, prayed, had tea with a cookie, kissed the Koran and drove away.[154] The cookies were laced with drugs which were administered by Dr. Aziz al-Abub (whose real name was Ibrahim al-Nadhir), an Iranian protege of Abu-Nidal and Fadlallah who had received "special training in the techniques of mind control" from the KGB in the USSR. In the mid-1980s, he emerged as the primary torturer of Western hostages.[155]

On October 23, 1983, at 6:17 AM, Martyr Chubtarasha crashed his Yellow Mercedes truck loaded with 300kg of high explosives into the U.S. Marines barracks. At 6:20 AM, Martyr Talabkaran crashed a small red truck loaded with 75 kgs of high explosives into the French headquarters. Both bombs were expertly made from Composition-B, a delicate combination of 60% RDX Hexogene explosive, 39% standard PTN and 1% fine wax used to coat and stabilize the sophisticated contours of the charge to enhance the blast.[156] At 6:32 AM, minutes after the bombings, several cars rushed from the Iranian Embassy in Beirut on their way to Damascus.[157] When the smoke cleared, the results were devastating and the casualties heavy: 245 Americans were killed and 146 were wounded; 58 French were killed and 15 wounded. The explosion in the Marines barracks was "the single largest non-nuclear explosion on earth since World War II," FBI forensic investigators eventually reported.[158] It is noteworthy that this bomb composition technique, with some improvements and variations, would remain the Islamists' preferred material and would be used, among other places, in the World Trade Center bombing in New York City on February 26, 1993.

Meanwhile, almost immediately after the explosions in Beirut, the unknown organization Free Islamic Revolutionary Movement claimed responsibility for the bombing and identified the drivers as Abu-Mazin and Abu-Sij'an.[159] The next day, Iran denied any involvement, but endorsed the attacks because they reflected "the crystallization of the growing anger of the Lebanese Muslims against the direct interference of Western colonial forces. It is the just right of a nation to inflict decisive blows by any means on intervention forces and aggressors, in order to end their interference," it stated.[160] Syria could understand the motives of the perpetrators. "The two operations carried out by the Lebanese national resistance forces must be viewed . . . as being perpetrated within the framework of confronting the forces of occupation, those who assist them and work to prolong their presence."[161] In Beirut, a caller speaking in the name of Islamic Jihad claimed the operations in the morning.

> We are the soldiers of God and we crave death. We are not Iranians, or Syrians or Palestinians. We are Lebanese Muslims following the tenets of the Koran. After our previous attack on the American Embassy we warned that our next strike would be even more powerful. Today, they [the multinational forces] comprehended with whom they are dealing. We do not want any [foreigner] to stay in Lebanon, not even Syrians and Israelis. We desire an Islamic Republic even if it leads to war. Violence is our only path and it will remain so if they [the multinational forces] do not leave the place. We are ready to turn Lebanon into a second Vietnam.[162]

In Baalbak, Sheikh Mussawi, who denied any involvement in the bombings in interviews with French newspapers,[163] stated:

> I hail this noble action. It is an action which Allah and his Prophet Muhammad have blessed. I bow in reverence for the souls of the martyrs who implemented this action.[164]

By now, Iran considered itself officially a party to the conflict in Lebanon. In mid-November, Tehran stated that "the Islamic Republic of Iran would defend the legitimate rights of the Syrians, the Palestinians and the Lebanese and would exploit all means at its disposal in order to totally drive the aggressive forces out of the region."[165] Within days of the Beirut attacks, Soviet and Iranian intelligence officers arrived in the Shi'ite suburbs of Beirut to organize and supervise additional terrorist operations against the multinational forces in case the anticipated retaliation escalated beyond token actions.[166]

On November 25, an Iranian delegation led by Mustafa Mirsalim, a presidential adviser, arrived for an inspection tour of the Iranian and *HizbAllah* installations[167], blatantly ignoring a Lebanese ultimatum to leave the Biqaa in 3 days.[168] The Iranians brought along additional senior terrorist trainers and weapons for Tufaily's and Abbas and Hussein Mussawi's men.[169] Emboldened by the Iranian and Syrian support, Sheikh Subhi al-Tufayli explained that the *HizbAllah* was aware that "our enemies will not leave our country unless we fight them; these [multinational] forces must leave Lebanon or else there will be nothing between us and them other than fighting."[170] Meanwhile, Mirsalim inspected the Israeli border on the Golan Heights in case Iran's help was needed in a major war with Israel.[171] Upon returning to Tehran, Mirsalim reiterated Iran's commitment to support its regional allies.[172]

Emboldened, the *HizbAllah* increased its activities and raised its profile.[173] The Iranian presence was a constant proof for the Lebanese Shi'ites of their role in the Islamic revolution and a guarantee of the protection of Iran. Sheikh Abbas Mussawi explained: "The presence of our brothers, the members of the Islamic Revolutionary Guards Corps in Lebanon, is the main support for our struggle against Zionism and imperialism."[174]

The shock of the suicide bombings in Beirut, and a smaller bombing of the Israeli headquarters in Tyre a few days later,[175] brought the *Islamic Jihad*, who claimed this operation as well,[176] to the fore. Sheikh Fadlallah claimed that *Islamic Jihad* did not exist and that "several parties are using it or its name as a cover." While *Islamic Jihad* was indeed "a movement name for several parties," Hussein al-Mussawi clarified, "the organization does exist and is a distinct group with ties to Syria and Iran."[177] Arab sources concluded that the name *Islamic Jihad* "is borne by a number of groups that employ violence and terrorism to achieve their aims and that their membership includes various forces that have no connection with one another and that avoid publicizing the identities of their organizations so as not to expose themselves to punishment, repressions and political embarrassments." In the early 1980s, *Islamic Jihad* displayed unique sophistication in such actions as the mining of the Red Sea or the suicide bombing in Beirut. "It is not strange if we say that the *Islamic Jihad* organization is a fictitious one that has no real existence." Some Arab sources even suggested that the U.S., Israel and other forces were using the label *Islamic Jihad* against the Arab world.[178]

It soon became clear that, for all intents and purposes, *HizbAllah* was *Islamic Jihad*. Iran, through the *HizbAllah*, was therefore responsible for the attacks on the U.S. in Beirut. Sheikh Fadlallah was identified as its leader.[179] In 1984, the *HizbAllah* was crystallized as the umbrella organization guiding and coordinating the predominantly Shi'ite Islamic activities. The *HizbAllah* "absorbed" such organizations as Islamic AMAL, *Al-Da'wa* (the Call), *Jundulah* (Soldiers of God) and the Forces of Hussein. "*HizbAllah* is not one party but four or five, a kind of Islamic front, very rigid and very strong,'' explained an AMAL official.[180] The cohesiveness of the *HizbAllah*'s factions was clearly demonstrated in their protest march in Beirut in late November 1983.[181]

The *HizbAllah* traces its roots to the Islamic Revolution in Iran.[182] Sheikh Hussein Mussawi compared Iran's relations with the *HizbAllah* to those of ''a mother to a son. We are her children.''[183] Sheikh Ibrahim al-Amin defined his capacity as the ''leader of the *HizbAllah*s of the Beirut region, appointed by the Ayatollah Khomeini.''[184] He defined the Iranian Revolution as ''an inspiration.'' Sheikh Ibrahim al-Amin explained that the *HizbAllah* was an integral part of a world order established by Khomeini. Its political unity with Iran was best expressed in their common struggle against tyrants all over the world. As a result of the Iranian Revolution, ''Islam acquired a political and international power base'' from which to spread the Islamic revolution.[185]

The *HizbAllah* is thus a ''universal'' entity, ignoring states and nationalism.[186] Islam and revolution have a universal character, Ibrahim al-Amin insisted. ''Our political work in Lebanon is not defined by the geography of Lebanon but by the geography of Islam, which is to say the geography of the world.''[187] This definition, however, did not prevent Sheikh Fadlallah from recognizing certain worldly realities. ''Obviously, the Syrian role in Lebanon is basic and realistic, and emanates from the nature of the Lebanese internal conditions and the conditions in the region as a whole.''[188]

Sayyid Muhammad Hussein Fadlallah differentiated between the common message of the Iranian Revolution and *HizbAllah* and their socio-political backgrounds. Fadlallah emphasized that Khomeini ranked ''at the top of the list of leaders of freedom in the world.''[189] His religious-political leadership was undisputed. ''Imam Khomeini represents an authority. He is a great and inspiring Islamic leader and, as such, we hold him in high esteem and believe that he represents a mature and inspiring Islamic leadership." Fadlallah explained that in Iran, "the revolutionary leadership advocated the concept that Islam should be the rule of life. This was similar to the Marxist revolution against the Czar." Inspired, the Shi'ites of Lebanon had burst into the open, establishing such organizations as the *HizbAllah* in reaction to the prevailing conditions around them. Fadlallah acknowledged that "Shi'ism has benefited from the state of violence that has prevailed in Lebanon. It became involved in violence in Lebanon, which, in turn, drew upon the violence in the region arising from the Palestinian problem and the Middle East conflict."[190]

The *HizbAllah* thus emerged as an integral component of a global Islamic Revolution led by Iran. Ibrahim al-Amin pointed out that the *HizbAllah* was "not a regimented party" in the conventional way if only because such westernized forms of organization were alien to Islam. He defined the *HizbAllah* as a "mission" and a "way of life."[191] Sheikh Fadlallah stated: "The *HizbAllah* is a party, just like other parties in Lebanon which resort to the use of arms. It might be responsible for infractions and violations of the law, and they might have made mistakes, even though their mistakes are far less than those of others." In contrast, he pointed out, "*Islamic Jihad* is a mere telephone organization."[192]

However, the ultimate objectives and goals of the *HizbAllah* were completely different than those of other parties in Lebanon. Sheikh Ibrahim al-Amin emphasized that the declared goal of the *HizbAllah* was the establishment of a "great Islamic state" uniting the entire region. The *HizbAllah* did not believe that it would be natural to establish an Islamic state in Lebanon alone and therefore "wished Lebanon to be part of the (universal) plan."[193] Sheikh Hussein Mussawi agreed that the establishment of an Islamic state in Lebanon "is not our demand" because the *HizbAllah* was committed to the establishment of an "all-encompassing Islamic state" that would include Lebanon.[194] Sheikh Fadlallah went even further, admitting that the Lebanese society was not ripe for the establishment of an Islamic republic. However, he did not rule out that Lebanon would "be transformed into an Islamic republic in the future."[195]

Thus, events in Lebanon in the early 1980s not only crystallized the radical militant Shi'ite community, but proved that, given the right professional assistance, the "Khomeini International" could affect world politics. The groups operating under the name *Islamic Jihad* were organized and institutionalized. The 1982 Israeli invasion of Lebanon broke the PLO-dominated system of international terrorism. Within a short time, the Lebanese network reconstituted itself around Iran and Syria and renewed its international activities.[196] Moreover, Tehran was able to utilize the relationships of Iranians with the most radical terrorist groups.[197]

The *HizbAllah* became the cornerstone of "Neo-International Terrorism." The new Iran-led multi-national terrorism, in fact, replaced the terrorist confederation created by the 1972 Baddawi Pact and instituted new modes for the exchange of experience, expertise, experts, intelligence and supplies between the involved movements and their supporting states in the battle against Western society.[198] As always, Syria remained involved in the background, as was the case in the bombing of the U.S. Marines barracks, providing extensive support for these attacks that end up serving Syria's interests.[199]

As for the *HizbAllah*, Sheikh Hussein al-Mussawi declared the movement's determination to spearhead Khomeini's global struggle. He explained that "nothing threatens the imperialist interests in the world except Islamic resurgence, namely, the revolutionary activity of Muslims under the banner of the Islamic revolution led by Imam Khomeini. . . . We in Lebanon are part of this line and loyal to it. They call us terrorists. We say, as we have said previously, that if terrorism means defense of religion and dignity and sanctities, we not only insist on being called terrorists but insist on being terrorists."[200]

IRAN'S GROWING ROLE

In 1984, Tehran took major steps toward the realization of Khomeini's global messianic mission. For Tehran, terrorism was also an intentional and pragmatic instrument of policy aimed at achieving through terror and blackmail whatever Iran could not get from the West through more conventional means. "If our wishes are not granted we shall drag you into a sea of fire and blood. We shall be at war with you, hitting you everywhere," Hashemi-Rafsanjani declared in December 1984.[201] Little wonder, therefore, that the seeming impunity of Iran and its proteges featured heavily in the Arab assessment of the emerging international terrorist campaign against the U.S. "America today considers itself at war with what it calls 'official terrorism' in the world. It believes that countries such as Iran, and perhaps Syria and Libya, are involved in the operations against it."[202] Under such conditions, little wonder that the anti-U.S. radical camp was willing to accept Iran's activist strategy.

Thus, combining Islamic zeal and cool pragmatism, Tehran assumed a leadership position in the new system of international terrorism. Iran was able to seize the initiative in the unfolding terrorist campaign because it had already demonstrated the commitment and zeal of its own terrorists in the *HizbAllah* attacks in such places as Beirut and Kuwait in the early 1980s, where they had confronted the U.S. directly and, by Arab standards, defeated it.

Ayatollah Muhammad Hussein Fadlallah emphasized the significance of the legacy of the Beirut bombings to the emergence of *HizbAllah*'s global role and awareness:

> When our people and *mujahideen* jolted the reality, they discovered that they had been living under a great delusion in falling prey to absolute fear. In its confrontation with the reality of the multinational force in Beirut and the Israeli reality in the South,

> the Islamic resistance was able to prove that there
> had been delusion and that those who feared [others]
> could frighten [others].[203]

In early 1984, Khomeini ordered the establishment of Iran's "independent brigade for carrying out unconventional warfare in enemy territory", that is, international terrorism.[204] The IRGC came up with an outline for a program and Khomeini approved it, stating: "Whatever is necessary to destroy them [the West] must be done."[205]

An organizational meeting took place on May 19/26, 1984. It was chaired by "Mirhashem," a pseudonym of the unit commander, and included Ayatollah Muhammad Khatami, Minister of Islamic Guidance, twelve ministers, military commanders, heads of departments and terrorist leaders. Khatami hinted that Mirhashem was a famous figure in Tehran, apparently Mir Hussein Mussavi, Iran's Prime Minister.[206] Other key participants were the "presidential advisers" Mustafa Mirsalim and Hussein Mussavi-Kho'iniha. Both were graduates of the Patrice Lumumba University in Moscow and also underwent terrorist training in the PDRY. In 1984, Mirsalim was put in charge of the terrorist training camps in Iran.[207] The terrorist unit was designated "The 110th Independent Brigade", put directly under the Iranian Government and made completely independent of both the Army Command and the IRGC.[208]

In order to expedite reaching operational status, it was decided to utilize some of the more active *HizbAllah* cells or branches as nuclei for this brigade. Khatami explained that the unit would be built around a nucleus of a few groups, each 10 to 20 men strong, "who are currently serving in Lebanon." Mirhashem discussed his forces in Lebanon that "are known to the outside world as suicide groups," and expected to have some 1,500 to 2,000 men assigned to the 110th Independent Brigade by the end of July 1984.[209] The first groups of suicide fighters, called the *Isargaran* (Lovers of Martyrdom), were dispatched to south Lebanon primarily in order to gain additional recruits from the local Shi'ite population.[210] In Lebanon, they joined the al-Hussein Forces, the organization overseeing the now institutionalized suicide operations, originally established by Haydar al-Mussawi. [211]

For overseas operations, the Brigade's intelligence agents were to be sent overseas under diplomatic cover, including as military attaches. One of the first of these agents was Mehdi Ahrari-Mostafavi, named as Iran's Ambassador to Austria. Mehdi Ahrari-Mostafavi had completed a special course with the George Habash PFLP and was also involved in the establishment of the brigade in Tehran.[212]

In mid-1984, Iran established a set of institutions to conduct infiltration operations of the target countries in the Near East and the Muslim communities in Western Europe. The coordination bureau in Tehran was under the direct control of Sheikh Taki ad-Din al-Mudarrisi who, in turn, answered to Ayatollah Montazeri. Mudarrissi maintained close links with a series of associations of political refugees, mainly in Western Europe. The ultimate objective of the "coordination bureau" is "the destabilization of the Middle East, the Mediterranean Basin and Europe by means of religious fanaticism and terrorism."[213]

The coordination bureau oversaw specialized training for operatives and terrorists in the as-Sayda Zaynab camp near Damascus, in Baalbak in the Biqaa and in Tehran. Two types of *Hizbollahi* were trained in Tehran: (1) operatives who will act directly on location, like the drivers of car bombs, those placing explosives, etc.; and (2) indoctrinators who, in the name of the Shi'ites, will penetrate the Sunni communities throughout the world, infiltrate them and win them over to Khomeini's world-wide revolutionary struggle.[214]

Sheikh Mudarrissi is proud of his "lovers of martyrdom" *Hizbollahi*, their professional capabilities and dedication. "In one week I can gather five hundred faithful ready to throw themselves into suicide operations. No frontier will stop them," he stated.[215] The indoctrinator *Hizbollahi* were organized in the new *Fadayeen-i-Islam*, the fanatic missionaries of a profound long-term *Jihad* that is being waged on a quiet and subtle front. This *Jihad* is waged on the "dogmatic and philosophical level." However, ultimately, and in the long run, these activities end up promoting, facilitating and expediting international terrorism.[216]

Meanwhile, the ideological motivation for the anti-U.S. global struggle also evolved during 1984. The scope of the ideological justifications and the rationalizations of the emerging world struggle widened with various movements and spokesmen borrowing ideological formulations from one another in order to portray a unified front. In late 1984, Sheikh Fadallah denounced "racism against the Third World" and presented it as one of the evils against which "Muslims" — that is, the *HizbAllah* — should fight.[217]

Similarly, the Libyans, who justify their anti-U.S. struggle in Islamic terms, defined their operations as revolutionary. "We must force America to fight on 100 fronts all over the earth," Muammar Qaddafi explained, "in Lebanon, in Chad, in Sudan, in El Salvador, in Africa." [218] Abd as-Salam Jallud went even further, declaring the active participation of Libyans in the anti-U.S. global revolutionary struggle: "There are Libyans now fighting in Salvador and in Nicaragua. The small Libyan Arab people are fighting in three continents for the sake of the revolution and tide of the masses. The Libyans have managed to fight on a front extending from El-Salvador, Nicaragua, Lebanon, Syria and Chad to South Africa. Why? For the sake of the revolution of the masses."[219] A North Korean official in Libya stated that the two countries "represent a natural alliance in confronting America."[220]

Little wonder that the Arab world was bracing for the escalation of state terrorism.

"All expectations indicate that a new undeclared war will hit the Middle East area. It is the war of 'official terrorism' or 'official violence' waged by regimes and intelligence services from within and without the area that has shed and will shed much blood and will claim the lives of agents and that of the guiltless and guilty alike. It is the other picture of the struggle between the axes and the ugly side of fragmentation in the Arab world.'' These terrorist attacks would constitute part of an anti-U.S. campaign. Some 205 out of the 500 ''violent acts undertaken in the world'' during 1984 were ''against Americans and American interests.'' Keeping up with the customary revolutionary rhetoric, the Arabs also pointed out that some of the surge of such violence in the Middle East and Third World should be considered as retribution against the legacy of oppression and violence of the once colonial and imperialist powers.[221]

CHAPTER 2

THE NEW SYSTEM OF INTERNATIONAL TERRORISM

Iran and Syria proved their basic argument in the ashes in Beirut — that international terrorism is an effective vehicle capable of delivering dramatic results that no other instrument of foreign policy could. The success of the Beirut bombings sent a surge through the ranks of the Islamists and their supporters.

In the next few years the Lebanon-based, Iranian- and Syrian-controlled terrorists would launch a series of spectacular terrorist operations against the West. Several of these strikes — most notably the bombing of the U.S. Embassy Annex in Beirut, the seizure and holding of hostages, the hijacking of TWA Flight 847, and the blowing up of Pan-Am Flight 103 — were directly aimed at Americans.

However, while world attention was focused on these spectacular terrorist operations another development, with far greater implications for the safety of America and Americans, was taking place out of the limelight. Iran, Syria, and their allies, operating under the cover of the *HizbAllah*, had embarked on a crash program to build a lethal terrorist force to carry out spectacular strikes at the heart of their enemies, especially the U.S.

The *HizbAllah* and other Islamic terrorists are a unique phenomena, combining ideological and religious zeal with cool, sophisticated professionalism. It is this special characteristic which makes them so dangerous to America.

Thus, it is impossible to comprehend the magnitude of the threat Iranian-sponsored terrorists pose without understanding the transformation they have undergone since the mid-1980s. Moreover, as detailed below, the extent of the commitment by both the sponsoring states and their terrorist agents to strike America is clearly reflected in the magnitude of their training and their ideological virulence.

THE INSTITUTIONALIZATION OF THE TERRORIST SYSTEM

By early 1985, both the Iranian Revolution and the *HizbAllah* inspired the entire international terrorist movement. A major step toward the recognition of the *HizbAllah* as the leading organization of international terrorism took place in January 1985, at a secret meeting in Hermel in the northern Biqaa, whose importance was comparable to that of the 1972 Baddawi conference. Present at this watershed meeting were senior officials of the Iranian, Syrian and Libyan intelligence services; the entire scope of terrorist organizations connected to Lebanon, including the Lebanese progressive organizations led by the LARF and the Islamist organizations led by the *HizbAllah*; and even European terrorist organizations such as Action Directe from France, the Red Brigades from Italy, the Combative Communist Cells from Belgium and the Red Army Faction from Germany.

Ibrahim Lakhis, a Shi'ite activist politician and drug smuggler from Shtura, in Lebanon, had been advocating the need to reexamine the division of responsibilities for terrorist operations against the West. In early January, at the Hermel meeting, Lakhis convinced those in attendance of the need to reexamine the objectives and roles of the various terrorist organizations. The decision was made to launch an ongoing campaign to destabilize Western Europe. In the first phase, the West Europeans would conduct terrorist operations while the Middle East groups would provide the logistical and material support. Ultimately, the Islamic Jihad would assume prominence in the conduct of terrorist operations all over the West. The conference also laid the groundwork for a new policy in Beirut: the kidnapping of hostages.[1]

Ironically, the Arab world's apprehension of the wrath and capabilities of *HizbAllah* contributed to improved ties between terrorist states. In December 1984, the U.S. had privately suggested to friendly Arab countries that Israel be encouraged to damage the Beirut International Airport, which would help avert some 70% of all air hijackings. Fearing retribution, there was a leak from one of the Persian Gulf states and, consequently, an important meeting took place in Tehran in January 1985 to discuss new methods of neutralizing U.S. policy. Officially, the foreign ministers of Syria, Iran, and Libya arrived there to discuss a military and political pact opposing the U.S. and Israel. However, simultaneously, a far more significant meeting of intelligence officers from the three countries concluded a series of agreements on such subjects as intelligence sharing, mutual aid in crossing international frontiers and producing forged passports, and mutual assistance in subversive operations.[2]

The outcome of these meetings was the formulation of a coherent terrorist ideology and strategy. For deniability and because the strategy was to be implemented in and from Lebanon its authors attributed it to the *HizbAllah* in Lebanon. Thus, on February 16, 1985 the international headquarters of *HizbAllah* in Tehran published an *Open Letter Addressed by the HizbAllah to the Oppressed/Downtrodden in Lebanon and in the World* which constituted its declared doctrine and outlined its objectives. The letter declared that the *HizbAllah* considered the U.S. to be the force behind all the catastrophes of the Islamic world and, therefore, their primary enemy:

> We are moving in the direction of fighting the roots of vice and the first root of vice is America. All the endeavors to drag us into marginal action will be futile when compared with the confrontation with the United States.

The *HizbAllah* emphasized that its struggle was an integral component of a wider struggle of global proportions against the U.S. For this struggle to succeed, there should be cooperation between all anti-imperialist forces based on the unity of objectives and the commonality of their enemy.

> We strongly urge on all the oppressed of the world the need to form an international front that encompasses all their liberation movements so that they may establish full and comprehensive coordination among these movements in order to achieve effectiveness in their activity and to focus on their enemies' weak points.

This approach opened the door for increased cooperation between *HizbAllah* and the USSR and its allies and proxies. Little wonder, therefore, that the *HizbAllah* was bracing itself for a long and arduous struggle in which "we will endure until *Allah* issues his Judgment on us and on the oppressors."[3] In such a *Jihad* there can be no compromises. Moreover, the lives of individuals, both *Hizbollahi* and especially their victims, are meaningless.

Meanwhile, Muammar Qaddafi increased his efforts to better coordinate and even unify the various terrorist organizations and revolutionary movements. On March 29-31, 1985, he organized the first conference of the pan-Arab Command for Leading the Revolutionary Forces in the Arab Homeland in Tripoli. In a speech on the eve of the conference Qaddafi pointed to the strategic significance of the example set by the *HizbAllah* in Lebanon.

> The lesson is that America was kicked out of Lebanon when an individual Arab was able to kill 300 Americans. . . One person in a car full of explosives will die, but 300 Americans will also die.

Qaddafi further emphasized Iran's role in the pan-Arab progressive revolutionary struggle. "We shall fight under the banner of Pan-Arabism," he declared.[4] At the end of the conference, the pan-Arab Command for Leading the Revolutionary Forces in the Arab Homeland published a communique which further specified the objectives of the pan-Arab revolutionary *Jihad* Qaddafi was determined to lead:

> To confront imperialism, especially U.S. imperialism, and work toward liquidating its military bases and foil its schemes and strike at its positions and interests wherever they might exist; to consolidate the alliance with the revolutionary forces and the peoples struggling for liberation and consolidate the ties of friendship with the bloc of socialist countries headed by the friendly Soviet Union.[5]

The growing importance of Iran in the terrorist movement was recognized by Qaddafi in early 1985. He discussed at great length the unique characteristics and bravery of Shi'ite terrorism.

> The Iranian Revolution has encouraged the Shi'ite in the Arab Homeland, who have regarded its uprising as a revolution in the name of Islam; not against the Sunnis but against reaction and against the United States. . . . The Shi'ite proves his heroism when he falls martyr. Nobody else except the Shi'ite would load his car with explosives and blow it up himself. In fact it was the Iranian Revolution that kindled this sense in the Shi'ites. . . . There may be a *HizbAllah*, but the fact is that they are all Shi'ites.[6]

Qaddafi soon committed huge sums of money to overturn "American-Zionist schemes" and allocated significant portions to finance the military build-up of the *HizbAllah*. "What is important is the launching of an individual suicide action," Qaddafi said.[7] In July 1985 the two countries agreed to jointly form and sustain "a powerful terrorist corps" that would struggle against the U.S. and Israel.[8] Thus, Qaddafi, in essence, recognized the leadership of Iranian-supported terrorism in the emerging new order of international terrorism.

In August 1985, Iran further elevated its involvement in international terrorism. Three Palestinian terrorist leaders —

Abu Mussa (Sa'id Musa Muragha) of the *Fatah* Rebels, Ahmad Jibril of the PFLP-GC, and Abu al-Hayja' of *al-Sa'iqah* — visited Tehran for a week. Iran agreed to give them several millions of dollars at Syria's request. In return, they agreed to help Iran in its international terrorist activities and to assign Palestinian experts to train cadres of the *Pasdaran* and the *HizbAllah*. An agreement was also reached on the use of Iran's diplomatic facilities in support of Palestinian operations, including the use of Iranian passports and diplomatic mail for these purposes.[9]

Consequently, the cooperation between Iran and several terrorist organizations throughout the world entered a new phase. With Palestinian help, representatives of 28 terrorist organizations arrived in Tehran to discuss and plan how to achieve better mutual cooperation. Some of the participating terrorist organizations were: West Germany's Bader Meinhoff gang, Italy's Red Brigades, Japan's Red Army, several Palestinian extremists,

HizbAllah, Islamic Amal, Spain's Basque separatists and the Armenian Secret Army for the Liberation of Armenia. The principal funds for these terrorist organizations would be provided by Iran and Libya while Syria would have an important role in providing weapons and expertise.[10]

Soon afterwards Tehran delivered diversified arms and ammunition worth millions of dollars to terrorist organizations all over the world. Radio Tehran is reported to have stated that Soviet-made weapons captured on the Iran-Iraq front "have been delivered to liberation movements around the world."[11] In reality, these Soviet-made weapons were provided by the USSR, partly via Afghanistan, for Iran and Syria to distribute to the terrorist organizations.[12]

In 1986, the new international terrorist movement was further consolidated at two conferences in Tripoli, Libya. The objectives of these conferences were to formulate the specifics of the forthcoming terrorist and revolutionary campaigns, and to finalize the responsibilities of the various participating organizations. Special attention was paid to facilitating the escalation of the terrorist campaign in Western Europe and the U.S. Several training seminars on, and demonstrations of, weapons and explosives were conducted during the conference under strict security, especially for the non-Arab and non-African delegations. These included the providing of SPETSNAZ (Soviet special forces, which utilized highly specialized weapons optimized for terrorist operations) arms and training to additional groups and organizations.[13]

These training sessions constituted an integral part of Qaddafi's decision to develop a Libyan elite force for deniable clandestine and covert operations all over the Third World, comprised of expert terrorists from the numerous organizations and movements already supported by Libya. Mussa Kussa, a senior intelligence official who became Libya's Vice Foreign Minister in charge of the Office for the Export of the Revolution and a specialist in international special operations, was put in charge of the project. He established the *Mathaba* under the Arab Liaison Bureau as a "liberation movement" with an internationalist character. Its formal establishment took place in early 1986 during, or soon after, the Second International Conference of the International Center for Combatting Imperialism, Zionism, Racism, Reaction and Fascism held in Tripoli in mid-March (see below).

Meanwhile, *Mathaba* members were recruited by Libyan embassies, in Libyan training camps and during the various terrorist and revolutionary conferences. The suitable candidates then received two years of extensive intelligence and terrorist training in Libya before being sent back to their countries to form dormant *Mathaba* networks and recruitment cells. Between 1986-88, the vast Libyan economic and financial assets in Africa, including more than 30 banks, transportation companies, commercial enterprises, and agro-industrial institutions, were ordered to employ and/or support many of the *Mathaba* members and supporters.[14]

Subsequently, when world attention was focused on Libya's support for international terrorism, Libyan and Third World propaganda equated the *Mathaba* with the International Center for Combatting Imperialism, Zionism, Racism, Reaction and Fascism, thus dating its establishment back to 1982 and claiming that this body was only engaged in educational, propaganda, and financial services and support.[15]

Qaddafi's first 1986 gathering was the Second Conference of the Pan-Arab Command for Leading the Revolutionary Forces in the Arab Homeland on February 2-4, 1986. Colonel Muammar al-Qaddafi remained "the brother leader in the leadership of the battle of national liberation of the Arab nation."[16] Leaders and commanders of at least 25 revolutionary and terrorist organizations participated in the conference. The participants studied confrontation with, and ways of "escalating" their terrorist struggle against, the U.S. and its allies.[17] Tripoli emphasized the fact that Muhammad Mahdi, a U.S. citizen who travelled to the conference from Athens, was in defiance of the U. S. order that Americans must leave Libya.[18]

The Closing Statement of the Conference of the Pan-Arab Command for Leading the Revolutionary Forces in the Arab Homeland outlined its goals, further defining the Command's objectives:

> The command has decided on a comprehensive popular pan-Arab reply to the U.S. and Zionist attacks at all levels — political, economic, military, and security — and to consolidate its policy of striking against U.S. interests in the region and in the world.

The Command also adopted a number of important resolutions on their future actions, which clearly emphasized their anti-American terrorist objectives. "The most prominent of these resolutions is the mobilization of the Arab Revolutionary Forces, equipping them and raising their combat capabilities in order to establish a striking revolutionary force and suicide groups to hit U.S. interests in reply to any attack against any Arab country.''[19]

Soon afterwards, the Second International Conference of the International Center for Combatting Imperialism, Zionism, Racism, Reaction and Fascism convened in Tripoli, Libya, on March 14-18, 1986.[20] Some 1,000 participants from over 300 states and organizations took part in the conference of ''international revolutionary forces,'' ranging from representatives of the Bulgarian Communist Party to fundamentalist guerrillas from the Philippines.[21] There were also representatives of several West European and U.S. organizations as well as African, Central American, Caribbean and Arab revolutionary and terrorist organizations.[22] By then, Libya had an annual budget of $100 million for the maintenance of 20 training bases in Libya and the support, training and sustaining of over 7,000 terrorists all over the world.[23]

Syria's importance in the emerging terrorist system was also growing. Since the early 1980s, terrorism and active measures constituted an integral, if not central, part of Hafiz al-Assad's policy in Lebanon and the entire Middle East.[24] By the mid-1980s, whatever the terrorist affiliation — the *HizbAllah*, Islamic Jihad, the PFLP or even *al-Fatah* Rebels, the planners and instigators of their operations were in Damascus. These diversified terrorist organizations became ''mere pawns on the chessboard of Syrian intelligence, which is the real one pulling the strings.'' However, the highly proficient Syrian intelligence did its utmost not to leave its fingerprints while making full use of the large diversity of groups available for credible deniability in overseas terrorism.[25]

Indeed, Damascus went to great lengths ''to emphasize the importance and need to dissociate between terrorist operations and acts of liberation,'' explaining that the recent attempts to implicate Syria, which was actively supporting "the struggle of people who are fighting for their freedom and independence," in international terrorism was an imperialist-Zionist conspiracy. Damascus did not deny supporting certain irregular groups, but vehemently protested "the imperialist and Zionist policy of branding the national struggle as terrorism." Special criticism was directed at the U.S.-Zionist plots against "the Arab national movement and the Palestinian revolution."[26]

Syria's declared stand on support for terrorist organizations in Lebanon was unequivocal: "Syria has never kept it a secret that it remains committed to supporting the peoples' rights and struggle or its complete support for the Lebanese and Palestinian resistance. Syria provided Arab resistance men with all the means of steadfastness and will continue to offer all the support it can to Arab resistance men in their confrontation with Israel and its forces of invasion."[27] Damascus also emphasized its leading role in sponsoring and supporting Arab and international revolutionary struggles beyond the Middle East:

> Syria never hides the fact that it supports people's national liberation movements everywhere... This support will also continue in the future. Syria is a pioneering national liberation force in the world; an important, integral part of the anti-imperialist anti-racist front; and a vanguard of Arab revolutionary force which leads a relentless struggle to liberate occupied Arab territory and regain the Palestinian Arab people's national rights and all Arab rights that have been usurped by imperialism and Zionism.[28]

Thus, by 1986, Tehran and its proteges were rejuvenated and eager to escalate the liberation struggle for the Muslim world. Mir Hussein Mussavi explained that "the export of revolution is in fact an effort to defend Islam everywhere." He acknowledged the Iranian export of revolution, pointing out that "what indeed upsets the superpowers is the very upsurge of Islam and Islamic values, as well as the awakening among

Muslims to Islam. This upsets them and compels them to react."[29]

In a Friday sermon in November 1986, the President of Iran, Ali Khamenei, linked the challenges facing Iran to its relentless confrontation with the U.S. and international terrorism. He deemed "the religious rite of unity among Muslim societies as being equal to *Jihad*" and other key tenets of Islam. "If the one billion Muslims in the world were to regain their unity they would be a tremendous power barring the path to wrong doers and oppressors!"

This pan-Islamic rejuvenation is of crucial significance in view of the ongoing confrontation with the U.S. "As long as the United States follows its bullying and hegemonistic policy and as long as it reacts in this manner toward the meek Palestine and Arab nations it will never meet with any flexibility or compromise from our side!" Khamenei saw little hope because "in his speech Reagan had once again confessed to Iran's military, economic, and political strength in the world and its influence in Islamic countries particularly in the oppressed and deprived nations." Therefore, stern measures were needed to face the U.S. In this context, Khamenei hailed "those Lebanese youth who are holding several American hostages in order to restore their rights."[30]

Little wonder that the Third World's radicals, and especially the Islamists led by Tehran, were confident that they were on the verge of a cataclysmic clash with what they considered to be a Western-dominated hostile world. This struggle would be characterized by a surge in terrorism on an unprecedented scale. Sheikh Fadlallah called it a form of defensive violence erupting as a result of the oppression and despair of the weak. "This violence began as the people, feeling themselves bound by impotence, stirred to shatter some of that enveloping powerlessness for the sake of liberty." Fadlallah pointed out that the unique aspect of the impending surge of terrorism was the intensity of the emerging reaction to the magnitude and depth of Western oppression. "For this reason I fear that if solutions based on realistic and practical study of each problem as it occurs on the ground are not found, we are heading for a Third World War. Rather than arising between the two superpowers, this will be a war of terrorism, not Islamic terrorism, but terrorism among all the peoples of the planet. The weak will fight to defend their interests, even if they have to use knives and stones to spread chaos throughout the earth.''[31] Tehran and its allies were determined to be better prepared for this inevitable global struggle.

ESTABLISHING THE CURRENT TERRORIST SYSTEM

Since the mid-1980s, the international terrorist system has been totally controlled by a few states and constitutes an instrument of their foreign policy. As far as terrorism originating from and/or sponsored by the Middle East, there are no exceptions to this phenomenon and no deviations are tolerated by the controlling states. With high quality operatives becoming available, and with international arrangements largely in place, the international terrorist system could institutionalize and escalate its operations. The mature international terrorist system is completely controlled by Syria and Iran, with other countries, notably Libya, providing crucial services and support.

Thus, the much vaunted *HizbAllah*-Palestinian terrorist menace is completely subservient to the whims of Tehran and Damascus. The terrorist organizations are fully aware of the importance of their relationship with the supporting states as reflected in their main ideological statements. After a January 1990 meeting of the Central Committee of the PFLP-GC devoted to reflecting "on the fate of our pan-Arab and Palestinian struggle," the Front issued a statement emphasizing its relationship with the three main terrorist sponsoring states. The PFLP-GC statement hailed "the importance of alliance with Syria based on the joint steadfastness and confrontation

... [and] reiterated its commitment to its alliance with the Libyan *Jamahiriyah* on the bases of the joint struggle,'' and, most importantly, ''emphasized the promotion of militant ties with the Islamic Revolution in Iran.''[32]

The terrorist sponsoring states are fully aware of their dominance. A Syrian intelligence officer explained the interrelationship between Syria, Iran and the role of the *HizbAllah* in international terrorism. He belittled the importance of such master-terrorists as Abd al-Hadi Hammadi and Imad Mughaniyah in determining the policy and doctrine of international terrorism. ''All that matters is what Tehran says,'' he explained. ''And that depends very much on what our president [al-Assad] has to say.''[33] PKK leader Abdullah Ocalan pointed out in early 1991 that the Syrian government was providing assistance to 73 liberation (terrorist) organizations. (PKK is the Kurdish People's Liberation Front, initially a Syrian controlled radical terrorist organization that is increasingly becoming Islamist as a result of Iranian dominance.)[34] Syria was also the dominant power concerning terrorism in Lebanon.[35] Although Libya tried to maintain a high profile, it was not the dominant power.[36]

The key to the success of the mature international terrorist system is that the well-organized system of control is consolidated on the basis of the ideological and professional character of the participating ''organizations.'' Thus, Tehran is the key to the new revolutionary organizations in the Middle East.[37] Iranian prime minister Mir Hussein Mussavi stated that Khomeini continued to insist on the predominance of ''exporting of the revolution'' and reiterated that Iran's policy would continue to be guided by this ''genuine principle.''[38] Islamic Jihad, the *HizbAllah* and the various martyr organizations ''obey'' Khomeini also on the basis of ideological affinity.[39] Sheikh Hassan Nasrallah explained that the *HizbAllah* was ''working in the interests of an Iran that has no interests but Islam and the Muslims in the world.''[40] Sheikh al-Tufayli described the relations between the *HizbAllah* and Tehran as

these "of a soldier to his commander."[41] Thus, the *HizbAllah*
is "totally controlled by Tehran" from an operational point of
view.[42] In addition, some expert organizations and teams are
totally controlled by Damascus and are entrusted with specialized tasks.[43]

EVOLUTION OF IDEOLOGY AND DOCTRINE

Because of Tehran's dominance over the international
terrorist movement, the ideological evolution of Iran and the
HizbAllah since the mid-1980s and the consequent refine-
ment of their world view are crucial to the understanding of
the formulation of the armed struggle doctrine of the Islamist
terrorist system. Because they must mobilize and convince
their followers, ideologically and theologically based organizations generally attempt to explain and justify their actions.

Thus the evolution of the *HizbAllah*'s ideology testifies to
the commitment of Iran and Syria to escalate the terrorist
campaign all over the world. The Islamic struggle thus reflects
more the vengeance of states than the export of revolution by a
subversive movement. A coherent terrorist ideology and strategy, attributed to the Lebanese *HizbAllah*, was published in
Tehran on February 16, 1985, under the title: *Open Letter
Addressed by the HizbAllah to the Oppressed/Downtrodden in
Lebanon and in the World*. The document covered the declared doctrine and outline of the objectives of Iran, Syria and
the terrorist organizations they were controlling.[44] Not by accident, the entire high-command of the Lebanon *HizbAllah*
appeared in public on the very same day for the first time as an
organized body. They attended a meeting in the *Husseiniyah* in
Shyah (southern Beirut) where Sheikh Ibrahim al-Amin read
the *Open Letter* ceremoniously.[45]

In the mid-1980s the *HizbAllah* emerged, in its own words,
as a unique entity with global pan-Islamic loyalties and commitments. Sheikh Nasrallah explained that "Islam is our religion; our path originates from it. We have no leader or source

but the Imam; we shall follow him. . . We pledge to the Imam to continue our fight for Islam to the last drop of our blood; we shall not stop fighting until an Islamic government, led by the Imam of the *Ummah*, is established.''[46]

The *HizbAllah* is committed to the pursuit of Khomeini's grand design. Sheikh Fadlallah emphasized that ''the resistance has not emerged as a reaction and does not operate as such.'' Instead, it is following ''a long-term plan'' in which ''the Islamic resistance is part of the general situation.'' Fadlallah sees in the *HizbAllah*'s operations in Lebanon a spark and a catalyst for a major process. He explained that ''the spirit driving the resistance is beginning to intensify and grow from being simply a combat state of mind into a political and ideological state of mind, if that is the right expression. As such, the resistance may be able to maintain its growth and enter the arena as a new formula in competition with other formulas in the future.''[47]

The *HizbAllah* considers itself a unique organization representing and standing for the entire Islamic liberation struggle and the struggle for Islamic self-identity. Sheikh Abbas al-Mussawi explained that the *HizbAllah* is ''not a party in the traditional sense of the term. Every Muslim is automatically a member of *HizbAllah*. Thus it is impossible to list our membership.''[48] Sheikh Fadlallah went further, dwelling on the essence of *HizbAllah* as God's Party in the context of the martyrdom operations in Beirut. He explained that ''the *Hizballah* in the broad Qoranic sense which includes all free, struggling Muslims who represent the whole nation and the whole people . . . has a basic connection with the [martyrdom] operations, since the oppressed people who are God's Party in the Qoranic sense are those who stood against Israel and the United States.''[49] Fadlallah also pointed to the *HizbAllah*'s unique role in the Arab revolutionary struggle: ''We are not like others who say that they are a part of a broader unified Arab strategy. We say we are the basis for an Arab strategy and its true defenders.''[50]

Indeed, the declared ultimate objectives of the *HizbAllah*

are global and maximalist. Sheikh Subhi al-Tufayli acknowledged that the ultimate objective of the *HizbAllah* is "to set up
an Islamic Republic in the world."[51] Sheikh Abbas al-Mussawi
explained that all the *HizbAllah*'s operations, starting with
clashes and skirmishes in southern Lebanon, "were part of the
plan launched by the Islamic resistance since its inception — a
plan to seize the initiative and to escalate the *Jihad* and the
qualitative operations until they are turned into lessons, rather
schools, for Muslims in all parts of the world."[52]

The Iranians equate the *HizbAllah* with the *Pasdaran* as a
single Islamic revolutionary entity. As such, the *HizbAllah* is
more than a prototype for the Islamic revolution all over the
world; it is the embodiment of the further development and
dynamism of Khomeini's Islamic Revolution beyond Iran.
"All those who love the revolution and Islam should know that
the continuation of the path of the revolution and the preservation of the banner of pure Islam can be achieved only by
complete support for the *HizbAllah*."[53]

As Iran is changing, the support for the Islamic revolutionary (i.e., terrorist) movement is the quintessence of Khomeini's
legacy. "The preservation and continuation of the revolution is
only possible through support for the *Hizbollahi*," argued
Ayatollah Jannati. He argued that "in order to export the
revolution to the entire world the forces who support the
revolution must be strengthened."[54] Mussavi-Kho'iniha explained that "the Islamic Revolution of Iran has become the
standard-bearer of a profound and far-reaching struggle throughout the world against world arrogance and against the Great
Satan."[55] Hashemi-Rafsanjani pointed out that "the flag-bear-
ers of the struggle against imperialism, hegemony and capital-
ism are the Muslim revolutionaries," because, under current
conditions, "Islam is now the only pivot capable of rallying
together all justice-lovers around the world."[56]

In the pursuit of this campaign, Tehran urged all Muslim
communities to "shoulder their responsibilities and set up
HizbAllah resistance groups throughout the world." Tehran

pointed out that in today's interdependent world, "proven methods of struggle can be applied everywhere, either as they are or with slight modifications taking into account cultural, political and social peculiarities." Under these conditions, the Lebanon *Hizballah* should "serve as a model for an Islamic revolution in other Muslim countries."[57] Mehdi Karrubi also "emphasized that *HizbAllah* cells should be organized world-wide to defend the rights of Muslims."[58]

Sheikh Fadlallah took a prudent approach toward the real-ization of these long term objectives of the *HizbAllah*: "We call for Islamic rule in every part of the world, but it is not enough to advocate such a rule for it to materialize but rather to know the ground on which you could make such rule exist."[59] The *Pasdaran* shares this appreciation of professionalism. In February 1990, Rahim Safavi, the IRGC Deputy Commander, declared that the IRGC "is ready to share with Islamic armies and movements across the globe the military experiences it has acquired during almost eight years of the Iraqi-imposed war."[60]

The Islamic Jihad against the U.S., which is expressed in the form of international terrorism, has remained a central theme in the formulation of the guiding ideology of the terrorist groups sponsored by Iran.

In the summer of 1986, the Revolutionary Justice Organi-zation, another front for Iran and the *HizbAllah*, outlined its political objectives, emphasizing the global character of their *Jihad* and the centrality of terrorism to its implementation. The revival of revolutionary Islam, "has been made possible with the blood of the revered martyrs who lit the path of the revolution and who strengthened the will of the people, who defeated the enemy and who forced Israel to accept indignity and defeat." Thus, the Islamist terrorism in the Middle East "has also caused the revolutionary path of the people to be opened up to the Third World, and the nations of the world will gradually take their historic opportunity in the face of dangers of the cancerous plans of the United States and its allies in the North Atlantic Treaty."[61]

With the growing success of the *HizbAllah* and the further clarification of its Islamist revolutionary message, Tehran's endorsement and encouragement was becoming more explicit. "By relying on Islamic ideals, we are extremely hopeful of the bright future of our struggles . . . against superpower plots," President Ali Khamenei stated. He defined "the struggles of the Lebanese *HizbAllah* and other Muslim revolutionaries" as "the true meaning of the words *Jihad* for *Allah*."[62] However, it was up to Sheikh Fadlallah to explicitly state that the key "lies in knowing the U.S. policy in the area and, consequently, knowing the true nature of international conflict."[63] Therefore, Islamic Jihad argues, the confrontation with the U.S., "the world oppression of the arch-Satan," is the common denominator that links the Iranian, Lebanese, and Third World revolutionary movements in a global pan-Islamic "*Jihad* and struggle."[64]

This time, however, with a rejuvenated self-confidence, the *HizbAllah* was seriously considering seizing the initiative in the global revolutionary struggle.[65] Sheikh Fadlallah hailed the steadfastness and resolve of the *Hizbollahi* whose struggle brought about "the fears the world oppressors have for the world liberating Islamic movement." Nevertheless, the Islamic revolution was still facing grave challenges. Fadlallah warned that "currently the Islamic *Ummah* in various parts of the world is facing massive threats from oppressors who are vainly trying to contain the growing Islamic movement."[66] The triumph of the Iranian Revolution serves as a precedent for and a proof of the potential of the Islamic struggle. "The Iranian revolution," explained Sheikh Fadlallah, "proves that an Islamic movement can materialize the wishes of a nation and disproves the myth of the invulnerability of the big powers of the world."[67] And the *HizbAllah* had a clear doctrine as to the future and fortunes of the ensuing global Islamic revolution, concentrating on a struggle against Israel and the U.S.[68]

In the late 1980s, the *HizbAllah* anticipated the escalation of its Islamic revolutionary struggle and the growing direct involvement of the sponsoring states. Sheikh Hussein al-Mussawi explained that under present conditions, "we must ask ourselves and our partners in the Islamic and national front, who are supported by Syria and the Islamic Republic of Iran, to translate this alliance into practical results and unify their ranks."[69] Sheikh Fadlallah emphasized that such effort was required in order to implement the *HizbAllah*'s commitment to the establishment of "Islamic condition" in Lebanon and subsequently the rest of the world. "The Islamic condition I am talking about is one that includes all Muslims and is open to all the dispossessed in the world on the basis of Islamic thought, Islamic doctrine, Islamic action, and Islamic life."[70]

The *Jihad*, the divine armed struggle in all its forms including terrorism, is more than just the prime instrument for the realization of the *HizbAllah*'s main objective. The *Jihad* is the only means of realizing Islam's message for, as the Arabs say, "*Din Muhammad bi'l-Saif*" (Muhammad's divine law can be implemented only by the sword). For the perpetrators it is the ultimate form of moral self-purification. The adoption of Islamic ways, namely, the conduct of a resolute armed struggle, is the only hope for the restoration of the Islamic world. This is an urgent task for, because of Westernization, "the armed forces of the Islamic peoples were divested of the only creed appropriate to their cultural character, namely *Jihad*."[71] Addressing the growing pressures stemming from Westernization, Fadlallah emphasized "the dangerous consequences of such an action if the Islamic movement senses a threat to its existence."[72]

Sheikh Subhi al-Tufayli, the *HizbAllah*'s Spiritual Guide, stressed that although "Islam seeks to build a society on the basis of good and justice," the armed *Jihad* is a must. Thus, when attacked, "the Muslim has a duty to defend himself." Currently, the Muslim world is under attack from the United States, Tufayli explained, and the *HizbAllah* has a major role in the struggle against it: "We boast and are proud of ourselves when we are the head of the Muslim spear in the chest of U.S.

authority."[73] Sheikh Fadlallah elaborated that it was only as a consequence of its involvement in Islamic terrorism that "this Islamic movement has been acknowledged and honored by all local, regional, and international forces, by both those who label it as terrorism and those who have friendly feelings towards it."[74]

Sheikh Abbas al-Mussawi of the *HizbAllah* acknowledged a connection with the Islamic Jihad and its terrorist attacks.[75] He explained that the *HizbAllah*'s objectives can be achieved through a combination of "armed activities and social activities." Terrorism is an inevitable and acceptable instrument, he explained: "We must harass Americans wherever they are found in Lebanon, in train stations and airports. You don't have any other way except belonging to the *HizbAllah*." Sheikh Mussawi stated that "in his eyes it is an honor to be called terrorist whenever the goal is to harass and expel oppressors."[76]

Sheikh Fadlallah also differentiates between the act of violence and the perpetrators' motivation and righteousness. For him, the moral characterization of violence depends on the latter aspect. Fadlallah believes that "terrorism is a relative matter. People who want to be free and want to confront the forces which stand in the way of liberation causes must look for all possible means to use for the liberation of their territory, economy, and policies. They do not consider anything forbidden in the pursuit of these objectives. The legitimacy of every means stems from the legitimacy of the end sought. The purpose of raising the issue of terrorism and the concentration on the Arab and Islamic worlds in particular is to protect Israeli and imperialist interests."[77]

Sheikh Abbas al-Mussawi was fully aware of the issue of hurting innocent people in the course of terrorist attacks and bombings and argued that they should not constitute a hindrance to the realization of a divine objective. "There are mistakes sometimes, of course, but our actions are justifiable because we are defending all Muslims in Lebanon against the United States and Israel."[78] All victims, innocent bystanders and *Hizbollahi*, are parts of the Shi'ite myth of martyrdom. Sheikh Hussein al-Mussawi emphasized the fundamental difference between the *HizbAllah* and other Muslim terrorist movements: "In the first case the interests of Islam are more important than anything else and in the second case the interests of a Muslim individual is given priority over the interests of Islam as a whole."[79]

The Shi'ite collective exaltation of the martyr as an emulation of the legacy of Imam Hussein is at the foundation of the *HizbAllah*'s approach to suicide terrorism. Sheikh Fadlallah provides the clear definition for the justified and intentional martyrdom at the heart of suicide terrorism:

> The martyr constitutes an offering to sacrifice himself for a cause worthy of struggling for. He contains the concept of sacrifice that is all the values of liberty in the world. The difference between [martyrdom and] suicide is in the goal, not in the act in itself. He who commits suicide kills himself for his own private reasons, such as a desperation with life, financial problems or comparable reasons. If the suicide is motivated by the defense of a cause, it becomes martyrdom. Within the religious vision of martyrdom there is a political dimension. The *par excellence* example is that of Imam Hussein who fought far numerous enemies for the values of justice, liberty and the truth.[80]

Indeed, Sheikh Fadlallah asserts that one's death is determined as martyrdom on the basis of the original intentions rather than the actual cause of death: "The Muslims believe that you struggle by transforming yourself into a living bomb like you struggle with a gun in your hand. There is no difference between dying with a gun in your hand or exploding yourself. . . . In a situation of struggle or holy war you have to find the best means to achieve your goals."[81]

In the first months of 1988, Tehran embarked on a thorough examination of Islamist terrorism, both doctrinally and practically (such as training efficiency, network organization, etc.). The conclusions were defined in the "strength resolution," which called for the escalation of the *Jihad* and for the expansion of required terrorist training and support, and which was adopted in the Third Revolutionary Conference held in Tehran in February 1988.[82] After consultations with many Palestinian and *HizbAllah* terrorist leaders, Iran decided to establish an Islamic organization for the Liberation of Palestine as a substitute for the PLO.[83]

The essence of the Tehran conclusions were closely studied by several leaders and scholars of the *HizbAllah*, the prime executioners of Iran's strategy.[84] Fadlallah concluded the process with a definitive study on the evolution of the Islamic revolution and struggle that saw no alternative to a global escalation. He anticipated that the forthcoming phase of the Islamic struggle will be a fateful development because of the gravity of the outcome for both sides: "The battle goes on with all means and methods... The coming phase is the phase of struggle — the phase of the great future that makes huge progress." Fadlallah was optimistic as to the ultimate and inevitable outcome of the confrontation with the U.S. because "we are also considering a plan to achieve our major objective of liberating the oppressed from U.S. and imperialist domination and of encouraging Islam to become the ruling force in life... Consequently, the word that embodies the real situation with the United States is the word 'struggle'."[85]

The doctrinal and policy deliberations of early 1988 led to a thorough reexamination of the Islamic terrorist policy and the formulation of a coherent program. On June 12-15, the senior commanders of the *HizbAllah*, led by Ibrahim al-Amin, Subhi al-Tufayli, Hussein al-Mussawi, and Hussein Khalil visited Damascus for consultations with senior Syrian officials on future operations.[86] A decision about the escalation of international terrorism with the U.S., Israel and Turkey as the primary objectives was reached on June 20, 1988 in a major conference of the *HizbAllah*. The main resolutions concerning the escalation of international terrorism were published in the name of *Islamic Jihad*:

> On 20 June 1988, the High Command of the Islamic Jihad Organization held a session in Beirut to review the situation . . . as well as to map the organization's operations in the future. . .

> The High Command of the Islamic Jihad Organization has decided to continue the holy *Jihad* by all possible means against American imperialism, the Zionist enemy, and traitors like Kenan Evran, (the president of Turkey).

> We shall continue hijacking aircraft and ships, and also killing enemies of the Islamic world, until the faithful children of *Allah* are released from prison, and the occupied lands of the Muslims are free. On with the holy struggle for the triumph of the Islamic Revolution! —The Islamic Jihad Act.[87]

Soon afterwards, once these resolutions became known, Syria floated rumors that Iran decided to disband the Islamic Jihad Organization primarily because of the lingering hostage crisis.[88] The primary objective of these rumors was to blunt the impact of the *Hizballah*'s declared future plans.

In the late 1980s, Iran and the *HizbAllah* foresaw an escalating and intensifying struggle with the West. Sheikh Fadlallah believes that the growing power of Islam has already transformed the confrontation with the West into an all-out struggle for the very existence of Islam, explaining that "when the Islamic revolution started, it opened the eyes of international arrogance to the elements of strength that Islam possesses through committed groups that believe that their religious commitments deepens their political commitment." Fearing the ramifications of the spread of Islam, "international arrogance has begun to besiege Muslims even in matters pertaining to worship and individual commitments because it feels that any position of strength for Islam in the life of the individual or society will gain for Islam possibilities of strength in other areas. . . The Arab regimes have thereby begun to admit that the danger lies in the mosques and in those who frequent the mosques — believing young men and believing young women."[89] Tehran believes that the West, especially the U.S., is still committed to the eradication of the Islamic revolutionary movement. However, the ideas of conspiracy and struggle have expanded and now include several other aspects, especially "cultural conspiracies" — that is, Westernization.[90]

Thus, the *HizbAllah* explains that "the change of tactics by the powers of arrogance and their reliance on proxies at home instead of direct intervention to achieve their goals will not change the pure nature of the blood that the martyrs pumped in the veins of their people and their nation, making them prefer pride of martyrdom to the humiliation of acquiescence. This noble blood will serve as an incentive to reject the positions of humiliation, regardless of the pressures and the sacrifices."[91] Ahmad Jibril of the PFLP-GC sees in the growing pressure and despair both the cause and justification for the expansion of international terrorism. "Terrorists are people who have lost the will to suppress their anger and patience any longer," Jibril explained. "They hit back right, left and center, so the world will take notice of their plight."[92]

Meanwhile, faced with the rejuvenation and resurgence of Islamic revolutionary movements and terrorist organizations all over the world, and the growing influence of Iran over this trend, Qaddafi decided to return to center stage through an international conference designed, like past conferences, to set a unified global terrorist agenda and solve various ideological problems.

Between March 19 and March 21, 1990, Muammar Qaddafi chaired a large conference in Tripoli aimed at escalating the anti-U.S. Islamic revolutionary struggle all over the world. The

Second General Conference of the World Islamic Popular Command convened in order to determine how to mobilize and incite the Muslim masses to unite in a decisive struggle against the U.S. and the Western world, and overthrow their own apostate leaders.[93] The World Islamic Popular Command determined that ''there is a real obstacle on the future path of the Arab people and the Muslims everywhere presented by the United States which is leading the 10th Crusader campaign.''[94] In his keynote address to the conference, Qaddafi emphasized that there can be no compromise in the *Jihad* against the West because ''Christianity does not recognize anything called Islam, its ideology, its Qoran or its Prophet!''[95] Specific objectives and priorities for the anticipated world-wide struggle were outlined in the conference.[96]

The World Islamic Popular Command determined that ''The U.S. is the devil on this planet.''[97] However, the Islamic struggle advocated by the conference is against the entire Western civilization. ''The so-called United States of America and its capitalist, imperialist gang — its allies — which it controls, in fact embodies the devil on earth,'' explained Qaddafi. ''The break between us and them should be permanent and decisive.'' The Muslim world, Qaddafi exclaimed, is already ''in a battle against the 10th crusader campaign led by the United States of America and its satanic allies.''[98] The conference urged all Muslims to isolate the West from the world and lay siege to the U.S., pressuring it into destruction. In order to realize these objectives, the World Islamic Popular Command called for ''the declaration of *Jihad* against crusading and Zionism.''[99] Qaddafi hailed the move, stating: ''If we did not declare *Jihad* against those, then against whom are we going to declare it?''[100]

The most important aspect of the Tripoli conference was that Qaddafi led the World Islamic Popular Command into making a milestone theological decision concerning the priorities and methods of this *Jihad* against apostates. The World Islamic Popular Command decreed a sharp deviation from the

doctrines of the predominantly Sunni Muslim Brotherhood to
a form of popular *Jihad* very similar to the Shi'ite *Jihad* as
defined by Khomeini. They decreed that this desired change in
the Muslim world should be achieved through the pressure of
the masses. Unlike the Muslim Brotherhood, who believe that
violence against apostates at home should precede any *Jihad*
against the infidels, the World Islamic Popular Command
decreed that Islamic terrorism should not be directed against
Arab regimes or the killing of Muslims, but rather concentrate
on the killing of Jews and/or Israelis who are the source of evil.
In his address, Qaddafi criticized the Muslim Brotherhood
activists for conducting terrorism against Arab regimes, even
secular ones such as Syria's and Egypt's, when they should
"cause an explosion in Tel Aviv" and kill Israelis wherever
they may be, particularly on Egyptian soil.[101]

In his keynote address, Qaddafi was very explicit in his
definition of the anti-U.S. and anti-West *Jihad* he intends to
lead. Qaddafi sees the party of God (*HizbAllah*) as the moral
and militant struggler (mujahid)-vanguard of the revival of true
Islam. "The Party of God are the Muslims; the Muslims are
the *HizbAllah*; non-Muslims are the Party of Satan. We have
declared that the Islamic nation is the Party of God (*HizbAllah*).
America, the Israelis, and their allies are the Party of Satan."
Qaddafi emphasized that the *HizbAllah* should lead a popular
struggle all over the world, including the forces of the Arab
states. "There is no army in Islam. There is militant-struggler
people, armed people." In conclusion, Qaddafi urged the
Second General Conference of the World Islamic Popular
Command "to establish a real Islamic renaissance and unity
and wage a real *Jihad*" until their ultimate objective is realized. He reiterated his and Libya's commitment to do their
utmost to realize these goals.[102]

Meanwhile, Tehran was also looking for a ideological
definition that would permit it to increase support for Islamic
terrorist and revolutionary movements while being able to
deny the export of the revolution. Mohtashemi addressed this

issue in March 1990, arguing that "there is no contradiction between national and ideological interests. As a whole the term 'outside interests' is a deviant thought as far as Islamic principles and the Islamic revolution are concerned, because Islam is an ideology that has set out to free the human race." Therefore, the foundation of any ideology of an Islamic state is a commitment to liberation of the entire nation. Because of the universal character of Islam and the Islamic revolution, there is no need for it to be exported.

"With regards to exporting the revolution," Mohtashemi explains, "this is not something that is under our [Iran's] control. One of the special aspects of the brilliant Islamic revolution is that it is aimed at liberating people and giving them dignity. It opens its own way in human society, all by itself. It has no limits and recognizes no boundaries. Not only the enemy, but even the leaders and supporters of the revolution will be unable to oppose its exportation, as long as its principles remain intact."[103]

The world view of official Tehran and its perception of the role and prospects of the Islamic Revolution in early 1990 emphasize the emergence of a global Islamic Revolution recognizing and accepting Tehran's leadership:

> The Islamic movement, the base of which is the Islamic Republic of Iran and the main basis of which is the Islamic revolution, is based on a divine world outlook. It is not only based on the interests of the masses, but it has been created by the people and rests on the shoulders of the people. In Asia, Europe, Africa, America, Oceana, and every corner of the world where a movement in the name of Islam exists, its banner is carried by the people who are motivated by their belief in God and opposition to materialism. It is exactly because of this that despite all the international pressure being inflicted on it, this great popular movement is constantly expanding, strengthening, and deepening.[104]

Tehran emphasizes that this anti-Western revolutionary trend is a direct continuation of the Islamic revolution incited by Khomeini:

> If the Great Satan and the other satans, especially in the West, feared Imam Khomeini, may his soul be sanctified, and lived in fear for a decade, then they continue to fear him today more than ever before, even though he is not among us. . . The Westerners have correctly understood that the world movement of Islam is the biggest threat to the 'corrupt Western empire.' It is we, the Muslims, who should — through our alert unity — prove that the West will be defeated by the world movement of Islam. *InshAllah* (God willing), we shall prove this.[105]

While Tehran defines the threat and challenges quite explicitly, it is up to the *HizbAllah* to bring up the issue of counter-measures.

Sheikh Fadlallah called for a new wave of *Jihad*, modified for new world conditions. He suggested that the Western hostages should be released simply because they had outlived their usefulness. "The issue has long been exploited by the West to distort the image of Islam and Muslims."[106] Under the current conditions, Fadlallah emphasized, "*Jihad* must take on a new impetus with new means and a new mentality."[107] Indeed, the Islamist revolutionary *Jihad* is still escalating. In a Beirut sermon endorsed by Tehran, Sheikh Fadlallah outlined *HizbAllah*'s confrontational goals for the Muslim world:

> Al-Sayyid Fadlallah called on Muslims to establish military, cultural and economic forces to achieve the goals of Islam and to confront the forces that are robbing the Islamic world. He warned against weakening and despairing vis-a-vis the forces of global arrogance. . . . He emphasized that the United States will stand with the Arabs only when this stand serves its own and Israel's interests.[108]

Tehran sees itself as the center of an Islamic world facing ever greater threats and on the verge of confrontation with the West. Under these conditions, Tehran is obliged to be involved in anything affecting Muslims, wherever they might be, in order to protect and further the interest of the global Islamic revolution. Hojjat ol-Islam Mehdi Karrubi defined Iran's position:

> It is only natural that, for an Islamic Republic that must be protected by all Muslims in the world, it is a duty to defend the rights of Muslim nations and not remain indifferent in the face of injustices that are being committed against them.[109]

Little wonder, therefore, that Mohtashemi is very optimistic as to the overall outcome of the world-wide Islamic revolutionary process:

> It is under such conditions — when the superpowers have their internal issues and problems — that the people of the Third World, especially the Islamic countries, will, within the next decade, become free of the control of foreign powers and their mercenaries and will be liberated. So the world is becoming multi-polar. Ultimately, Islam will become the supreme power and will play a decisive role on the international scene.[110]

LEADERSHIP AND FORCE STRUCTURE

The top of the formal command structure and organization of the *HizbAllah* and the rest of the Islamic terrorist system is in Tehran. Syria, although maintaining equally tight control over the terrorist system, never placed Damascus in the formal command structure or organizational charts.[111] Because of Iran's dominance, the evolution of the leadership in Tehran in the mid 1980s is a key to understanding the development of the mature international terrorism system.[112] This trend was clearly reflected in widespread domestic changes in Iran. Most important, the rise of Shi'ite militancy in Iran was reflected in grass roots changes in the mosque where the teaching of the Qoran was giving way to practical sessions on the art of bombing. Iran's terrorist center is thus a state within a state.[113]

Changes in the supreme leadership in Tehran thus reflect the evolution of the Iranian terrorist policy. The rise of Ali Khamenei, then the president of Iran, served as an indication of the escalation of Iran's involvement in terrorism.[114] The leading leaders in Iran's Supreme Defense Council — Khamenei, Hashemi-Rafsanjani and the IRGC's Mohsin Reza'i — are also empowered to issue directives to the *HizbAllah*.[115] (Reza'i replaced Rafiq-Dust who was nominated Chairman of the Oppressed Foundation in September 1989.[116]) As of early 1986, routine coordination with Syria and Libya was conducted by a committee of three: Mirsalim, Reza'i and Jallaludin Farsi.[117]

These trends were further intensified following the formal removal of Ayatollah Montazeri as Khomeini's designated successor in mid-October 1986.[118] Conservative ayatollahs such as Golpayegani, Najafi, Qomi and Kho'i were supporting the rise of confrontational terrorism. Other leaders, notably Hashemi-Rafsanjani and Velayati, were considered moderates because of their pragmatic approach to policy. Moreover, the practitioners, led by Mussavi-Kho'iniha, had a meteoric rise to power under Khomeini on the basis of their operational successes.[119] During this power structure formulation, several circles in Tehran were aware that ''terrorist attacks against Western countries in the name of Islam bring a great deal of satisfaction to the leaders of Moscow.''[120]

Ultimately, the control over the *HizbAllah* served as a major stepping stone to power by members of the Iranian elite, most notably Hojat ol-Islam Ali-Akbar Hashemi-Rafsanjani, who used strategy and foreign policy, of which international terrorism was a prime instrument, as his main vehicle in his climb to power despite his relatively low formal religious education.[121] This aspect of the Tehran power struggle was emphasized by Ali Kent who was in charge of the intelligence arm of *Islamic Jihad* in Turkey in the early to mid-1980s.[122] Already in 1986, Ali Kent explained that "Hashemi-Rafsanjani is the true leader of Islamic Jihad. He is very strong. Hashemi-Rafsanjani will come to power after Khomeini. The majority of members of the Iranian *Majlis* support the Islamic Jihad."[123]

Indeed, the office of the Islamic Liberation Movements was separated from the IRGC in 1985-86,[124] and the center of Islamic Jihad was located in the 'Guidance Ministry' of the Islamic Republic in Tehran where Hashemi-Rafsanjani was in direct command,[125] with active support from the Ministry of Intelligence.[126] In 1987, Hojjat ol-Islam Hadi Khosrowshahi, a protege of Hashemi-Rafsanjani, was nominated to be the new head of the office of the Islamic Liberation Movements.[127] This moving of the office facilitated the strengthening of official Tehran's control over the terrorist infrastructure.

Consequently, in 1987, Iran publicly reiterated its support for the Islamic struggle and declared that this would dominate its foreign policy. "We cannot maintain peaceful relations with satans and those who have gone astray; indeed, we cannot coexist with them. Islamic governments have charged us with fighting against all errant and irreligious people everywhere in the world."[128] Simultaneously, Tehran set up an integrated Iranian terrorist organ to supervise terrorist operations abroad that was headed by Hashemi-Rafsanjani. The other officials in charge were IRGC Commander Muhsin Rafiq-Dust, Information Minister Ali Fallahiyan, Interior Minister Abdollah Nuri, and Muhammad Hashemi Bahramani, the president's brother. The organization had an independent budget, and a special section inside the Council of Ministers was overseeing it.[129]

Then, Deputy Foreign Minister Javad Mansuri consolidated and expanded the use of Iran's diplomatic missions as centers of terrorism. He also built a cadre of diplomat-terrorists from the ranks of the SAVAMA and IRGC-intelligence who became his disciples. "Our glorious revolution can only be exported with grenades and explosives," Mansuri wrote in his book *Revolution and Diplomacy*. In the late 1980s, Mansuri was made Ambassador to Pakistan, a center for the export of the revolution into the U.S. He was then assured by Ali Khamenei, Iran's spiritual guide, that the apparatus he had set up to export the revolution would remain under his control and that Iranian embassies abroad would continue their work according to the programs that Mansuri had especially designed for each of them.[130]

Indeed, Prime Minister Mir Hussein Mussavi complained on September 5 or 7, 1988, in his resignation letter to Ali Khamenei that the terrorist campaign was being run by Khamenei and Hashemi-Rafsanjani without the participation of the government.

> External/Overseas operations are carried out without our knowledge and without our orders. You know how damaging the effect of this situation has been for our country. Only after an airplane is hijacked are we informed. Only when a machine gun opens fire in a Lebanese street and the sound of it echoes everywhere do we find out about the incident. Only after explosives are discovered in the possession of our pilgrims in Jiddah [Saudi Arabia] do I find out about it. Unfortunately, and in spite of the damages and harm caused by these actions to the country, such operations can take place, at any hour in the name of the government.

Mussavi confirmed in his letter that these terrorist operations were being conducted under the direct command of Khamenei, and that consequently Mussavi and others are "deprived of any power in the foreign policy sphere."[131]

By early 1989, a stronger Hashemi-Rafsanjani was "moving toward the extremists' camp in the Iranian government."[132] Official Tehran was extremely preoccupied with furthering the Islamic revolution throughout the Arab world and the armed struggle [terrorism] against the West.[133] Hashemi-Rafsanjani and Khamenei strengthened their hold over Iran in late 1989, establishing a committee of 40 clerics, most of them hard liners, that in effect runs the country, pursuing a confrontational policy.[134]

In mid-1989, Hashemi-Rafsanjani assured a delegation of the *HizbAllah* and pro-Syrian Palestinian commanders that Iran "will remain on the side of the Lebanese Muslims" in their struggle.[135] Iran continues to emphasize the centrality of the export of the Islamic Revolution in its policy. "Today, Tehran is considered as the main backer of the Shi'ite world community, though the Islamic Revolution of Iran has a wider scope which includes all Islamic schools of thought."[136] Sheikh Fadlallah was encouraged by these developments in Tehran, which he attributed to Khamenei's policies. Fadlallah explained that "the Islamic line that is open to Islamic liberation movements is still the line that is in the mind of the Islamic leadership, especially Ayatollah Khamenei, who has experience with the ideology of Islamic political movements. He has also been able to deepen his experience and has begun to experience broad responsibility in his high position."[137] Nevertheless, as post-Khomeini Tehran was being consolidated, the leadership of the *HizbAllah* and the other Islamic "liberation movements" also reiterated their loyalty to both Hashemi-Rafsanjani[138] and Khamenei.[139]

Since 1988, the Iranian-controlled terrorist high command has remained fairly stable. Hashemi-Rafsanjani is the senior commander. His undisputed authority is reflected in his communications with the "front" where he uses the code name *Sheikh*. He is supported by an integrated terrorist organ that consults and supervises terrorist operations abroad. The 110th Independent Brigade and Iran's vast terrorist training infrastructure are directly under Hashemi-Rafsanjani. The operational command and control over international terrorism under

Hashemi-Rafsanjani is divided into two branches: (1) Iranian direct supervision under Muhammad Rayshari; and (2) preparation of and control over the terrorists under Muhsin Rafiq-Dust.[140] Muhsin Reza'i replaced Rafiq-Dust in September 1989.[141]

The consolidation of the *HizbAllah* "High Command" in Lebanon was indeed simultaneous because, for Tehran, the terrorist build-up in Lebanon was only the first phase in the implementation of Khomeini's grand design to export a global Islamic Revolution.[142] In mid-1986, the *HizbAllah* was transformed into "a broader, umbrella organization comprising of all extremist groups and organizations" in Lebanon. Its Iranian-controlled revolutionary cells include Shi'ites, Sunnis and members of politicized minorities such as Armenians and Palestinians.[143] These cells were represented in the consultative council that first adjourned on May 28, 1986.[144]

However, the web of myriad mini-organizations claiming operations should not be confused with their being dependents of a single entity, namely, the Iranian-dominated central leadership. All major terrorist operations originating from Lebanon are carried out on order from Iran or, at the least, detailed consultation with Tehran.[145] Sheikh Subhi al-Tufayli explained that *Islamic Jihad* was merely a name "used by all those who want to disguise their true identity."[146] Indeed, the secret services of both Iran and Syria use the cover of *Islamic Jihad* to shield their covert operations.[147] Tehran makes most of the meaningful decisions for *HizbAllah*, and "their real leader appears to be Khomeini."[148] At the tactical and professional high command levels, the authority is strictly in the hands of professionals with strong influence, dominance and supervision being exercised by outside professional experts such as those of Syrian intelligence.

The force structure is on the basis of personal relationships. "Militiamen are very loyal to their commanders and religious leaders. As in Iran, martyrdom is a sacred duty."[149]

Salah Khalaf (Abu-Iyad) pointed out that Islamic Jihad, the *Islamic Jihad* for the Liberation of Palestine, and Revolutionary Justice "are the names of one organization, expressing the currents inside *HizbAllah* which have repercussions in the Lebanese arena and extensions in the Iranian arena."[150] *HizbAllah* is organized on the basis of Lebanon's Shi'ite clans.[151] Officially, *HizbAllah* is but a part of the web of myriad mini-organizations rather than a single entity, all functioning under the jurisdiction of the Iranian-dominated central leadership.[152] The clan leaders among themselves make up an ordinary and well organized command structure with specific responsibilities.

Sheikh Muhammad Hussein Fadlallah is effectively the chairman of the *HizbAllah*. Sheikh Fadlallah is recognized as the highest spiritual leader in both Syria and Lebanon. He also exercises some control over the *HizbAllah*, the Imam Hussein Suicide Team, the Lebanese Muslim Students Associations and a few other specialized organizations. Abd al-Ilah al-Mussawi (Abu-Haydar) is in charge of the practical aspects of the Imam Hussein Forces. Second in command is Sheikh Hasan Nasrallah who runs military and terrorist operations. Sheikh Zuhayr Kanj is his deputy. Third in command is Sheikh Subhi al-Tufayli, the spiritual guide of the *HizbAllah*, who is close to Fadlallah. Nasrallah and Tufayli are directly in charge of key activities including the hostage holding. Hussein al-Musawi heads Islamic Amal. Sheikh Ibrahim al-Amin is the *HizbAllah* spokesman and a key leader. Imad Mughaniyah is in charge of practical military affairs and special operations. Mustafa Shihadah and Abd al-Hadi Hammadi are the main intelligence interrogators and investigators. Abd al-Hadi Hammadi is chief of security of *HizbAllah* in Lebanon. Khalid Assaf is the *HizbAllah*'s information official. The *HizbAllah*'s internal security officials are Salah Nun and Muhammad Hammud. Until his death in February 1992, Sheikh Abbas Mussawi, was the "maestro" of operations in Beirut.[153]

The Shi'ite *JundAllah* (The Soldiers of Islam) that works directly for the Iranian intelligence is under the command of the brothers Yussuf Hassan al-Hakim and Hussein al-Hakim, as well as Muhammad Ahmad Sallam, the *Jundullah*'s chief of military and terrorist operations, Ali Hussein Karaki, Fu'ad Ali al-Qasri, and Hussein Qassim al-Hussein.[154]

Reflecting Tehran's preferences, Fadlallah, Abbas Mussawi and Isa Tabataba'i of the Iranian Embassy in Beirut led a *Pasdaran-HizbAllah* military march in the Biqaa.[155]

Major terrorist operations are conducted by the Special Operations division established by Col. Muhammad Awa'i.[156] The force is under such a direct and tight control of Hussein Niknam, the Iranian charge d'affaires in Beirut, that Sheikh Fadlallah privately described the force members as "nothing more than the Iranian 'hunting dogs.'"[157] The *HizbAllah* special operations division is a highly professional team of no more than 25 experts, all of whom are Shi'ites who received lengthy training in Iran.[158] In late 1989, Imad Mughaniyah was *HizbAllah*'s Chief of Special Operations, having completed intensive training in Iran,[159] and Abd al-Hadi Hammadi, a senior official of the *HizbAllah* security apparatus in Beirut, was his closest assistant mainly on Lebanese related issues.[160] Other key members are Sheikh Hussein Ghabris, who acts as the commander in Beirut when Mughaniyah is away, and Sheikh Hussein Khalil who is the contact man with *HizbAllah* security and intelligence.[161]

The majority of Lebanese personnel of *HizbAllah* special forces and elite terrorists come from the Mughaniyah and Hamadah clans and are personally loyal to the senior commanders.[162] The specialized equipment and weapons, and the target-instruction intelligence folders are delivered to *HizbAllah* special operations directly from Tehran on Iran Air flights to Beirut. Ambassador Dastmalchian inspects the unloading of these items in person in the Beirut airport.[163] Islamic Jihad announcements accompanying these operations are written by the *Shura Majlis* (the Assembly Council, *HizbAllah*'s supreme ruling body of 12 members) in consultation with the Iranian ambassador to Damascus.[164]

FORCE STRUCTURE AND TRAINING INFRASTRUCTURE

In mid-1985, Iran decided to markedly increase its terrorist training program. By then, there were already some 37 training bases for terrorists in Iran. The instructors for general subjects were already mainly Syrians, Libyans and Palestinians.[165]

In February 1986, the *HizbAllah* Supreme Council held the Fourth Islamic Conference in the former Intercontinental Hotel in Tehran. It was chaired by Hojatolislam Muhammad Rayshari, Iran's chief of intelligence. Several representatives of the Iranian Government and several Islamic terrorist organizations, mainly from the Middle East (Iran, Lebanon, Tunisia, Kuwait, Bahrain, Saudi Arabia, Iraq, etc.), took part. The participants came with a very clear understanding of Tehran's global aspirations. Iranian speakers stressed that the sophistication and effectiveness of the recent acts of terrorism were directly proportional to the increase in courses and specialized training sponsored by Iran and Syria. Rayshahri told the participants that he gave his permission to open special courses on "Training and Security" beginning in April 1986, and that they would be held in a special school set aside in Shiraz. In addition, some of the key participants were taken to a visit to the "Gardens of Manzarieh," Iran's suicide school.[166]

Indeed, since mid-1985 Iran was increasing its specialized terrorist training program for foreigners prepared for high-risk operations overseas. Among the first to receive these training was a group of Afghan *mujahideen* in the Mashhad area who were transferred to a camp in the Quchan district and given intensive terrorist and clandestine work training under the command of Muhammad Ali Kolahduz. Following their initial success, Tehran decided to use several groups of Afghans for overseas terrorist operations. Some of these Afghans were prepared for terrorist operations in the U.S.[167] Similarly, when General Al-Khouli decided to integrate the ASALA operatives into the Syrian- and Iranian- controlled network in Western Europe, ASALA moved its headquarters from Talabia, in the Biqaa, to Tehran where many of its operatives underwent additional training before deployment to Western Europe.[168]

Since the late 1980s, Tehran continued to significantly expand the training infrastructure for highly sophisticated clandestine and terrorist operations in the West. Most important is the new SAVAMA school established in 1986 at the Aqdassiah base near Tehran. It is the training site for death squads and assassination teams for the elimination of the regime's enemies overseas, mainly in Western Europe and the U.S. At the Chamran base, the specialized training in sophisticated explosives and sabotage training for IRGC operatives for overseas operations was markedly expanded.[169] In the Manzariah Camp near Tehran there was a further expansion of the terrorist and sabotage training for terrorists recruited overseas (not from the Middle East) as well as an expansion of suicide training. Iranian and Arab hit teams for overseas operations, mainly Western Europe and the Far East, are also trained there.[170]

The special *Imam* school in Shiraz, whose opening was announced by Rayshahri, specializes in espionage and counter-espionage techniques aimed at helping the graduates run clandestine networks overseas. Each class has an average of 250 students, 200 of whom are members of the security-intelligence service of the IRGC. The other 50 are from Persian Gulf countries, mainly Kuwait, Saudi Arabia and Bahrain, who return to their home countries after completing their training. A few Soviet Central Asians had enrolled in each class as of 1986. The IRGC operatives also receive in Shiraz specialized training in foreign languages, principles of espionage and counter-intelligence, code making and breaking, low intensity warfare, deep penetration into and survival behind enemy lines and sophisticated terrorist operations such as sabotage and assassination. The trainees receive advanced military training in a camp in Persopolis. Instructors in Shiraz include foreign experts such as North Koreans and Syrians. [171]

In the fall of 1989, Tehran decided to further expand the high quality terrorist and guerrilla warfare training of the IRGC, and established a dedicated battalion that would specialize in such operations. Ahmad Jibril and Muhsin Reza'i signed an agreement for the PFLP-GC to provide trainers and instructors for this battalion. Training takes place in a new garrison east of Tehran. In return, Tehran increased its monthly support for the PFLP-GC from $3 million to $5.5 million. [172]

Kuwaiti, Lebanese and Iraqi terrorists also have training bases in the Mashhad area where they are taught various subjects ranging from sophisticated sabotage techniques against oil installations to ways to strike civil aviation. [173] The IRGC also provides advanced training in terrorism and sabotage at the Imam Hussein school in Eshratabad for terrorists recruited in Arab countries. [174]

Since early 1988, there has been a surge in the Iranian preparations and training for terrorist strikes against Western civil aviation. [175] Terrorists specially trained in surveying and preparing terrorist attacks on civil aviation (aircraft and airports) are deployed as crew members on Iran Air aircraft for flights all over the world. They also recruit airport workers or neighbors and create cells for future operations. [176] Highly trained expert terrorists and hit teams [men and women] are deployed as Iran Air stewards so that their official uniforms would enable them to move freely around the airports. They arrive unarmed on Iran Air flights and retrieve their weapons and explosives from operatives and/or caches on-site. [177]

There was a corresponding expansion of the specialized training in Wakilabad (a major Iranian airport near Mashhad, a major city in northeast Iran) with a growing emphasis on placing bombs on aircraft. In a significant development, detachments of two to three Westernized female terrorists are trained on actual aircraft.[178] Moreover, teams of Kuwaiti, Lebanese and Iraqi terrorists are provided with intense and concentrated training in the Wakilabad airport. Some of these graduates have already participated in the hijackings of Kuwaiti aircraft. One of the reasons a hijacked Kuwaiti aircraft landed in Mashhad was to enable the trainees to closely examine operations in progress.[179]

In February 1988, Tehran decided to significantly increase the number of women terrorists. Their training is coordinated by the International Revolutionary Muslim Women's Organization. Consequently, the number of Shi'ite female terrorists trained under the leadership of Zahra Rahnavard, the wife Mir Hosayn Mussavi, increased to 400 per class. Khomeini's daughter Zahra Mostafavi is also a senior official of the organization. Zahra Rahnavard concentrates on special training camps in Iran where sabotage training are provided to females, including suicide attacks. The main camps, all under SAVAMA supervision, are at Manzariyeh, Wakilabad, Salehabad, and Marudashi. Most women are from Iran, the Gulf sheikhdoms, Pakistan and Bangladesh.[180]

Iran also continued to expand the training infrastructure for comprehensive operations in the Third World. There has been a marked expansion of the Najafabadi Camp in Qom under the command of Mullah Ha'eri, specializing in ideology, recruitment and network control training for *HizbAllah* operations in Muslim communities in non-Muslim countries, mainly sub-Saharan Africa and South East Asia, but also in Western Europe.[181]

Most important, though, is the Imam al-Sadiq University in Qom dedicated to furthering the export of the revolution. It is a highly professional institution preparing operatives for Third World assignments, mainly the education, agitation and organization of communities into supporters of Iran and the global

Islamic revolution. Yussuf al-Badri, an Egyptian visitor, pointed to the professionalism and expertise of the students. He explained that these students "know the language of every country to which they will go, and speak it like natives. They master the dialect and understand the habits of peoples in these countries, their likes and dislikes. They learn everything about them. . . They gather information on a certain region as if they were living in it. It is a dangerous group."[182]

The Melli University in Evin, near Tehran, was expanded and converted into an advanced, highly specialized training site for foreigners. Since the mid-1980s, there have been approximately 1,000 operatives studying there at any given time, including members of the Irish Republican Army, ASALA, and Syrian-controlled Palestinian groups. Special attention is paid to selected individuals from Sri Lanka, Senegal, Brazil, Paraguay and Mexico, who are expected to establish networks in their countries and then move on to the American South and West, establishing networks under the protection of Hispanic communities. North Korean intelligence operatives, who would operate with these groups and in other dangerous missions, are also being trained in Melli. In the U.S., these Koreans melt into the numerous Korean communities.

Emphasis is put on clandestine operations in Westernized urban centers. Operations aim for the disruption of normal life through diverse methods, including gaining access to and sabotaging computerized networks, and exploiting politicians, journalists and members of the clergy. Several Europeans serve as senior faculty as well as guest speakers in highly specialized sessions. Military and sabotage training are provided in facilities in Firuzkoor (in the desert near Tehran) and, in special cases, in Manzariyah. Reportedly, in Manzariyah terrorists study how to brainwash, control and activate suicide terrorists while in the West.[183]

Another highly specialized center in Tehran, on Takht-e-Tavous Street near the Libyan Embassy, concentrates on spe-

cial intelligence and clandestine operations training, mainly for
agents recruited from Western countries. The center also oversees the Iranian part of special projects conducted in cooperation with Libya.[184] Among the first such projects was the
training of Polisario (the Western Sahara liberation front)
terrorists. On May 2, 1986, the first class of some 80 members
of the Polisario Front left Iran, having completed intensive
advanced training.[185] These international operations were further expanded in 1989 with the recruitment of some 300
foreign Muslim students for studies in the International Islamic
University in Tehran. In mid-1990, the building of a permanent
site for the university began near Qazvin.[186]

All of this training and all these preparations are to serve
the anticipated escalation of *HizbAllah* terrorism under the
command of Imad Mughaniyah.[187] Toward that end, Tehran
allocated $90 million in late 1987 for the "military enhance-
ment" of *HizbAllah* that "will bring about a comprehensive
change in the nature of the *HizbAllah's* military actions in the
near future," including "the consolidation of the *HizbAllah*'s
nerve center with all the new strength it needs." Former
Harakat Amal commander Aql Hamiyah and Mughaniyah
were nominated for senior positions in the new command.[188]
Imad Mughaniyah himself arrived in Tehran and stayed during
October-December 1987 for intensive training in the Iranian
special operations schools north of Tehran.[189] In January 1988,
he attended school in Qom.[190] Abd al-Hadi Hammadi also
arrived in Tehran in late 1987 for a few months[191], but reportedly did not stay as long as Mughaniyah. Both Abd al-Hadi
Hammadi and especially Imad Mughaniyah continued to make
frequent trips to Tehran to oversee terrorist preparations.[192] It
can be said that Imad Mughaniyah, in effect, stayed in Tehran
for three years, making short visits to Syria and Lebanon for
special operations or high-level meetings. Imad Mughaniyah
returned from Iran to Lebanon in early July 1990, assumed
command and then inspected key *HizbAllah* installations in-

cluding the Western hostages and their guards.[193]

As part of its deniability policy, Syria tried to minimize the presence of large terrorist-related installations on its soil and instead concentrate them in the Syrian-controlled Biqaa, ostensibly Lebanese territory. Major terrorist headquarters remained in the Damascus area as part of Syria's focus on control through the monopoly of specialized key functions. For example, in the mid-1980s, Syria undertook to expedite, streamline and simplify communications and travel between the *HizbAllah* and Tehran. A new transfer point was organized by the Syrian army in Mansa', and Ayatollah Karrubi used it on an inspection tour in the Biqaa.[194]

Syrian intelligence holds the Palestinians under tight control through their Damascus headquarters. When the Syrians need an overseas terrorist operation they call in a terrorist leader and order the operation. The Palestinian will ultimately get some favors. Now the Palestinian leader pulls out some "sub-contractors" from among the foreigners in his training camps and uses them for the expendable aspect of the operation. In return, the foreign terrorist organization will receive additional weapons, false documents and shelter. Thus, the Syrians are capable of conducting deniable operations from Damascus.[195] Similarly, and for security reasons, some of the most sensitive Iranian operations are also conducted from Syria. For example, the Shi'ite *JundAllah* is actually an arm of the SAVAMA but received its weapons and training from Syria.[196] Meanwhile, the Biqaa itself is totally dominated by the Syrian Armed Forces and the security forces of Rifa'at Assad.[197]

Hafiz al-Assad himself emphasized the importance of *shahadah* (martyrdom, that is suicide) terrorist operations in a speech to Syrian students. "Such attacks are aimed at causing the enemy heavy losses," he explained. "[T]hey are also spreading terror among the enemy ranks on the one hand, and raising the morale of the people and enhancing their awareness of the importance of the spirit of sacrifice, on the other hand.

Thus, waves of popular *fiday* (singular of *fidayeen*) sacrifice will follow successively and the enemy will not be able to endure them." Assad anticipates that such *fiday* and *shahadah* operations will spearhead "the battle against Zionism [which] is a fatal battle — to be or not to be."[198] Toward that end, Syria maintained its own "school for militants", also known as "the big struggle school", where elite terrorists, including suicide drivers for the Lebanese National Resistance Front, are trained and especially prepared for their suicide attacks. Among the trainees were Syrians committed to Greater Syria.[199] Damascus highlighted the existence of this school in order to demonstrate that the Shi'ites did not have a monopoly on suicide attacks. Indeed, the suicide car-bomb that crashed into an Israeli convoy near Jezzine in mid-March 1985 was driven by a Druze member of the Syrian Socialist National Party trained near Damascus.[200]

Syria has always been an ardent supporter of Palestinian terrorism. The bulk of the Palestinian terrorist organizations that joined the anti-Arafat Rejection Front maintain headquarters in the Palestinian Quarter of Damascus. Most important are al-Saiqa, the *Fatah Intifada* of Abu-Mussa, the PFLP of George Habash, the PFLP-GC of Ahmad Jibril, the PSF of Samir Gawshah, the PLF under Talat Yaqub and Abu-Layl, and others.[201] George Habash hailed the PFLP's cooperation with Syria and emphasized the important role of Syria in the pan-Arab struggle.[202] In mid-1988, most Palestinian terrorist organizations were discussing new levels of mutual cooperation, as well as a new relationship, with Syria toward the escalation of their common anti-Israeli struggle.[203] While "Mother" Syria would have liked to support even more terrorist groups, its economic crisis prevented this. Consequently, Syria concentrates on supporting only the most operationally effective and loyal groups and encourages Iran and Libya to help finance the others. Thus, Abu-Mussa and even *al-Saiqa* have financial problems. However, the PSF of Samir Gawshah and the PFLP-GC of Ahmad Jibril are in a unique position due to their Iranian financial patronage, but tight control is maintained by Syrian intelligence. Moreover, in September 1989, Ahmad Jibril brought back to Damascus hundreds of his best trained terrorists who were, until then, based in Libya.[204] The main base of the PFLP-GC is still some 15 miles north of Damascus.[205]

An emerging trend in Syrian direct support for international terrorism is the providing of highly specialized services, both in Syria and overseas. Terrorists sent for operations in the West go for their final preparation in Syria. For example, the Abu-Nidal terrorists who attacked the Rome airport in December 1985 received their commando training near Isfahan, Iran, and then their advanced, pre-departure training in Syria.[206] Syrian military intelligence continues to provide genuine Lebanese passports and UNRWA identity cards to members of Palestinian terrorist organizations such as Abu Nidal's.[207] An advance terrorist training center optimized for preparing operatives for operations in the Arabian peninsula was established by Syria and Iran near Damascus in the summer of 1989.[208]

Syria also expanded its role in mediating between the USSR and the terrorists. KGB experts continue to direct, assist and support terrorist training and operations in the as-Sayda Zaynab camp near Damascus.[209] Walking around in uniforms, Soviet military instructors and experts also supervised the training of Syrian, Lebanese and Palestinian terrorists by the Syrian army in Homs, in northern Syria. Training includes basic intelligence work, small arms usage, sabotage and hand-to-hand combat.   Graduates are sent to join key terrorist formations or even infiltrate organizations considered hostile to Damascus and Tehran such as *Harakat Amal*.[210] Syria was also the gateway for advanced and highly specialized terrorist training in the USSR. For example, in the late 1980s several highly trained terrorists of the Lebanese Communist Party were sent for three to six month courses in sophisticated sabotage, sniping techniques, assassination and psychological conditioning for agents' deep penetration in the USSR. A few graduates took part in terrorist attacks that were launched from Lebanon as of 1988.[211]

Meanwhile, the marked expansion and improvement of the terrorist infrastructure and installations in the Biqaa started in mid-1985 in the wake of the January 1985 conference in Tehran. Ministers from Iran, Syria and Libya agreed to cooperate in facilitating the crossing of international frontiers and with other forms of mutual assistance. Toward that end, Syria undertook to expedite and simplify communications, supply routes and travel between the *HizbAllah* in the Biqaa, Lebanon and Tehran.[212] Iranian personnel are still processed at al-Zabadani base.[213] Noting the growing importance of states exporting terrorism, Kuwaiti Assembly member Khalaf al-Ghaza pointed out that "the training camps in south Lebanon are no longer targeted against Israel, but rather aim to create discord among the Arab peoples."[214]

The most significant development of this period was the expanding cooperation between the Islamists and numerous international terrorist organizations in the Biqaa. In the summer of 1985, there was an increase in the numbers of members of international terrorist organizations receiving advance training at special centers in the Biqaa under Syrian control, such as the JRA (Japanese Red Army), the RAF (the Red Army Faction, an extremist terrorist organization in [West] Germany), the Italian Red Brigades etc. "These forces are the Palestinians, who are the principal of the Palestinian Revolution, and they are also the Arabs and the Lebanese. In Beirut, there were people from more than 50 minority ethnic groups," explained Fusako Shigenobu Oko Daira, the leader of the JRA.[216] Other Islamic terrorist groups training in the Biqaa under Syrian-Iranian control include Yemenis, Pakistanis, Libyans, West Europeans and Americans.[217] The JRA had established a "sui-

cide corps'' in Lebanon that took active part in the fighting in
Beirut. After the 1982 siege of Beirut, the JRA relocated to the
Biqaa and established their headquarters with the PFLP's near
Baalabak. There the Japanese terrorists supervise and train
many Asians ''such as people from the Philippines, Bangladesh,
etc.''[218] Indeed, the JRA's manifesto emphasizes its internationalist character:

> The Japanese Red Army is maintaining a position to
> carry out the fight. Together with the revolutionary
> forces of the world we join the broad movements of
> the anti-imperialist united front. . . . We will fight
> together with the fighting people of the world and
> Palestinians so that we can share the realization of
> anti-nuclear disarmament in the name of peace.[219]

CHAPTER 3
IRAN AND THE NEW MUSLIM WORLD ORDER

Iraq invaded Kuwait in the early morning hours of August 2, 1990. American forces were quickly deployed to Saudi Arabia, the United Arab Emirates and the Persian Gulf in Operation Desert Shield. In early 1991, U.S. forces led a multinational coalition in Operation Desert Storm, an air and ground campaign that led to the eviction of Iraqi forces from Kuwait.

Throughout the Gulf crisis, Saddam Hussein and numerous Palestinian terrorist leaders repeatedly threatened to use international terrorism against the U.S. and its allies, at first to compel the withdrawal of their forces and, later, to avenge the Iraqi defeat. The U.S. and Western Europe braced themselves for a wave of terror that never came. Ultimately, the terrorist strikes were few and sporadic. None took place in the U.S.

Some critics suggested in the aftermath of the Persian Gulf War that the inaction of Iraqi-sponsored terrorism proved that international terrorism was no longer a viable threat, and that the law enforcement and security forces in the West were capable of neutralizing terrorism.

Nothing could have been further from the truth. The terrorists' relative inaction during this period marked a major phase in Iran's consolidating its dominance over the entire Middle East terrorist movement, primarily the Sunni Islamist movements. This development would have a profound impact on Iran's ability to strike in America.

BACKGROUND

Saddam Hussein's real war was for the heart, soul and future of the Muslim world, especially of the Arabs. The invasion of Kuwait which led to the Gulf War and the subsequent missile attacks on Israel were means toward this end of domination. In the summer of 1990, immediately after his invasion of Kuwait, Saddam Hussein tried des-perately to draw the Arab world into the fold of fundamentalist Islam which was, ironically, dominated by his arch enemy, Iran.

The only way Saddam Hussein could reverse the trend toward Iran was to lead an anti-American *Jihad* of his own. Baghdad's strategy called for compelling the conservative Arab regimes, through the demonstration of Iraq's overwhelming military might, to recognize Saddam Hussein's leadership and join him in a renewal of an Arab war against the West.

The anticipated role of international terrorism had a major impact on Baghdad's willingness to compromise with Iran. Saddam Hussein openly made the terrorists "the back-up force" for his assault on Kuwait. Only terrorism could bring the war to his enemies anywhere in the world.[1] The Iraqis realized that the most committed terrorists were motivated by Islamic zeal. Saddam Hussein would have to establish Islamic credentials before he could get Islamic terrorists to operate and die for him. Sheikh Asa'ad Bayud al-Tamimi of the Palestinian Islamic Jihad provided a first opening when he declared that "Iraqi President Saddam Hussein has the opportunity now to become a second Salah ad-Din [Saladdin] in Palestinian history if his threat to use chemical weapons against Israel is true."[2]

Thus, already on the eve of the Gulf Crisis, Baghdad had to come to grips with the dominant power of Islam in the ranks of virtually all Arab radical organizations. Since Iraq could not strike at the conservative Arab regimes without the support of the radicals, Saddam Hussein made a far-reaching strategic decision.

In order to increase popular support for his Great War, Saddam Hussein contemplated a call for a Shi'ite-dominated All-Islamic Jihad against the Great Satan (America), for the destruction of Israel, and for the restoration of a Khomeini-style traditional ecumenical Islamic rule over the Holy Shrines in Jerusalem, Mecca and Medina. Baghdad believed that such a grand design would be too irresistible for Tehran and Damascus to avoid. Indeed, strategic arrangements along these principles were reached between Baghdad and Tehran (then speaking also for Damascus) in the summer of 1990, leading to a formal pact signed on July 28, 1990, and to Iraq's ceding to Iran, on August 15, 1990, some of the fruits of its victory in the Iran-Iraq War. Both Hashemi-Rafsanjani and Hafez al-Assad supported wholeheartedly this grand design. All indications from the Arab world pointed to massive popular support for any pan-Arab/pan-Islamic eruption.[3]

The Iraqi agreement with Iran called for Tehran to provide Baghdad with diversified vital support without becoming directly involved in the Gulf conflict.[4] Primarily, the agreement gave Iraq access to the Iranian and Syrian international terrorist system which controlled an extensive, well organized support infrastructure in Western Europe and the U.S. This network was originally established to support the operations of Ahmad Jibril, Abu Nidal, *HizbAllah* and many of the PLO-affiliated terrorist organizations.

In June 1990, Barazan al-Takriti, Saddam Hussein's half-brother and Iraq's ambassador to Switzerland, was designated to become the senior commander of the terrorist network and personally negotiated the cooperation and coordination of European terrorist operations with Cyrus Naseri in his capacity as a special representative of Hashemi-Rafsanjani.[5] Concurrently, in the summer of 1990, Saddam Hussein intensified his efforts "to woo radical Palestinian factions to Baghdad in an attempt to realize his dream of becoming the unchallenged leader of the Arab world." A major aspect of this effort was the courting of radical factions through lavish financing, even though these moves "undermined Arafat's influence" over the Palestinian terrorist movement and Arafat was one of Saddam Hussein's most vocal supporters.[6]

In late May to early June 1990, Tehran convened a major conference of Islamic terrorist leaders to discuss the future course of the struggle. Key participants included Sheikh Muhammad Fadlallah, Sheikh Sa'id Sha'ban, Sheikh Subhi al-Tufayli, Sheikh Hussein al-Mussawi, Sheikh Ibrahim al-Amin, Husayn Ra'd, Imad Mughaniyah, and several other *HizbAllah* notables from Lebanon. From the Palestinian ranks several delegations headed by senior commanders, including Ahmad Jibril of the PFLP-GC and Sa'id Mussa Muragha of the Palestinian Liberation Front (sic), took part. Key members of various Palestinian *Islamic Jihad* factions, notably Sheikh Asa'ad Bayud al-Tamimi, Sheikh Abd-al-Aziz Awdah, Fathi al-Shqaqi also participated in the conference, as did representatives of Islamist terrorist organizations in Egypt, Thailand and India (Kashmir).[7]

The conference "centered on the coordination of the future method of operations of the terrorist groups", including escalating the Islamic revolt in Egypt and Jordan as well as disrupting the *Hajj* (religious pilgrimage) processions in Saudi Arabia.[8]

Four of Tehran's closest Sunni allies — Jibril, Tamimi, Awdah and Shqaqi — stayed behind for a series of discussions with senior Iranian officials, some of which also included Sha'ban.[9] In a key strategy formulation meeting with Khamenei, they defined "the struggles of the Islamic republic of Iran against global arrogance, especially the Great Satan, the United States, and its illegitimate child, Israel, as a strategic posture." They further reiterated that "waging a *Jihad* and moving along the path of *Allah* are the foundational elements of the Islamic revolution," and committed their respective organizations to a further escalation of their common struggle.[10]

Meanwhile, at a *HizbAllah* rally in Beirut, Sheikh Sayyid Barakah anticipated imminent momentous events altering the region because "the outbreak of the Islamic revolution and the struggling *intifadah* clearly affirm that the artificial entities in the region could be broken." Sheikh Fadlallah echoed these sentiments, stressing that "*Jihad* against arrogance is as essential a duty as prayers and knowledge."[11]

After he returned to Beirut from the Tehran Conference, Sheikh Tufayli elaborated on the regional character of the impending struggle, reflecting the essence of the Tehran-Baghdad agreement. "We must follow the example of *Allah*'s messenger . . . and bring back the cities of Mecca and Medinah to the bosom of Islam so that the banner may fly high again over Mecca and the Holy Shrines." Tufayli expected an escalation of the crisis. "The war on the Islamic resistance will remain because the war order comes from Washington," he explained. "It is the same war waged by the agents of the West in Mecca, the Gulf, Palestine, and Lebanon."[12] In June and July, several hundreds of *Pasdarani* arrived in Lebanon and deployed "in fighting groups for operations of a special nature," in order "to carry out their operations under the *HizbAllah* umbrella" once the crisis erupted.[13] Hussein al-Mussawi said that the *HizbAllah* "announced" new operations against the U.S., Western Europe and Israel.[14]

In the early summer, Tamimi travelled to Tehran and Tripoli to urge Khamenei and Qaddafi to actively join and support the impending regional *Jihad*. "My task is instigation — instigating the *Ummah* to *Jihad* for the liberation of all of Palestine," he explained.[15] Indeed, soon afterwards, Qaddafi convened the executive bureau of the International Islamic Popular Command to discuss recent developments and devise future activities.[16] Qaddafi also convened the pan-Arab General People's Congress Permanent Secretariat who decided that Libya would "provide more support for the revolution of the generation of anger with the aim of bringing about an effective pan-Arab participation in the struggle to achieve the goals."[17] Tehran also called for the escalation of fighting, and sent a message to the *HizbAllah* urging "our *mujahideen* to remain the leading force against the Zionist enemy."[18]

Tamimi's priorities were reflected in the Islamic Jihad Movement — Bayt al-Maqdis' call for first "confronting the U.S., striking against U.S. interests" because the U.S. "is the deadliest enemy of our people," and only then for "armed

Islamic Jihad and for escalating the *intifadah.*"[19] Reflecting popular sentiment, the *HAMAS* echoed the Islamic Jihad call, "urging our heroic Palestinian people to press ahead with their *Jihad* and sever any link with the United States." (HAMAS is the Islamic Resistance Movement, the clandestine terrorist arm of the Palestinian Muslim Brotherhood, organized in Gaza in early 1987.)[20]

Dr. Abd-al-Latif Arabiyat, the speaker of Jordanian Parliament and leader of Islamic Movement, reiterated that "*Jihad* is the only way to restore our rights in Palestine from the River to the Sea." He joined an emerging consensus that such a *Jihad* is possible only as a part of a larger confrontation with the U.S. "The U.S. hostility and arrogance must motivate our Arab and Islamic Nation to put an end to the course of begging and capitulation that it is immersed in." Instead, he urged the "remobilizing of the Arab and Islamic nation and preparing it for *Jihad* and martyrdom."[21]

Meanwhile, Iraqi and PLO intelligence, in close cooperation with the East Germans, reexamined their contingency plans and operational options in Western Europe. They soon discovered that virtually all the local terrorist infrastructure and support systems were firmly in the hands of networks controlled by Syria and Iran. On the eve of the crisis, Baghdad realized that close cooperation with Iran and Syria was a must for any terrorist operations in the West, and thus intensified its efforts to ensure meaningful Iranian-Syrian support. (Terrorism in Western Europe is discussed in Chapter 5 below.)

As the tension grew, Tehran also moved quickly to put the final touches on its role in the terrorist plans. Pursuant to the agreement with Baghdad, Iran made arrangements with Fadlallah to transfer the most militant elements of the anti-Saddam Shi'ite Iraqi *Hizb al-Da'wah al-Iqlimi* to HizbAllah bases in Lebanon so that they could take part in the impending struggle while appeasing Iraq.[22]

Meanwhile, Iranian ambassadors and *charges d'affaires* arrived in Tehran for a special seminar on July 25-26 that was also attended by most of Iran's supreme leaders.[23] Tehran anticipated a worldwide escalation of the export of the revolution in the context of the impending global crisis. Toward that end, the seminar provided the diplomats with instructions on how to "accomplish the heavy duty of defending the Islamic Revolution against the aggression of its hostile enemies."

The diplomats were told to prepare for the unleashing of a terrorist offensive. "If the Islamic Republic is to preserve its offensive policy toward the ringleaders of infidelity and oppression, as the leader Ayatollah Ali Khamenei has said, the implementation of such a policy would be possible only through revolutionary and competent forces who are nonchalant towards worldly pomps and seriously devoted to the principles of the Islamic Revolution."[24] Thus Tehran, in effect, ordered an escalation in international terrorism.

France, having been forewarned about Iraq's plans and fully aware of the potential of Iranian-supported terrorism on its soil, moved to unilaterally remove a major "cause" for terrorism. Anis Naccash and his four accomplices, whose release had been demanded by Tehran since 1981, were suddenly pardoned on July 27, 1990, and immediately flown to Tehran. Tehran interpreted the release as a "humanitarian and positive gesture" by Paris aimed at improving relations.[25]

IN THE WAKE OF THE INVASION

Immediately after the invasion of Kuwait, Baghdad went out of its way to appease the Iranians. For example, the Iraqis released several Shi'ite prisoners, including the Kuwait 17, took them to Baghdad and then to Iran. (The Kuwait 17 were the 17 members of *HizbAllah* and Islamic Jihad who were captured on December 12, 1983, after a series of car bombings in Kuwait and sentenced to death or lengthy prison terms. Their release had been a consistent demand of the *HizbAllah* in the 1980s.)[26] Some of the prisoners made it to Iran and Lebanon on their own, using Iranian and Lebanese documents provided by the Iranian embassies in Kuwait and other Gulf States.[27] Essentially, Saddam Hussein released these terrorists in order to persuade the *HizbAllah* to "carry out suicide attacks for him."[28]

Indeed, once the Kuwait 17 were safe in Tehran, Hussein al-Mussawi issued a call "for all Muslims to fight the Western military deployment in the Gulf through suicide operations."[29] "We must confront America in the same way the Muslim confronted the American marines and the French paratroopers in Lebanon," he explained.[30]

HizbAllah also publicized and endorsed the series of *fatwa*s issued throughout the Muslim world urging and authorizing strikes against the U.S. and coalition forces in the Arabian Peninsula and the Persian Gulf. (*Fatwa*s are religious decrees written by high religious authorities authorizing specific actions such as terrorist operations.)[31] Simultaneously, Hashemi-Rafsanjani issued an order to the Iranian armed forces to avoid any action that might seem as a provocation to, or a threat against, Iraq.[32]

Meanwhile, the PLO-affiliated terrorist organizations immediately rallied to Iraq's support. Since early August 1990, the vast majority of the leaders of the Palestinian terrorist organizations had reiterated their support for Saddam Hussein and their commitment to the anti-U.S. *Jihad* he declared. For example, Abu al-Abbas's PLF issued a communique in Beirut on August 8 in which the PLF stated: "We, in performance of our national and pan-Arab role, declare to our Palestinian people and nation that we will strike at U.S. and colonial interests once a foreign soldier sets foot on Arab lands." Muhammad Abbas issued an order to "strike with . . . strong arms at all U.S. interests" all over the world.[33]

A PLO official in al-Baq'ah refugee camp (Jordan) warned that the organization "will strike the United States and its allies in any place we can reach."[34] George Habash of the PFLP issued "a call on Arab masses to resist the U.S. invasion of the Arab Gulf by all means and methods," and urged "confront-

ing U.S. aggression on Iraq and Kuwait.''[35] Nayif Hawatimah
of the DFLP urged the unity of all Arab nationalist forces to
confront the U.S. presence and expedite the liberation of
Palestine.[36]

Palestinian terrorist leaders rallied to the banner of *Jihad*
despite the declared political position of Syria and Iran. George
Habash acknowledged that he was ''very disappointed over
Syria's stance in the Gulf crisis.''[37] Indeed, he continues to
consider Syria ''the heart of Arab nationalism.''[38] Habash's
position was closer to Iran's: ''We do not support Saddam's
invasion of Kuwait. On the other hand, we support the Iraqi
president and the Iraqi people against the U.S. invasion of the
Arabian Peninsula.'' Habash showed understanding of
Saddam's move and blamed Kuwait and the Gulf states for
inciting the crisis.[39]

Nevertheless, the PFLP ''denounced the U.S. military presence in the Arabian Gulf and the Arabian Peninsula and
considers it a military invasion of the Arab land — an invasion
which defies and directly threatens our Arab nation's aspirations and hopes for liberation and democracy.''[40] Habash visited Baghdad on September 2 and met Saddam Hussein and
other senior Iraqi officials, but reiterated his intention to keep
his base in Syria and Jordan.[41] Habash urged ''all Arab liberation movements to strike U.S. and Western interests.''[42]

Even the PFLP-GC expressed its support for the Iraqi
confrontation with the U.S. and criticized the rest of the Arab
world for not mobilizing against Israel.[43] However, Ahmad
Jibril emphasized that he did not travel to Baghdad to demonstrate his support for Saddam Hussein.[44] The PFLP-GC called
''for studying all ways to confront the U.S. forces that seek to
occupy the Arab oil fields and recolonize the region.''[45]

Ultimately, despite its pact with Baghdad, Tehran was
ambivalent toward the unfolding of events in the Persian Gulf.
This ambivalence led to its indecision on the role of Iranian-
controlled terrorists in the anti-West campaign advocated by
Saddam Hussein. Tehran and its proteges could not ignore the

Islamic mobilization and rejuvenating aspect of the anti-American wave that was sweeping the Arab world. Sheikh Sa'id Shaban saw in this phenomena the hope for the future: "If all Muslims including the Arabs were to unite against Imperialism and Zionism, countries such as the United States of America and Israel would no longer exist in the world."[46]

Sheikh Hussein al-Mussawi's initial reaction reflected the duality of Tehran's approach to the unfolding crisis in the Persian Gulf: the Islamists "urge our kin everywhere to confront the Saddamite aggression without seeking the help of the arrogant, and to confront the colonial U.S. invasion in every way that could remind them of the lesson taught by the sons of Islam in Lebanon, who forced the Americans, French, and multinational forces to leave their territories by means of martyrdom."[47] Sheikh Fadlallah took this argument further, advocating an all-encompassing Islamic drive with the aim of bringing back to the fold wider segments of the Muslim world.[48]

Claiming to be the region's leading power, Tehran began issuing statements reflecting the new status. On September 12, 1990, Iran's spiritual leader, Ayatollah Ali Khamenei, declared that Tehran "will never permit the American to establish a foothold for themselves in the region . . . where we have influence and any place" in the Muslim world. Moreover, he decreed that, "Anybody who stands up to fight and confront America's aggression, greed, plans and policies aimed at committing aggression in the Persian Gulf region will be participating in the *Jihad* on the path of *Allah*, and anybody who is killed on that path is regarded a martyr."[49]

This *fatwa* sanctioned fighting and resisting the U.S. not only for Iraq's large Shi'ite population (over 60%) but was also addressed to the al-Hassa Shi'ite nation in Saudi Arabia and to the Shi'ite majority (or near majority) in most Gulf states, all of whom follow Tehran's religious guidance.

In his statement aimed at the Shi'ite population of the Persian Gulf states, Khamenei invoked the importance of Shi'ite terrorism of the kind practiced in Beirut. "It's surprising how the Americans don't learn lessons from past events. They saw how vulnerable their presence can be. They saw how in Lebanon a handful of committed and Muslim youth ... swept them away and evicted them from Lebanon. Have they forgotten it?'' Khamenei also reiterated Iran's desire for ''cooperation with Persian Gulf countries'' against all aggressors, but especially against the U.S. because reaching a solution to the question of Iraq's invasion of Kuwait ''is the duty of regional countries,'' and not the U.S.[50]

Jordanian Islamists saw in Khamenei's statement a milestone in the effort to consolidate a unified pan-Islamic stand.[51] Belatedly, even *HAMAS* ''praised'' the statement.[52] Sheikh Fadlallah, however, stressed that although fully justified, Khamenei's *fatwa* had little practical implications for the *HizbAllah*. Sheikh Tufayli concurred.[53]

Thus, after the immediate reaction to the crisis passed and the region settled down to coping with the new realities, Fadlallah gave a more balanced and sophisticated analysis of the situation that clearly recognized the potential of international terrorism. ''Faced with the mobilization of U.S. forces,'' he explained, ''we say that the small can destroy the games of the big.'' Fadlallah saw in terrorism the only viable response to the U.S. buildup. ''The small can't destroy a house but they can make it untidy, and we're teaching Muslims to sabotage America's scheme of things. . . When Muslims reject the U.S. presence and policy they must think of ways to counter America, but how, when and where will be determined by developments.''[54]

Fadlallah explained that the *HizbAllah* was compelled to take this position because of the overall Islamic ramifications of the U.S. build-up and despite its opposition to Saddam Hussein and Iraq's policies. ''We believe a psychological war is being waged to destroy the soul of the Islamic Nation, and that is what we aim to counter.'' Moreover, terrorism might be a lesser evil than a full-scale war in the Middle East that would bring widespread destruction. Fadlallah warned that ''a military confrontation would make Saddam a hero for the Arabs and Muslims and create problems for the United States with the Soviet Union, Europe and Japan, which consider the Gulf region vital."[55]

Consequently, terrorist organizations affiliated with Iran and Syria urged participation in the anti-U.S. terrorist struggle not so much because of their support for the policy of Saddam Hussein or his legitimacy, but out of apprehension of the adverse long-term ramifications of the U.S. and coalition deployment to the Arabian Peninsula. The centralized command of Palestinian terrorists in the Biqaa issued a statement calling the deployment of U.S. forces to the Persian Gulf "a grave danger to all liberation movements in the Middle East, the *intifadah* in particular." They invited all conscientious Muslims to "join forces against the U.S. and to destroy the vested interests of international imperialists."[56]

Similarly, Fathi Shqaqi of the Islamic Jihad for the Liberation of Palestine issued a leaflet in the territories in which he declared "a campaign of terror against the Americans, Israel, Saudi Arabia, and Egypt," yet without expressing support for Saddam Hussein or Iraq.[57] The *HizbAllah* issued a call "for the unity of all Muslims to confront the presence of U.S. forces in the region."[58]

PREPARING THE TERRORIST ASSAULT

After August 1990, Iraq launched a major effort to organize a large anti-Western terrorist force and initiate a unified concentrated terrorist campaign against the U.S. "Iraq has always been a land of asylum for terrorist movements. Now it is up to them to show their gratitude" to Saddam Hussein, commented a French journalist.[59] The terrorism campaign was coordinated by the *Estikhabarat* (military intelligence) and the *Mukhabarat*.[60] Egyptian sources revealed an Iraqi plan to launch organized terrorist operations in a number of Arab and European capitals. Terrorist groups were being trained in special camps in Iraq for these strikes.[61] Col. Hawari of the PLO was a major organizer and commander of this terrorist buildup and especially the preparations to operate in the Middle East and Western Europe.[62]

Consequently, Baghdad was able to threaten terrorist attacks against U.S. and other installations world-wide. Baghdad declared that "the vital interests of the United States and its institutions throughout the globe will all become military targets which the *Fadayeen* of the gathering of the believers will attack with the fire of justice and capability."[63] "Hundreds of thousands of volunteers are now at the highest state of readiness to fight against the alliance of evil and aggression," in a *Jihad* where "the confrontation will not be confined to the battlefield."[64]

Abu al-Abbass stated that "the striking Palestinian groups have defined American and Western targets" including "U.S. installations and interests spread all over the globe."[65] Other reports suggested that "as many as 14,000 commandos trained to carry out suicide operations had been dispatched to the front line facing Saudi Arabia."[66] They included PLO pilots and special forces.[67] In addition, some 1,500 Palestinian terrorists, 300 of them Abu Nidal's experts, were ready in Iraq to implement the "global conflict" on behalf of Baghdad, including assassinating Saddam Hussein's "enemies."[68]

In order to execute the terrorist campaign, especially overseas, Iraq established a comprehensive command, control and communication system coordinated by the *Estikhabarat* (military intelligence) and the *Mukhabarat*.[69] Two Saddam loyalists and intelligence experts, Fadel Barak and Ibrahim Sebahoui, were put in command of the campaign in Baghdad.[70] Ilich Ramirez Sanchez, a.k.a. Carlos, was in Baghdad as a key expert assistant and consultant. He was using an Iraqi passport under the name Mahmud al-Bakr.[71] Barazan al-Takriti, Saddam Hussein's half-brother and, as previously mentioned, Iraq's ambassador to Switzerland, was the senior field commander. Under him was a network of Iraqi intelligence and special forces officers deployed in all of Iraq's embassies and other diplomatic facilities throughout Europe.[72]

According to the Iraqi plan, the terrorist operations were to be conducted in accordance with a three-phase strategy of gradual escalation aimed at saving and securing quality assets until the extent and effectiveness of the reaction by local security forces were ascertained:

1. Use of local assets all over the world in order to demonstrate action while creating problems for the local security forces;

2. Quality attacks in Western Europe and the Middle East by Palestinian and Iraqi organizations living off of and gaining operational support from the locally-based dormant networks; and

3. Spectacular strikes, including suicide attacks, against civilians in Western Europe and the U.S. in order to avenge and demonstrate the extent of the despair of the defeated Arab World.[73]

As a direct result of the Gulf Crisis, *al-Fatah* overtly returned to active terrorism.[74] Toward that end, *al-Fatah* decided to transfer personnel to Iraq where they formed the Al-Aqsa Mosque Battalions, under the command of Hajj Ismail but trained with the Iraqi Army under Iraqi officers.[75] The PLO's Muhammad Milhim declared: "Our people are ready to fight everywhere against the Arab coalition of Egypt and Syria, against the United States, and against Europe."[76] Several other Palestinian organizations declared their commitment to the Iraqi cause[77] and established training facilities in Iraq.[78] The main Palestinian organizations prepared by Saddam Hussein for attacks on the West were the PLF under Abu al-Abbas, May 15 under Abu-Ibrahim and the Special Command under Salim Abu Salim.[79]

In the fall, Abu al-Abbass continued to threaten dire ramifications of direct U.S. involvement in Middle East fighting.[80] Dr. Nadir al-Tamimi of *Islamic Jihad* — Bayt al-Maqdis announced that "clear instructions have been given to the *Islamic Jihad* cadres operating in the West to strike at any foreign state that takes part in the aggression and buildup against Iraq."[81] The increase in Hussein al-Umari's activities and preparations meant that airline sabotage was a primary objective.[82] Indeed, the Arab Liberation Front threatened strikes against Western and Gulf aircraft in case Iraqi airliners were intercepted.[83]

THE RISE OF TEHRAN

In the fall of 1990, Baghdad's determination seemed to be wavering. Concurrently, the Arab masses were demonstrating ever greater support for the anticipated anti-U.S. and anti-Israel *Jihad*. Hashemi-Rafsanjani and Hafez al-Assad saw no reason why the Tikriti Sunni, Saddam Hussein, should lead and dominate such a *Jihad* (Tikrit was the village from which he came). In mid-November, Iraq tried desperately to avert a strategic realignment by sending a high level military delegation led by Izat Ibrahim to Tehran, but to no avail. In late 1990, Tehran and Damascus decided not to join Iraq, but only after Tehran had convinced Baghdad to evacuate to Iran much of Iraq's strategic equipment, such as aircraft, tanks and artillery, which were ultimately confiscated by the Iranians.[84] However, Tehran declared its neutrality in case of a war against Iraq only on December 31.[85]

Tehran's position now was that its agreement with Baghdad on the danger of the U.S. presence in the region should not be confused with acceptance of Saddam Hussein's leadership or support of Iraq. Discussing the U.S. danger in the Persian Gulf, Fadlallah stated, "The fact that we agree with Saddam on this issue does not make him an Arab hero. For this he lacks the format and the moral standing."[86] In an appeal to Arab rulers and masses, the *HizbAllah* expressed a concern of Tehran and Damascus: "Do not urge war and threaten to wage it, for war will force everyone to stand by Saddam's side, and you may end up turning him into a national hero."[87]

In order to avoid such an eventuality, Tehran suggested the establishment of an international force with troops from Iran, Yemen, Libya, Algeria, Sudan, Cuba, North Korea, and Vietnam "for the defense of Iraq," but not "a defense of Iraq's occupation of Kuwait," and "deployed only in Iraq proper" because, Tehran warned, "an American victory will be parlayed, in effect, to destabilize all the regimes deemed hostile to U.S. purposes," while the deployment of such an international force "will act as a credible deterrent to Mr. Bush's dreams of turning the entire Persian Gulf into an enormous and oil-rich banana republic."[88]

By now, Tehran, Damascus and their proteges were seeing in the upheaval in the Muslim world caused by the Gulf crisis a golden opportunity. They felt they could direct what they thought were the frustrations and hostilities of Muslims into an anti-Western struggle leading to "a new Muslim world order" under their hegemony. Sheikh Sayyid Abbas al-Mussawi anticipated that the Gulf Crisis would further polarize the world into "only two blocs — the bloc of blasphemy and the bloc of Islam," with "the bloc of Islam comprising all the revolutionary movements" throughout the Third World.[89]

HizbAllah leader Sheikh Hussein al-Mussawi expected Iran to assumed the leadership of this emerging trend:

"We hope that the Islamic Republic [of Iran], with the cooperation of Syria and Muslims in Lebanon and Palestine as well as all Muslims throughout the world, will be able to establish an Islamic world order. This can prevent the U.S. from imposing its power and order on Muslims. In this regard we hope that all Muslims cooperate with Iran, because Imam Khomeini's path is still continuing. This path is being continued by the leader of the Islamic Revolution Ayatollah Khamenei. We hope the Muslims will be able to stand up against their enemies."[90]

THE FALL OF IRAQ'S TERRORIST CAMPAIGN

In early January 1991, Iraq believed it had in place a major terrorist infrastructure under the direct control of Baghdad in order to conduct terrorist operations in Western Europe and the U.S. The centralized command and control component under Barazan al-Takriti were completed and made operational in Western Europe several days prior to the outbreak of the war. He controlled a network of Iraqi intelligence and special forces officers deployed in all of Iraq's embassies and other diplomatic facilities throughout Europe. Each of these officers controlled a locally based terrorist network and had large weapons caches in place, both in storage and in Iraqi embassies. Large numbers of weapons were brought to Europe via Iraqi diplomatic mail in recent months in anticipation of the operations.[91]

On December 24, 1990, Saddam Hussein chaired a meeting of the Revolution Command Council that examined the status of the preparations for international terrorism. Consequently, Baghdad issued urgent orders in Cable No. 138 of December 27 for its "diplomatic missions to facilitate the tasks of the persons who will carry out the attacks in coordination with intelligence officials in these missions."[92] The Iraqi Ambassador to Spain, Arshad Tawfiq, warned of terrorist operations in Europe: "We do not want terrorism, but if there is war, there may be these movements."[93]

This Iraqi terrorist infrastructure dominated the most radical Palestinian and Islamist terrorist networks throughout Western Europe. These terrorists were a mixture of pro-Saddam extremist groups associated with the PLO, such as the PLF under Abu al-Abbass (charged in the death of Leon Klinghoffer on the Italian cruise ship *Achille Lauro*), the Special Headquarters/Command under Salim Abu Salim and the 15 May Organization under Abu Ibrahim, combined with the vast and highly effective terrorist infrastructure controlled by Syria and Iran (such as the *HizbAllah*, *Islamic Jihad*, the PFLP-GC under

under Ahmad Jibril, the PFLP under George Habash, the Abu Nidal Organization, and many more). Baghdad was certain of the support of the terrorists controlled by Iran because in June 1990, Barazan al-Takriti had personally negotiated cooperation and coordination in Europe with Cyrus Naseri.[94]

Most of these terrorist networks also have close working relationship with the various West European terrorist groups and could rely on their assistance in case of attacks on American targets. However, as Baghdad examined the operational terrorist networks it became clear that they were actually controlled by Iran and Syria. For example, Abu Nidal was calling in "favors" from networks and supporters on behalf of Saddam Hussein in Egypt Morocco, Saudi Arabia, the Philippines, Thailand, and even Norway, Sweden, Denmark and the Red Army Faction in Germany.[95]

The PLO's terrorist network was truly subservient to Baghdad, but Arafat was having problems delivering it. From the beginning of the Gulf crisis there had been a widening gap between Arafat and Abu Iyad, who tried to maintain a semblance of neutrality. Hani and Khalid al-Hassan also tried to contain the pro-Iraqi policy and sent feelers to Abu Mussa and Khalid al-Fahum (the former chairman of the Palestinian National Council). Several terrorist leaders conceded that "there is no faith in Arafat."[96] Several PLO officials tried to reconcile the "undeclared disagreement" between Arafat and Halaf, who objected to the PLO's all-out pro-Iraqi stand, in order "to prevent an eruption" within the Palestinian leadership once hostilities began.[97] Khalid al-Fahum even strongly denounced Saddam Hussein and the damage he was causing to the Palestinian cause. He urged an escalation of the "Palestinian struggle" and increased "resistance" on the West Bank instead of overseas adventures.[98]

Ultimately, the PLO leadership supported participation in the terrorist struggle on Iraq's side. Abu Iyad suggested that, in the case of a regional war, the Palestinians should concentrate on fighting Israel rather than the Gulf states,[99] but predicted that once the war broke out "all Arab nations would side with Iraq to face the U.S.-Atlantic onslaught."[100] Abu Iyad stated: "It is an honor for the Palestinian revolution to stand at Iraq's side in case the war breaks out."[101] Farouq Qaddumi warned the U.S. and Europe that in case of a war "hell would break loose against U.S. and Western" interests because the Palestinians "would fight with all our might to defend the dignity and pride of the Arab nation."[102]

Then, in January 1991, just prior to the outbreak of the war, there emerged a potential complication in Iraq's ability to control and conduct a massive terrorist campaign in Western Europe. Part of Baghdad's last-minute scare campaign was a threat by Yassir Arafat to mobilize his assets and renew the terrorist campaign in the West. However, Arafat also claimed control over the anticipated terrorist operations as part of the Palestinian contribution to the pan-Arab struggle led by Saddam Hussein. On January 14, 1991, Arafat urged his followers to strike deep in the West and all over the world.[103]

Zaid Wahba, the senior PLO commander in Lebanon, declared that once the war began the Palestinians would operate all over the world. "All American interests throughout the world will be targeted and suicide attacks will not be limited to the Gulf and Palestine," he declared.[104] "We'll act from Lebanon, Amman, Cairo, and Damascus and orders have been given to attack U.S. and British interests around the world." Wahba warned that "the war has already begun."[105]

Now, there emerged a potential for a major strain between the various components of the terrorist offensive because of past struggles between the PLO and the vast majority of the terrorist organizations participating in the Iraqi-controlled infrastructure. Arafat and his aids created the impression that he and the PLO would become the leaders of the terrorist forces in the anticipated campaign. Salah Halaf (Abu Iyad, second in command in the PLO and Arafat's deputy), Hayil Abd al-Hamid (Abu al-Hawl, third in the PLO command and its intelligence and military commander), and Fathi al-Amri

(Abu Iyad's deputy and principal military aid) would be among the commanders of the Iraqi-led terrorist campaign.[106]

However, most Palestinian terrorists were associated with anti-Arafat groups. They mistrusted and even hated Abu Iyad, whom they accused of betraying operations to the French and other Europeans as part of the power struggles in the Palestinian movement.[107]

Meanwhile, Saddam Hussein needed Arafat only as a figurehead for world consumption. It was unacceptable to the more radical terrorists to cooperate with the commanders Arafat wanted to impose upon them. Thus, Arafat's commanders had to go before Baghdad could launch the terrorist offensive.

It was in this context that three PLO senior commanders — Salah Halaf, Hayil Abd al-Hamid, and Fathi al-Amri — were assassinated in the pre-dawn hours of January 15, 1991, in Tunisia during a late night strategy session. The meeting was to be a milestone in the anticipated terrorist campaign. Abu al-Hawl had just returned from Baghdad and Abu Muhammad had just returned from Cairo where they had gone to coordinate terrorist operations. They expected Abu Mahir, the head of Lebanon operations, and Farouq Qaddumi to join them around midnight. In the session, Abu Iyad was in favor of the PLO supporting Baghdad because the masses were demanding it, but was "extremely worried about the consequences of the war for his people." He had already assigned Abu al-Hawl the task of further coordinating and supporting the *intifadah* to cope with the rise of the Islamists.[109] Now, Abu Iyad was discussing with his senior aides their command, control and coordination of the international terrorist campaign that, if successful, would place the PLO once more in the role of undisputed leader of the Palestinians.[110]

Then, just before 11:00 PM, Hamzah abu-Zayd, the bodyguard of Abu al-Hawl, walked into the meeting room and emptied an AK-47 magazine into the three leaders from point blank range. Hamzah abu-Zayd was identified as Hamzah

Abdallah, an undercover agent of Abu Nidal's *Fatah* — Revolutionary Council. Several months earlier, he had claimed to have defected from Abu Nidal Organization to the PLO. In reality, he had been sent as a deep penetration agent controlled by Abu Nidal's chief of intelligence, Samir, whose mission was to assassinate Abu Iyad and other key leaders. A few weeks beforehand, Hamza had travelled to Libya, ostensibly for family reasons, where he made contact with a controller called Raghib who gave him the final instructions for the assassinations.[111]

These assassinations were a milestone in Iraq's planned launching of the worldwide terrorist campaign, because they both streamlined the upper-echelons of the Iraqi-dominated terrorist command structure and created a very strong motive for vengeance against Israel and the West.[112] At one stroke, they removed both the source of discord with Iranian and Syrian controlled terrorists and the PLO's real challenge to the Iraqi terrorist command system, while retaining Yassir Arafat as the leader of the PLO. In the past, such assassinations always meant internal purges executed by Iraqi agents and/or hard-core Palestinian terrorist professionals operating on behalf of several states and organizations under the cover of the Abu Nidal name. Moreover, in January 1991, Abu Nidal was closely cooperating with Baghdad.[113]

Indeed, it was soon learned that "the order for the[Abu Iyad] murder was given by Saddam Hussein."[114] Immediately, some 14 of Abu al-Hawl's loyalists based in Kuwait were assassinated by Iraqi intelligence.[115] Moreover, young PLO commanders still blame Arafat for Abu Iyad's assassination.[116] The only group to claim responsibility for the killing, in mid-April 1991, was the Martyr Abu Jihad Group [*Majmu'at al-Shahid abu-Jihad*] in Beirut.[117]

The unfolding of the terrorist campaign since the outbreak of Operation Desert Storm demonstrated more than anything else the extent of the tight control exercised by Syria and Iran over the international terrorist network. Some 120 terrorist attacks took place all over the world between mid-January and mid-February 1991. The number had increased to some 200 attacks, mostly amateurish and ineffective, by mid-March 1991. More than half were directed at American targets.[118] These operations were conducted in accordance with a three-phase strategy of gradual escalation aimed at saving and securing the network's quality assets until the extent and effectiveness of the reaction by local security forces were ascertained. The delays in escalating into the second phase were due to the inability of Damascus and Tehran to relinquish their control over international terrorism and their refusal to coordinate operations with Baghdad, although they continued to use Iraq's clandestine assets, money, and training support.

Indeed, the terrorist network in Europe remained controlled from the Middle East. Irrespective of Barazan al-Takriti's designs, Beirut was still the forward control point at the insistence of Damascus and Tehran. Thus, despite its impressive capabilities, the *HizbAllah* remained "very discreet," although its activist commanders supported Mohtashemi's call for "holy alliance" with Iraq against the "American Satan." But they patiently waited for orders from Tehran. Similarly, in Jordan, *Islamic Jihad* for the Liberation of Palestine, under Sheikh Asa'ad Bayud al-Tamimi, spearheaded the Sunni Islamist contribution to the Iraqi terrorist effort by "laundering" Iraqi intelligence, PLF, 15 May, and even PFLP-GC teams on their way overseas, and activated his vast network in North Africa, Egypt and Yemen.[119]

Ultimately, Palestinian *Islamic Jihad* became the primary vehicle for Iraqi terrorists. In early 1991, "terrorist groups, using religious slogans as a cover and Baghdad as their terrorist activity headquarters, received intensive training in acts of assassination and ways of planting explosives in public places from Iraqi officers of the intelligence organs specializing in terrorism." Many of these squads, along with their Iraqi intelligence control officers, then travelled to Jordan, preparing to launch operations against both Israel and Syria.[120]

The Palestinian Islamists utilized their relationship with other communities in the Arab world to spread terrorism on behalf of the Iraqi war effort. In Algeria, Islamic Jihad worked in cooperation with the Islamic Salvation Front. In Egypt, they cooperated with the local Islamic Jihad and off-shoots of the Muslim Brotherhood. In Sub-Saharan Africa, a major support and back up infrastructure dominated by the *HizbAllah*, Iran and Libyan was readied. But, with the exception of Egypt, none of these networks carried out any operations, not having received authorization from the controlling states. In contrast, in Turkey, the leftist Dev Sol (Revolutionary Left) was activated through old PLO contacts and claimed a few bombs thrown at American interests.[121]

Events in Vienna serve as an indication of the collapse of the "arrangement" with Iran and Syria and a confirmation of Iran's mistrust of Baghdad and its decision not to cooperate with Iraq. Abu Nidal's Fatah Revolutionary Council, the Iraqi sponsored *Mujahideen ul-Khalq* and the Iraqi *Mukhabarat* considered Vienna "a stronghold of Arab terrorism."[122] The commander in Vienna was Saad Majid, ostensibly a worker in the Iraqi Embassy, who also controlled the *Mukhabarat*'s hit teams.[123]

In mid-January 1991, a group of 11 Iranian terrorists was arrested in Vienna while waiting for their attack plans, weapons and explosives. They were a "dormant cell" activated to carry out terrorist strikes in Austria as part of the pro-Iraqi campaign. What was notable about this situation was that these terrorists were members of the anti-Tehran *Mujahideen ul-Khalq* organization then operating in Iraq along the border with Iran.[124] Since Tehran and Damascus would never tolerate cooperation with, and the participation of, the *Mujahideen ul-Khalq*, the activation of the latter indicates that already at that point Baghdad had given up on cooperating with Iran and Syria.

CONSOLIDATING THE NEW
MUSLIM WORLD ORDER

In the aftermath of the Gulf War and the consequent major shock suffered by the Arab and Muslim world, the rise of widespread pan-Arab/pan-Islamic sentiments has been exploited by Damascus and Tehran to further implement a bold strategic move, namely, the consolidation of an anti-American Muslim bloc stretching from Lebanon to Pakistan and dominated by Shi'ite-Allawite leadership (Hafez al-Assad comes from the Allawite sect of Islam). Behind the appeal of the new regional bloc was the realization that the Arab world would retain its overall anti-U.S. character in spite, or even because, of the defeat of Iraq. Ayatollah Muhammad Hussein Fadlallah pointed out that "although some Arab states have sided with the U.S., they nevertheless have many differences with Washington." Fadlallah explained that "America's Arab policies are not based on principle, but on manipulating the facts in such a way as to preserve its interests."[125]

As the Gulf War was winding down, Tehran warned that the impression that "Saddam has returned to Islam" was but "a misgiving [sic] which will not last long." Instead, Muslims were urged by Tehran to "continue to preserve our divine rage against world arrogance and especially criminal America and bloodthirsty Zionism so that at the right time and under the orders of the leader of Islam — and not on Saddam's front — we can rub the noses of the enemies of Islam into the dirt."[126] Nevertheless, Fadlallah warned that in view of widespread rage and despair, "Muslims will respond to Iraqi President Saddam Hussein's call for a *Jihad* against the coalition led by the United States, even though Saddam does not have the right to make such a call."[127]

As before, terrorist leaders closely associated with Tehran and Damascus were the first to explain the policies of the controlling states. Thus, a highly important statement explaining the evolution of the Islamist regional strategy was issued in Amman on January 20, 1991 by Ahmad Jibril's PFLP-GC.

The PFLP-GC examined the outbreak of war in the Persian Gulf "from a position of national and pan-Arab responsibility" and concluded that "the U.S.-NATO aggression against our people in Iraq [is] seen as a U.S. effort to strike the Arab nation and the battle of its liberation and Islamic awakening through what America calls the new world order — which America is beginning to implement in our region." The ultimate U.S.-Zionist objectives in their aggression against Iraq were "to strike, intimidate, and contain all countries of the region: Syria, Jordan, the Islamic Republic of Iran, and the Libyan Arab *Jamahiriyah*, and to quell and finish off the heroic *intifadah* and liquidate the Palestinian issue and the rights of the Palestinian people." In view of these threats, the PFLP-GC declared its commitment to a "firm confrontation of U.S. imperialism and Zionism" wherever they might be in order to derail "their policy of world hegemony . . . and aggressive strategy and policy."[128]

Syria expressed its support by allowing the Damascus-based DFLP to call the U.S.-led ground offensive "a criminal act" against all Arabs and to urge Arab countries to sever diplomatic and economic ties with the coalition nations. (The DFLP is the Democratic Front for the Liberation of Palestine, a radical leftist organization led by Nayif Hawatimah and sponsored by Syria.)[129] Tehran was encouraged that an Islamist conference convened in Islamabad in mid-February 1991, although supportive of Iraq, concluded that "the revival of Islam will gain momentum as a result of this war."[130]

THE GLOBALIZATION OF THE STRUGGLE FOR *AL-QUDS* — JERUSALEM

The Iraqi defeat in the Gulf War was a rude awakening for the Palestinians. Growing numbers sought solace in the fold of Islam. Consequently, the war not only did not harm the position and hold over the population of HAMAS and Islamic Jihad, but actually helped the Islamists. Moreover, the damage to the PLO's image would strengthen the Islamists' power and especially give more credence to their arguments.[131] Thus, in early 1991, even the radical Palestinian terrorist organizations that had supported Iraq were convinced of the inevitable rise of radical Islam as the dominant trend in the Middle East.

An Islamist, Mu'ayyin Tahir of the mainstream of *al-Fatah*, issued a telling analysis. The radicalization of the Palestinian movement in Jordan greatly benefitted the Muslim Brotherhood and especially the HAMAS. Tahir believes that "the progress of Islam is the direct result of the failure of Arab nationalisms and the parties of the left." He explained that, rhetoric aside, "*al-Fatah* in the occupied territories and Jordan is essentially Islamist and that this is a trend that is constantly growing in all Palestinian organizations." Tahir believes "the new Islamic order" is inevitable and imminent.[132] As'ad Abd-al-Rahman, a member of PLO Central Committee, acknowledged that the PLO was losing the Palestinian leadership to the Islamists:

> Our whole region is slipping toward radicalism, including the Palestinians. What will happen if Saddam Hussein is not totally vanquished or if he wins? In either case, extremism will make immense progress. Officially, the PLO controls its strategy, but it is questioned more and more. Since August 2 (the date of Iraq's invasion of Kuwait), the Palestinians have been coordinating their efforts with a view of helping Saddam Hussein. However, while united against the Israelis and the Americans, they no longer agree on the political agenda.[133]

Meanwhile, after mid-January 1991, once the magnitude of the Iraqi defeat was becoming clear, the Islamists in Jordan shifted emphasis in their agitation. They now considered the Iraqi defeat at the hands of the U.S.-led coalition as the spark that would ignite a cataclysmic clash between revivalist Islam and the West, and especially the U.S. On January 21, 1991, Sheikh Nadir al-Tamimi of the Palestinian Islamic Jihad declared that Muslims "are entitled to strike back in the Western countries. This is our reaction to the bombardments."[134] The next day, Sheikh Asa'ad Bayyud al-Tamimi anticipated that "many volunteers for suicidal attacks against Western interests will launch their operations shortly." He had given them spiritual guidance and issued *fatwa*s encouraging such strikes. Sheikh As'aad al-Tamimi predicted that once confronted with the Islamists' wrath, the U.S. will "face its end in this war against Islam in spite of its strength because *Allah* is greater and stronger."[135]

Iran was the dominant force behind and in control of this anticipated rejuvenation of Palestinian-Islamist international terrorism. In mid-March 1991, Tehran convened a major terrorist conference with most terrorist leaders in attendance, including Ahmad Jibril, Subhi al-Tufayli, Fathi al-Shqaqi and Sa'id Barakah. Iran's leaders, led by Khamenei and Hashemi-Rafsanjani, personally supervised the Iranian side.[136] The conference concluded that it was imperative for the Islamist organizations to seize the initiative and launch a struggle against the U.S. in revenge for the situation in the Middle East and toward the restoration of their dominance over the region's policy. "Only the Arab masses are capable of defending their dignity. It is time for the Arab masses to take immediate action and for Arab organizations, wherever they may be, to strike at anyone and anything American until they stop their aggression against us in Iraq, Palestine, and elsewhere," explained a Jordanian Islamist.[137]

Khamenei held a series of meetings with several terrorist leaders. Tehran emphasized his direct involvement with and control over the assembled leaders: "While giving them certain instructions, he said that to overcome the enemies of Islam it is necessary for the faithful to be aware of truths and realities of the contemporary world, not to fear death and not to be concerned with worldly goods... During each meeting, the leaders of combative Palestinian and Lebanese groups submitted reports to the leader of the Islamic Revolution on the developments and situation in their regions."[138] In order to accelerate the struggle, the IRGC was ordered in early 1991 to establish the Quds Forces in order to "advise and train Muslims all over the world" as well as carry out special operations on behalf of Tehran.[139] Akhmad Khomeini's Service to Islam Organization[140] was incorporated into the new organization.

A PFLP-GC high-level delegation, headed by Ahmad Jibril, remained in Tehran longer than the others. It met with a high-level Iranian group headed by Hashemi-Rafsanjani for additional consultations to discuss the Palestinian question and especially Tehran's assistance and contribution to the efforts to "restore the Palestinian national struggle's cohesion, unity, and ability to continue the struggle."[141] Indeed, the Islamic Jihad for the Liberation of Palestine emerged as an important player in the Iranian system of international terrorism beyond the struggle against Israel and the *intifadah*. In a meeting between Hashemi-Rafsanjani and the organization's leaders Fathi al-Shqaqi and Sa'id Barakah, Shqaqi stated: "Thousands of real Muslims who consider themselves the children of the Islamic Revolution of Iran are now ready for *Jihad* and martyrdom until the liberation of *al-Quds*."[142]

The Gulf Crisis was thus the catalyst for a milestone development in the Islamists', and especially Iran's and *HizbAllah*'s, grand design in more than one respect. Saddam Hussein's survival after the War was used increasingly to incite and agitate the Muslim world (even beyond the Middle East) against the Arab regimes that sided with the West and betrayed the "noble cause".[143]

The Islamists sought to capitalize on the shock and humiliation suffered by the Muslims. Sheikh Sa'id Sha'ban expressed his "hope that Iran will be able to convince certain Arabs to break their alliance with the West and instead form an Islamic front to counter conspiracies of imperialism and Zionism in the

Middle East, especially Palestine, Iraq, Kuwait, Afghanistan, and Kashmir.''[144] Indeed, Tehran was beginning to formulate its perception of the future course of the region, and the Muslim world as a whole, in the wake of the Gulf Crisis. The strengthening (and, in Kuwait, the restoration) of conservative-royal regimes in the Gulf by the U.S. was seen as a most dangerous development.[145]

SUBVERTING THE PLO

In the spring of 1991, the possibility of a marked escalation of anti-Western international terrorism loomed high despite, or actually because of, the terrorists' inability to launch the massive campaign they and Saddam Hussein promised as part of the Arab reaction to the Gulf Crisis. The West averted some acts with a massive expulsion and containment of possible perpetrators. Moreover, Arafat's PLO and Iraqi-controlled elements were torn from within by the mistrust and lust for power that led, in the wake of Abu Iyad's assassination, to near paralysis as Operation Desert Storm was escalating.

However, the most important reason for the failure of the anticipated terrorist campaign was that Iran and Syria had reneged on their deal with Saddam Hussein and actively prevented their terrorists from supporting the Iraqi cause. Since the international terrorist system controlled by Iran and Syria is the best organized and most capable in the industrialized West, there was not much the Iraqis could do once they were denied access to this infrastructure.

The Iraqi defeat, and the ensuing quest for revenge by both Arafat and Saddam Hussein, rejuvenated the Palestinian-Iraqi preparations for an escalation of the terrorist campaign. A clear indication came in mid-April 1991 when Arafat ordered the transfer of the majority of the PLO's fighters from Tunisia to the Sara camp in Libya, some 1,000 kms from Tripoli, for intensive training. The terrorists' families were not permitted to join them in Sara so as not to distract them from their arduous training.[146] It did not take long for Libya to realize that these terrorists were essentially Islamists. Soon afterwards, Qaddafi consulted with key allies and terrorist leaders about what to do about them. In mid-May 1991, Shqaqi and Mohtashemi met in Tripoli, Libya, to discuss unifying and closing the ranks of the Islamist struggle in the region. They also met with several high-level Libyans and other officials.[147]

Having been identified as one of the prominent sponsors of international terrorism, and on a campaign to establish a new "moderate" image, Syria's Hafez al-Assad found an ingenious way to revive international terrorism under his control, yet in a deniable manner. Toward this end, Syria has intensified its efforts to take over the PLO from within,[148] leaving Assad's nemesis Arafat as a token head so that future terrorist operations will be attributed to the PLO and not to Syria. The power-hungry Arafat goes along with the plan because the alternative is a sure assassination. Indeed, Arafat began hinting at the resumption of international terrorism by PLO members, ostensibly as a result of the world's failure solve the Palestinian problem. "I do not know for how long I can prevent them from resuming hijackings," he warned in the spring of 1991.[149]

Meanwhile, Syria and its supporters held several meetings in Damascus with high level representatives of Arafat's PLO in an attempt to restore unity.[150] Faruq Qaddumi, himself a former member of the Syrian *Ba'ath* Party, visited Damascus in late May on behalf of Arafat to "negotiate" under what conditions Assad would tolerate Arafat's continued "leadership" of the PLO.[151] Qaddumi also met with Ahmad Jibril and the PFLP-GC leadership, all tightly controlled by Syria and Iran, to discuss closer operational cooperation.[152] Damascus added some "incentives" by unleashing Lebanese forces on PLO strongholds in southern Lebanon, resulting in the destruction of PLO forces and assets, including their main command room, the confiscation of their weapons, and the incarceration of many commanders.[153] Soon afterwards Arafat accepted the

Syrian conditions and agreed to form a Syrian-Palestinian coordinating committee with Syrian Vice-President Abd-al-Halim Khaddam as his counterpart, a clear dishonoring by Syria of the claimant to Palestinian presidency.[154]

These actions stand is sharp contrast with the treatment of *HizbAllah* and other pro-Syrian terrorists in the area. They were simply moved to new camps in the Biqaa with all their weapons.[155] Meanwhile, on July 3, 1991, Syria signaled to Israel its control over terrorism by sending a DFLP squad to ambush soldiers near the IDF (Israel Defense Forces) Hermon stronghold, causing one fatality. The significance of this DFLP ambush is that the perpetrators came from and withdrew to Syria in a path passing through several Syrian military positions. Thus, the DFLP could not have conducted this operation without direct support from the Syrian Armed Forces.

Damascus thus delivered a clear message that an escalation of terrorism from the Syrian border is always possible given the right political circumstances, and that the key to such an escalation is in Assad's hands.[156] Another DFLP squad tried to repeat the operation on September 23 but was engaged and destroyed at the Lebanese/Israeli/Syrian border near the Hermon mountains.[157]

Meanwhile, the new arrangement was working and the PLO was on the verge of escalating international terrorism. In mid-June 1991, Hakam Bal'awi, the head of Arafat's office in Tunis, chaired a meeting in Tunis of senior commanders of *al-Fatah*, the *Fatah* Revolutionary Council, and other Palestinian terrorist organizations, most of whom "have led and carried out several terrorist operations in Arab and Western capitals." The subject of the meeting was international terrorism. "On Arafat's personal orders, they decided that the return to terrorism and violence is unavoidable in order to draw the world's attention to the PLO again," and then discussed the expansion of specialized terrorist training toward the launch of the campaign.[158] The younger generation of the PLO considers Hakam Bal'awi their preferred candidate to replace Arafat and rejuve-

nate their struggle.[159] Bal'awi was expected to assume Abu
Iyad's post.[160]

Meanwhile, George Habash, an Assad loyalist who had
maintained close relations with Saddam Hussein during the
Gulf Crisis, held meetings with Saddam Hussein in Baghdad to
discuss the emerging course of the terrorist struggle.[161] Soon
afterwards, Saddam Hussein held meetings with other terrorist
leaders that have camps and assets in Iraq and promised
Baghdad's support for their renewed operations.[162] These negotiations culminated in a secret agreement between Saddam
Hussein and Yassir Arafat to transfer some 10,000 PLO fighters to Iraq in order to bolster a "special force" formed by Iraqi
intelligence in the Ramadi camp near Baghdad, now including
the "special guards" commando of the Iraqi Republican Guards
as well as Palestinian, Yemeni, Sudanese, Jordanian, and other
Arab terrorists.[163]

The next major phase in the consolidation of the terrorist
front took place in the first week of July in Rifa't al-Assad's
villa in Marbala, Spain. Abdul Sallam Jallud, second to Qaddafi
in Libya, secretly arrived in Marbala for discussions with
Syrian officials. Libya was assured of the impending escalation
of the armed, that is terrorist, struggle and that the suppression
of the PLO in Lebanon should in no way be interpreted as a
threat to international terrorism from Lebanon. The Syrians
and the Libyans then discussed Libya's role in, and contribution to, the new phase in international terrorism.[164]

The results of these negotiations were immediately reflected in Libya's public posture. In mid-July, Tripoli announced that "the Arabs now have no alternative but to launch
a popular war against the foreign forces occupying the Arab
land in order to preserve their dignity, restore their rights, and
be worthy of occupying their place on earth under the sun."[165]
Qaddafi repeated the call to arms, explaining that "the Arabs
have nothing left but to wage a popular war to confront this
conspiracy being hatched against this nation. The Arabs have

no choice but unity to confront the U.S.-Zionist attempt to corner Iraq and humiliate the Arabs."[166]

Meanwhile, the PLO also escalated the terrorist warnings. In early July, Muhammad Milhim of the PLO Executive Committee issued a statement in which he warned "the United States and the European countries" that unless a comprehensive solution to the Palestinian problem, acceptable to the PLO, is found, "the next year would be a black one." He emphasized that in "giving peace a final chance," the PLO insists on being the full and sole representation of the Palestinians. Milhim stated that if these conditions were not met immediately, "a new action strategy will be adopted (by the PLO) based on the military option for as long as the Zionist enemy continues to occupy our land."[167]

Faced with a widespread rejection of his "moderate" line, Arafat attempted a desperate move to restore his Islamic credentials. On July 29, he sent a conciliatory note to the *Ulama* in Qom, appealing for help "to confront the American-Zionist plot in the form of a Arab-Israeli compromise." While the Islamist leadership was in full agreement concerning the threat in the peace process, they would not endorse Arafat. Tehran would not help Arafat, but instead urged his followers to return to the fold of the true, that is Islamist, Palestinian resistance in order to escalate their common struggle.[168] Tehran conditioned its support of the PLO on the ouster of Arafat, and notified several Palestinian leaders affiliated with the PLO, including Faruq Qaddumi, that "Arafat need be ousted from PLO leadership and removed from the political arena, so that it [Tehran] can fulfill its commitments to the fraternal Palestinian people."[169]

CONFRONTING THE *PAX-AMERICANA*

Although apprehensive about growing challenges, the Islamists were determined to capitalize on the upheaval and rage in the Middle East in order to expedite the march of

Islam. In April 1991, the *HizbAllah*'s Sheikh Na'im Qassim stated: "No one should think at any moment that we will abandon the march of Islam, irrespective of the difficult conditions and magnitude of the plots against it. We will continue to bear the trust of the blood which was shed in the name of Islam."[170]

Sheikh Fadlallah explained that the region provides unique circumstances and conditions for the resurrection of the Islamic Revolution on a global scale:

> The Middle East is the base of the Islamic fundamentalist movement, which has expanded to reach various regional and world locations at interlinked levels of security, politics, and culture. The Middle East is a strategic region. . . Only the Middle East could unsettle the world's political centers and affect them adversely. No region other than the Middle East could enable the United States to control the world economy and political conditions and, therefore, control the world's security game.[171]

It was possible to measure Khamenei's power in late May 1991 when Sheikh Abbas al-Mussawi was elected as the new Secretary General of the *HizbAllah*[172], replacing Sheikh Subhi al-Tufayli. Sheikh Mussawi was a devotee of Ayatollah Muhammad Baqir al-Sadr, the founder of the Iraqi *Al-Dawah*. Khamenei is also a devotee of al-Sadr. He and Mussawi have been close since their days in Najaf, a Shi'ite holy city in southern Iraq which has become a religious and educational center for young Shi'ites from all over the world. At the time, Abbas al-Mussawi was considered Khamenei's staunchest ally in Lebanon. Mussawi's confidants insist that he has the "spiritual fanatic support necessary for the jurisprudent's governorship" since the 1970s. ("Jurisprudent's governorship" is Khomeini's concept of the rule of the religious leader as the supreme authority in Islam; Mussawi was committed to Khomeini's ideology since the 1970s.)

Similarly, Sheikh Ibrahim al-Amin, the newly elected deputy secretary general of the *HizbAllah*, is another devotee of al-Sadr.[173] Thus, the election of Khamenei loyalists with common religious backgrounds as the new leaders of the *HizbAllah* clearly demonstrates the new power and authority of Khamenei. They will assist him significantly when the time comes for him to compete for the top position in the Shi'ite world.

The Second Congress of the *HizbAllah* and Islamic Jihad took place in late May in Bir al-Abd and was devoted to discussions about the future. Some 300 representatives of the factions and institutions affiliated with the *HizbAllah* took part. They formed the future leadership: Sheikh Abbas al-Mussawi was elected the Secretary General and Sheikh Ibrahim al-Amin is his deputy. Other key members elevated within the *Shura* are Hassan Nasrallah, back from advanced studies in Qom, Hussein al-Khalil, Muhammad Funaysh, and Subhi al-Tufayli. Special attention was paid to "the need to mold the organizational body in a manner that makes it compatible with the emerging regional and international developments and harmonious with the new Iranian leadership."[174]

In his speech, Sheikh Sayyid Barakah of the Islamic Jihad Movement in Palestine declared that "this is the beginning of the era of Islam and the end of the era of the Americans and the Jews. There is no room for reconciliation with these enemies." He anticipated a major escalation in the fighting against Israel. Sheikh Subhi al-Tufayli discussed the apparent consolidation of pro-Western regimes in the Middle East that would not cooperate with the Islamists. Tufayli had no doubts as to the next steps. "We will not wait until the rulers make a gesture to us and open the borders. We must destroy all the idols, who are led by the American beast." Tufayli stated that the primary challenge facing them is to "unite in order to liberate our land, and establish a resistance movement to defend our dignity."[175] Sheikh Fadlallah defined these Arab leaders as "agents of the CIA" and enemies of Islam, thus sanctioning their destruction.[176] Indeed, the new leadership of the *HizbAllah* was committed to a major escalation in its armed struggle against Israel and the U.S. in accordance with a doctrine that had been agreed upon between Hashemi-Rafsanjani and Hafez al-Assad during the former's visit to Damascus. [177]

The region's radicals, led by Iran and Syria, remained committed to a major terrorist campaign against the U.S. For the radicals, the mere existence of U.S. influence in the Middle East and the legitimization of Israel by merely acknowledging its right to exist are perceived as a major direct threat to their vital interests. Therefore, they are willing to take drastic measures — primarily anti-American international terror — to counter this threat. Indeed, as of the summer of 1991, once it was clear that the U.S. succeeded in its efforts to convene a peace conference, the Middle East's radicals, led by Iran and Syria, began a hectic campaign to confront the West and prevent, virtually at all costs, its return to the Islamic Middle East. This policy was guided by Iran.

Iran intends to realize the new Muslim world order by mobilizing the masses toward a common noble cause with as little (overt) direct challenge to existing regimes as possible. In early June 1991, Khamenei explained that the process was irreversible but urged prudence because the process is so fateful. He pointed out that "looking at the world one feels that the great Islamic movement is growing bigger and stronger every day." Khamenei anticipated a major struggle against the U.S. because of the dire ramifications of the triumph of Islam for the West. But, he concluded, "if the Muslims are wise, have self-esteem, and believe in the glory of Islam and their own strength, no doubt this movement will attain its goals."[178]

Meanwhile, by mid-summer, a coherent Islamist assessment and doctrine were being consolidated. Fadlallah pointed out that the Gulf Crisis has proven once more that the West considers the oil resources as its own property and that the West's "program is that it seeks to block the emergence of any liberation movement in these countries so their peoples cannot free themselves from the shackles of Western colonialist hegemony. . . The Muslim people of the Middle East and the rest of the Islamic world, particularly those in Islamic Iran, thus have a duty to find the levers of power and sources of strength that will enable them to control their own destiny."[179] The alternative would be disastrous in view of the long-term objectives of the U.S. "By raising the issue of a new world order, America wishes to destroy the Islamic and revolutionary movement through a comprehensive disarmament and to control the fate of the world community," Ahmad Khomeini explained.[180]

Sheikh Fadlallah urged the mobilization of the Muslim world to confront the danger. "The world's Islamic movements, chief among which is the Islamic Republic of Iran, have a clear and great duty to bring about the defeat of U.S. plots."[181] Ahmad Khomeini believes that Iran was already pursuing these objectives. "The Islamic Revolution as the main focus of liberating revolutions is the only power which is properly confronting world blasphemy and the arrogant camp and will not allow America to achieve its evil aims," he explained.[182] Fadlallah anticipated an imminent escalation because "Muslim *mujahideen* all over the world have no recourse but to reach an understanding with the Islamic Republic of Iran and to make long-term plans to combat the U.S. plots and transform the American era into an Islamic one in which Islam's sovereignty can be extended throughout the world."[183]

Sheikh Fadlallah saw a very distinct role for the *HizbAllah* in the emerging Islamist struggle. "We, the oppressed Muslims of the Third World, believe that the United States is not invincible and it is possible for us, even though it is in the long term, to foil the U.S. tyrannical plots and plans by all means possible," he explained. However, for such a struggle to be successful, it must be waged under a unified leadership. Such leadership, Fadlallah acknowledged, can be found only in Tehran, because only the Iranian support system proved capable of transforming the Muslims into "revolutionary Muslims who can confront world arrogance."[184]

The profound strategic objectives of Tehran and Damascus, namely eradicating the Western presence in the Middle East, have not changed since the 1980s. Moreover, the Gulf War and the consequent increase in U.S. influence in the Middle East only marked a rejuvenation of the campaign to expel the U.S. Tehran warned that the U.S. "cannot emerge as the sole power determining international issues." In order to prevent such a course, "a strong Islamic revolution and the thoughts of revolutionary Islam in their capacity as a superior idea have been revived in the world instead, and these are moving forward to emerge into a viable power in the face of the dominant atheism and insecurity by communicating their universal message to the oppressed masses."[185]

In order to expedite the anti-U.S. struggle, Hojjat ol-Islam al-Muslemin Sayyid Ali Akbar Mohtashemi was nominated in early August 1991 as Chairman of the Defense Committee of the *Majlis* (the Iranian Parliament), a major improvement of his political power.[186] Moreover, Iranian sources insist that Hashemi-Rafsanjani's "struggles with Mohtashemi are over methods, not aims."[187]

The official position of Iran was outlined by Iran's supreme leader, Ayatollah Ali Khamenei, in a speech on August 19, 1991, in which he urged Muslim youth to act against the U.S. "Are the zealous Muslim youths of Palestine and other Islamic countries dead so that America can easily settle the biggest problem of the Islamic world in its own interest?"[188] The *HizbAllah*'s Abbas Mussawi enthusiastically endorsed Khamenei's urging of "the Islamic *Ummah* and the Muslims in the region, particularly those in the *HizbAllah Ummah*, the Islamic Resistance, and the Islamic *intifadah* in Palestine, to shoulder their responsibilities" in confronting the U.S. and Israel, and vowed to follow these directives.[189]

It would not be long before Iran would begin formulating and implementing a global terrorist master plan that would ultimately bring terrorism to America.

DECLARING WAR ON AMERICA

Beginning in October 1991, an assertive Tehran was taking credible steps to revive and markedly escalate the Islamist anti-American *Jihad*. An international terrorist conference was convened in Tehran in order to formulate strategy and tactics for an unprecedented escalation of a worldwide *Jihad* against the U.S.

On October 4, Ayatollah Abdul Qarim Mussavi Ardebili devoted his Friday sermon to "this great calamity of American domination" which he called "a catastrophe, a disaster for Muslim peoples." Therefore, all Muslims must "attack American interests and take away their peace," he decreed. "What I say to you is a duty, a religious and obligatory duty. Muslims must take away their security, just as they have taken security away from Muslims." Ardebili favors the escalation of international terrorism. "The Kuwaitis, the Iraqis, the Pakistanis and the Iranians should form resistance cells and endanger American interests," he explained. "They should make life difficult for them. We do not know about classical warfare, but we know about this sort of thing," that is, terrorism. He assured that whoever "is killed in the process, he will be a martyr." Ardebili then urged immediate action, especially by trained terrorists such as the *HizbAllah*'s, to whose action he alluded in his call for arms. "If this is delayed even by an hour, it will be too late. The youths, those who have so far proved in the arena that they are capable of it, they should form resistance cells and attack them, their properties, their interests, deprive them of their peace and security."[190]

The importance of Ayatollah Ardebili's call to arms and terrorism was reflected in the extensive coverage the sermon received in the Iranian media and especially the international broadcasts and IRNA (the Islamic Republic News Agency, the official news agency of Iran).[191] In Beirut, the *HizbAllah* was in full agreement with Tehran. "In the *HizbAllah*, our strategic policy has always been persistent,'' Sheikh Abbas al-Mussawi explained. ''The great achievement of the *HizbAllah* is that through two operations of sacred martyrdom against the American Marines and the French paratroopers, the organization was able to evict America and the multinational force from Beirut.''[192]

In essence, Mussawi reaffirmed the validity of a long-standing strategy of the *HizbAllah* and the states sponsoring it. The Islamic Jihad Forces — Bayt al-Maqdis of Sheikh Asa'ad Bayud Tamimi — announced their formal joining of the *HizbAllah* and the consequent change of the organization's name to *HizbAllah*-Palestine.[193]

As the Madrid Peace Conference was becoming a reality, Tehran clarified its strategic posture and objectives. On October 16, Khamenei explained that fearing the rise of Islam, the Americans ''are in a haste to strengthen their foothold in the region to enable them to halt the Islamic uprising of the nations'' before it is too late to save the West. ''The struggle and *Jihad* will remain with great vigor,'' Khamenei declared.[194] He then urged all Muslims not to surrender to the ''American threats'' but to take part in the *Jihad* so that ''the Israelis will not feel secure in any place all over the world.''[195]

On October 18, 1991, Iran convened the International Conference in Support of the Islamic Revolution of the People of Palestine. Over 400 delegates from 45 countries attended the conference. Participants included members of parliament and government officials from all the Arab and many Third World countries, including senior officials from Syria and Jordan, Islamist leaders from several countries including the U.S., and a large number of Palestinian, Lebanese, Afghan and other Muslim terrorist leaders and commanders.[196] A concluding report claimed that the conference ''was attended by ministers, parliamentarians and revolutionaries from 60 countries.''[197]

Hojjat ol-Islam Ali Akbar Mohtashemi, the head of the Defense and Islamic Revolutionary Guard Corps Committee in the *Majlis* explained that the conference brought together all who can contribute to, and take part in, "the all-out battle between us as an Islamic nation and the global alliance of arrogance."[198] Mehdi Karrubi, the speaker of the *Majlis*, was the president of the conference. In his opening speech, he called on the participants to "take decisive actions against the greatest problem which faces the world of Islam," and vowed that Tehran would provide "extensive support" for all the Muslim *mujahideen*.[199]

Hojjat ol-Islam Abdul-Vahed Mussavi-Lari, the conference chairman, explained that "in the three-sided committees to be set-up in the conference, means of giving aid in terms of finance, arms, training Muslim Palestinian resistance fighters, as well as ways of countering the dangerous phenomenon of Jewish migration to the occupied territories, will be examined."[200] The president of Iran, Ali Akbar Hashemi-Rafsanjani, delivered the first opening speech in which he announced "Iran's readiness to join the *Jihad* for the liberation of Palestine. . . Iran is even ready to dispatch troops to fight Israel along with the Palestinians," he added.[201]

In the other opening speech, Iran's spiritual leader, Ayatollah Khamenei, explained why the issue of Palestine is so crucial for Iran and the entire Muslim world. "The issue is that the world of arrogance needs the land of Palestine, which is the geographical heart of the Islamic World, in order to crush Islam; in order to put pressure on Islamic nations; in order to check the Islamic movement." He emphasized that there is no substitute to an armed struggle against Israel, and urged the gathered to activism. "You must be decisive here, you must take decisive actions," Khamenei told them.[202]

Subsequent speakers from highest levels of the Iranian leadership were more practical. Maj. Gen. Mohsen Reza'i, the IRGC commander, urged the formation of an Islamic army to liberate Palestine.[203] Reza'i sees the IRGC as the core of such an army because of its declared internationalist role of "helping Muslims everywhere, since we are an Islamic army."[204]

Ahmad Khomeini clearly stated the ultimate strategic objective of Tehran and its allies — attacking America. He emphasized the fatefulness of the inevitable struggle with the U.S.: "We should realize that the world is hostile toward us only for [our commitment to] Islam. After the fall of Marxism, Islam replaced it, and as long as Islam exists, U.S. hostility exists, and as long as U.S. hostility exists, the struggle exists." He explained that "the struggle against Israel is a war against the U.S. and Europe with no short end." Alluding to the forthcoming terrorist campaign, Ahmad Khomeini told the participants in the conference, "You should decide behind closed doors how much arms and ammunition the Palestinians need, and the Iranian Armed Forces and Revolutionary Guards will do their best."[205]

Several Middle Eastern and Third World speakers urged, in the words of Hojjat ol-Islam Muhammad Baqir ol-Hakim of SAIRI, the formulation of "a common strategy for all Muslims and combatants so that all of them will move in one direction" because "America's objective is . . . to annihilate liberation movements . . . all of which are carried out with Islamic aspirations." This theme was concurred with by several dozen speakers.[206] Several participants asked Tehran for additional budgets for the escalation of their struggles.[207] Two days later, Khamenei opened accounts in Iranian banks to collect donations and transfer money to the Islamist struggle.[208]

Many terrorist leaders rallied behind Tehran's call for escalating the armed struggle. Sheikh Asaad Bayud al-Tamimi, now of the *HizbAllah*-Palestine, declared that "we back the Islamic Revolution to the hilt, and I believe that Israel will not be able to continue its existence." He anticipated that as a result of the rejuvenation of the struggle made possible by the "crucial" conference in Tehran, "we will finally enter al-Aqsa mosque, and this should be done with the help of guns."[209]

Abu Mussa, the leader of the Syrian-controlled *Fatah-Intifadah*, described "the armed struggle as the sole alternative to confront the Zionist enemy." He called on Muslims everywhere to participate in that *Jihad*. He also called on "Iran, Syria and Libya to take the first steps in forming a Palestinian army." He then urged all terrorist organizations to unify their operations for better results in the upcoming fight.[210] Ahmad Jibril urged all Muslims to "thwart" the American schemes.[211] Sayyid Abbas al-Mussawi, the head of Lebanon's *HizbAllah*, accused the United States of harboring an "open enmity with Muslims."[212] "The *HizbAllah* will hold out its struggle against the Zionist regime until the city of *Quds* (Jerusalem) was liberated," he vowed. He added that "Iran will continue to support all strugglers who are fighting for the liberation of Palestine."[213]

Official Tehran warned that any country or person that helped strengthen Israel "has in fact endorsed the suffering of the Palestinian nation and must be confident it will have to pay back dearly." These comments were "not a threat, but the expression of a reality."[214] Tehran called for "practical measures to be taken for the enrollment of Muslim people in an 'Islamic Army'" committed to battle so that "the cancerous tumor of Zionism be eradicated."[215] Mohtashemi concluded that the conference "stressed the need for continuing struggle of the world Muslims against the U.S. and the Zionists."[216]

The Conference decided to establish a permanent secretariat and staff in Tehran under Mussavi-Lari to coordinate the operations decided upon.[217] The conference also decided on "the formation of a united Islamic Army to liberate *al-Quds* from the Zionist usurpers."[218] In its formal resolution, the conference also called for an "all out *Jihad*" against Israel and the West.[219] Most PLO factions signed the Tehran declaration.[220]

The conference in Tehran was also used for consultations

and coordination between senior commanders of the various terrorist organizations that are members of the Iranian- and Syrian-controlled network.[221] Sheikh Fadlallah hinted at the possibility of international terrorism: "We expect to adopt secret resolutions that will materialize publicly at the appropriate time as procedural steps against efforts at settlement."[222] Abbas al-Mussawi suggested that the *HizbAllah* would resort to violent methods, even in Europe.[223]

Mohtashemi stated that "it is necessary to target all the U.S. objectives throughout the world."[224] He emphasized that Iranians and Muslims are prepared to carry out worldwide terrorist attacks. Toward this end, Iran "would have more than five million trained fighters who already had eight years of combat experience," he explained. "Iranians are ready for sacrifice and Holy War, either through organized warfare . . . or by martyrdom [suicide] missions worldwide, not only in Palestine but against Zionists throughout the world."[225]

Mohtashemi anticipates a major eruption of the all-out *Jihad*. His perception of the upcoming *Jihad* is explicit and demanding from an Islamic legal point of view while being, at the same time, rich in Shi'ite symbols and strongly invoking emotional commitments: "The count down has begun; the zero-point is approaching; the children of Ashura and Karbala are ready, and the bloody destiny-making Husseinite battle against global blasphemy is before us, and the promise of justice based on the victory of the oppressed over the arrogant is certain. The moment of justice has arrived. Peace and *Allah*'s Mercy be upon you."[226]

The resolutions of the Tehran conference were not idle talk. Almost immediately there was a spate of terrorist attacks in the region. In Beirut, Sheikh Abbas al-Mussawi, the "maestro" of operations, brought with him instructions from Tehran to activate the *HizbAllah*'s special operations command. The Syrian Special Forces protect and shelter the main *HizbAllah* facilities in Beirut and the new stockpiles in the Biqaa, delivered via Damascus. Imad Mughaniyah was put in charge of special operations such as aircraft hijackings and bombings, overseas sabotage as well as kidnappings. He was assisted by Abd al-Hadi Hammadi and Mustafa Badr-ad-Din, Mughaniyah's brother-in-law who had been in command of the Kuwait 17 and was released from jail in August 1990. In the first phase, they would concentrate on launching operations in Western Europe, with Spain and Germany being among the initial objectives. The latter is Hammadi's personal obsession because of his brothers' continued incarceration there.[227]

But, as Mohtashemi has stated repeatedly, this time the ultimate objective is the U.S. itself. Both Tehran and Damascus have realized that U.S. influence in the region, being demonstrated and enhanced in the peace process, would not enable the realization of their strategic designs — the New Islamic World Order. The U.S. must be evicted from the Middle East and South-West Asia as a precondition for the rise of the Islamist bloc. Thus, a confrontation with Washington is inevitable. Damascus and Tehran believe, on the basis of their experience in Beirut in the early 1980s, that it is possible to compel Washington into drastic changes in its policy by a few spectacular terrorist operations, especially if the carnage is massive. This time, however, they would do it on U.S. soil.

CHAPTER 4
THE NEW ISLAMIST INTERNATIONAL

The February 26, 1993 bombing of the World Trade Center in New York was but one of the first events in a new phase of the Islamist *Jihad* against the West, one that if carried out as planned, will be characterized by a spate of terrorism throughout America and Western Europe.

As mentioned earlier, since the Fall of 1992 there has been a marked increase in Islamist terrorism, subversion and violence in many countries around the world, including the U.S. and Israel. These recent, seemingly disparate incidents are not isolated cases that by chance happen to have occurred more or less simultaneously. They are in fact the first acts in an intensified *Islamist Jihad* against the Judeo-Christian world order.

The importance in these incidents is that they are being carried out by Sunni networks affiliated with the new Islamist International, the umbrella organization of the various "Jihadist" organizations that operate within the theological framework of the International Muslim Brotherhood. Essentially controlled and sponsored by Iran, and run via Sudan under the leadership of Sheikh Hassan Abdallah al-Turabi, the Islamist International is the realization of Khomeini's original vision of an ecumenical all-Islamic Revolution that does not distinguish between Sunnis and Shi'ites. This new Islamist International has been consolidated only since the fall of 1991.

The Armed Islamic Movement, popularly known as "the International Brigade/Legion of Islam," spearheads the new international terrorism wave. The leading terrorists are known as 'Afghans,' having been trained with the *mujahideen* in Pakistan. Some fought in Afghanistan. The Islamist legion sends its fighters all over Asia, Africa, Europe and America to support, further, incite, and facilitate what the leadership considers Islamic liberation struggles. Affiliated Islamist groups and organizations are currently active in Israel, Jordan, Iraq, Kashmir, Egypt, Algeria, Tunisia, the Philippines and, increasingly, Bosnia-Herzegovina. The Islamists have bases and support facilities in Sudan, Iran, Afghanistan and Pakistan where they also receive advanced military, terrorist, clandestine and subversion training from an international cadre of expert trainers. They deploy to their destinations via Tehran and Khartoum.

The current rise of Islamist terrorism in its Sunni variant is an expression of a profound socio-political process throughout the Muslim world, with special importance in the Arab world where the tradition of political terrorism was most active. During the 1980s, radical leftist Arab terrorism was slowly collapsing. The overall failure of the Arab revolutionary trend and the lack of charismatic young leaders had diverted the radicalized and frustrated youth away from the socialist-nationalist movements into the fold of revivalist radical Islam.

In contrast, the Islamist movement provides its followers with young charismatic leaders, divine guidance and assurances of high rewards in eternity. The suffering and frustration of this world are presented as trials on the road to martyrdom and paradise, so that the more the believer suffers and sacrifices, the better his eternal reward. Consequently, the radicalized youth join the banner of Islam in unprecedented numbers. Radical Islamist terrorism is the wave of the future. The current wave of Islamist violence and terrorism is but the first hesitant phases in a future campaign.

ROOTS

The rise of Islamist terrorism, and especially the Armed Islamic Movement, is the result of the convergence of several trends:

* The aggregate impact of the Islamic Revolution in Iran, especially its call to arms, on the Sunni Islamist movement dominated by Muslim Brotherhood and its specific ideology.

* The appeal and impact of the rise of the radical international terrorist movement dominated by Iran and Syria, the most notorious component of which is the *HizbAllah*, and the ensuing transformation of leftist Palestinian organizations that "discovered" Islam.
* The lingering impact of the war in Afghanistan and the presence of Arab volunteers in the ranks of the *Mujahideen*.

As discussed in Chapter 1, from the very beginning the Islamic Revolution in Iran emphasized its internationalist characteristics and its commitment to an all-Islamic revolutionary process. Moreover, Tehran considered the support of and its participation in *Jihad*s and revolutionary struggles abroad not just its moral obligation but a vital step to ensure the very existence of the regime.

At first, the Sunni Islamist elite, especially the Muslim Brotherhood with their own rich theological and ideological heritage, were apprehensive about Khomeini's self-declared leadership of the Muslim world. Indeed, Egypt's theological elite received the Iranian Revolution with a mixed reaction. Islamist activists had a variety of opinions about the legality of a Shi'ite revolution as a precedent and inspiration for a Sunni movement. A wholehearted endorsement was expressed by Umar al-Tilmisani of the Muslim Brotherhood who expressed his delight with the victory of the Islamic Revolution in Iran.[1] He predicted that the victory of one Islamic Revolution and the establishment of one Islamic Regime would incite an Islamic revolutionary process leading, within a short time, to the eradication of the rule of non-Muslims over Muslims.[2]

However, most controversial was the question of the legitimacy of the ecumenical message of Khomeini, namely, his call for a joint and unified Islamic world. Some interpreted the ecumenical message as a rallying cry for the rejuvenation of Islam. For example, in his introduction to Khomeini's book *Islamic Government* that he translated and edited, Dr. Hassan

Hanafi emphasized that the differences between Sunni and Shi'ite Islam "has been played with by imperialism and Zionism . . . but Khomeini . . . leads a truly Islamic revolution that surpasses these sectarian borders. . . . Its *elan* goes back to the first revolutionary achievements of the earliest phases of Islam."[3]

However, in the early 1980s, Egyptian Islamists were preoccupied with internal problems and their reaction to Khomeini's call for the worldwide export of the Islamic revolution was dictated by their own priorities. Indeed, the sharpest opposition to the Iranian Revolution, including even a denial of its Islamic nature, came from the ranks of the militant revivalists. For example, during their trial after the assassination of Sadat, members of the *Jihad* Organization, including declared followers of Abd al-Salam Faraj, protested that "to compare us to Khomeini is like trying to discredit the authentic Islamic regime that we strive for."[4]

At the same time, Faraj himself endorsed Khomeini's concept of the supremacy of the *jurisconsult* as a leader and the centrality of the *Jihad*. Faraj wrote in *The Absent Percept* that "learned men of religion today have ignored *Jihad* as the way of *Allah*, despite their knowledge that it is the only way to restore and raise the edifice of Islam again, and that the devils on this earth can only be removed by the power of the sword."[5] Moreover, the militants of the *Jihad* Organization were paying close attention to the operational lessons of underground activities, clandestine organization building, and mass proselytizing in Iran in the period leading to the revolution. They would use the Iranian experience with great success in planning and carrying out the assassination of Egypt's President Anwar Sadat on October 6, 1981. Indeed, during his trial, Lt. Col. Abbud al-Zumur explained that the *Jihad* Organization was determined to incite a mass revolt by assassinating Sadat because the conspirators "learned from Iran that the army and police cannot withstand a popular rebellion."[6]

Meanwhile, Iran had become the Mecca of young radical Islamists, both Sunni and Shi'ite, who were integrated as individuals into the rapidly expanding international terrorism system. For example Sunnis from the *Maghrib* were active members in Iranian-led terrorist groups in Western Europe. From there they supported and led "pro-*HizbAllah*" organizations of religious extremists and took part in most Iranian-sponsored operations from Morocco to Djibouti, as well as in France. The *Maghribi* Islamist "is connected with terrorism, especially since he was molded in Iran to aid and abet extremist terrorist organizations," concluded Mustafa al-Zaanouni, a Tunisian official.[7]

Similarly, with the growing involvement of Iran in the terrorist infrastructure in Lebanon, numerous Islamist Sunni groups and organizations were now enjoying Iranian and Syrian financing, training and assistance to the point of their becoming an integral part of the international terrorist network controlled and sponsored by Iran and Syria. Consequently, there has been a marked intensification of the growing Islamicization process of the extremist Palestinian terrorist organizations which had been previously dominated by revolutionary, leftist, and even near-Communist ideologies. Inspired by the commitment and zeal of the *Hizbollahi*, growing numbers of Arab terrorists were becoming Islamists, initially as individuals, but ultimately in such numbers that they were drawing the leaders into the fold of Islamism.[8]

Consequently, traditional radical Palestinian terrorist organizations who enjoyed Iranian support and sponsorship, mainly in Lebanon, ultimately "discovered" Islam. For example, the PFLP-GC's Ahmad Jibril emphasizes the inevitability of the rediscovery of Islam and the return to a pan-Islamic unity: "We have reached total conviction that we, as an Arab generation that was a victim of a false culture — a Western culture and a poisonous culture since the beginning of this century — should search for sources of power under these difficult and tough circumstances to face our enemies. In other words, we must search for sources of power in the Arab and Islamic nation in order to mobilize them in the battle of confrontation with the Zionists. . . We must review this issue, and Islam must be given its spirit, that is, politics. . . Islam made our grandfathers the leaders of the world."[9] It is highly significant that Jibril sees the essence of his revolutionary struggle as the resurrection of a pan-Islamist super-state, the Islamic nation (*Ummah*).

Meanwhile, in the mid-1980s, Tehran tried to translate the transformation of individuals into an institutional development, and decided to establish "an expanded Islamic front" that would include Sunni Islamists. Tehran's idea was received positively by several clergy groups, especially those affiliated with the Islamic Unification (*Towhid*) Movement.

"Imam Khomeini insisted on forming an expanded Islamic movement in Lebanon to consist of those who agree to join it, ignoring the opposition group."[10] In the fall of 1984, Sheikh Sa'id Sha'ban travelled to Beirut and met with Iranian officials to examine "the possible formation of an Islamic front with *HizbAllah*" toward the formation of "a united Islamic leadership."[11]

Although Sheikh Fadlallah emphasized the close relations between the Shi'ite *HizbAllah* and the Sunni Islamist *Towhid* Movement and its leader "Brother Sa'id Sha'ban,"[12] the *HizbAllah*'s Islamic *Jihad* commanders mistrusted the Sunnis. Khomeini then charged Ayatollah Mehdi Karrubi, the head of the Martyrs Foundation, with winning the support of the Shi'ite leadership.[13] Karrubi travelled to Lebanon where he met with Fadlallah and other leaders and "reviewed the Lebanese Muslims' situation."[14] Karrubi also met Sheikh Hassan Khalid, the Sunni Mufti of Lebanon,[15] and Sheikh Sha'ban in an effort "to unify Shi'ite and Sunni *ulama* in Lebanon."[16] Indeed, Sheikh Hussein al-Mussawi soon stated that "our relations with Sheikh Sha'ban are excellent and strong because he is not only a servant of the Lord, he has also closed ranks with Imam Khomeini. Although he is Sunni and we are Shi'ites,

I have to say that his goals and ambitions are the same as ours."[17]

THE AFGHAN EXPERIENCE

Soon after the Soviet invasion of Afghanistan in December 1979 Egypt's President Anwar el-Sadat, at the request of the U.S., agreed to help the fledgling Afghan resistance by supplying it with weapons. Sadat acknowledged that the Egyptian military assistance was provided "because they are our Muslim brothers and in trouble." This definition enabled the Islamists in Egypt to agitate in the name of Afghanistan. It also enabled them to send some of their agents there, especially after their assassination of Sadat. Muhammad Hasnin Heikal observed that since "Afghanistan was to be helped in the name of Islamic solidarity, that was playing into the hands of the unofficial Muslim groups which were in a much better position to exploit it."[18] Indeed, a few Islamist Egyptians, some of them former officers in the Egyptian army, began arriving in Afghanistan to share their military knowledge with the *mujahideen*.[19] Many of the first Egyptians to arrive, led by Ahmad Shawqi al-Istambuli (the brother of Khalid al-Istambuli, Sadat's assassin) were fugitives from purges in Egypt. In 1983, Istambuli organized a network in Karachi for the smuggling of people and weapons to and from Egypt.[20] Nevertheless, solidarity within the Arab world was an illusion.

However, the impact of Afghanistan on the Muslim world became strong around the mid-1980s. Then, hundreds of Arabs, predominantly fundamentalists, began joining the Afghan resistance to fight in their ranks.[21] Indeed, if in the early 1980s there were some 3,000-3,500 Arabs in Afghanistan, in the mid-1980s their numbers reached some 16,000-20,000 with *Hizb-i Islami* alone.[22] Moreover, Arab Islamist organizations sent some of their commanders to Afghanistan "on a mission to study the *Jihad*." They also engaged in Islamic education.[23] The foreign 'volunteers' were absorbed very well into the

Islamic environment in Pakistan because of the all-Islamic ideological character of the Afghan resistance.[24] All of these social values and objectives were identical to the aspirations of the Arabs, especially those from the Muslim Brotherhood and the various Jihadist organizations.

Indeed, it was not long before Egyptian and other Arab Islamist groups began using Peshawar, the center of the Afghan resistance in Pakistan, as a center for their exiled headquarters. As a result of their growing cooperation they established an "International *Jihad* Organization" using Pakistan and Afghanistan as their springboard. One of the first *Jihad* Movement Bureaus was opened there for the Islamic *Jihad* Movement of Abbud al-Zumur in 1984 by Dr. Ayman al-Zawahiri, who had escaped from Egypt during the post-Sadat purges.[25]

Meanwhile, in order to expedite and expand its own terrorist support programs, Pakistan's Inter-Service Intelligence (ISI) encouraged the expansion and internationalization of the Islamist training and support effort. Muslim volunteers from several Arab and Asian countries were encouraged to come to Pakistan and join the Afghan *Jihad*.[26] Arab trainees included several Commando officers (both active duty and "recently retired") who were sent to acquire combat experience.[27] Since the mid-1980s, the ISI was training an average of 100 Arab *mujahideen* a month. They received military training in Peshawar and Afghanistan, and, after their return from Afghanistan, refresher and advanced training instruction at special camps in Sudan and Yemen.[28]

Although the Arabs (especially Egyptians, Palestinians and Jordanians) were provided with intensive training, not all of them were sent to fight inside Afghanistan. Instead, many would disappear soon after their training and practice period were over. These foreign volunteers received specialized training in such topics as the use of shoulder-fired SAMs and sabotage (especially the use of sophisticated remote-control detonators and advance explosives). They also underwent extensive Islamic indoctrination which makes them devout and overcommitted zealots.[29] The role of such trainees in the PLO-Islamic *Jihad* system was exposed with the arrest of a member of Islamic *Jihad* who was planning to blow up a sophisticated car bomb in the middle of Jerusalem or Tel Aviv in Israel in early August 1987.[30] These trainees thus became elite cadres of Islamist international terrorism.

Thus, in the quest for Islamist violence, the camps of the Islamist Afghan resistance in Pakistan have become to Sunni Islamist terrorism what Lebanon used to be for radical leftist terrorism. Pakistan has become a place of pilgrimage for aspiring Islamist radicals. Islamist terrorists have always looked for semi-autonomy — a sort of a state within a state — as the ideal circumstance for their training and center of operations.

The most devout and radicalized challenged the concept of an Islamic state under contemporary conditions. Consequently, during the 1980s, all Sunni states were considered apostate entities, and thus enemies. The Afghan community was conducting a *Jihad* in pursuit of a utopian Islamic state, and therefore was the closest to a true Islamic community that could harbor and support radical-militant Islam. Such autonomy has also some practical benefits, such as lesser dependence on states and their intelligence services, and feelings of accomplishment and independence.

Thus, by the late 1980s the Afghan camps in Pakistan had turned into the center of Sunni Islamist terrorism, the melting pot of the Sunni *Jihad*. The entry of the *Mujahideen* into Kabul added a whole vast area for the support of the *Jihad*. Consequently, in the early 1990s, Afghanistan and Pakistan are to Islamist terrorism what Lebanon used to be to radical and progressive terrorism. And as the center of gravity of Islamist terrorism is shifting to 'holy terror', so the significance of the Pakistani-Afghan infrastructure is increasing.

SUDAN: THE LEADERSHIP AND HIGH COMMAND

Meanwhile, during these years, there has been a marked rise in the power of the International Muslim Brotherhood (MB) under Hassan Abdallah al-Turabi, a Sudanese politician and Islamist activist. Already in the mid-1980s, he was active in the formulation of a global Islamist doctrine with emphasis on utilizing the MB's infrastructure in Egypt. Turabi established close relationships and alliances with Islamist movements in Algeria, where Abbas Madani, the leader of the Islamic Salvation Front (FIS), and Turabi co-authored a book on the functioning of Islamist movements under the military regimes of Tunisia, Pakistan, Afghanistan, and several Persian Gulf States. The International Muslim Brotherhood also supported several clandestine and semi-clandestine Islamist communities in the U.S., Western Europe and Africa.[31]

By then, Sudan was ripe for becoming an active outpost for the dissemination of the Khomeini-ist Islamic revolution. The transformation of Sudan from a Libyan-Iraqi ally to an Iranian fiefdom was not a mere change of hegemonic power, but rather a profound process with far reaching ideological ramifications for the entire Muslim World. This is because of the character of both the military regime in Khartoum and the Sudanese Islamist movement. After his rise to power in a military coup on June 30, 1989, Gen. Umar al-Bashir tried to impose an Islamist regime in Sudan.[32] Bashir repeatedly emphasized his support for pan-Arab causes and hoped for Arab support.[33]

Soon after he seized power, Gen. Bashir invited Turabi for consultations on Sudan's role in furthering the spread of the Islamic revolution. Following his discussions with Bashir, Turabi notified the IMB leadership that they had a firm hold in Sudan. They met in London in early August 1989 and decided to transform Sudan into a base for Islamist movements in the Arab world, Africa and Asia. Khartoum and the MB reached an agreement whereupon Sudan would become a "springboard to Arab and African countries" in return for substantial financial assistance. An International Muslim Brotherhood leadership board of 19 was established in Khartoum under Turabi in August 1989.[34]

Col. Sulayman Muhammad Sulayman, member of the RCC, was sent to Tehran on October 1, 1990, to seek military assistance and strategic guarantees. In Tehran, Col. Sulayman "expressed hope that as a result of the significant and foremost role of the Islamic Republic of Iran, proper grounds for closer relations between the two Muslim nations of Iran and Sudan be prepared by means of his trip."[35] Col. Sulaymen brought with him a special written message from Gen. Bashir to Hashemi-Rafsanjani, stating Khartoum's recognition of "the significant role of the Islamic Republic of Iran in guiding the Islamic nations." Col. Sulayman added that the Sudanese "consider the Islamic Republic of Iran as the hope and bulwark of the Islamic nations and the harbinger for bringing to victory the efforts of the oppressed peoples."[36]

While in Tehran, Col. Sulayman also raised Khartoum's request for military assistance in its fight against the Christian south. In his response, Hashemi-Rafsanjani assured Col. Sulayman that, "For the sake of *Allah* and discerning the experience of Islam, the Islamic Republic of Iran is ready to help the Sudanese Muslims."[37] In a meeting with Dr. Akbar Torkan, the Minister of Defense in charge of armed forces logistics, Col. Sulayman also asked for Iranian support for Sudan's lingering war against the SPLA in the south. Dr. Torkan promised comprehensive support from Iran because Tehran "considers this issue as a problem for all the Islamic nations and supports the Sudanese government's efforts in this respect."[38]

However, Sudan's profound shift toward Iran occurred in the early spring of 1991, in the wake of the Gulf Crisis, and especially Saddam Hussein's failure to conduct the war as a genuine Islamic *Jihad*. Turabi declared the creation of "a

universal framework for the Islamic movement" operating
from sanctuary in Sudan. The Islamic Arab Peoples' Conference was established in Khartoum in the spring of 1991 with
Turabi as permanent leader. The exact mandate and character
of operations were decided in a meeting in Turabi's home in
Manshiyah, Khartoum, on the eve of the conference. Turabi,
Bashir, Abbas Madani (Algeria), Rachid Ghannouchi (Tunisia), and Mahdi Ibrahim (responsible for foreign affairs in
IMB) took part in this crucial meeting. The movement's offices in Khartoum became in effect "an operation room" for
numerous Islamist subversive movements. Bashir vowed that
Sudan would take a direct role in enhancing revolution.[39]

The Arab Islamic Peoples' Conference took place in
Khartoum on April 25-28, 1991. It was a congress of a wide
variety of terrorist organizations and popular Islamist movements from 55 countries. It was the first serious attempt to
coordinate a Sunni Islamist assault on the Muslim world and
against the West in revenge for war with Iraq.[40]

High level delegations from terrorist supporting states such
as Iraq, Iran, Libya and Somalia, participated in the Khartoum
conference.[41] The other participants included several veteran
Palestinian terrorist leaders and emerging younger Islamists.[42]
Delegations of revolutionary Islamist movements from Algeria, Tunisia, and Yemen attended.[43] The Palestinians were
represented. Daud Mussa, the leader of Britain's Muslims, also
participated.[44]

The Palestinian Islamists were clearly identified as the up-
and-coming force in the struggle against Israel and the U.S.[45]
Returning from the conference, the Jordanian MB (Muslim
Brotherhood) published a statement identifying the U.S. as
"the number one enemy of Arabs and Muslims." The only
viable solution is "mobilization of the nation for *Jihad*, and
unification of its word on Islam doctrine and law, thus
advancing it to confront and uproot this danger."[46]

The Arab Islamic Peoples' Conference resulted in the

establishment of the first real Sunni Islamist revolutionary international called the Popular International Organization (PIO). Turabi stressed in his address that the PIO's "objective is to work out a global action plan in order to challenge/defy the tyrannical West, because *Allah* can no longer remain in our world, in the face of the absolute materialistic power." The PIO established in Khartoum a permanent council of 50 members, elected for 3 years, representing 50 states where Islamic struggles take place. A provisional general secretariat of 15 members would be the operational executive body.[47]

The Iranians were duly impressed with the zeal and commitment displayed during the Islamic Arab Peoples' Conference, and Tehran decided to provide al-Turabi with professional assistance that would enable him to effectively spread the Islamist revolution. Most important was the establishment of a headquarters for the PIO. The PIO HQ, formally known as Bureau No. 7, is located in the Hall of Friendship in Khartoum. Turabi's own heavily-guarded offices and a sophisticated communication center are located there, as well.[48]

In order to establish this HQ, Col. al-Fatih Urwah of Sudanese intelligence travelled to Tehran in April 1991 immediately after the conference. There, he took several courses on staff management and communications techniques. He brought back communications systems, including "electronic jamming equipment," for the PIO in order to facilitate secure communications with the numerous Islamist movements. Clandestine techniques and communication codes were also taught in Khartoum by newly arrived experts from Iran and the *HizbAllah*, as well as Egyptians who had defected from the *Mukhabarat*. With their help, al-Turabi was able "to create a code which would allow him to contact fundamentalist organizations in the Arab world and abroad without being decoded by the (Western) security organs."[49]

Thus, in the summer of 1991, Sudan was already committed to slide in the Iranian direction. The most important phase in the transformation of Sudan took place when Bashir recognized the importance of the Khomeini-ist principal of *wilayat-i faqih* (the rule of the jurisconsult) and made Turabi the spiritual head of Sudan. Turabi presents his role in Sudan in terms almost identical to Khomeini's position in Iran. "I have no role in managing the regime, but, when necessary, I do play a general intellectual role," Turabi explained.[50]

The Sunni Islamist leadership was in a state of near euphoria in the early fall of 1991. Turabi and the PIO were recognized as an up and coming international revolutionary power, and Islamist movements throughout the Third World were paying attention to the ideological deliberations in Khartoum. However, the euphoria was short lived.

On October 18, Iran convened the International Conference in Support of the Islamic Revolution of the People of Palestine, with over 400 delegates from 45-60 countries attending.[51] (For details see Chapter 3.) The PIO took an active role in Tehran as an important organization in the Islamic revolutionary movement. Several PIO-affiliated leaders, including Turabi, were prominent in the proceedings. The Islamist terrorist and subversive groups affiliated with the PIO were, in effect, integrated into the Iranian-led and sponsored system of international terrorism without challenging Turabi's supreme leadership from a religious point of view, thus maintaining the uniquely Sunni character of the PIO.

Further coordination and cooperation with Iran were promised.[52] Indeed, after the completion of the Tehran Conference Iran dispatched three delegations of experts to numerous Asian, Arab and African countries "to follow up the adopted financial, political and economic decisions" reached in Tehran pertaining to the escalation of the Islamist struggle.[53]

However, despite the superb Iranian hospitality, Turabi and his aides were shocked by what they saw in Tehran. The wide gap in professionalism between the terrorist organizations controlled by Iran and Syria and their Sunni organizations became apparent. An *ad-hoc* 40-member council, then the highest echelon of the Islamic Front, returned from Tehran and met for a critical strategy formulating session in Khartoum on October 23, 1991.

Turabi acknowledged that the Islamist drive had so far failed to deliver the anticipated results, and that there was an urgent need for an escalation of the Islamist struggle, especially in promising countries such as Egypt. He assured the council that "there was no going back on the policy of giving assistance to the soldiers of Muhammad in Egypt, and that Islam is coming eventually, no matter what." The support being given to "the *mujahideen* in Egypt" included allocation of specific training camps, and the promise of more being established. Turabi concluded by emphasizing the importance of Iran to Sudan's security and the Islamist revolutionary movement worldwide.[54]

Turabi then moved to improve the leadership, command and control elements of the Islamist movement. In late 1991, Turabi established a supreme council for the PIO and the International Muslim Brotherhood in Khartoum. Some 350 functionaries and leaders from several countries who were now residing in the city were to receive specialized training so that they could carry out these roles. The main leaders of the movement were Dr. Umar Abd-al-Rahman (Egypt), Hasan al-Turabi (Sudan), Rachid Ghanouchi (Tunisia), and Abbas Madani (who was jailed in Algeria). Rachid Ghannouchi, exiled in London, and Umar Abd-al-Rahman, exiled in New York, were nominated as senior members of the leadership entrusted to act as the senior representatives overseas. These leaders task their cells to commit specific terrorist attacks in accordance with a master plan and agreed upon priorities and strategy.[55]

Turabi also convinced Gen. Bashir that it was imperative for Sudan to become a genuine Islamic republic if the spread of the Islamist trend was to succeed. Consequently, on November 15, the Sudanese government imposed the *Shari'a* (Islamic law) in its most fundamentalist interpretation as the law of the land.[56]

Most important, however, are the changes in Sudan's perception of international relations, especially within the Arab and Muslim world, even though Bashir's Sudan had already been actively involved in supporting terrorism and subversion in the Middle East. The new Pan-Islamic objectives were outlined by Turabi in mid-November 1991. He argued that Sudan, and for that matter any other Islamist entity (state, movement), has both the right and the obligation to interfere in the internal affairs of other Muslim states. These principles underline the relationship between Turabi and the other Islamist movements.[57] This understanding and definition of inter-Muslim relations is essentially Khomeini-ist.

Thus, by late 1991, the time was ripe for Tehran to move boldly and consolidate the strategic alliance with Sudan. Both countries already enjoyed very good relations and close cooperation on such issues as defense and support for Islamist terrorism. Once Turabi found the ideological compromise between the approaches of Qutbism and Khomeini-ism to the Islamist revolutionary process, the road was open and mutual relations were developing and expanding rapidly. (Qutbism is the quintessential doctrine of the Muslim Brotherhood, named after Sayyid Qutb, a most important Egyptian ideologue of the Muslim Brotherhood who elucidated its position against Gamel Abdul Nasser and the modern Arab state.)

The final consolidation of the strategic alliance that made Sudan Iran's fiefdom was completed in mid-December during the visit to Khartoum by a huge Iranian delegation led by Hashemi-Rafsanjani.[58] The Iranians arrived on 12-13 December to "boost relations between the two fraternal countries and widen horizons of cooperation and cohesion."[59] Bashir defined the visit as a key event in an attempt to break out of the blockade against Sudan inspired by the U.S.[60] The Iranian delegation included 157 senior officials, including Ali Akbar Velayati (Foreign Minister), Akbar Torkan (Minister of Defense and the Military's Commanding Officer), Ali Fallahian (C.O. Intelligence), Muhsin Reza'i (C.O. IRGC), Zulradr'

(Chief of Staff of the IRGC), Gholam Reza Foruzesh (Minister of Construction Jihad), Abdol Hussein Vahaji (Minister of Commerce), and Massud Roghani-Zanjani (head of the budget office).[61]

They signed several agreements on comprehensive defense/terrorism cooperation, economic agreements whereby Iran would provide oil (free or very cheap to compensate for the reduction of Libyan supplies), and food and diversified economic assistance. There were discussions on the modification and Islamicization of the Sudanese educational systems, especially universities, on the basis of the Iranian experience.[62] Both sides also "reviewed military cooperation between the two countries and ways of improving them."[63] Taken together, these agreements would expedite the transformation of Sudan into an Iranian clone.

Thus, in early 1992, Sudan emerged as an Iranian strategic outpost and key infrastructure for the export of the Islamic revolution throughout the Near East and Africa. Khartoum is committed to its role in Tehran's grand design. Dr. Mustafa Uthman Ismail, the secretary general of the Khartoum-based International People's Friendship Council, declared that, in pursuing its commitment to furthering the Islamist cause, "Sudan is standing up to the enemies of peace and freedom."[64] Turabi emphasized that Sudan was "establishing a model Islamic system in a country which is said to be backward and weak" rather than a terrorist haven.[65]

In view of the still wide qualitative gap between the Iranian sponsored terrorist movement and the fledgling Sudanese sponsored movement, Tehran decided to closely examine the progress of the implementations of the October conference and the state of preparations for the unleashing of the Islamist *Jihad*. Toward this end Tehran convened an international terrorist conference involving 80 senior participants from 20 terrorist organizations in early February 1992. In a speech on the eve of the conference, President Hashemi-Rafsanjani announced "Iran's readiness to put its experience at the disposal of any liberation movement" and reiterated that "the Islamic revolution was not confined to Iran but rather is a base which must be preserved." The terrorist conference was held under guise of the commemoration of the Ten Days of Dawn (the victory of the Iranian Revolution). An indication of the importance of the conference was that Ahmad Khomeini personally took the participants to the tomb of his father.[66]

The terrorist leaders met with senior officials of Iranian intelligence, security services, the IRGC, Islamic propaganda organizations, the Shahid Foundation, the Imam's Foundation, etc. Together, they formulated a combined joint doctrine for the future of *Jihad*, and decided on the means towards its implementation. Tehran asked the participating organizations to temporarily refrain from attacking Western objectives and interests of the West in order not to attract attention to the Iranian-supported build-up until they were ready to strike. The organizations reiterated their commitment not to do anything without prior notification of Tehran. They agreed on the forms of reorganization and improvement of their organizations and on enhancing their capabilities. These steps would be taken immediately with full and generous Iranian financing.[67]

Meanwhile, the Iranian build-up in, and supplies of weapons to, Sudan accelerated immediately after Hashemi-Rafsanjani's visit, and continued to grow in 1992.[68] In the spring of 1992, Iranian expertise and know-how were being implemented and felt. Turabi and his deputy Ali Uthman Taha made secret visits to Tehran, the last in early February, asking for increased assistance. Tehran agreed to provide training for the Sudanese intelligence with military and interrogation techniques.[69] In late February, the IRGC took over the Kabar prison in Khartoum and converted it to their central headquarters in Sudan, thus providing a clear indication of Tehran's long-term intentions.[70]

The extent of Tehran's involvement continued to increase. Gen. Muhsin Reza'i, Commander in Chief, IRGC, secretly visited Sudan at the head of a senior military delegation on

March 11. He came to inspect and approve the Iranian and Sudanese military preparations for the offensive in southern Sudan, as well as discuss with the Sudanese authorities the requirements for weapons, training and logistics support for forthcoming operations.[71] He also visited terrorist training camps where Islamists receive "high-level training" from the IRGC experts.[72] Upon his return to Tehran, Reza'i delivered a very positive and upbeat report. Consequently, Iran further increased its direct involvement in, and massive support for, both Khartoum and the Islamist terrorist movement.[73]

A new "Islamist International" thus emerged in 1992, unifying and better coordinating the various Sunni militant Islamist movements from West Africa to the Far East, now spreading rapidly throughout the Muslim world as well as through non-Muslim areas. This new "Islamist International" is the dominant force in, and spearhead of, widespread Islamic proselytizing and is actively involved in numerous armed clashes and subversions all over the world. The new organization is an outgrowth and expansion of the already extensive military-political networks of the Muslim Brotherhood.[74]

Turabi also maintains senior and trusted aids in key positions overseas to ensure the global character of the Islamist movement. Most important are Rachid Ghanouchi (London), Umar Abd-al-Rahman (New York), and Muhammad Abd-al-Salam al-Istambuli (Peshawar and Kabul).[75] They constitute the supreme leadership. Another member of the supreme leadership who joined only in mid-1992 is Sheikh Naim Qasim of the Lebanese *HizbAllah*.[76] His membership in Turabi's intimate entourage is of paramount importance to the understanding of Iran's dominance over the Islamist movement. Sheikh Qasim is a loyalist of Sheikh *Hajj* Hussein Khalil[77] who is the chief of the *HizbAllah*'s central intelligence center and headquarters and the contact man of the *HizbAllah* and Iranian intelligence with the *HizbAllah*'s special operations command responsible for international terrorism.[78] Thus, Qasim is Turabi's point of contact with the innermost circles of Iran's international terrorist system.

The Popular International Organization (PIO) acts as the supreme coordinating body for the numerous militant Islamist organizations supported by Tehran and Khartoum.[79]

THE TRAINING INFRASTRUCTURE IN IRAN

During 1992, Iran intensified its active preparations for the expansion of the Islamic revolutionary struggle in and beyond the Middle East. These preparations reflect the new regional strategic realities and the dramatic The New System of International Terrorismrise of the Sunni Islamist militancy.

Sudan serves as Iran's main training and deployment facility for Sunni Islamists. Indeed, the Bashir regime in Khartoum offers sanctuary to virtually any movement and individual supporting and furthering "radical Islamism." Turabi's Islamist campaign is conducted with "Tehran as instigator and Khartoum as executor" of a grand design in which Sudan is little more than "a pawn in the hand of the (Iranian) *mullah*s."[80]

Nevertheless, Turabi provides Tehran with vital services. Despite the profound ideological and theological evolution in Sunni Islamism, Tehran has not completely solved the disputes with the Muslim Brotherhood. Therefore, the Iranians are using al-Turabi "to bridge the gap" between the two Islamist doctrines. Sudan, therefore, serves as a safe place for these Sunnis who still feel uncomfortable about Shi'ite Iran.

Similarly, there are residues of mistrust of Sunni Islamists among the *mullah*s in Tehran. Therefore, in addition to sponsoring the training infrastructure in Sudan, Iran trains its own Sunni terrorists from Egypt, Algeria, Tunisia, and other states "in the framework of their future operations." The training is provided in Iran and in the Biqaa (Lebanon) by *Pasdaran*, *HizbAllah* and PFLP-GC trainers and experts.[81]

The cadres directly controlled by Tehran are divided into two main groups: those organized within Iranian-controlled organizations, and individuals who are to be integrated into

Sudan-based groups, primarily in senior command and supervisory positions. The training of Sunni Islamists in Iran is aimed at providing Tehran with elite terrorist cadres for use as the core of the effort to overthrow Arab regimes from the inside and not through external invasion or intervention.[82]

In conjunction with the organization and expansion of the Turabi networks, Tehran has expanded, reinforced, and consolidated the *HizbAllah* networks in Yemen, Egypt and several Persian Gulf countries. These networks come under Tehran's direct control and are aimed at furthering and realizing Tehran's own strategic objectives. The leader of the Yemeni *HizbAllah* explained that the various branches of the *HizbAllah* "have short term objectives and strategic ones. Among the short-term ones are resisting world Zionism and fighting Israel. Our strategic objective is to achieve power. . . Activities within the *HizbAllah* go on at two levels. The first is that each party has its own plans and objectives. The second is that we are issued direct instructions from Tehran. We are committed to implementing these instructions without thinking or arguing. Iran is the *HizbAllah*'s main headquarters and the others are branches. We are working to achieve our objectives and are using all means, including armed force."[83]

Meanwhile, the training of Sunni Islamists in Iran also continues to expand. By late 1992, there were some 9,000 Arab 'Afghans', mainly from Egypt, Jordan, Algeria and Tunisia, in IRGC training camps in Mashhad and Qom. In addition, there were some 1,200 additional 'Afghans' in Pakistan who were involved in drug smuggling from Pakistan to Western Europe and the U.S., in order to finance the local Islamist networks. These 'Afghans' constitute the core of the Tehran-controlled individual cadres integrated into the Sunni international terrorist network. Indeed, many of these 'Afghans' are being transferred to Sudan in preparation for their use in the anticipated Islamist struggle.[84] Simultaneously, since the late Fall of 1992, intelligence officials of Pakistan and Iran have been "making hectic efforts" to purchase left-over Stinger missiles held by the Afghan *Mujahideen*.[85]

Meanwhile, the IRGC has markedly increased its training of elite Sunni terrorists in Iran. At the main center, the Imam Ali Department in Saadabad (the former palace in northern Tehran), the *al-Quds* forces are trained. The chairman is Gen. Muhammad Shams (of the Iranian Army), and his deputy is Gen. Aruji. The commander of *al-Quds* Troops is Gen. Ahmad Vahidi, formerly the head of the Information Department of IRGC General Command responsible for export of the revolution. At this center terrorists are primarily trained as instructors and commanders to run and expand networks in their homelands as well as receive sophisticated sabotage training.

Other Sunni terrorists are trained in Qom, Tabriz, and Mashhad. Candidates from "secular" states first receive theological and ideological instruction in Qom, after which they are sent for military training in the Saadabad camp near Tehran. Follow-up courses are provided in Lebanon and Sudan by IRGC and *al-Quds* officers. Graduates, including terrorists recently captured in Egypt, are provided with very specific operational plans before leaving Sudan.[86]

Meanwhile, Tehran made special efforts to align the leading Sunni organizations, primarily those with ideological standing and popular support, with the Tehran-led terrorist establishment. A major breakthrough took place in July 1992 when Dr. Ayman al-Zawahiri, one of the leaders of the Egyptian Islamic *Jihad* based in Peshawar, arrived in Tehran after mediation by Turabi. Tehran agreed to provide advanced training in Iran (mainly in Mashhad) for about 800 of his people who were stationed in Pakistan and Afghanistan; transportation to Sudan; training by *HizbAllah* and *Pasdaran* in the Shandi and Omdurman camps; and financing and weapons for the escalation of the *Jihad* against Cairo. Tehran conditioned its support on the Islamic *Jihad* joining the Arab Liberation Battalions of the IRGC Intelligence.[87]

In the late summer, at Tehran's invitation, Muhammad

Shawqi al-Istambuli travelled to the Biqaa to inspect the *HizbAllah* facilities and discuss their assistance in training Egyptian *mujahideen* already in Sudan who would constitute the first Egyptian Liberation Battalion. In addition to the Egyptians sent to Iran, some 500 terrorists were sent to Sudan where they joined *HizbAllah* training program.

Thus, by the fall of 1992, the main Egyptian Islamist groups were being integrated into the Iranian-*HizbAllah* terrorist system.[88] It is, therefore, not by accident that the Egyptian Islamic *Jihad* began issuing communiques from Tehran in December 1992.[89] This Egyptian-Iranian agreement will have long-term direct ramifications for the security of the United States because of the predominance of Egyptian Islamists from the Jihadist organizations in the Islamist terrorist organizations in the U.S.

Meanwhile, Tehran continues to improve terrorist training provided to the Islamists in the vast infrastructure in Sudan. With the anticipated U.S. intervention in Somalia in mind, Ayatollah Muhammad Yazdi arrived in Sudan on November 28, 1992, for a four day visit ostensibly aimed at "expanding bilateral judicial relations and cooperation." His delegation included Muhsin Reza'i (IRGC Chief of Staff), Adm. Abbas Muhtaj (Deputy Commander of Navy), and Dep. Adm. Ali Shamkhani (the Commanding Officer of the IRGC Navy) as well as some 30 members of "the intelligence, security and military services, economic experts and diplomats," who were to assist the Sudanese in better implementing its Islamic government and overcoming its initial difficulties.[90]

The Sudanese asked Yazdi for larger financial assistance and more weapons, and promised that they would provide even more assistance and support for the *HizbAllah*, *al-Tawhid*, HAMAS, and the various Islamic *Jihad* organizations all over the region and the world.[91] As a result of Yazdi's visit, a new "protocol for security cooperation" between Iran and Sudan was signed in Tehran by the two intelligence services. The primary objective of the new agreement was to expedite

Tehran's support for the Sudanese security agencies in sponsoring terrorism against, and subversion of, both domestic opposition and "other Arab regimes." Sudanese teams are being trained by the IRGC Intelligence in Mashhad and Qom. A special coordination bureau is to be opened The New System of International Terrorism at 50 Mir Street, in north Tehran.[92]

THE TRAINING INFRASTRUCTURE IN SUDAN

The terrorist infrastructure in Sudan serves as the strongest example of the cooperation between Tehran and Khartoum. Its expansion as of the Spring of 1991 has been not just in size, but also in quality and, significantly, the terrorists' objectives. This terrorist infrastructure was built on foundations established by the International Muslim Brotherhood leadership board in the aftermath of the coup that brought the National Islamic Front (NIF) to power in Khartoum in the Summer of 1989. The coup turned out to be a milestone in the surge of militant Islamism.[93]

The MB (Muslim Brotherhood) opened 3 training camps for Islamic revolutionaries — on the Red Sea coast, in Kaduqli, and in al-Jarif (near Khartoum) — where assassinations, clandestine organizing, sabotage, and arms smuggling were taught by Sudanese and other Arab instructors. Khartoum provided the graduates with extensive assistance, including Sudanese passports.[94]

The organized training of Egyptian Islamists in Sudan began in the early summer of 1990[95] in the aftermath of an agreement on joint operations signed in April 1990 by Dr. Umar Abd-al-Rahman and Dr. Hasan al-Turabi in a house north of Khartoum. It was decided that the National Islamic Front would assist the Egyptians with funds, training, weapons, and the production and distribution of cassette tapes and other propaganda materials.[96] In return, Arab graduates were dispatched as assassination squads to kill "enemies" of the Bashir regime in Saudi Arabia, Egypt, and Ethiopia after the

April 1990 coup attempt by leftist officers against the Bashir regime and Islamicization. Coup leaders had received assistance from Egypt and Saudi Arabian intelligence.[97]

The terrorist infrastructure in Sudan expanded between April and November of 1991.[98] Existing installations and several new training camps were part of the growing mission of the People's Defense Forces (PDF), the goal of which was to become "the Third World's leading edge of popular defense."[99] Turabi explained that "in Sudan we opened popular defense bases based on the *Jihad* idea."[100]

In mid-December Iran agreed to help Sudan "set up military training camps for the Popular Defense Forces."[101] Ultimately, the IRGC-trained forces would become a Sudanese Revolutionary Guards Corps, committed to both securing the Turabi-Bashir regime and exporting the Islamic Revolution.[102] Indeed, a qualitative milestone was the arrival of Iranian trainers and financing from the IRGC. First to arrive were terrorist experts and combat veterans, including several members of the *HizbAllah*, who arrived from the Biqaa.[103] During the summer, they were joined by a growing number of Iranian *Pasdaran* and *HizbAllah* experts from Iran.

By November 1991, Iran already assisted in the establishment of 30 terrorist training bases for Muslim terrorists from all over the world in several parts of Sudan. Iranian staff and financing dominated this infrastructure. Special attention was paid to the expansion of the HAMAS principle, namely, having a dedicated armed branch of the Muslim Brotherhood. General training include advanced sabotage with SEMTEX, armed ambushes, clandestine activities and counter-political work (subversion and the disruption of political rallies, etc.). (SEMTEX is a Czechoslovak-made plastic explosive, perhaps the best in the world. It is extremely powerful and undetectable by most detection machines.)[104]

The training infrastructure in Sudan is under the direct supervision of Col. Abdallah al-Hadi (a.k.a. al-Hadi al-

Nakkashah) who is one of the most powerful figures in the Sudanese defense establishment and a devotee of Turabi.[105]

Several of the 30 terrorist training bases in Sudan have unique missions and roles.[106] For example, Palestinian members of *HAMAS* are trained in advanced sabotage in the Khartoum area under the command of Commander Jabr Ammar. Immediately after the Tehran Conference, one of them was dispatched to assist the Turkish Islamic *Jihad* in carrying out Iran's instructions to strike. On October 28, 1991, two well-placed explosive charges killed a U.S. serviceman and badly injured an Egyptian diplomat when they started their cars. "We will not allow the imperialist powers to divide up the Middle East at the peace summit," announced the Turkish Islamic *Jihad*, claiming responsibility for the bombing.[107]

The two most important sites are the al-Shambat and al-Mazra'ah camps where terrorists from Tunisia, Algeria, France, and Belgium receive advanced terrorist training. At these camps plans have been made for long-term terrorist operations in Western Europe. The subjects taught in these camps include the use of small arms, self-defense, explosives, laying ambushes, "manufacturing of explosives from local materials," topography, and using night-vision equipment. In the summer of 1991 there was a delay in sabotage training due to shortages of SEMTEX, but Iran ultimately supplied large quantities.[108]

Specialized training for Egyptian and other Islamist terrorists was developed by Abbud al-Zumur, a former Egyptian military intelligence officer now in jail for the Sadat assassination who continues to lead Islamic *Jihad*. In order to enable the terrorists to operate in Western society Zumur insists on having the young Islamists "wear ordinary clothes like jeans, shave their beards, and hang out in cafes."[109] These instructions are already being implemented by members of the Islamist terrorist networks in the U.S., Canada and Western Europe.

The growing importance of planning for operations in Europe became apparent in October/November 1991 when the newly promoted Brig. Gen. Bakri Hassan Salih was nominated as Chief of Security Agency of the Sudanese RCC (Revolutionary Command Council). He was put in charge of "the Islamic Tide Brigade in Europe," the organization responsible for training and preparing Islamist terrorists, mainly Algerians and Tunisians, for long-term operations in Western Europe.

The first group of trainees was chosen from those who participated in a three month course that began on May 23, 1991, in the al-Shambat camp, a.k.a. the Farm. The purpose of this course was to train "65 *mujahideen* who will act as a nucleus for Islamic action in Europe." These candidates were personally selected by Dr. Umar Abd-al-Rahman (Egypt), Sheikh Rashid al-Ghannush (Tunisia) and Sheikh Abbas Madani (Algeria). In addition to extensive terrorist training, they also received psychological and Islamic conditioning courses to enable them to sustain clandestine operations under conditions of "materialistic Western slavery" without losing their identity and Islamist zeal.[110]

The groups and target countries were: 25 Algerians and 10 Tunisians to France; 12 Algerians and eight Tunisians to Belgium; five Algerians and two Tunisians to Holland; and 13 Egyptians divided between 'the Islamic Group' and the 'Martyr Dr. Ala-al-Din Group' to England.[111]

In late November 1991, a group of 16 Tunisian terrorists left Khartoum for Paris and Tunis. It was a high quality assassination squad with a mission to kill 14 Tunisian senior security officials — "the formidables" — that al-Ghannouchi considers most threatening to his movement, *al-Nahdah*. These Tunisians were trained in the al-Ma'aqil camp near Shandi (170 kms north of Khartoum). Subsequent detachments still being trained there will try to assassinate the president of Tunisia.[112]

Once the direct and dominant role of Iran was finalized in mid-December 1991, additional *Pasdaran* and *HizbAllah* expert trainers arrived to train the Sudanese armed forces, terrorists, intelligence services, and the PDF. Some 3,000 IRGC troops arrived late December 1991. They are based in a camp near al-Shambat, in the "Farm," and in a special camp in Kart,[113] where they "train and plan to export terrorism throughout the world."[114]

Special installations for the officer corps were established in Riyad for climatization preparations prior to their dispatch to several remote areas. Militant clergy of the IRGC arrived to help Islamicize the Sudanese Armed Forces.

Khartoum also intended to transform the PDF into an IRGC-type force under the effective control of Turabi.[115] In late November 1991, a new *Jihad* Call Organization, aimed at "building to *Jihad* of the forces and the population", was put under the PDF.[116] In late December, there were some 5,000 IRGC troops in Sudan.[117]

Meanwhile, the number of trainees increased in late 1991.[118] In the second half of 1992 there was an expansion of the Sudanese training camps, with 13 camps built especially for Arab and African trainees, including 900 Arabs returned from Afghanistan to prepare for further assignments.[119] Additional Islamic Front training camps were opened and expanded in Sudan under the direction of Dr. Ali al-Haj for fighters from Africa.[120]

Altogether, in the pursuit of this expansion program, Iran established 25 training bases in Sudan for the Islamic underground throughout the Middle East. Tehran's direct involvement included the sending of Arabic-speaking IRGC officers, many of whom received extensive training and operational experience in Lebanon, in senior supervisory positions of terrorist training programs.[121] Thus, lament Egyptian sources, "the Sudanese regime is indeed the country that sold the Sudanese people's sovereignty by letting the Iranians build terrorist camps on Sudanese territory" in order to further what is essentially an Iranian strategic aspiration.[122]

Further expansion of the Sudanese camps is planned for 1993 because many of the over 10,000 'Afghans' currently in Iran and Pakistan are being transferred to Sudan in preparation for their use in the anticipated Islamist struggle.[123] Indeed, in the late fall of 1992, the Sudanese government evicted all civilians from the Arusah area in east Sudan, on the Red Sea, and turned it into a headquarters and assembly point for terrorists from Egypt, Tunisia, Algeria, and Palestine. In these centers they will get specific instructions from Iranian experts before operations. Some 250 terrorists were already based in the area as the first phase of the program.[124]

IRAN'S HAND

Tehran has already developed close relations and co-operation with the Sunni Islamist movements, mainly through the Turabi and Sudan channel. However, because of the enduring ideological differences with some of the Islamist movements, most notably the Egyptian organizations drawing on Qutbism, Iran's involvement has been limited to controlling and influencing highly trained terrorists as well as providing overall logistical, weapons, and financial support. These arrangements enabled Tehran to dominate and influence the Sunni organizations and movements. Moreover, Turabi, who enjoys strong ideological and theological influence over these organizations and move-ments, essentially represents Tehran's strategic interests. Consequently, Tehran is in a position to determine and dictate the overall character of the subversive operations even of Islamist movements which it does not dominate ideologically.

Iran is optimistic about the prospects of an Islamic Revolution in Egypt. The continuing crackdown on Islamists "will only multiply the problems of this regime in a society already replete with instability and tension, as this will make the Muslim *mujahideen* of this country more determined to fight against the tyranny and oppression of the Cairo regime." Tehran is most encouraged by what it sees as clear parallels between the socio-political situation in the Egypt of 1981, on the eve of Sadat's assassination, and the current situation. Indeed, the Islamist armed movements are incomparably better organized, trained and prepared for the assault on the Cairo regime.[125]

This basic analysis is shared by the Egyptian Islamists. "Yes, we are terrorists against the enemies of *Allah*," explained one of the Islamist ideologues. The terrorism, violence and assassinations they advocate are presented as a direct continuation of the insurrection of the early 1980s: "The wheel of *Jihad* turned by al-Istambuli and his comrades [Sadat's assassins] will not stop. . . In the distant past it was al-Sadat; in the not distant past it was al-Mahjub [the Egyptian parliament speaker assassinated during Operation Desert Storm]; and tomorrow it is anybody who is hostile to Islam."[126]

Since the summer of 1992, there has been a profound change in the theological position of the Egyptian Islamists that closely reflects the position of Iran. Through that summer, several large-scale Islamist terrorist networks were exposed. And all had close ties to Sudan. These networks planned to "strike at tourism, sabotage important installations and assassinate important figures" in an effort to destabilize Egypt. They "smuggled weapons, ammunition, and explosives overland from Sudan, entered Egypt with false passports, and carried sums of money in U.S. dollars."[127]

Islamist terrorists captured in Egypt in the late fall were better prepared professionally. They were also provided by the intelligence centers in Sudan with very specific operational plans, including detailed assassinations lists and objectives for sabotage. Many were trained during the summer of 1992 northeast of Khartoum to carry out specific missions. Most significantly, however, is the fact that these Egyptian terrorists worked closely with religious and military instructors from Iran who also discussed ideological issues with them as well as providing extensive advanced terrorist training. The Egyptian Islamists were struck by the close similarities between their Qutbism and the Khomeini-ism preached by the Iranians.[128]

This exposure to Iranian Khomeini-ism filtered upward

through the ranks of the Egyptian Islamists and soon had an impact on the theological pronouncements of the leadership. During the summer, an unidentified leader of the Islamic Group repeated some of the Khomeini-ist tenets. Like the Iranians, the Egyptians believe that "*Jihad* is a sixth duty" after Islam's Five Pillars. "We believe that there is a need for *Jihad* to change the non-Islamic society and establish an Islamic state. Our method is similar to that of the Islamic movement in Iran, namely, popular Islamic revolution. We are responsible for the assassination of a number of policemen and state officials," the leader of the Islamic Group confirmed.[129] Even Dr. Umar Abd-al-Rahman, the spiritual guide of Egypt's militant Islamists, hailed the Iranian experience and success though he denied having operational cooperation. His prescription for Egypt's future is identical to Khomeini's approach to the Islamic Revolution. "The regime must be removed and the *ulema* should take over and implement *Allah*'s *Sharia'*," he explained in December 1992.[130]

THE BIG PICTURE AND BEYOND

The magnitude of the threat that the new Islamist International presents is far beyond the actual ability of their terrorists — not that this is something to ignore. The essence of the threat facing the West lies in the integration of the solutions advocated by the militant Islamists into the main socio-political developments in the Muslim world in the last five years, and their accumulating impact on the Muslim world beyond them. Being Sunni and professionally educated (doctors, lawyers, engineers), and thus better integrated into urban society in the Muslim world, the radical Islamists are capable of influencing and mobilizing the masses far better than Khomeini's original message.

However, the most distinct doctrinal-theological development in Turabi's current Islamist message — the centrality of international solidarity to the Muslim Brotherhood *Jihad* — is directly derived from Khomeini's analysis and world view. It is noteworthy that Sheikh Dr. Umar Abd-al-Rahman, who had been arrested during the 1981 purges after Sadat's assassination, has undergone since the mid-1980s the same kind of doctrinal and theological development, thus becoming one of the most prominent spiritual leaders of Islamist international terrorism.

Back in the early 1980s, radical militant Islamism was preoccupied with the transformation of society at home. Abd al-Salam Faraj, the ideologue of the Egyptian Islamic *Jihad* trend on the eve of Sadat's assassination, argued that "the liberation of the Holy Land is a legal precept binding upon every Muslim . . . but let us emphasize that the fight against the enemy nearest to you has precedence over the fight against the enemy farther away. All the more so as the former is not only corrupted but a lackey of imperialism as well."[131] The Islamists' initial approach to the establishment of a Muslim society was influenced by the Marxist liberation theories of the 1960s and 1970s. They anticipated that, as more countries became truly Muslim, under Islamic rule, their regimes would willingly gravitate into a single *Ummah* as a political framework. Thus, the primary role of the Islamists was to condition their own states.

However, during the mid-1980s there was a profound deviation in that doctrine, largely influenced by the Iranian experience, especially its growing theological influence. The revived Islamist doctrine was based on the inherent enticement and allure of Westernization in the Muslim World. In their quest to cling to power, various rulers and regimes in the Muslim world willingly accepted the patronage of the West, and, in so doing, succumbed to the alien un-Islamic doctrine of statehood. Such a challenge, the Islamist ideologues argue, must be addressed on a global scale. The concurrent cataclysm in Afghanistan, which was transformed into a an Islamist *Jihad*, strengthened and confirmed the centrality of the global aspect to the Islamist doctrine.

A notable effort to codify the role of the *Shari'a* in the modern state is the *Model of an Islamic Constitution* developed by the Islamic Council in the mid-1980s. This Islamic Constitution asserts the Muslims' "disillusionment with secular ideologies and their firm resolve to build their society on the foundations of Islam." It concluded that Islam cannot be practiced completely under the conditions of a modern Westernized state because "unless there is an Islamic state, part of the *Shari'a* will remain in suspension."[132]

Consequently, the underlining principles of the nation-state — nationalism — are defined as "heresy." Indeed, the Muslim Institute concluded, after a major study of nationalism and Islam, that "modern nationalism is a peculiar product of Western political development" that remains "an all-pervasive instrument of colonial and neo-colonial policies of *kufr* (heresy)." That definition alone ensures that the laws enacted by the state, especially the liberal and secular Western states, are also heresy and thus forbidden to Muslims.[133]

Concurrently, as the Afghan resistance was collapsing and the Islamist leaders were finding it harder and harder to mobilize their followers into a futile *Jihad* and certain martyrdom, they sought new outlets for their rage and frustration. Concentrating on international terrorism was a natural development because the Afghan Islamist *Jihad* had always been but a part of a global Islamic Revolution aimed at the root of all evils, Westernization. "As a political, social and cultural response," wrote Gerard Chaliand, "Islamicism is characterized by a global rejection of the West and its value system. In political terms, the return to fundamental Islamic values can be seen as a rejection of existing constitutions, of institutionalized Islam and of those regimes that claim to draw their inspiration from Islam." (Chaliand is a noted French expert on guerilla and terrorist movements.)[134]

The believers thus become preoccupied with the fundamental roots of their plight and commit themselves to utopian solutions of comparable magnitude. The rage of radicalized Islam, fueled by the "gloom and doom" mood of the Muslim world, has already begun to simmer. The return to the basic roots of Islam, in the quest for guidance for the future, brings with it a total rejection of the state-system in its contemporary connotation.

The Islamists developed the 'fulcrum theory,' arguing, in essence, that in order to take on the Muslim world, the Islamists must first have a solid base from which to effect the rest of the world. Dr. Fathi Ibrahim of the Palestinian Islamic *Jihad* explained that Islamist globalism is the main ideological point of the Muslim Brotherhood, including *HAMAS*. The *Ikhwan* (literally brothers, Arabic for the Muslim Brotherhood) "do not make a distinction between the Palestine question and any other Islamic issue such as the issue of the Muslims in the Philippines, Kashmir, or Eritrea." They are waiting for the emergence of an Islamic state that would "undertake the responsibility of raising the banner of *Jihad* and march toward the liberation of Palestine as an Islamic land just as any other colonized or occupied Islamic territory."[135]

Bassam Jabbar, one of the most militant *HAMAS* leaders, emphasized its global identity and aspirations. He explained that "the Islamic Movement not only aspires to conquer all the areas of Palestine from the Jordan River to the Mediterranean Sea, but the whole world." Jabbar stressed that the Islamic Movement would "impose Islamist regime" over all the territories ruled or inhabited by Muslims wherever they might be.[136]

The establishment of an Islamist regime in Khartoum in 1989 provided the militant Islamists with the long sought-after fulcrum. Indeed, under the guidance of Turabi, Sudan has been transformed into a center for the exportation of the Sunni Islamist Revolution.

The Gulf Crisis of 1990-91 was both a distraction and a crisis that rejuvenated and incited ever wider circles of the population throughout the Muslim world into adopting an anti-Western position. After the Gulf War, the Islamists sought to capitalize on the widespread communal shock and humiliation suffered by the Muslims. Sheikh Sa'id Sha'ban expressed his "hope that Iran will be able to convince certain Arabs to break their alliance with the West and instead form an Islamic front to counter conspiracies of imperialism and Zionism in the Middle East, especially Palestine, Iraq, Kuwait, Afghanistan, and Kashmir."[137] Subsequent events in the Middle East and Central Asia seems to have confirmed the Islamists perceptions of a revived Muslim wave.

In the summer of 1992, Turabi was convinced that his base in Sudan was so solid as to support a marked escalation of the Islamist struggle worldwide. This was expressed in an interview Al-Turabi gave in Khartoum aimed at the local audience. Turabi declared Sudan to be "free of foreign exploitation" and that "the realization of a truly Islamic state is inevitable." Echoing Khomeini's concept of Islamic rulers, Turabi explained that Islamist leaders (like Turabi himself) should be "in influential positions (where) they can advance the Islamic cause."[138]

Indeed, Khamenei, Hashemi-Rafsanjani, Turabi, and their followers have grand designs for the new Islamist front. Turabi considers the Higher Liaison Committee, the supreme council for the PIO, the first phase toward the establishment of "a world fundamentalist organization" tailored after the Soviet Comintern of the 1920s-30s. Its activities would overlap those of the International Muslim Brotherhood, but will center on bringing together movements and groups "who resort to violence as the way of fulfilling objectives. One of its characteristics is close coordination among its members in more than one Arab country."[139]

Khartoum has always been preoccupied with the subject and potential of pan-Islamic unity. Gen. Bashir attributed the confrontations with the West to the fact that "the West was aware that the rapprochement between Muslims will lead to the creation of a superpower which could defy Western civilization."[140]

Turabi repeatedly complains about the Western characterization of Sudan as a terrorist-sponsoring state and himself as being involved in terrorism. He argues that the West "found 'terrorism' to be a suitable word with which to brand the Islamists."[141] However, the essence of the Turabi doctrine for the imminent *Jihad* is "using religion for political purposes, acting against the current regimes, and calling for their downfall by force and violence through political assassination." The Islamist movements affiliated with Iran and Sudan will be identified by such names as *mujahideen, HizbAllah, Jihad* and other religiously oriented names. Their activities will take place in three tiers:

1. The mosque — in order to reach the popular masses.

2. The universities — the first line of the 'Islamic rebels' because the largest groups of the best educated and motivated militant Islamists can be found there.

3. The opposition community and pressure groups through taking over social and humanitarian services, social work, trade, etc., in order to insert secret cadres and better penetrate and subvert society from within.[142]

This long term plan is not an abstract conceptualization. Many of the practitioners within the ranks of the Islamist militants have already formulated plans for the implementation of Turabi's doctrine. Most important is a document by Abbud al-Zumur about "Total Confrontation" smuggled from jail in the summer of 1992. Zumur stresses that the Islamist struggle should be carried out through such measures as "armed popular revolution," "the military coup," "the civilian coup," and "escalation of combat through special operations," that is, terrorism. Although Zumur defines the Islamicization of the Middle East as the major priority, his document stresses the crucial significance of confronting and fighting the root causes, namely, the West.[143] This is a fundamental deviation from the tenets of the Egyptian *Ikhwan*, primarily Faraj, Zumur's own mentor. Zumur accepted it as a reaction to the Gulf Crisis. (Abd al-Salam Faraj is discussed at the beginning of this chapter.)

Islamist leaders are convinced that the escalation of the armed struggle is imminent and desirable. For example, Ibrahim Ghawshah of *HAMAS* anticipates a lengthy struggle because it is the only viable option open to the Islamists. He argues that the peace process and reconciliation "threaten penetration of the Arab and Islamic world as a civilization," which must therefore be resisted virtually at all cost. Ghawshah stresses the unique appeal of "the alternatives of *Jihad*, struggle, reliance on one's own available forces (Arab or Islamic)" to defending Islam.[144] The Islamists are also convinced that the conditions throughout the world are ripe for the beginning of the implementation of their grand designs. Various consultations about future plans and operations are already taking place.

The Islamist terrorist strategy for the forthcoming terrorist campaign in the West, and especially the U.S., underwent a major revision in a special conference of some 300 senior terrorist commanders and Iranian intelligence officials held in Tehran in early February 1993. The primary objectives of this conference were to formulate and define the grand strategy of Iranian-sponsored international terrorism and to set operational guidelines for all other Islamist terrorist organizations. These guidelines will be presented to the other organizations in a forthcoming follow-up conference in Khartoum, Sudan.[145]

In Tehran, the Iranian and *HizbAllah* leaders conceded that Iran's policy of "moderation" failed to attract economic assistance and investment from the West, and that instead the West, and especially the United States, were paying increased attention to Iran's growing power and to the spread of Islam. U.S. policy in the Middle East and the Balkans was identified as a reflection of its growing threat to Islam.[146]

Therefore, the leaders decided that there was no alternative to the resumption of the classic uncompromising terrorist struggle against, and in, the West and particularly America. Because of its far reaching strategic ramifications, this new terrorist campaign will be conducted under the tight control of Iranian intelligence. Special attention has been paid to discussing the revival of spectacular terrorist operations such as kidnapping foreign (mainly American) hostages, political assassinations of the "enemies of Islam", hijacking or blowing up transport aircraft, and major sabotage operations.[147]

In this context, Sheikh Fadlallah delivered a major sermon in which he justified and legitimized the resumption of international terrorism from the Islamist point of view. He dwelled on the theological bridging of differences between Shi'ite and Sunni Islam with emphasis on key aspects of international terrorism such as martyrdom (suicide) operations and the cross-trend issuing of *fatwas*, a crucial issue for authorization of spectacular terrorist operations in the West. The conference also decided that many of the terrorist attacks will be attributed to various Islamic "causes" worldwide in order to create the impression of a joint pan-Islamic struggle against the U.S. and the West.[148]

During the Tehran conference, a very small select group of senior Iranian and *HizbAllah* commanders held separate discussions concerning the most expedient and effective methods to take revenge against the U.S., including the escalation of terrorist operations in the U.S. itself. They resolved that only a series of major shocks will curb the U.S. drive into the Muslim world.[149]

Indeed, Tehran is making arrangements to hold a major conference of Islamist organizations in Khartoum, originally planned for February 1993 but now postponed. The primary aim of this conference is to form a "general world secretariat" to better coordinate the terrorist and subversive operations of the Iranian supported groups. At present, 19 organizations in Lebanon, Iraq, Algeria, Egypt and Sudan, as well as in other countries and the West Bank and Gaza, are already active members in this alliance. They all intended the Khartoum conference to result in specific plans of action.[150]

Muhammad Javad Larijani is very optimistic about the outcome of the struggle ahead. "The cresting of the Islamic movement will soon transform the face of the world in the same manner as the Renaissance changed the face of Europe." In reference to the various Islamist "organizations" and their impact on the Muslim world, Larijani concluded: "*InshAllah* (God willing), the new Islamic movements will also change the face of Islam."[151]

The real challenge and threat in these plans and designs of the Islamists lie not in the question of whether radical Islam is going to triumph over Western modernization. So far, political Islam has largely failed to establish and sustain Islamist regimes. Only Iran and Sudan claim to be genuine Islamic states. Some forms of political process based on Western institutions remain even in Iran and Sudan. Even such Islamist movements as FIS (Islamic Salvation Front, Algeria's Islamist movement), *al-Nahda* (Tunisia's Islamist movement), the *Ikhwan* in Egypt and Jordan, the *HizbAllah* in Lebanon, have as part of their strategy joining in the political system as a way of subverting it from within. There is no indication that there will be a profound change in the near future.

The lack of success of the Islamist political elites must not be confused with widespread popular sentiments. Even in the pseudo-democracies in the Muslim world, the masses are not really represented because the real power remains the domain of very limited elites, and the "parliaments" are limited to symbolism and titular procedures. The masses are disenchanted and, due to a widespread social and economic malaise in the Arab world, increasingly withdraw into the panacea of the absolute solutions offered by radical Islam. They are drawn into, and won over by, radical Islam, in part through comprehensive and widespread Islamist programs of social services and welfare. This popular transformation is increasingly strong among the urban population, including very young professionals and intellectuals. The young militant leaders are convinced they are empowered to lead an Islamist revolution and wrestle power from the established elites in order to establish an Islamic society and state.[152]

It is in the process, in the attempts to seize or influence power, that the real challenge and threat lie. The Islamists consider their quest for power so divine as to justify and sanctify any conceivable means, primarily violence. That alone petrifies the already inherently unstable local leaders and regimes who, in turn, increase oppression and suppression, as seen in Algeria and Egypt, thus playing into the Islamists' hands while further destabilizing themselves. The ensuing violent outburst is the real threat of Islamist revivalism.

Furthermore, the Islamist failures to realize their dreams lead to despair and a thirsting for revenge which are increasingly expressed through terrorism and subversion. Taken together, these socio-political processes feed a vicious cycle with no end in sight, and only promise to grow in intensity, accompanied by more violence and more terrorism. And, with the Islamists blaming the West, and particularly the U.S., for supporting the hostile regimes, their rage and craving for retribution in the form of international terrorism are increasingly aimed at the U.S.

The militant Islamists are increasingly convinced that only a total disengagement from, and a major confrontation with, the hostile world order will deliver salvation. The Islamists are waging a ceaseless struggle against any manifestation of Westernized culture — clothing, music, or other form of daily life except for science and technology, including military applications, which are also twisted to fit their prevailing ideological constraints. Further, the Islamists consider the regimes in the

Muslim world, especially in the Middle East, as being totally dependent on, and beholden to, the West.[153]

The hated regimes survive only because of the West's commitment to saving its own puppets, as clearly demonstrated recently during *al-Az'ma*, or "The Crisis"— the Persian Gulf War. It is a term of severity second only to *al-Naqba* in describing calamities befallen on Islam or Believers. *al-Naqba* translates as the "holocaust", what Muslims refer to for the establishment of the State of Israel in 1948. Therefore, the only viable strategy is for the vanguard of believers to take on the West, and especially America, in order to wrest from them their divine right to establish Islamist societies and regimes.

CHAPTER 5

IN WESTERN EUROPE (I)

A close study of the development and performance of Islamist terrorism in Western Europe is extremely important for the comprehension of the terrorist threat to and in the United States. In essence, Western Europe serves as a testing ground for Islamist terrorism. Many operational and organizational concepts have been first refined in Europe before being implemented in the U.S. Thus, the current state of Islamist terrorism in Western Europe is also a forecast of the Islamist terrorism awaiting America.

Western Europe, like North America, is a sophisticated, open and liberal society. Professionally, the terrorists' operational conditions in Western Europe are not unlike those in the United States and Canada. Nevertheless, the intensity and magnitude of Islamist terrorism in Western Europe has been far greater than in America.

In the early 1980s, it was easier for the Islamists to operate in Europe than in the U.S. for numerous reasons. There is a legacy of Arab terrorism in Western Europe that functioned in the 1970s in cooperation with numerous European radical leftist terrorist groups which provided a pool of expertise and knowhow. There is a large, well-organized Muslim emigre community in Western Europe in which Islamist terrorists could easily hide. Terrorists could also find shelter, support and professional assistance in Eastern Europe. Finally, Western Europe is relatively close to the Middle East and there is frequent travel between the two regions.

For these reasons, Western Europe was an appealing theater of operations for the fledgling Islamist terrorist movement. At present, having honed its skills in Western Europe, the Islamist terrorist system is accelerating its assault on America.

ROOTS

From the very beginning, the Islamist movement was determined to export the Islamic Revolution to Western Europe. This drive was furthered by Tehran when the newly established Supreme Council of the Islamic Revolution was given the mission to coordinate terrorist operations in Western Europe in September 1981.[1]

However, in the early 1980s the masters of Islamist terrorism were confronted with the contradiction between ideological commitments and practical considerations. Islamist leaders, and especially those who were European-based, urged Tehran to export the Islamic Revolution to Western Europe. "In the sphere of theology there is no giving up the battle," warned one British Muslim leader.[2] At the same time, however, Tehran was fully aware of the complexities involving the conduct of terrorist operations in Western Europe. Therefore, out of pragmatic considerations, the *HizbAllah* decided to consider the early 1980s as "an era of sowing the seeds of tomorrow,"[3] namely, establishing a major terrorist infrastructure in Western Europe.

Nevertheless, Tehran was determined to escalate the Islamic struggle against Western Europe because of its ideological imperatives. For example, the Muslim Socialist Revolutionary Organization threatened in 1984 that it "decided to score hits on tourist and entertainment centers where nationals of Arab and Islamic countries congregate in West European countries, especially Britain and Spain," because they constituted insults to all Muslims and source of Westoxication, the Iranian term for all the evils from the Western ways of life.[4] However, in the absence of indigenous Iranian assets, the struggle would be fought by the emerging terrorist alliance of Iran, Syria and Libya. For example, the terrorist squads that arrived in Italy, Switzerland, Belgium and France in late 1983 and early 1984 were actually terrorists and operatives trained in Libya but working for and in the name of Iran and Syria.[5]

Thus, Iran was attempting to continue the struggle against the enemy in Western Europe while the Islamic terrorist infrastructure was being built. Toward that end, Tehran decided to first employ a dual strategy:

1. To escalate the armed revolutionary struggle — terrorism — in Western Europe through assassinations, bombings and hijackings by utilizing small cells and/or autonomous organizations with diversified ideologies as long as they were totally controlled by the intelligence services of Syria, Libya or Iran.

2. To consolidate a comprehensive, Islamist terrorist infrastructure in Western Europe, building on and exploiting the growing Muslim communities in the West.

Because of the importance to the leaders in Tehran of a proper Islamist ideological motivation, the Iranians concentrated at first on the long-term building of a terror support system. They left much of the routine conduct of terrorist attacks to the discretion of the Syrians. Pierre Marion, the head of French intelligence from 1981 to 1982, identified Rif'at Assad, then head of a Syrian intelligence branch, as having control over Arab terrorists in France during these years.[6]

Tehran was willing to totally rely on assets in place, all of which were under the control of Syrian and Libyan intelligence. These networks would carry out most of the world terrorist operations in the early 1980s. However, Iran did not remain out of the picture. Gradually, a growing number of Islamist terrorists, mainly Iranians, Lebanese and North Africans, joined in the operations once their training had been completed.

By the mid-1980s, the well-trained Islamists became the dominant element of international terrorism. The ensuing campaign of Islamist international terrorism became an integral part of the new strategic struggle in the West characterized by the systematic conduct of low-intensity conflict everywhere, including Western Europe. Each terrorist attack constitutes an element of a coherent strategy because no act of terrorism in this campaign, be it in Western Europe, the Middle East, or in the Third World, is "due to chance or the imagination of an insane person. Cold logic and professional agents are always at work; there are no self-taught individuals or amateurs in this business."[7]

Behind the romanticized *kaffiyas* (Arab scarfs) and the myth of terrorist freedom fighters are well-trained soldiers — supported, equipped and programmed by states. Closely examining the terrorist attacks of the mid-1980s, "the Europeans, dumbfounded, discover the Lebanese hornet's nest and the power of the Islamic faith." Iran emerged as the new guide of terrorism because of its ability to provide the committed fighters with operations all over the world. Furthermore, Qaddafi and Assad pursue their own grandiose expansionist designs through the conduct of international terrorism, and therefore contribute money, training, equipment and expertise. The origin and commonality of the skills and equipment utilized indicates that "the USSR was unquestionably the supervisor of terrorism."[8]

INITIAL OPERATIONS

In the early 1980s, the conduct of terrorist operations in Western Europe was shifted from the faltering Palestinian network, which included elements of radical Palestinian organizations as principal operatives, to a new network directly controlled by the intelligence services of Syria and Libya. As a rule, most operations were carried out by small autonomous detachments led by professional veteran terrorists.

In retrospect, the operations of the Lebanese Armed Revolutionary Faction (LARF) during the early 1980s, under the leadership of the Greek Orthodox George Ibrahim Abdallah, constituted a milestone in the development of Islamist terrorist capabilities in Western Europe. George Ibrahim Abdallah defined himself as an "Arab Fighter" and stated: "The fact that

I am charged with complicity in voluntary manslaughter is an honor for me as a fighter for the Arab cause. It [the charge] is a part of the war against our people but I have not had the honor of participating in these acts either directly or indirectly.'"[9]

Because LARF helped supply, finance and train the "classic-left" West-European terrorist organizations, they came to play crucial roles in introducing the Islamist terrorism into Western Europe.

The Islamic *Jihad* worked closely with Iranian, Syrian and Libyan intelligence services, as well as Palestinian groups such as the PFLP, and the ASALA. The Islamic *Jihad* also provided various Palestinian organizations, the pro-Syrian *al-Saika*, the Lebanese Shi'ites of Islamic Amal and *HizbAllah* as well as Iranian *Pasdaran* and Iraqi Shi'ites from Iraq's Islamic Amal and *al-Da'wah* operating out of Tehran. Subsequently, Islamic *Jihad* began claiming responsibility for anti-French murders in Beirut in a communique in which it called the victims "NATO spies," a Libyan-style phrasing.[10]

Sabri al-Banna (Abu-Nidal) was the other great influence on the fledgling Islamist terrorist movement. He brought with him a proficient and tested terrorist network. The organization had the expertise to plan operations "with the greatest precision." Special attention was paid to operative and agent selection, training and indoctrination. Agents and weapons were planted well in advance of potential attacks. A locally-based detachment that would not be involved in the operation conducted target reconnaissance, prepared papers, itineraries, safe houses, etc. This group always cooperated with a locally-based embassy. It was Abu-Nidal's golden rule: never operate without the complete backing of the security and diplomatic services of at least one state. Another group, in operational facilities in a safe area, patiently prepared the terrorists, psychologically and militarily. Abu-Nidal then dispatched them to their objectives where they were guided through the operation by the local cell that then melted into the background.[11] This approach to mission organization and conduct characterizes the Iranian-led networks.

Thus, the terrorist alliance that emerged in Western Europe as a result of this campaign included Abu-Nidal's group, Carlos's group, the ASALA, some Lebanese Shi'ite organizations and Iranian organizations including SAVAMA, all of which relied generally on radical Arabs as operatives. They also maintained close cooperation with radical European organizations.[12]

In 1985, with the collapse of LARF, Abu-Nidal became the primary Palestinian organization coordinating and cooperating with other terror groups such as Action Directe (France), the Combating Communist Cells (a Belgian radical terrorist organization), the ETA (Basque), the Red Army Faction (Germany), the Irish Republican Army and "all extremist leftist groups", fronting for the supporting states. LARF (the Lebanese Armed Revolutionary faction, was a Syrian-dominated and Iranian-sponsored small elite terrorist group that operated in Western Europe during the early 1980s under George Ibrahim 'Abdallah.)[13]

Abu-Nidal had a preoccupation with close relations with the states that could be relied upon to support his operation. He would provide clandestine "services" to their intelligence operations, allowing them to contract for assassinations and murders which the agencies and states could then disavow. His operatives were the best trained and his dependence on the supporting state suited the Iranians very well.[14]

Through the 1980s, Iranian intelligence operatives and senior Arab terrorists working with them studied the internal operations of the Palestinian terrorist organizations, their West European allies, and, their relationship with, and dependence on, the intelligence services of both Middle East states and those of the Eastern Bloc. Tehran concluded that the establishment and consolidation of a comprehensive support system was imperative for the success of any terrorist campaign in the challenging environment of Western Europe.

THE SUPPORT SYSTEM

By 1990 Tehran had in place a fully-developed Islamist terrorist network in Western Europe. Since the late 1970s, the Iranians had been infiltrating the Muslim immigrant circles throughout Europe in order to export the Islamic revolution. Simultaneously, a propaganda campaign with the strategic objective of replacing the "Islam of the Corrupted" (Saudi Arabia's) with the "Islam of the Disinherited" (Khomeini's) was launched.

This relentless campaign began in France as early as 1980. In 1979, Iran concentrated on the establishment of a "dormant network." This network would be kept in place for years until the arrival of "executors" with specific targeting information and their own ammunition and explosives. After the completion of an operation, another "dormant" net takes over while the original net returns to "normal life" until the next operation. For example, a network placed in France in 1979 was not exposed until March 1987.[15] Similarly, a Lebanese network in Spain in 1980 was not exposed until November 1989.[16]

The Iranian penetration in the early 1980s was systematic and quiet. In France, recruitment concentrated on Sunni minorities such as Moroccans and Tunisians whose communities in France were relatively stable. Only proven devotees were actually recruited after a lengthy period of observation by Iranian agents. They were then sent for training in Iran. Similarly in West Germany, the Iranians concentrated on the Turkish community. In the United Kingdom, the Iranians targeted the Pakistani and Benghali communities, in Scandinavia the Palestinians and the Kurds.[17]

An important element of Iran's long term penetration of Western Europe was the use of *HizbAllah* operatives as students. On August 8, 1981, the Iranian government appropriated approximately one billion Iranian rials (hundreds of millions of U.S. dollars) to finance these operations. On August 12 the Iranian consulate in Bonn received a Top Secret note instructing officials that "the money is to be distributed among the *HizbAllah* members who are dispatched to foreign countries as students to try to render futile all the demonstrations of those students who are anti-revolution and anti-Islamic."[18]

Indeed, between 1982 and 1985, Tehran consolidated a network of Iranian terrorist bases and sympathetic leaders in Western Europe using its embassies, consulates and cultural centers for conducting terrorist activities and engaging in arms smuggling.[19]

Virtually all the Islamic centers in Western Europe, as well as the Shi'ite propaganda and agitation network, were penetrated by Iran. In 1982, the deteriorating situation in France prompted France's internal security service (the DST) to conduct a thorough study of the local Islamist community. The DST report, submitted to Prime Minister Pierre Mauroy on January 21, 1983, warned of the long-term dangers of the Iranian-supported network. "Initially embryonic, this network has been methodically organized and now covers, if not the entire country, then at least all the regions where sufficiently large Muslim communities live."

Iranian influence was constantly growing through its relentless propaganda. "Iranian propaganda, circulating clandestinely in the immigrant workers' centers or in their mosques, engages in violent criticism of the socialist government of France, attacking the social, economic and financial policy of the President of the Republic as well as his pro-Zionist and anti-Arab international policy." Simultaneously, growing numbers of Iranian operatives and controllers were being infiltrated into France, providing the Islamist network with teeth. "One can consider the organization set up as 'operational' and ready to respond to all requests," the French internal security service concluded.[20]

Meanwhile, Libya also established a comprehensive support system in Western Europe in cooperation with the intelligence services of the terrorist-supporting states. However, this Libyan infrastructure was originally organized to facilitate Qaddafi's relentless drive to assassinate his real and imaginary foes. During 1980-1984, Musa Kusa of Libya's Ministry of Religious Affairs established an efficient network in Europe.[21] By the mid-1980s "Qaddafi already had the infrastructure for his hit-squads in place." These professionals controlled and could activate Libyan students in place in the West, acting "as 'sleeping' revolutionary committee members."[22] In early 1984, Qaddafi organized and began deploying suicide squads in order to hunt down opponents and carry out operations "anywhere in the world."[23] In order to sustain these operations, Libya established diversified front organizations. In the mid-1980s, they were also being used for the support of international terrorism. Qaddafi was using East European-style commercial, cultural and other fronts identical to those established by the intelligence services of the Eastern Bloc.[24]

By the mid-1980s, the Shi'ites were everywhere in Western Europe, quietly infiltrating the local Muslim communities in order to gain control and subvert them from the inside.[25] Toward that end, Iran established a solid interwoven web that included several student organizations, Arab Friendship associations, and diversified agents of influence and espionage. Virtually all Iranian institutions, including international organizations, banks, students and schools and transport companies (shipping, airlines, etc.) received formal instructions from Tehran and were required to participate in this campaign.[26]

A late 1986/early 1987 circular signed by Mussavi-Kho'iniha ordered these bodies to do everything possible to "assure the supremacy of Islam in the struggle against the West and Zionism."

Another method used to infiltrate Islamist operatives and terrorists is the sending of Iranian-trained agents, including Iranians, Lebanese, Palestinians, Tunisians, Africans or Sri Lankans, to the West, requesting political asylum. All of these individuals establish themselves in "dormant nets" until activated on behalf of Iran.[27]

Once Tehran committed itself to the escalation of international terrorism in 1984, an all out Shi'ite "infiltration" of the Muslim community in Western Europe began and has since markedly intensified. As of the mid-1980s, Iran established several institutions to conduct these operations. In Tehran, a coordinating bureau under Mullah Sheikh Taki Ad-Din al-Moudarissi links a series of associations of political refugees, mainly in Western Europe. He oversees the training of two types of *Hizbollahi* in Tehran: terrorist operatives, and those who, in the name of Shi'a Islam, will penetrate the Sunni communities throughout the world, infiltrate them and win them over to Khomeini's cause. These *Hizbollahi* are the fanatic believers who work subtly on the philosophical level to transform Sunni Muslims, with or without their awareness, into devoted adherents of Khomeini's doctrines and dedicated supporters of the *Jihad.*[28]

The cultural attack in Western Europe constituted the first phase in the implementation of Khomeini's grand design to export a global Islamic Revolution. Iranians opened their own cultural and agitation centers and wrested control of existing Islamic centers from the Saudis. These centers are also used to shelter terrorists.[29] Thus, ultimately, these activities all end up promoting terrorism. Indeed, SAVAMA Colonel Sa'id Moghaddam explained that Islamic terrorists "enjoy three logistical and support centers —Rome, London and Brussels. They operate under the cover of cultural centers and are still directed by high-ranking religious leaders."[30]

The *HizbAllah* penetration activities in Belgium are characteristic of other West European operations. The *Hizbollahi* are young Sunnis who underwent thorough indoctrination and religious training, mainly in Iran. They join a local immigrant community as "undercover agents" and begin the slow conversion process. They are aided in their climb to leadership by large sums of money they can spend on communal assistance and welfare projects. These *Hizbollahi* are never Iranian. The "holy men" who, on Tehran's behalf, frequent the Belgian and Dutch predominantly Sunni Muslim communities and preach a return to a pure and austere Islam, are never Iranian. They never talk of Shi'ism but rather of a greater love for *Allah*. As they stay longer and longer in one place, they gradually become spiritual counselors of individuals and ultimately of the entire community.[31]

The *Hizbollahi* implement psychological indoctrination. Within a short time a new concept of religious fanaticism insinuates itself insidiously into the minds of the local faithful. It is a fanaticism that, once accepted, allows them to turn upside down their ordinary scale of values, that is good versus bad. Since the Muslim immigrant communities in Western Europe are already isolated and under pressure, they are very susceptible to such indoctrination. Moreover, it is difficult for the established religious leadership to oppose these operations because they are built around a return to pious and traditional Islam.[32]

The early Iranian success quickly caught Qaddafi's eye. Consequently, Qaddafi decided in July 1984 to expand his European operations beyond neutralizing his opposition in Europe into building an Islamic constituency that would influence Western policies vis-a-vis Libya. It was not long before Libya constituted an integral part of the Islamist subversion of Western Europe under the cover of cultural-religious activities. Consequently, the Islamic Call Associations, established back in 1975 as a propaganda tool, were taken over as instruments of subversion. The Islamic Call Association is presently a front of the Libyan Government that oversees the establishment of fictitious branches and Islamic associations throughout Western Europe in such countries as France, Italy, Belgium and West Germany.[33] The Libyans joined the Iranian-led campaign with money and access to local assets and agents.

The first Iranian "cultural" operations were aggressive. In 1982, for example, they spent $8 million on recruitment of Muslim workers in France. Initially, the Iranians competed with the Saudi, Libyan and Algerian Islamist networks for control of the Islamic centers. However, by the mid-1980s, the terrorist alliance was consolidated and began working closely together, preaching Islamic Revolution.[34]

Consequently, the established Muslim leadership in most of Western Europe was helpless against the destabilization campaigns by the spiritual messengers of Khomeini. There was always the underlying threat that the *Hizbollahi* and their masters are quite dangerous and that they would strike and kill anybody standing in their way. It did not take long for Belgium to become not just the center of terrorism in Europe but also the center for "the all-out 'Shi'itization' of immigrants," with representatives of the Iranian "coordination bureau" in Brussels put in charge of a web covering Belgium, Holland, Germany, Luxembourg, France and Italy. Syria provided clandestine conspiratorial assistance and Libya began footing the bills of some of the Iranian operations.[35]

Everybody involved recognizes Tehran's leadership. In August 1989, Ayatollah Rohani, the head of the Shi'ite community in Western Europe, alluded to this when discussing the hostage crisis. He pointed out that the solution to the hostage crisis "is in the drawer of the Iranian president's desk." Ayatollah Rohani emphasized that "Hashemi-Rafsanjani is the key to the problem, by 100 percent, even if there are several decision centers in Iran."[36]

Thus, between 1982-1985, Iran consolidated a comprehensive network of terrorist bases and leading individuals in Western Europe. As a rule, Tehran is using its embassies, consulates, and cultural centers in Western Europe for conducting terrorist operations and arms smuggling. This network still constitutes the core of Iranian-supported international terrorism in Western Europe.[37] France is used as an organizational and transit base because Paris has "guarantees" that French territory will not be used by Syria and Libya "to settle inter-Arab disputes with guns." Therefore, France is lenient about the travelling and presence of terrorists who can coordinate operations there. In 1985, France negotiated an arrangement with Iran comparable to those with Syria, Libya and the PLO.[38] These attempts would soon not only fail but would lead to the escalation of Iranian and Islamist terrorism in France because of the nature of the terrorist states.

Little wonder therefore, that in the mid-1980s, when the Supreme Council of the Iranian Revolution established two standing committees to oversee and conduct "the operational leadership of terrorism," the one in charge of European operations was based in France.[39] The Iranian Embassy in Paris is therefore the center for Iranian and Arab terrorists in Western Europe.[40] The Muslim cultural and religious associations already recognized by the French government were all taken over by Iran.[41] Already in 1985, Iran-style Islamic student associations were flourishing in Strasbourg, Nice, Reines, Lyons, Annecy, Bagnolet and Clichy.[42]

Ayatollah Khomeini had maintained a contingency force in France since he arrived in Paris in 1978. The force was placed under the control of Massud Hendy, Khomeini's 'nephew'. Hendi (b. 1957) had been in France since 1974 as an electronics student. After the revolution he became the Iranian Press Attache and a top official of the Iranian Cultural Committee in Paris and immediately began taking over Muslim cultural and religious associations already recognized by the French government. He was personally involved in the planning of violent demonstrations and terrorist operations in Paris. These operations were conducted by some 300 young dedicated but inexperienced *Pasdaran* sent to Paris as students.[43]

In early 1986, all of these activities and assets were fully integrated into a single Iranian-controlled support network in France. The network was divided into key elements, each of them comprised of sub-elements, the most important of which is the Muslim fundamentalist movement directly supported by the Iranian Embassy in Paris.[44] Radical Muslims specializing in agitation, incitement and recruitment continue to infiltrate the Muslim religious organizations in France and Western Europe as a whole. Their importance grows as the Muslim community and its religious awareness grows. [45]

The impact of these activities is most evident in Belgium because of its small and predominantly Sunni Muslim community. This coincides with the opening of an Iranian Cultural Center at the heart of the Muslim immigrant district. An intense propaganda campaign is conducted from the center, hailing the achievements of the Iranian Revolution and spreading the message of Islamic revolution. In effect, there is a Shi'ite "infiltration" of the Muslim community in Belgium. By 1985, a significant proportion of the Belgian Sunni community had been won over by the Shi'ites without even realizing it. Consequently, portraits of Khomeini are appearing more frequently at Islamic demonstrations and events. [46]

From an operational point of view, the Iranian Embassy in Bonn is "the biggest center of terrorism in Europe." [47] It is also the center of Iranian commercial activity in Western Europe. Iranian agents are dispersed, and propaganda is distributed, from Bonn. [48] Bonn is also the center for diversified Iranian clandestine activities conducted in other countries. For example, in the Bonn Embassy Begdeli planned the March 1983 hijacking of the Air France flight between Vienna and Paris that ended up in Tehran. [49]

Terrorists and potential recruits easily melt into Germany's largest community of Iranians in Europe. The key installations are the Iranian Embassy in Bonn, the House of Iran in Cologne (a center of Iranian Shi'a militancy in Europe), as well as the Islamic centers in Munich and Hamburg. It is highly significant that the leader of the Shi'ite mosque in Hamburg since 1984 is Imam Hussein Moghaddam, a former militant Marxist who developed into a religious fanatic. He is one of the leaders of the Shi'ite-Iranian religious hierarchy in Europe. [50] In 1985, he established a center of operations in the Islamic Institute in Bonn. [51]

The Iranian Embassy controls a series of "cultural" and "religious" institutions all over Germany. The Center for the

Union of Islamic Leagues in Europe receives direct orders from the Revolutionary Guards in Tehran. The Center's primary role is financing the Islamic federations loyal to Iran all over Western Europe. Other installations, such as the Hamburg Mosque, the office of Iran Air in Frankfurt, and the House of Those Aspiring for Martyrdom in Olsching near Munich are key centers for sheltering terrorist operations.[52] The Iran House in Cologne is one of the most active support centers for all of Europe. It operates the Islamic Organization of Khomeini-ist Students.[53] The Iranian Consulate in Frankfurt and several Iranian institutions also serve as transfer points for clandestine operations, issuing false papers and arranging flights and other trips.[54] Leaflets and other kinds of literature for Western Europe are printed in and distributed from Germany.[55]

Some of the initial organizing of the Iranian networks in Western Europe was conducted by the Narachan brothers. Hamid Reza Narachan was the first Iranian ambassador to Vienna. His brother, Mohammad Reza Narachan, was the Ambassador to London. A third brother was jailed in France for participating in the first Bakhtiar assassination attempt. (Bakhtiar was the last Prime Minister under the Shah who tried to block Khomeini's rise to power; he was considered the archenemy of the Islamist regime. The attempted assassination was significant because it was the first major assassination attempt in Europe by the Khomeini government. As will be discussed in Chapter 6, a second assassination operation succeeded; Bakhtiar was brutally killed in August of 1991.

An Iranian detachment led by Annis Naccache tried to kill him on July 18, 1980. Naccache was a close personal friend of Rafiq-Dust, who was in charge of the operation. The attempt failed and all members of the assassination team were jailed until 1990.[56])

Despite their credentials, the Narachan brothers had a mixed record. The Iranians succeeded in establishing a network in London. Thus, when the *HizbAllah* threatened government buildings in early November 1984, a *HizbAllah* member explained: "We have people in place. They are just waiting for orders."[57]

In 1985, London became an intelligence and oversight center. Ayatollah Shahabadi of London's Islamic University runs an Iranian espionage network and "determines the missions and the operations in Europe in the name of Tehran."[58] The Iranians also established a "terrorist command center" for worldwide operations in their embassy in Vienna in the early 1980s.[59] However, it never became fully operational. For the early part of the decade Vienna was subsidiary to the Bonn network.

The role of Vienna changed in May 1985 when Mehdi Ahrari-Mostafavi (b. 1953) became Iran's new ambassador to Austria. An expert terrorist and intelligence operative, he was sent to Vienna to build up the Iranian terrorist and intelligence infrastructure for all of Europe from Austria, exploiting its neutrality.[60] Consequently, Vienna has become one of the main control centers of Shi'ite terrorist activities directed against Western Europe.[61] Vienna's new prominence was reflected on June 23, 1986. The Iraqi Embassy was hit by a missile launched by Iranian operatives. The attack served as a "terrorist demonstration" and a warning to the Iraqis.[62]

In late 1984, Iranian agents gained control of the Muslim Council of Lisbon (CIL), taking over its budget, the construction of a new mosque, etc.[63] Since 1985, Tehran became the main purchaser of Portuguese arms. Its military agents are present in Lisbon and have influence. Their work is facilitated by a general lack of control on these affairs in Portugal.[64]

Libya also launched a major recruitment effort in Portugal. In early 1985 Qaddafi dispatched several "special delegates" to Lisbon to rebuild contacts and his intelligence network. These special representatives were European citizens, stayed in the best hotels and operated strictly by the KGB handbook. Their primary objective was to recruit among university students by using "the classic means of Eastern Bloc services," but they demonstrated a lack of imagination and discretion.

The Libyan recruiters first tried to charm candidates with the "glory of the Green [Libyan] Revolution," but exaggerated to such an extent, and were so incapable of taking criticism, that they were ridiculed. They then switched to several means of entrapment and extortion, as well as outright bribery. They also became involved with common criminals including thieves and pimps.[65]

Nevertheless, with ample money, they had some successes; their recruits were directed to the Iranians. Consequently, by the late 1980s, Lisbon was becoming a center for trafficking in and the smuggling of weapons, drugs, and other contraband for the international terrorist movement.[66]

Since 1985, and increasingly since 1986, Qaddafi financed an Islamist group, The Islamic People's Conference, that was working to penetrate and influence the Islamic community of Norway, especially the Oslo congregation of 10,000 or so. Money was channeled through the "cultural" Islamic Call Society based in Tripoli. In December 1986, The Islamic People's Conference established the Islamic Information Council of Norway to distribute and disseminate Islamist propaganda and agitation material throughout Scandinavia.[67]

Meanwhile, since the fall of 1985, Denmark has been infiltrated by several agents of Islamic Amal, *HizbAllah*, the Syrian Socialist Party, the Syrian Secret Service and the PSP. These networks operated within the Lebanese refugee community and made contact with known addresses in Germany associated with the Iranian terrorist network. These agents supervise the activities of their countrymen in the Danish refugee camps and use them as bases for recruitment and operations.[68]

Italy is another key base of Iranian-supported terrorism in Western Europe. The Iranian Embassy to the Vatican is the headquarters for action in Italy. It is a huge building containing a place of refuge, an arsenal and a command center. The commander is Hojatolislam Hadi Khosroshahi who was described by an Iranian defector as "a kind of travelling salesman for Shi'ite subversion." The embassy is well protected. Although it has an extremely large staff, it maintains few or no relations with the Vatican. The Iranian building is contiguous to the Libyan Embassy. Italian authorities believe that there are two large underground tunnels connecting the two buildings.[69]

An Iranian employee who defected provided details about the embassy. The embassy was the source of weapons for most terrorist operations in Italy. The hand grenades used in the September 1985 attack on the Cafe de Paris on the Via Veneto and the assault on British Airways came from a shipment of weapons that arrived at the embassy in June 1985.

On September 16, 1985, a Syrian terrorist, Ahmad Hussein Abu Siriya, threw a grenade into a Rome cafe full of tourists, 39 of whom were wounded. The operation was claimed by the Revolutionary Organization of Socialist Muslims.

The British Airways attack took place on September 25, 1985. A bomb, including hand grendades as part of the charge, exploded in the airline's Rome office, killing one and wounding 13. Responsibility for the operation was claimed by the same organization. The 16 year-old perpetrator - Asan Atab - was a Libyan trained by Abu-Nidal.

The weapons for the hijacking of the *Achille Lauro* were also supplied from this arsenal. The Kalashnikovs used in the Rome Airport attack in December 1985 also came from the Iranian stockpile. The embassy was full of various small arms, offensive and defensive hand grenades, explosives of all kinds, thousands of cases of ammunition, rocket-launchers, small missiles. It provided false passports (Moroccan, Tunisian, Jordanian, Lebanese, Egyptian and Kuwaiti) for operatives. The passports were produced in the so-called 'national university' in Tehran, a major production center for papers and documents under the direct supervision of Ayatollah Montazeri.[70]

The situation at the Iran embassy in Rome has worsened

through the years.

The Iranian Embassy in Rome also directed various clandestine operations, including finding and assassinating anti-Khomeini Iranian exiles. The Iranians maintained a network of Iranian and Lebanese operatives who operated alone as well as in cooperation with the Italian neo-fascists. The most important group was led by Abedi Tari and included eight to ten Iranian "students", one Syrian and one Lebanese. The group was very active and highly mobile, organizing "Islamic Seminars" all over Europe, mainly Italy, France and West Germany. Operating since 1984, they accumulated "an impressive stock of file cards on enemies of the revolution." Other key operatives in Italy include Kanso Kamal of the *HizbAllah* in Lebanon and Iravani of the *Pasdaran*. Ayatollah Hussein Ali Montazeri personally supervised their progress.[71]

The exposure of a *HizbAllah* network in Spain in late November 1989 provided an indication of the magnitude and sophistication of the current Iranian-*HizbAllah* support infrastructure in Western Europe. Spanish authorities apprehended "a most important *HizbAllah*-related sabotage cell in Europe." The network belonged to "*HizbAllah*'s most radical branch" and included some eight terrorists from several countries, including one who held a Brazilian passport and a Lebanese who had been a legal resident of Spain since 1980 — a dormant agent. The eight suspects carried a variety of passports. More than 1,000 kgs of explosives were found concealed in some 30,000 cans of preserves that would have been then exported from Spain to other countries in Europe as the operational needs required. France and U.S. targets in Europe were to be the first objectives of this *HizbAllah* network.[72]

The explosives uncovered in Spain were for the West European network of the *HizbAllah*. They were concealed in a 19-ton shipment of canned goods from Sidon, Lebanon.[73] The Spaniards captured 1,600 boxes, each containing six cans with an average of one kilogram of explosive per box. Also captured were 258 electronic detonators, mostly French made, as well as grenades. At least 2.75 kgs of liquid explosives were found in soft drink cans. These were to be used by *HizbAllah* throughout Europe.[74] A close examination of the food/explosives suggests that some of the sabotage products were made in Iran.[75]

It was a highly professional operation, for the *Hizballah* was in effect the owner of both the Qirtas Conserve Company in Shtura, where the canned "food" was packed, and the Al-Yasar (Alissar) Importing and Exporting company that imported the shipment and was to further distribute it through Western Europe. The three owners of the Alissar/Al-Yasar company were Ali Muhammad Subayti, a Lebanese resident of Spain for some 10 years; Abbas Muhammad Hallal, a Kuwaiti of Lebanese origin and a long term resident of Spain; and Hasan Ra'd, a Brazilian citizen. The owners of the Al-Yasar were members of the *HizbAllah*. (Subayti claimed that he was only a sympathizer of the ideology.) The *HizbAllah* chose Spain as the starting point because of its relatively weak security and its ease of access to the rest of Western Europe.[76]

A close examination of the captured *Hizbollahi* points out the high quality of the operatives and their preparations. The eight-man *HizbAllah* net captured in Spain was about to enter France. Its members had passports from Brazil, Sudan, Kuwait, Iraq and Iran. Of the eight *HizbAllah* terrorists captured, four spoke French remarkably well and two of them had good-quality false French residence papers. The other two had already been to France and roomed in the Paris Islamic Center, a hub for Islamist activities supported by Iran.

In Paris, they were to activate a "sleeper" support network already in place. The *Hizbollahi* were to travel clean while the Alissar Import-Export was to ship the "food containers" to a Paris-area address for pick-up.[77] The composition of the group also indicates that the *HizbAllah* was very active and quite successful in recruiting Arab Muslim students in Spain and preparing them for operations in Western Europe.[78] The European *HizbAllah* networks prepared to attack U.S., Israeli and

French interests and targets throughout Western Europe. Another target was the U.S. embassy in Rome. Western air carriers were targeted. Persian Gulf targets were also planned.[79]

In the mid-1980s, as a direct result of Iranian agitation, there was a politicization of the Islamist cause in Western Europe. Jean Paul Mazurier, the lawyer of both *HizbAllah* and the Belgian Combating Communist Cells, explained: "There are two and one-half million Arabs in France who have a developed political conscience. They can feel united and commit attacks."[80] Indeed, there is a persistent radicalization of the West European Muslim community, especially in France, which is reflected both in everyday life and the emergence of activist Islamist circles. Tunisians are very active in "pro-*HizbAllah*" organizations in France.[81]

The local communities, long ripe for the absorption of Islamist theories and tendencies from the Middle East, and especially the Maghrib, now react to political Islamist developments at home. Thus, for example, a suppression of the Islamic Salvation Front[FIS] in Algeria, "would cause a resurgence of terrorist attacks in France. The FIS has an armed wing and could attack Algerian diplomats. Within the fundamentalist sphere in Paris, some Algerian Islamists are in contact with persons close to the *HizbAllah*."[82] The same applies to the Tunisian and other Arab communities.

Thus, an escalation of Islamist terrorism in Western Europe in the 1990s is anticipated. Syria and Iran have worked in the last few years to consolidate networks and plan sabotage actions, especially against France. The previous waves of terrorism in the 1980s, culminating in the Spanish capture of explosives, show a constant improvement in the skills and expertise of the *HizbAllah* nets and operatives in Europe. Moreover, the real quality nets, at least in France, are yet to be uncovered. Members of these "sleeper" nets have perfectly authentic French identity papers and have been in the country for years. Additional authentic papers were issued by French embassies overseas, especially in Senegal, Tunisia and Guinea where French diplomats and local workers were agents of *HizbAllah*. There is also a systematic and quite effective campaign to eliminate DGSE (the French foreign intelligence service) anti-terrorist agents in the Third World, especially in Lebanon and Africa which have become the *HizbAllah*'s staging areas.[83]

THE ESCALATION AND ISLAMIZATION OF THE TERRORIST OFFENSIVE

Once Iran committed itself to the escalation of the terrorist struggle in 1984, Tehran moved quickly to implement decisions and establish a coherent terrorist movement worldwide. Close cooperation with other states supporting terrorism was established through a series of international conferences, mainly in Libya. Consequently, there emerged a centralized leadership and command structure for the international terrorist movement. The consequent improvement of C3I (command, control, communications and intelligence) capabilities, and the professionalism and expertise of the international terrorist movement constitute the key to its growing success, deadliness and effectiveness. Only in the late 1980s, in such incidents as the blowing up of Pan Am Flight 103, did the true capabilities of the new command structure of international terrorism begin to be felt in the West, especially in Western Europe.

The command structure of the new international terrorist system and the cooperative elements between its various components evolved and were perfected through a series of conferences held in Europe and Iran in 1985-86. During this period Libya assumed a high profile through the conduct of international conferences in Tripoli (discussed in Chapter 2) dedicated to strategic issues such as policy formulation and the organization of training and logistical supply. The Iranian conferences, on the other hand, were relatively small and quiet, and concentrated on studying and solving the practical aspects of conducting and escalating the terrorist struggle against the West. The Iranians chose to rely on and adapt existing and operationally proven methods and structures for the new terrorist strike system in Western Europe.

Tehran approached its new responsibility very seriously. Hojatolislam Hadi Khosroshahi convened a major terrorist conference in Geneva in December 1985 with high level officials of the Libyan secret service, a Syrian intelligence official, an Algerian devotee who had converted to Shi'ism and "the top official of an international organization" to better study the problems and challenges facing the operatives in Western Europe on a first hand basis. The data brought by Khosroshahi was studied carefully by the two standing committees of the Supreme Council of the Iranian Revolution which were established to oversee and conduct "the operational leadership of terrorism."[84]

In February 1986, the Iranian Supreme Council held a conference in the former Intercontinental Hotel in Tehran. The conference was chaired by Hojatolislam Mohammad Raishari, the Minister of Intelligence. A primary objective was to develop "a great plan of action for Europe." The Council came up with specific plans to send emissaries responsible for indoctrinating the masses, ship arms and explosives, and activate dormant networks. The participants decided to make their campaign one that was "all embracing . . . of anti-Western terrorism" that would attract all the groups and organizations already operating in the West. The subsequent bombings in Europe, irrespective of the claimants, were largely a result of this conference.[85]

The decisions of the Tehran conference were soon translated into intense activities by Islamist leaders all over Western Europe intended to transfer these principles to actual operations. In May 1986, a critical 4-day secret meeting took place in the house of Ahmed Ben-Bella in Lausanne, Switzerland. A veteran of leftist revolutionary and terrorist campaigns, Ben-Bella "has reconverted to Shi'ite militancy since his mystic crisis," namely his 1983 expulsion from France after a cache of Libyan weapons was found in his house.

Ben-Bella, a former FLN revolutionary and leader of the Algerian revolt against France, is the exiled former president of Algeria. He evolved from a far-left ideology to Islamic fundamentalism. At first he lived at his banker's house in Switzerland from where several Syrian and Lebanese terrorist operations were coordinated. Ben-Bella emphasized the importance of his relations with Libya and Iran and reiterated his support for Khomeini's revolution.[86]

The goal of the May 1986 meeting at Ben-Bella's house was to further integrate the diversified activities of radical Islamist movements all over the world. Special attention was paid to the intensification of the revival of Islam in the Middle East and to the expansion of radical Islamist activities, that is Islamist terrorism, in the West, primarily Western Europe. The main participants were Yussuf Nadah, the leader of the International Muslim Brotherhood; Muhammad Shamkh'ani, one of the leaders of the Iranian Revolutionary Guards and intelligence services; Sheikh Muhammad Hassayn Fadlallah, the *HizbAllah* spiritual leader; Ga'al Hamasah, one of the leaders of the Muslim Brotherhood in Syria; Sheikh Umar Abd-al-Rahman of the Egyptian *Al-Jihad Al-Islami* organization; Salem Azzam, the general secretary of the London-based Islamic Conference; and several representatives of Islamist subversive organizations, mainly from the Arab world.[87]

The primary objective of the conference was to revitalize the Islamic world and escalate "the March of Islam" to global glory and power. Muslims would assume the role of global leadership and domination once they overcame the current hurdles, primarily the apostates in their midst and the poisoning influence of the Zionist entity and the corrupting West.

These negative trends would persist as long as they exist. Therefore, the conference dealt both with the cleansing of the Islamic world from apostates, and with the conditioning of the West to its eventual liberation "by the sword".[88]

Under Salem Azzam, the Islamic Council of Europe advocates the resurgence of Islam in Europe along with the modification of the Arab regimes along the traditional lines of Islam. Azzam believes that having gone through the ordeals of "gloom and doom" instigated by the Westernization of the Arab world, Islam is on the rise, stronger than ever and ready to assume its global position of power. Azzam leads a major movement to introduce Islamic culture to Western Europe, which is in essence a massive Islamic missionary effort. The council builds mosques and cultural centers throughout the West[89] which are then used by Islamist terrorists.

Meanwhile, as the organization of the Iran-led international terrorist system was being consolidated, the Iranians and Libyans continued to conduct sporadic terrorist operations in Western Europe. The terrorists demonstrated a continued acquisition of professionalism and expert knowledge. They also continued to expand their cooperation with locally active organizations. In the summer of 1984, there were indications that ETA members were being trained in southern France by Iranian experts. An ETA network dismantled in Madrid was financed by Iran through the embassy.[90]

Similarly, Portugal's PF-25, although dependent on Communists, also sought Iranian support. In 1983-84, a delegation of the Portugese Communist Party travelled to Lebanon to inspect three training camps used by the *HizbAllah* and its Palestinian allies for PF-25 terrorists. Moreover, "at least one PC 'submarine' is active within the PF-25, passing to them timely information. This 'submarine' comes from the directing rungs of the terrorist organization."[91] In return, the Spanish and Portugese terrorists assisted the Iranians in conducting operations in their countries.

An Iranian terrorist network whose members bombed the Saudi Arabian and American embassies in Madrid in 1983 was exposed in Barcelona on July 16, 1984. They were betrayed when another courier member of the network was arrested at Orly Airport in France carrying six kilograms of TNT and 9mm ammunition. The group's leaders were Sayyed Jabbar Husseini, the official supervisor of Iranian wounded receiving treatment in Spain, and Sohrab Dezfuli, an Iranian student also working as a translator in Iran's Madrid Embassy. (Badly wounded Iranians, primarily those suffering from chemical weapons and similar wounds, were treated in Spain.)

In the spring of 1984, another Iranian, Hassan Husseini, arrived and rented an apartment in the same building as the other two. He belonged to the Iranian Martyrs Establishment [92]

Although Hassan Husseini is the brother of Sayyed Jabbar Husseini, they avoided meeting each other. The network was receiving instructions from Mohammad Ja'far Niknam, the Iranian press attache in Madrid. Weapons were discovered in Hassan Husseini's office and in bags the others were carrying: 20 rounds of ammunition; 3 RPG-7s with shells, hand grenades and revolvers. Hidden in the house was "a cache full of light weapons and quantities of rockets." Two pistols in Jabbar's apartment disappeared the same day that a "Gulf citizen" was assassinated in Madrid.[93] The victim was an adviser to the Emir of Kuwait.[94]

When exposed, the network was planning the assassination of an Arab ambassador. It was to be carried out on July 23, 1984, by Mohammad Rabbani, an Iranian with a Tunisian passport. The group's other objectives included the assassination of an Arab leader and of Shapur Bakhtiar during their visits to Spain.[95] The network was actively planning to hijack a Saudi plane and attack the Saudi embassy and abduct its employees during the pilgrimage. Hassan Husseini confessed that they received orders from Tehran through Ja'far Niknam who told them "Imam Khomeini himself had issued the orders on the need to hijack an airplane and blow it up at Riyadh Airport."[96]

The Iranians were also operating in Italy. Operational support was provided via Switzerland, thus shielding other Iranian assets in Italy. Seven young Lebanese were arrested at Ladispoli (Rome) and an eighth was arrested in Zurich on November 27, 1984. All were members of Islamic *Jihad*. They planned to drive a suicide truck into the U.S. Embassy in Rome.[97] The Italian police found Islamic *Jihad* propaganda material in the apartment then used by the seven Lebanese. Additional documents provided proof that they were planning to drive a truck bomb into the U.S. embassy.[98] In Beirut, Islamic *Jihad* denied the accusations, explaining, "When we decide to undertake a suicide operation, we entrust it to one single person."[99] However, on December 15, 1984, a man identified only as Abu-Jihad stated, "The Islamic *Jihad* organization warns Italy for the last time that it must release the eight people it is detaining. If it fails to do so, goodbye to its embassy in Beirut."[100]

Another Iraqi "Khomeini-ist" network was discovered in Greece, comprised primarily of Arabs. The network already had the basic structure that would characterize the mature Iranian-sponsored networks. This was learned from the investigation of the explosion and bombs found in the Iraqi Embassy and diplomatic cars on December 3, 1984. The perpetrators melted into the Arab community of Athens. The Greek security service believes that "some of these Arabs make up a team for receiving terrorists who have been arriving in Athens over a period of time for the purpose of carrying out special missions."[101]

By the time the terrorists arrived in Athens the support system was already activated. Local Arabs put up the operatives in homes within the Muslim community, helped them to get around the city, furnished them with maps and diagrams of various target areas, and even equipped them with weapons and bombs once they were ready to go into action. The four bombs were constructed in Athens from high-powered explosives which "do not exist in Greece" and must have been smuggled in, but the cheap watches used as timing devices were purchased locally. The fuses included boobytrapping.[102] An Iraqi group naming itself after "the Martyr Ibrahim Salman" claimed responsibility for the attack and threatened to escalate its campaign against Iraqi objectives in Europe. (Ibrahim Salman was killed in November 1983 while planting a bomb in a Baghdad police building.[103])

In early 1985, Western Europe was bracing for "a new wave of assassination squads coming from the Middle East to carry out operations in which Arabs liquidate other Arabs." These operations were to be run in West European cities as well as a few Arab capitals by the secret services of Syria and Libya. In early 1985 there was a security alert in Europe concerning Arabs travelling on forged Gulf, Saudi, Tunisian and Lebanese passports. The first victim of this team was Faraj Umar Makhyun, assassinated in Rome on January 13, 1985 with a 7.65mm Walter with silencer, one of the assassins' weapons of choice. Makhyun was a Libyan diplomat suspected of betraying the Qaddafi regime, which asked for the help of the Iranians and the Syrians in killing him.

The network was exposed when the British detained an Arab with a forged Gulf passport who travelled to London to prepare for the arrival of a hit squad whose targets were senior Arab diplomats in London.[104]

Soon afterwards, eight members of an Arab hit team arrived in London with Syrian diplomatic passports. Among them was a technician responsible for assembling bombs who had traces of explosives on him when he was arrested. Although the team belonged to Ahmad Jibril's PFLP-GC, they intended to operate in the name of Black September. They were expelled in February 1985 before they could carry out any of their missions.[105]

Meanwhile, on January 25, 1985, a *Pasdaran* hit team with assistance from Abu-Nidal assassinated Rene-Pierre Audran, a key weapons supplier to Iraq, in front of his Paris home. *Action Directe* published a communique taking responsibility for the assassination, thus demonstrating once more the closeness of the new system of international terrorism. *Action Directe* was also responsible for concealing the weapons used.[106]

THE PYRAMID COMMAND SYSTEM

The outcome of the conferences and consultations in 1984-86 was the emergence of an entirely new three-tiered pyramid-type organization for the coordination of and control over terrorism in Western Europe. The pyramid consisted of: 1) the centralized high command; 2) the field officers; and 3) the expert trigger-men.[107]

In the mid-1980s radical Islam was on the rise. Its leaders were more self-confident and active than ever before. Moreover, the growing role of the militant youth within the Islamist movement brought about the adoption of "the armed struggle" as the primary tool for the resurgence of Islam all over the world.[108] This militancy determined the character of the leadership of the renewed Islamist international terrorist movement.

A committee of 15 strategists who include leaders of various Palestinian organizations and highly placed political figures in Iran, Libya, Syria and other Arab countries constitutes the upper, or first, tier. These "politicians," being "above all suspicion" because of their level in their governments or states, make constant trips between their countries and Western Europe, where they are often received with deference by the highest Western statesmen.[109]

The Iranians insisted on having members of the high command travel to the places in which actions would take place, citing the importance of past trips for on-the-ground oversight. For example, Hadi Ghaffari was in France in July 1981, 24 hours after Bani Sadr arrived in Paris, to examine the possibility for an assassination attempt.[110] Similarly, Mohammad Mussavi-Kho'iniha arrived in London in November 1983, using a false name and a Syrian passport, to review preparations for a massive increase of Iranian activities in the United Kingdom.[111] Mussavi-Khoeniha then travelled to France and was there on December 25, 1983, to make final inspection of the bombing plans for December 31st.[112]

Even senior terrorist commanders exploited the leniency of several West European governments to make inspection trips. For example, the *HizbAllah*'s Imad Mughaniyah travelled to France in November 1985 to inspect the local conditions and networks.[113]

Altogether, more than 150 high- and mid-level Iranian officials associated with terrorism visited Britain, France, Italy, Belgium, Spain, Switzerland, Austria, West Germany, Denmark and Sweden for periods ranging from a few days to a couple of months between 1981 and 1986. They reached more than half a million Muslim students and workers in 10 countries.[114]

Following the organization of the new high command, visits by senior commanders of Islamist international terrorism have been further refined. Enjoying diplomatic immunity and the reluctance of West European governments to face terrorism, these commanders stayed for lengthy periods, coordinating subversive activities virtually in the open. For example, when Hojatolislam Hadi Khosroshahi visits Paris, he shuts himself for days in the Ambassador's quarters and receives a string of visitors including Syrians and Libyans. From there he also sends messengers to other centers of Shi'ite terrorism, such as Brussels, Hamburg and Vienna.[115]

Libya's Qaddaf ad-Dam also personally oversees covert operations and terrorism. He conducts periodic conferences in

Paris with his Syrian and Iranian counterparts in order to exchange information on West European activities and coordinate operations. Of significance is their coordination of support and shelter systems for "armed men" from among the members of the various Islamic societies based in Europe.[116]

The second tier is comprised of field officers in charge of preparing and carrying out the operations and assaults. Most of these officers are highly trained Caucasians who appear to be Europeans. For example, a male-female team known as "the Belgians" was in charge of the late 1985 attacks in Rome. They provided the trigger men with detailed instructions and weapons and then disappeared before the attack.

The expert trigger men constitute the third tier. They are sent from training camps in Iran and Syria to Europe prior to the intended operations. In Europe, they are "stored" for months in safe locations by the local support system, often in a nearby country, until activated by the field officers.[117] The professionalism and expertise of the terrorists comprising these tiers has improved tremendously since the mid-1980s as a direct result of the high quality recruitment and training policies of Iran and its allies.

The primary targets of the *HizbAllah* recruiters in Western Europe are the young second and third generation Muslims who are familiar with Western life but also suffer from high rates of unemployment and economic deprivation. This community stratum constitutes a fertile ground for Shi'ite propaganda.[118] At first the Iranians make "efforts to hide behind religious activity to: incite sedition among emigres; become involved in hostile activities against one or another regime; or attempt to buy over people inside the country." Sources among emigres from Persian Gulf countries pointed out that "fomenting unrest and resorting to violence are not alien to the philosophy of the Iranian regime which is supporting such cells." At first the Iranians claim to be cooperating with the Arabs in Europe in revolutionizing their home countries. This approach reduces fear among the immigrants and helps create "an integrated Arab cell" from these Islamist revolutionaries. "People from different Arab countries are associated with these activities."[119]

The impact of the Iranian financial assistance is great in the impoverished Muslim communities. Consequently, it is not difficult for the *Hizbollahi* to organize a large recruitment pool from among the unemployed and radicalized youth. When some of these Muslim youth are judged ready and ripe for recruitment they are contacted by Arab "businessmen" from outside the community and usually even outside the country, who offer them tempting education and job offers, usually in a foreign country, at first, and then in the Middle East. These Arab "businessmen" promise to compensate the families of the recruited youth so that by signing up they also help their relatives who remain in Europe. Once vetted, cleansed and agitated, those recruited end up in the *HizbAllah* training camps in Lebanon or Iran.[120]

After basic training and indoctrination, the trainees are dispatched to camps in Syria, Iran or Libya where they receive expert and specialized terrorist training.[121] The Palestinians are also provided training facilities in Iran where they complete their basic training and drills. Advance training is completed in Syria and Libya where specialized detachments are prepared for specific future operations overseas and then infiltrated into Western Europe where they wait for their activation.[122]

Hadi Ghaffari is responsible for the training of the emigre recruit groups for overseas terrorist operations. Average courses have 300 trainees each. They are taught to use explosives, handguns and knives as well as "the latest technology of death."[123] Most important is the Tehran Khomeini training camp where they are thoroughly trained, after being brainwashed by Vietnamese specialists.[124] Iran has succeeded in organizing a molding system for the prospective trigger men by which, from the very beginning of their training, they are turned into fanatics, bewitched through the use of slogans. The process of conditioning goes even into creating a false, politically explosive, biography for each of the trainees.[125]

From there, the terrorists are sent on daring, and even suicidal, missions overseas. In the mid-1980s, the Muslim recruits from Europe were tested in the relatively secure environment of the Middle East. For example, the two terrorists who were killed in the assassination attempt on the Emir of Kuwait in 1985 were two young unemployed Moroccans who had been recruited in Belgium for work in Lebanon, then trained in Iran, and sent to Kuwait with forged Iraqi passports.[126]

Overseas, the graduates of the Iranian-controlled schools work closely and coordinate operations and activities with local Arabs. They use phony organizations that have been created for that purpose as their cover.[127]

In Europe, the trigger men are virtually "stored" in monastic conditions in safe locations such as cheap motels for a long time where they are left to meditate and study their material until activated. At times, such "storage" periods might take more than a month. They are "programmed" mentally and prepared for their mission in these days.[128]

For the field commanders, the Islamist movement is always searching for high quality recruits. A mix of the top graduates among the immigrants recruited in the West and highly trained experts from within the Muslim world constitutes the field command of the Islamist international terrorist system. Most important are those identified as future commanders. A most significant development in the international Islamist movement is the rise of a younger extremist generation that was exposed to the sinful West and the apostasy of the contemporary Arab world. They believe that there is no alternative to a revolutionary armed struggle along the Islamic principle of "let the sword talk." These youth are better educated and come primarily from both local and foreign universities as well as the junior officer corps. Therefore, these individuals are not only committed to their cause, but they are highly trained professionals who can operate in Western Europe.[129]

Indeed, there was a major improvement in the quality of Middle East terrorists operating in France. They came to be real professionals who were living isolated lives and were well versed in the techniques of secret operations. For security reasons, they use pseudonyms among themselves, call each other at very late hours from pay phones, and use only conventional phrases. Their notes are always in code.[130]

The field commanders constitute the vital link between the elaborate support system, the operatives and the high command of the terrorist movement. The Shi'ite support network is based on the immigrant clubs run by Iranian "students" who are enrolled in French universities on scholarships from Tehran and which membership include agents from Iraq, Syria, the Maghrib, etc. The Sunnis have a comparable support net based on the traditional mosque system, which, in turn, is based on the proven conspiratorial methods of the Muslim Brotherhood. Ongoing supervision is maintained by respected religious activists from the Middle East through frequent rounds of preaching and agitating in West European mosques.[131] The support network shields a clandestine cell structure adopted from the proven cell structure developed by the KGB, introduced by Wadi Haddad and Carlos in 1972, and used by ASALA since the early 1980s.[132]

Every overseas branch is comprised of two parallel sections, political and military. Only the section heads know the identity of another. Operating through front organizations, the political section provides general support ranging from propaganda to searching for and indoctrination of potential recruits. The military detachment under a field commander is made up of about 10 professional operatives supported by at least 20 personally loyal individuals who provide logistics and specialized services. The military cell is self-sufficient in communications, military skills, and intelligence. The main cadres are Turks, Iranians, Lebanese and West-European Armenians. The arsenals routinely maintained by these cells include combinations of weapons used by local security authorities and standard Soviet-made weapons and equipment. [133]

However, although these cells are capable of conducting terrorist operations, the terrorist leadership decided to make an effort not to risk its concealed infrastructure if possible. Thus, professional operatives, who form the third tier, are sent for specific operations and put under the local field commanders. In Europe, they live off the operational support system, getting diversified assistance including intelligence. An *Islamic Jihad* operative in Denmark explained that "the Islamic *Jihad* has secret agents in many major cities of the world. These agents have precise information about the detailed political policies, sensitive strategic points and military secrets in the country of their residency. Also there are 'submarines' who guide the special sabotage agents, bomb installers and commandos dispatched on special missions." These professional operatives must "act fast and accurately" at their destination, and therefore must "know the detailed specific actions of the place and disappear immediately after the bomb explosion."[134] The further away the operative gets from the place of operation, the wider is the circle of support available for exfiltration back to the Middle East.

Terrorists attacked the Rome and Vienna airports on December 27, 1985, causing a total of 18 fatalities and wounding 122.[135] The ultimate objective of the Rome detachment was for a suicide squad to seize an El Al plane and blow it up above Tel Aviv.[136] Libya hailed the attacks as "heroic operations."[137] Although claimed by Abu-Nidal, "the attacks were carried out by agents of the Libyan and Syrian governments, using Nidal's group merely as a cover."[138] These attacks serve as an example of the operations by the new terrorist infrastructure. The attacks in Vienna and Rome were "but the prelude to a wave of assaults destined to affect several European countries, including France."[139]

Libya was the immediate power urging these operations. Colonel Hasan Ashqal and Abu-Nidal met in the fall of 1985 and agreed on the establishment of "high powered" hit-men teams for operations in Western Europe. Ashkal himself was executed on Qaddafi's orders on November 23, 1985 because of the failure of the hijacking of an Egyptian Boeing 737 to Malta. The deal with Abu-Nidal remained in effect.[140] However, the professional support for the operation was provided by Iran and Syria. Indeed, Ahmad Jibril claimed in early 1986 that Abu-Nidal did not have bases in Libya or Syria and that he was spending most of his time in Tehran.[141]

In early 1986, PLO sources pointed out that there were some 300 followers of Abu-Nidal in Western Europe ready to strike. They also claimed that Abu-Nidal, ostensibly dead since 1983, is a cover name for "the secret services of some Arab countries."[142] (Indeed, soon after the Rome and Vienna attacks, there were rumors that Abu-Nidal was hospitalized in Yugoslavia.[143]) Dr. Nabil Sha'th of the PLO stated:

> Abu-Nidal is an alias given to Arab terrorist groups that operate in collaboration with Arab intelligence services. . . . But certain Arab intelligence organs spend large funds in order to maintain his alias, in order to use it in crimes they commit against the Palestinian people in particular and the Arab people in general, so that such crimes will not be traced back to the actual perpetrators.[144]

The Rome and Vienna operations were conducted under the personal command of Rashid al-Khmaydah, a senior aide of Abu-Nidal. He personally travelled to Rome and gave the order to carry out the mission, but faded into the background once the shooting started.[145] The terrorists in Vienna were Palestinians and those in Rome were Palestinians and Tunisians.[146] The two terrorist groups were trained in Iran under the

auspices of the 'Intervention Squad' created in early 1985 by
Tehran in order to carry out destabilization operations in the
West.[147] They received their commando training near Isfahan.[148]
Specialized training was provided in the main training facility
"some scores of kilometers" from Tabriz in a complex where
potential objectives, including Fiumicino airport, "are reconstructed in the minutest detail." Once they graduated from
Tabriz, they were sent to Tehran for final inspection and then
to Damascus.[149]

The terrorists received additional advance, pre-departure
training in Damascus from Syrian intelligence.[150] Additional
training was provided near Beirut.[151] In Damascus, they were
provided with passports. The terrorists heading for Rome
received Moroccan passports that were from the same batch
used by the hijackers of the Achille Lauro.[152] The terrorists
heading for Vienna received Tunisian passports that had been
seized by the Libyan government from Tunisian workers expelled in the fall. Since these Tunisians were illegal workers,
their passports had no sign of their entry into Libya.[153]

Funds and documents were smuggled from safe caches in
Europe prior to the arrival of the terrorists. The primary sources
were the Libyan and Syrian embassies in Rome and Vienna.[154]
For example, on November 22, 1985, Italian police discovered
20 Moroccan passports and large sums of money in a routine
random search at the La Speszia train station, left in a plastic
bag for pick-up.[155] Similarly, in October 1984 the Austrian
police stopped a car loaded with weapons; the driver claimed
he was transferring diplomatic cargo to the Libyan Embassy.[156]

The terrorists flew from Beirut to Switzerland and proceeded from there by train to Rome and Vienna. They arrived
at their destinations on November 27, 1985, and waited until
December 26, 1985. Lodgings were ready, booked and paid
for, and the terrorists already had addresses with them.[157] In
Vienna, a locally-based FRC commander acting as a pointer
met the three terrorists for breakfast on the morning of the

attack, gave them last minute instructions and then took them to the airport to ensure that they knew what to do. He disappeared the moment the shooting started. The weapons arrived from stockpiles of the Libyan Embassy.[158]

In the case of the Rome detachment, the terrorists seem to have used different passports for entering Italy and different passports for renting lodgings in Rome. They moved several times in Rome, about once a week, using false Moroccan passports.[159] The senior field commanders and coordinators of the operations in Rome were a blond man described as "Palestinian-Belgian" and his "French" female companion who arrived from Brussels. The Belgian was crucial in supporting the Rome attack by coordinating the hiding of the terrorists and the various local assets that provided them with weapons and intelligence.[160]

The terrorists received their weapons the day before they attacked the airport from individuals residing permanently in Rome. Just before the attack in Rome's Leonardo da Vinci airport, the two pairs of terrorists met with a woman who pointed the specific objectives to them and then disappeared before they opened fire.[161] Some of the Moroccan passports and the Kalashnikovs used in the Rome airport attack came from the stockpiles at the Iranian Embassy in Rome.[162]

Apparently, the Iranian embassy provided passports as a replacement for those found in the La Speszia train station back in November. However, there is no evidence that the terrorists had the slightest contact with the Iranian Embassy or any terrorist cell in Rome. The go-betweens arrived especially from Brussels and, with the exception of the pointer, all contacts with the terrorists were either by their coordinators or in an indirect manner. Thus, the captured operatives could not expose anybody in Rome or Vienna. The trail to the Iranian Embassy was established by comparing the weapons and passports captured on the Achille Lauro and in the Rome airport, not as a result of anything said by the surviving terrorist.[163]

Once the safety of the main networks was ascertained, there was no need to maintain the Abu-Nidal cover. In Damascus, Walid Awdah, a spokesman for *Al-Asifah*, the Abu-Nidal organization, expressed support for the attacks, which he called "a legitimate form of our revolutionary struggle." He insisted that they were the first operations carried out by Arab Fidayeen Cells. However, he did associate Abu-Nidal indirectly with the attacks, as well as the supporting states. "The Arab Fidayeen Cells is a group of Palestinians and Lebanese who have undergone long training. Now they are ready to strike. We are coordinating every action with this group," Awdah explained. He added that his organization was "getting political support from all revolutionary Arab states, among them Libya."[164]

However, Sabri al-Banna, a.k.a. Abu-Nidal, "confirmed" that it was his group which carried out the Rome and Vienna airport attacks. "The attempts were of our making," he said. "We have committed others in Brussels, Madrid and elsewhere." He also praised the Libyan assistance. "Qaddafi has provided us with extensive support so far. He is an honest man and we have close ties with him," Abu-Nidal explained.[165] In Beirut, Atif Abu-Bakr, claiming to be a spokesman for the Fatah Revolutionary Council, denied that Abu-Nidal gave this interview.[166]

THE IRANIAN-SUPPORTED OPERATIONS

The leaders of Radical Islam who convened in May 1986 decided on "the armed struggle" as the primary tool for the resurgence of Islam worldwide. Following that meeting, they issued guidance papers intended to ensure that their *Jihad* would be conducted in the most professional and effective manner. They emphasized that it must be conducted by "cold logic and professional fighters." Regardless of one's commitment or dedication, in the forthcoming struggle there would be no place for self-taught individuals or amateurs.[167] This requirement essentially reflected a strong trend already being implemented in Western Europe by the terrorists supported by Iran and Syria.[168]

Thus, an active "cooperative of violence" emerged in Western Europe, mixing diversified and often contradictory ideologies while still maintaining tight operational cooperation and a virtually identical perception of immediate objectives and the means of attainment, that is, through terrorist violence.[169] The Iranians united several and diversified terrorist movements in Western Europe, including Muslim Arabs, Armenians and other Middle Easterners, into a radical front that conducts operations with the support of other veteran groups already active there. The terrorist operations of leftist West European groups and Middle Eastern radicals are coordinated through the Iranian support system. The internationalization of terrorism in Western Europe is also apparent from the emergence of joint committees such as the "Support Committee for Arab Political Prisoners" and the sharing of funds and lawyers by the various groups, irrespective of their ideologies.[170]

The unified terrorist command in Western Europe was immediately reflected in the similarity in weapons and explosives used throughout the continent by seemingly unrelated groups ranging from Abu-Nidal, to CSPPA (the Committee for Solidarity with Arab and Middle Eastern Political Prisoners, a bogus cover name for Iranian-controlled terrorism in Europe, mainly France), to the Iranians. This unity pointed to a centralized supply and training system.[171] For example, on February 7, 1986, French police came upon a red Opel with two Iranians inside who eventually escaped on foot. Many documents, a Polish WZ 63 (9mm) and a Czech CZ Vzor 50 automatic pistol (7.65mm) were found. Both weapons are known to be favorites of the Iranian-supported terrorists.[172] The Vzor 50 was LARF's favorite weapon while the WZ 63 was Abu-Nidal's. Moreover, the two Iranians in the Red Opel were based in West Germany, near Frankfurt.[173]

Terrorist operations in Western Europe escalated considerably in 1986. A close examination of the networks exposed in the United Kingdom, West Germany and France clearly demonstrated the high level of professionalism of the Iranianstyle neo-international terrorism.

In early 1985, the Syrians and their allies decided to activate another network in Western Europe in order to ensure the availability of a high-quality terrorist arm. This Syriandominated network was centered on a small family living among the vast Muslim emigre community in Western Europe. This time, the core was the Hindawi clan from northern Jordan — the brothers Nizar and Ahmad Hazi and their cousin Awni.

The Hindawis were refugees who had fled Israel in 1948 and settled in northern Jordan, a radicalized area. The three were born and grew up as Jordanians. In the Palestinian myth, the Hindawi youngsters became committed to a ceaseless struggle against Israel after their parents were killed and their house destroyed in an Israeli strike during the fighting with Palestinian and Iraqi forces in 1967. In the early 1970s they vowed ''to spill as much Jewish blood as possible.'' However, in reality, the Hindawis began as local revolutionaries. Despite the massive presence and activities of radical Palestinian organizations in the camps in northern Jordan, the teenage Hindawis did not join them. They did, however, establish contact with several European terrorists then being trained in Jordan to learn about world revolution and global struggle. Although orphans with no visible source of income, the young Hindawis did not join the Palestinian exodus after Black September. Instead, they established the Revolutionary Movement for the Liberation of Jordan and yearned for action.[174]

With little or no reaction from the radicalized Jordanian street, the Hindawis decided to further their ''revolution'' in the global arena. On the advice of local underground circles, Nizar went to Lebanon and contacted Wadi Haddad, a front for Syrian Military Intelligence. Nizar received basic training in

Lebanon and Syria and the names of contacts in Western Europe. Nizar Hindawi then went to West Germany and got in touch with former friends. To prove his loyalty to the revolutionary cause, he began taking part in small-time terrorist activities, as a look out, for example, and as a weapons and explosives carrier between terrorist organizations in Western Europe. Then he was sent to Eastern Europe to smuggle weapons and explosives to the West. Meanwhile, the Syrians reported to the HVA about the promising youngster. It was not long before Nizar was sent by the HVA for ordinary sabotage and clandestine training in Poland. Nizar Hindawi stayed there long enough to marry a Polish girl he would later abandon in Warsaw.[175]

Around 1980, the HVA and the Syrians decided to establish a terrorist cell in Europe around the Hindawis. At first, they established Nizar Hindawi in London as a long term plant. By 1981, Nizar Hindawi was a low-level political journalist in London. Simultaneously, he was being paid small sums of money by Libyan intelligence for low grade information. Once established in London, Nizar began bringing the rest of his family to Europe. His brother, Ahmad Hazi, was sent to West Berlin where the Arab terrorist network is tightly controlled by Syria through the PFLP and living off the 100,000 strong, predominantly Palestinian Arab community. Cousin Awni became a student in Genoa, Italy. Moreover, another Hindawi brother, Mahmud, although not a revolutionary or terrorist, was brought by Nizar to London to serve as his own personal back-up. By the mid-1980s, Mahmud was working for the Qatar Embassy in London. For reasons of security and expediency, contacts with the HVA and the Syrian intelligence were maintained by Ahmad Hazi in Berlin, although Nizar was the network's head.[176]

By 1985, Nizar Hindawi was becoming impatient and bored with his uneventful stay in London. Libyan intelligence, always eager to conduct operations against the U.S., invited the

agitated Nizar Hindawi to discuss operations in Tripoli. In
July-August 1985, Nizar went to West Berlin and, after consultations with Ahmad Hazi, the two Hindawi brothers travelled
to Tripoli. They brought with them detailed plans of potential
American and Jewish targets in Berlin. The Libyans agreed to
sponsor and finance terrorist attacks against Jewish targets
once the Hindawis prove their capabilities. The Libyans had an
objective in mind — the La Belle disco in Berlin frequented by
American servicemen. The brothers promised to carry out the
operation.[177] Back in Berlin, they reported to their East German
and Syrian handlers. The East Germans promised to study the
idea.

Ahmad Hazi remained in a safe house in East Berlin while
Nizar returned to London. All this time, Nizar Hindawi was
having a series of affairs in London, including one with a young
Irish woman, Ann Murphy, who fell in love with him, became
pregnant and decided to keep the baby and marry the father.[178]
In Damascus, the Syrian Military Intelligence was alarmed by
the visit to Libya. Syrian, and most likely Soviet, experts
concluded that the Hindawis were rapidly becoming uncon-
trollable. Damascus decided to activate them in a series of
major operations before they were burnt out.

In December 1985, Ahmad Hazi invited Nizar to return to
Berlin. In West Berlin Nizar conferred with his brother Hazi,
and Farouq Salameh, a Palestinian PFLP operative. (Though
there is no known family relation, Farouq Salameh and
Muhammed Salameh, arrested in the New York World Trade
Center bombing, come from the same area of northern Jordan.)
In East Berlin, they met with a Syrian liaison officer who
invited them to come to Damascus for important consultations
on future operations. The Syrian officer promised that they
would get extensive support for operations under their original
name, the Revolutionary Movement for the Liberation of Jordan, ostensibly an anti-Hussein revolutionary organization.
Salameh and Hindawi flew to Damascus in January 1986.[179]

Nizar Hindawi went to Syria in January 1986, ostensibly to cover the Afro-Arab Unity Association conference in Damascus. He spent some 13 days there with Khalid Dandash who prepared him for both smuggling drugs and terrorist activities. He was told that drug trafficking was needed to finance the revolutionary struggle in the West Bank and Gaza.[180] In Damascus, the Hindawi operation was taken over by the all-powerful Syrian Air Force Intelligence. In Damascus, Hindawi met Gen. Muhammed al-Khouly, Brig. Okurah and Lt. Col. Said Haitham of Syrian Air Force Intelligence. By then, Gen. Mohammad al-Khouly had already directed 29 terrorist operations. Haitham was al-Khouly's closest aide and director of terrorist operations. As the Syrian military attache to Paris, under the pseudonym Hassan Ali, Said was responsible for the bomb on rue Marbeuf on April 22, 1982, that left one dead and 63 wounded. He was then expelled from France. Al-Khouly offered Hindawi a chance to make history by blowing up an El Al plane in mid-air. Nizar Hindawi and Farouq Salameh were then taken to a base near Damascus where they were shown the suitcase bomb. Lt.Col. Haitham arranged advanced training for Hindawi. Salameh was also trained on handling sophisticated explosives.[181]

Nizar Hindawi then returned to London for two weeks to make arrangements, and returned to Damascus for further training. This time, Lt. Col. Said Haitham of Syrian Air Force Intelligence was also waiting for Hindawi in the Damascus airport. He received a new Syrian passport with the name of Issam al-Shaar already stamped on it, and with entry visas to Italy, France, West Germany and Italy. (Isaam al-Shaar has been identified as a family member of the Syrian Foreign Minister.) Col. Haitham personally trained Nizar Hindawi and prepared him for the El Al bombing attempt. Hindawi also received a sophisticated detonator concealed in a pocket calculator from Dandash, who described it as an instrument aimed at shielding drugs from the X-Ray machines in airports. Hindawi was also told in Damascus that he was to go immediately to the Syrian embassy in London in case of trouble.[182]

Nizar Hindawi also learned in Damascus that the Syrian Air Force Intelligence would be glad to assist them with the bombing of the La Belle disco provided that they blew up another objective for the Syrians. The operational control over the terrorist operations in West Berlin was tightly held by Syria, but conducted through such radical organizations as Abu Nidal's, Wadi Haddad's and George Habash's. A wide variety of front organizations, such as 'Lebanon Aid' charities, was used for support, and the youth projects of the PFLP were actively recruited.

However, as a result of massive financial support from Bonn and conservative Arab states, the German Arab Cultural Organization was moderating the Arab community. The Syrians decided to neutralize the Center in West Berlin before it could influence their support infrastructure.[183] This was to be Salameh's mission.

In early 1986, the East German intelligence and security service approved the operations in West Berlin in principle and began assisting in the active preparations for the operation. Consequently, the HVA became "directly involved" in the bomb attack on La Belle disco. Its agents assisted Libyan intelligence in the execution. The HVA insisted that Nizar and Ahmad Hazi Hindawi, whom they considered "Syrian-controlled Palestinians," carry out the bombing. Ali Mansur, a Lebanese who had become a West German citizen, was the contact man for the East German State Security Service (Stasi) in West Berlin. 'Ali Shana' was a liaison officer between the Stasi and the Libyan intelligence and the terrorists. The La Belle operation was finally approved by the highest levels of government in East Germany, including President Eric Honecker, on March 20, 1986. The bombing was originally planned for March 26 but, because of technical reasons, took place on April 5, 1986.[184]

The bombing of the German Arab Cultural Organization Center in West Berlin was to be conducted by three operatives — Ahmad Hazi Hindawi, Faruq Salameh and Fajes Sahauna — all of whom were provided with Jordanian passports. The SEMTEX for the bombing operations in Berlin was supplied by the Syrian embassy in East Berlin. Col. Said Haitham was in East Berlin to inspect the bomb for the Cultural Center. The bombs were smuggled through Checkpoint Charlie in a Syrian diplomatic car. The bomb for the cultural center was planted twice but failed to explode. Ahmad Hazi retrieved it and notified East Berlin. Abu Ahmad, a Syrian bomb expert and a diplomat accredited to the Syrian Embassy in East Berlin, arrived from East Berlin to fix and fine-tune the bomb. It exploded successfully on March 29, 1986.[185] Reportedly, it was Said Haitham himself who operated under the alias Abu Ahmad and was frequently posted to Syria's Embassy in East Berlin to personally oversee terrorist operations in Western Europe.[186]

Meanwhile, Tripoli, through its embassy in East Berlin, was supposed to provide only financial and logistical support. But the Libyans were excited by the prospect of hitting U.S. soldiers and maintained extensive oversight of the preparations. Libyan operatives were seen all over West Berlin. On the eve of the operations, and especially on April 4, 1986, there were numerous explicit communications about the impending attack between Tripoli and the People's Bureau in East Berlin.[187] Ahmad Hazi reconnoitered the disco in advance of the attack and made a sketch of the place. The bomb was expertly placed. The explosion on April 5, 1986, killed two Americans and left 229 wounded.[188]

Although Syria and East Germany were also directly involved in the bombing, the U.S. immediately led a campaign to blame Qaddafi for the attack. The American reaction culminated in the U.S. bombing of Libya on April 15, 1986.

Libyan intelligence decided there must have been a leak. They identified Muhammad Ashur, a young Libyan, who panicked. The Libyans suspected that he might have been in contact with the U.S. and warned Stasi that he was going to divulge the DDR's role. Consequently, Stasi assisted the Libyans in assassinating Muhammad Ashur in East Berlin in late April 1986.[189] Moreover, as a result of the Libyan actions, West German investigators exposed a Libyan terrorist coordination office in West Berlin concealed as an information service for Third World interpreters run by an African. Calls were made from this office to Abu-Nidal's office in Damascus and to the Libya People's Bureau in East Berlin.[190] Therefore, the Stasi sheltered five Libyans, led by Musbah Abdul-Ghasim (Dervish), at least until June 1990, enabling them to continue operations against the West.[191]

As the bombs were exploding in West Berlin, Nizar Hindawi was back in London preparing for his own history-making operation. According to some reports, Hindawi and his cousin Awni flew back to Damascus in late March to prepare for the El Al attempt.[192] There is no confirmation for that report. Moreover, Hindawi had already brought with him the sophisticated calculator-fuse from Damascus. A three pound SEMTEX charge was smuggled to London via Syrian Arab Airlines. Bomb experts arrived as the security personnel on the Syrian Arab Airline flights to London to help Nizar Hindawi in his final preparations. They also brought the double-bottom suitcase in which he would conceal the bomb. Hindawi would later claim that he did not know that it was a bomb. The fuse was calibrated to explode at 13:40, at 39,000 feet above Austria.[193]

Apparently, Gen. al-Khouly expected Nizar Hindawi to personally carry the bomb on board. However, Hindawi decided to kill two birds with one shot. He "agreed" to marry Ann Murphy but only in "his parents' home" in Israel. At first, they were to fly together, and he bought tickets for the El Al

Ali Akbar
Hashemi-
Rafsanjani,
the President
of Iran.

HizbAllah fighters marching over U.S. flags lying on the ground
in Lebanon, in 1992/93.

Sheikh Hassan Nasrallah the Secretary General of the *HizbAllah*.

Sheikh Muhammad Hussein Fadlallah, the spiritual leader of the *HizbAllah*.

حسين فضل الله : انفتاح على الموارنة

فان حزب الله هم الغالبون

حزب الله

الثورة الاسلامية في لبنان

Symbol of *HizbAllah* — includes: (at center) the writing ''*HizbAllah*'' integrated into a combination of a hand holding an assault rifle (the symbol of the armed movement); the Holy Quran (symbol of Islamic association); the branch (symbol of renewal); and the globe (symbol of the universality of the movement). Underneath the *HizbAllah* name: ''The Islamic Movement in Lebanon''.

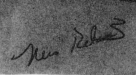

جيش التحرير
الفرقة الخامسة
الفريق المركزي أبو بكر المكي

New York Times
229 West 43rd Street
New York, NY 10036

The following letter from the *LIBERATION ARMY* regarding the operation conducted against the W.T.C.

We are, the fifth battalion in the *LIBERATION ARMY*, declare our responsibility for the explosion on the mentioned building. This action was done in response for the American political, economical, and military support to Israel the state of terrorism and to the rest of the dictator countries in the region.

OUR DEMANDS ARE:

1- Stop all military, economical, and political aids to Israel.
2- All diplomatic relations with Israel must stop.
3- Not to interfere with any of the Middle East countries interior affairs.

IF our demands are not met, all of our functional groups in the army will continue to execute our missions against military and civilians targets in and out the United States. This also will include some potential Nuclear targets. For your own information, our army has more than hundred and fifty suicidal soldiers ready to go ahead. The terrorism that Israel practices (Which is supported by America) must be faced with a similar one. The dictatorship and terrorism (also supported by America) that some countries are practicing against their own people must also be faced with terrorism.

The American people must know, that their civilians who got killed are not better than those who are getting killed by the American weapons and support.

The American people are responsible for the actions of their government and they must question all of the crimes that their government is committing against other people. Or they -Americans-will be the targets of our operations that could diminish them.

We invite all of the people from all countries and all of the revolutionaries in the world to participate in this action with us to accomplish our just goals.

". . . . IF THEN ANYONE TRANSGRESSES THE PROHIBITION AGAINST YOU TRANSGRESS YE LIKEWISE AGAINST HIM . . ."

LIBERATION ARMY
FIFTH BATTALION

AL-FARUK AL-ROKH, Abu Bakr Al-Makee.

Sheikh Umar Abd-al-Rahman:
The spiritual leader of the American Islamist community, and the senior leader of the Armed Islamist Movement in the US.

Muhammad A. Salameh:
The expendable martyr of the Islamist network. He performed these tasks, such as renting the bomb-carrying van and the storage site for the chemicals — services that would ultimately expose him as a participant in the network.

Mahmud Abdouhalima:
An 'Afghan', who was one of the principles of the Islamist network, the on-site professional leader activated for the operation against the World Trade Center.

Nidal A. Ayyad:
A chemical engineer and another expendable martyr of the Islamist network. He was implicated to appear as the network's bomb-maker.

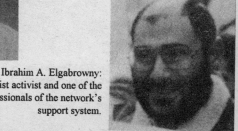

Ibrahim A. Elgabrowny:
An Islamist activist and one of the senior professionals of the network's support system.

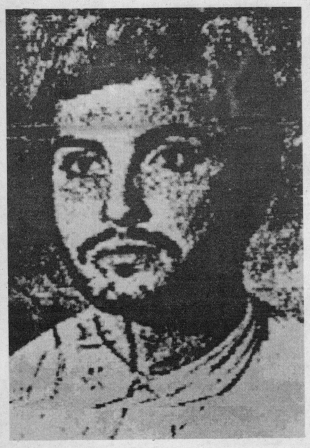

Imad Mughaniyah, of the *HizbAllah* Special Forces. This photo was copied from Mughaniyah's passport. *(courtesy Mednews)*

Sheikh
Hassan
al-Turabi,
the spiritual
leader of
Sudan.

JANIN/AFP

Emblem to the right:
The Armed Islamist Movement —
in the center, the crossed Swords
of Islam; above, the Holy Quran;
writing in the center "The
Muslim Brothers"; at the
bottom "The Call [of Islam]".

بسم الله الرحمن الرحيم

الإسلام طريق شعبي فلسطيني

{So when the second of the warnings came to pass, (We permitted your enemies) to disfigure your faces, and to enter the Masjid as they had entered it before, and to visit with destruction all that fell into their power.}   (17:7)

Islamic Committee for Palestine

Second Annual Conference

Palestine, Intifada and the Horizons of the Islamic Renaissance

Friday-Monday, December 22-25, 1989

McCormick Center Hotel
Chicago, Illinois

Invited Speakers

Sheikh Muhammad Al-Ghazali (Egypt)
Dr. Ahmad Sodki Dajani (Palestine)
Dr. Abdalla El-Nafisi (Kuwait)
Dr. Fathi Abdulaziz (Palestine)
Sheikh Maher Hammoud (Lebanon)
Mr. Fahmy Howaidy (Egypt)
Mr. Salah Jourachi (Tunisia)
Mr. Azad Garmiani (Kurdistan)

Sheikh Abdulaziz Odah (Palestine)
Sheikh Rashid Ghanoushi (Tunisia)
Mr. Adel-Hussein (Egypt)
Dr. Taha Jabir (USA)
Dr. Muhammad Sakr (Palestine)
Mr. M. Abulgasim Hag Hamad (Sudan)
Sheikh Abdulhadi Awang (Malaysia)
Mr. Hussein Ashur (Egypt)

And many other speakers from the USA and abroad

For More Information Please Call: 1-813-980-AKSA, in Chicago call 404-AKSA

TOPICS

● Intifada and Jihad: Concepts and Principles ● The Contemporary Islamic Movement and the Renaissance ● Intifada and Current Affairs ● The Ummah, the Islamic Movement and the Challenges of the Palestinian Issue ● Muslims in America & The Palestinian Issue ● The Quranic Dimension of the Palestinian Issue ● The Linkage between the Liberation Strategy and the Revival of the Ummah ● Towards an Islamic Strategy for Confrontation ● The Renaissance and the Challenges of Unity ● Political Initiatives and Social Changes in Palestine ● Islamic Causes: Kurdistan and Africa

Invitation Flyer of the Islamist conference in Chicago, 1989.
Invited guests included such terrorist leaders as Fathi Abdulaziz (Shqaqi) of the Islamic *Jihad*; Ghanoushi from Tunisia; and Odah (Awdah) of the Islamic *Jihad* in Gaza. Also note the preoccupation with the *Jihad* issue.

Ahmad Jibril, the
Secretary General
of the PFLP-GC.

بسم الله الرحمن الرحيم

إخبارية أسبوعية

المجاهد

صوت المجاهدين في فلسطين

To the right, the symbol of the
Palestinian Islamic *Jihad*. Note
their themes: knives (stabbing);
dome of the rock (the claim for
Jerusalem); clenched fists
(steadfastness); A map of Israel
(claim for all of Palestine).

CHARTER
OF
THE
ISLAMIC
RESISTANCES
MOVEMENT
(HAMAS)
OF
PALESTINE

THE ISLAMIC ASSOCIATION FOR PALESTINE

The Charter of *HAMAS*, published in Dallas, Texas.

סמל תנועת החמא״ס, המורכב מן הכתובת חמא״ס המשולבת: בספרה כסמל לאללה הוא אחד, ובתוכה מופיעה מפת פלסטין. בתוך שם התנועה כת... הים עד הנהרי״. מתחת לכתובת חמא״ס כתוב: תנועת ההתנגדות האסלאמית.

Symbol of *HAMAS* — The symbol of the *HAMAS* movement: The map of Palestine in its entirety (Land of Israel) is inside the number ''1'' (symbol of Allah is One) is imposed on the letter 'A' ... Inside *HAMAS* is written ''from the sea to the river'' meaning from the Mediteranean Sea to the Jordan river ... Under *HAMAS* is written ''the Islamic Resistance Movement'' ... The text below shows the back page of the Charter of *HAMAS*.

تم اعادة طباعة هذا الميثاق في امريكا الشمالية
تحت إشراف

الاتحاد الاسلامي لفلسطين

يطلب هذا الميثاق من

I.A.P. INFORMATION OFFICE
P.O. Box 741805
Dallas, TX 75374-1805, USA

حركة المقاومة الاسلامية

«حماس»

خلفيات النشأة وآفاق المسير

إعداد: أحـمـد بـن يوسـف

المركز العالمي للبحوث والدراسات

الإصدار الثاني

المركز العالمي للبحوث والدراسات

ICRS
P.O. Box 100
Worth, IL 60482

The title page of the key ideological text of the HAMAS called *The Islamic Resistance Movement "HAMAS"* by Ahmad bin Yusuf. Note the segment from the back of the title page that notes that the book was printed in the U.S. The books were then smuggled into Israel.

Masthead of Al-Sabil, the periodical of the Muslim brotherhood in Scandinavia, published in Oslo, Norway.

Masthead of the Bulletin of the Islamic Center in Washington, D.C. This specific issue focused on the topic of *Jihad*.

THE BULLETIN
OF
THE ISLAMIC CENTER
"UNDER SIEGE"

P.O. Box 32343 / Washington D.C. N.W. 20007

Vol. 5 No. 49   Thul Hijjah 16, 1406   August 22, 1986

"Therefore let those fight in the way of Allah, who sell this
world's life for the hereafter; and whoever fights in the way
of Allah, then be he slain or be he victorious, We shall grant
him a mighty reward."   (Quran 4:74)

JIHAD, THE FORGOTTEN ISLAMIC OBLIGATION

NEW ISLAMIST TERRORIST COMMAND STRUCTURE
(as of 1993)

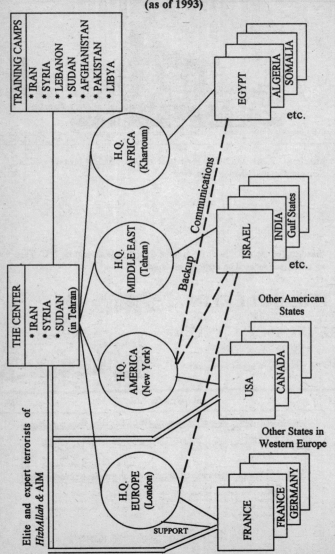

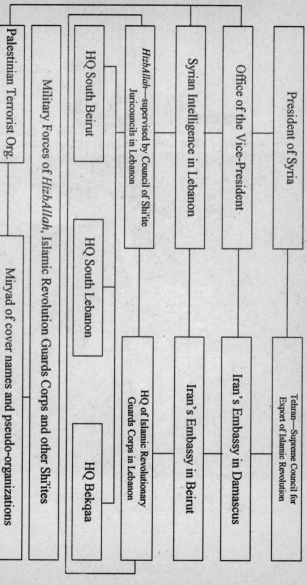

COMMAND STRUCTURE OF THE *HIZBALLAH* IN LEBANON

President of Syria

Office of the Vice-President

Syrian Intelligence in Lebanon

HizbAllah—supervised by Council of Shi'ite Juricouncils in Lebanon

HQ South Beirut

Military Forces of *HizbAllah*, Islamic Revolution Guards Corps and other Shi'ites

Palestinian Terrorist Org.

Tehran—Supreme Council for Export of Islamic Revolution

Iran's Embassy in Damascus

Iran's Embassy in Beirut

HQ of Islamic Revolutionary Guards Corps in Lebanon

HQ South Lebanon

HQ Bekqaa

Miryad of cover names and pseudo-organizations

The cover of *Al-Jihad*, the mouthpiece of the Palestinian Islamic *Jihad*. This issue was devoted to the evils of Judaism and Israel.

flight on April 17, 1986, the Syrian National Holiday. He then claimed to Murphy that he had to remain in London for urgent business, and promised to join her within a few days. On their way to the airport Hindawi gave her a special bag and a calculator as presents for the trip. The bag with the bomb passed through all the mechanical security checks only to be discovered by an Israeli security officer in a hand check just before Ann Murphy boarded. The shocked Murphy identified Nizar Hindawi.[194]

Nizar Hindawi rushed to the Syrian embassy as he had been told to do in Damascus. The Syrian ambassador, Dr. Lutfallah Al-Haydar, immediately called Col. Said Haytham (whose Damascus phone number is 336068) to report the failure. He then arranged a safe house for Hindawi. At first Nizar changed his appearance and dyed his hair. He received new documents and a Browning handgun. Two or three Syrian intelligence operatives were to escort Hindawi and guard him in the safe house until he could be smuggled out of the country by Syrian Airways. However, he became afraid that they were about to kill him in order to shield Syria's direct involvement. In Damascus, Gen. al-Khouly had told Hindawi that the punishment for betrayal was death. Nizar Hindawi managed to escape to his brother Mahmud Hindawi, who persuaded him to surrender to the British police as an alternative to a certain death.[195]

Sentenced to 45 years in prison, Nizar Hindawi then tried to get the Syrians to help him. He tried to smuggle a letter to his cousin, Awni Hindawi, in Genoa, Italy urging a prisoner exchange involving him as well as Western hostages kidnapped in Beirut. Col. Said Haitham was identified in the letter as the only man who could get in touch with the general secretary of the PFLP-GC, Ahmad Jibril, and compel him to exchange the four Israelis it was holding for himself and others. It is noteworthy that Nizar Hindawi was confident that Syrian intelligence had, in effect, control over the Western hostages to the

point of arranging their release in a trade for him if needed.[196]
The letter read:

> Dear Brother,
>
> Many greetings, it is time to act. I write to you
> hoping you won't disappoint me. Go to Damascus
> and talk to brother Abu and Ahmed-Haithan of the
> following: "Ahmad Jibril has two Israeli prisoners.
> Haithan has his word. Thatcher will be visiting
> Israel next Saturday. He has two Israeli prisoners.
> Abu has their words as well. A prisoner exchange
> should be organized which must include my brother
> Hazi. If necessary this can be accomplished in
> Thatcher's visit. Tell Haithan if necessary to include
> some foreigners from Beirut in the exchange." Have
> them give you 15,000 Deutschmarks (about
> $10,000) for my brother's lawyer and the same
> amount for my family. You are authorized to study
> any solution. Time is running out quickly.[197]

Syrian sources "firmly denied" any involvement with
Hindawi and the bombing attempt of El Al plane in London.[198]
Still, the interrogation of Hindawi in London after the failed
attempt to blow the El Al plane in mid-April 1986 clearly
revealed the extent of Syrian involvement in terrorism. A
major terrorist meeting took place in Damascus in late April
1986 in which George Habash demanded the escalation of
terrorist actions against the U.S. and Israel.[199]

Hafiz Assad was personally following the unfolding of the
Hindawi affair, and was especially interested in the conduct
and performance of Dr. Lutfallah Haydar, who was expected
to erase all traces of Syrian involvement.[200] In late 1986, Syria
represented the reaction in Europe to the Hindawi affair as part
of an all-out neo-imperialist campaign aimed at curbing its
important support for the Third World liberation movement all
over the world. Damascus also hailed the USSR's support and
its stand on Syria's side.[201]

Simultaneously, Syrian intelligence prepared to revitalize its infrastructure in Western Europe. Gen. al-Khouly remained a personal confidante of Assad.[202] The capture of Nizar al-Hindawi in London was the main reason why Syrian Air Force Intelligence changed the team operating in the Beirut International Airport. The task of the Syrian team is to send terrorists abroad through Beirut. They provide them with forged Moroccan, Lebanese and Yemeni passports. After the capture of Hindawi, President Assad ordered his Air Force Intelligence to clean up all evidence that might implicate Syria's activities in both Beirut and Tehran. The responsibilities of Gen. Muhammad al-Khouly were restricted to the Air Force. The performance of Brig.Gen. Ghazi Kan'an was also investigated closely in Damascus. New teams were sent in to rejuvenate the terrorist activities.[203]

In the haste of clean up operations, an Iraqi who headed a "sleeper" terrorist cell was exposed and deported from the United Kingdom to Syria in October 1986.[204] The Syrians also sent new people to West Germany. Palestinian killers guided by Syria (Abu-Nidal's men) infiltrated West Germany in the fall of 1986 and established a safe network with the assistance of the RAF (Red Army Faction) from where they could attack and attempt to assassinate leading politicians.[205] However, ultimately Iran would take over. *HizbAllah* operations in West Germany became the responsibility of the Gossen and Hammadi clans, of which Abbas Hammadi was the senior commander.[206]

CHAPTER 6
IN WESTERN EUROPE (II)

THE WORKING OF A MATURE NETWORK

In early 1985, Tehran was becoming impatient with the progress of negotiations with France regarding growing French military support for Iraq in the midst of the Iran-Iraq War, and prospects for the release of Anis Naccache, Rafiq-Dust's friend who had led the assassination attempt on Bakhtiar. Tehran made his release from jail a major issue in its relations with Paris.

According to Syrian intelligence sources, Tehran decided on March 15, 1985, after lengthy deliberations, to start kidnapping French citizens in Lebanon. Iran unleashed Islamic *Jihad* to perform these tasks.[1] Meanwhile, Iran also began preparing for an escalation of terrorist acts in Europe. At least one *HizbAllah* dormant net was activated in early 1985 and was ready for operations by late 1985. An expert terrorist was infiltrated to Paris in early 1986 to assess the network's operational status.[2] Thus, Tehran's primary theater of operations was in the heart of Western Europe.

A terrorist wave was revived in Paris in late 1985 with the December 7 explosions in two major department stores.[3] Reflected in communiques regarding their own prisoners in the West and Western hostages held in Lebanon, the objective of the participating terrorist organizations — LARF, ASALA, CSPPA and others — was to impose a change in French and Western policy in the Middle East, especially toward Iran and Syria.[4]

The character of Tehran's policy was implied by Hussein Mussavi when he warned that "France had to be realistic in its relations with the Middle East, the Islamic revolution on the world level and with Iran on the regional level."[5] As always, Damascus remained involved in the background, making sure that these attacks would end up serving Syria's interests. Hafiz al-Assad, the patron of the main terrorist organizations, insisted on coordinating the operations, controlling the professional side and, thereby he in effect consolidated a new policy of terror aimed at Israel and the United States.[6]

When the seizure of Western hostages did not produce the anticipated results, Tehran and Damascus unleashed the *HizbAllah* in a terrorist campaign in France. These were the first major operations of which Iran would be the undisputed leader.

Active preparations began in the summer of 1985. The organization of the new terrorist campaign was the responsibility of Imad Mughaniyah, who played a key role in the TWA hijacking in June 1985. Mughaniyah was identified in Paris but allowed free movement between November 10 and 16, 1985. By then he was already recognized as the most dangerous *HizbAllah* terrorist in Beirut and as having very close relations with the Iranian *Pasdaran*.

Officially, Mughaniyah came to Paris in November 1985 for some form of negotiations on the fate of the French hostages. At the very same time, however, Mughaniyah was serving as an inspector of the local conditions and networks, and supervising the delivery of money and weapons from Iran to the various Shi'ite groups. He also utilized his stay in Paris to make contact with various Iranian student groups.[7] Paris denied reports that Imad Mughaniyah was allowed to enter and leave France.[8] The *Pasdaran*, under Mohsin Rafiq-Dust, would play a central role in the negotiation-terrorism cycles aimed at freeing Naccache, and also conducted their own regional study. In January 1986, Rafiq-Dust sent his aide, Mohamad Salek, to Paris for "negotiations" and the personal inspection of the local terrorist infrastructure.[9]

A key strategy formulation session was convened in Damascus in January immediately after Salek's return. Attending were Gen. Muhammad al-Khouly and Col. Said Haitham for Syria, Muhsin Rafiq-Dust for Iran, a Col. Saleh for Libyan intelligence, and a senior commander of Abu Nidal's Fatah Revolutionary Council. All the participants stated that their respective governments were having problems with France. Syria feared French support of the Maronites in Lebanon; Libya was confronting France in Chad; Iran bitterly resented the French support for Iraq; and Rafiq-Dust was personally committed to Naccache. The Abu-Nidal commander attended the session to take orders concerning the implementation of the strategy.[10]

It was decided to unleash a terrorist campaign by utilizing existing dormant networks associated with progressive Palestinian organizations. Toward that end, Samir Abdallah, a nephew of Abu-Nidal, and an Armenian named Grigorian were dispatched to Paris to activate the dormant networks. Members of several compartmentalized cells, operating separately, began depositing components of bombs in pre-selected lockers in train stations. An expert bomb maker then constructed the bombs and made them available for operatives who would place them.[11]

Meanwhile, in early 1986, Iran, Syria and their allies were ready to resume their struggle against the West. The wide array of terrorist activities in Western Europe, irrespective of their ideological profiles, were directed and supported from Damascus, Tehran and Tripoli. Irrespective of the declared objectives of the specific attacks, most notably the demands for the release of prisoners, the ultimate objectives were far more fundamental.[12]

The intensity and significance of the terrorist operations were skillfully concealed through a massive campaign of disinformation and deception. From Beirut and Damascus, political and spiritual leaders, including Sheikh Fadlallah, repeatedly brought up offers for compromises and promised solutions to the cyclic crises — if Paris cooperated. Similarly, Hafiz al-Assad periodically offered to join with France in a combined military operation to release hostages if France's policy was amended to suit his strategic and regional objectives. Assad claimed that he was apprehensive about the growth of the Shi'ite terrorist forces, which Syrian sources claimed numbered some 20,000 fighters in the Baalbak complex alone. However, nothing happened, though the French hostages were known to be held by Hussein Mussawi and his Islamic Amal in a small village south of Baalbak, an area tightly controlled by the Syrian military and quite close to the Syrian border.[13]

The terrorists launched their first strikes by detonating three bombs (a fourth was safely dismantled) in crowded locations all over Paris between February 3 and 5, 1986.[14] Even then, the Iranians sought to maintain a deceptive line. The Committee for Solidarity with Arab and Middle Eastern Political Prisoners (CSPPA) emerged in February 1986, demanding the release of three terrorists in held in French jails: Anis Naccache, Varoudjian Garbidjian, and George Ibrahim Abdallah.

At first, the CSPPA appeared to be a front for LARF. French sources pointed out that this opinion was strengthened after the March 21, 1986, communique by CSPPA claiming that the organization "has no connection with religious movements and therefore no responsibility for the kidnapping of French spies. Our attacks are in no way linked to the existence or the non-existence of French hostages, wherever they may be." Although the CSPPA communiques also demanded the release of Anis Naccache and Varoudjian Garbidjian, the emphasis was always on George Ibrahim Abdallah.[15] Initially, Paris suspected the LARF and the Abdallah brothers and implicated Syria through General Muhammad al-Khouly, whose direct involvement in terrorism had been discovered in London and West Berlin.[16]

However, in retrospect, the timing of CSPPA's first really big attack clearly pointed to greater objectives. A major bomb exploded on March 17 on the Lyon-Paris train, followed by a massive bomb in the Champs Elysees on March 20, 1986, which killed 10 and wounded 28.[17] It was on the very same day that Jacques Chirac became the Prime Minister of France. The

Iranians were sending a message to the new French government. Behind the mysterious CSPPA actually stood an Iranian-dominated coalition led by the *HizbAllah*, and including the Marxist LARF, the ASALA-Hagopian faction and even several West European leftist radicals such as AD (Action Directe) and CCC (Combatting Communist Cells, referred to in Chapter 5), all supported by Iran and Syria.[18]

Indeed, it was the *HizbAllah* that assumed a higher profile in the ensuing political agitation. In late March 1986, Sheikh Fadlallah confirmed that "the issue of the French hostages is part of the French-Iranian conflict."[19] Fadlallah aimed high, explaining that "the abductors of the French hostages will release their captives as soon as the socialist regime in France falls."[20]

Even as the bombs were exploding in Paris, Tehran and Damascus were closely examining terrorist operations and considering the next phase. An important input about the political situation in France and Western Europe as a whole was provided by Fredrich Oriach, a French terrorist who had been a contact man between LARF and *Action Directe*. Immediately after he was pardoned and released from jail on March 16, 1986, Fredrich Oriach made a hasty trip to the Middle East. His reports served as the basis for the study of the new terrorist campaign.[21]

The highest levels of the alliance of Iran, Syria and Libya then decided to escalate the cycle of violence in Western Europe and the Middle East. Iran insisted that emphasis be put on France. In Tehran, Khomeini personally activated both the dormant terrorist networks in France and SAVAMA's control and support mechanism operating from the Iranian embassy in Paris.[22]

Syria was responsible for the organizational aspects. Brig.Gen. Ghazi Kan'an, close to Hafiz al-Assad, "personally supervised aspects of the planning, coordination, and execution of these acts and visited Tehran and Libya for this purpose." A major meeting chaired by Kan'an took place in Damascus on June 1, 1986, with Iranian and Libyan senior officials coordinating the terrorist campaign for late 1986. They decided to use the diversified infrastructure of training camps in Lebanon for the launching of terrorist campaigns, mainly against France, Italy, Cyprus, Greece and Spain.[23] Indeed, operatives later to be associated with CSPPA intensified their training in facilities in Lebanon run by the Iranian-dominated Anti-Imperialist International Brigade and used by other Syrian-supported terrorist groups.[24]

The 1986 bombings in Paris were the operations of a small but mature Iranian-Syrian network that included all the components of the mid-generation network in Europe. The operation included characteristics of Iranian-Syrian operations, such as the activation of a long-dormant network with some components that had been put in place as early as 1979; the use of expert operatives; the delivery of a clear political message without endangering the operatives in place; the shielding of the operation by deception and diversion without losing the key political message; and the maintaining of tight operational security. This was of particular importance to the planners for the network would be betrayed by a Tunisian Islamist (not a member) who had earlier defected for ideological reasons.

In early 1986, the Iranians succeeded in infiltrating the Muslim movements in France. They had already united various terrorist movements, particularly Arab groups. The Muslim "street" knew that they were preparing "torrents of blood" for the West. Indeed, attacks in early 1986 would confirm that the terrorists had become well-organized. There were doubts about Iran's role because it had previously "specialized" only in the assassinations of political opponents. Though by the mid-1980s they had diversified their activities with a clear predilection for Europe, the extent of their capabilities was not yet clear.[25]

The Paris network had three leaders, each responsible for specific aspects of operations:

1. Wahid Gordji, an Iranian diplomat stationed in Paris, who had extensive experience in Europe, had diplomatic cover and was responsible for command, financing and oversight on behalf of Iran;

2. Fuad Ali Salah, a Tunisian graduate of special training in Iran who had legal residence in France, was the commander of the 'dormant' support network and was in charge of interactions with support system;

3. Muhammad al-Muhajir, a Shi'ite from Baalbak and senior member of the *HizbAllah*, who was the network's expert in military affairs, operations, clandestine activities, recruitment and vetting, as well as the trusted contact man with the *HizbAllah* in Lebanon and the on-site coordinator between the dormant network, Iran and Lebanon (including the expert bombers arriving for specific operations)[26];

4. Ahmad Kan'ani, former IRGC commander in Lebanon, who was, while serving as Iran's ambassador to Tunisia, the back-up controller of the Fuad Ali Salah network ready to take over communications with the outside world in case the terrorists lost contact with the Iranian embassy in Paris.[27]

The success of the Paris network lay in the careful selection of its leading members and the methodical way in which they were settled in Paris. In the mid-1986 operations, Iran was more responsible than Syria for the bombing wave in Paris. Despite the Islamist character of the operatives, the exposed Iranian-supported terrorist and intelligence networks were organized exactly like the East European/Soviet intelligence networks.[28] The Paris network were responsible for 15 terrorist attacks between December 1985 and September 1986 in which there were 13 fatalities and 303 injuries.[29]

Wahid Gordji, acting as a translator in the Iranian Embassy in Paris, supervised the network and was the SAVAMA resident in charge of sabotage operations. Wahid Gordji was born in Tehran between 1960 and 1963, and arrived in France as adolescent with his father. The elder Dr. Walid Gordji was a reputed physician and businessman who treated Khomeini when he was in exile in France. The future prime minister Alireza Mo'ayyeri, then the Iranian chargé d'affaires in Paris who was posted as an interpreter at the Iranian embassy, took note of Wahid Gorji. Gordji's knowledge of French and French customs made him invaluable to the Tehran-supported international terrorist campaign. He was nominated as the SAVAMA resident in France, and was later put in charge of the SAVAMA all over Western Europe.

In this capacity he was in close contact with Mamoucheh Taleh, Iran's consul in Geneva, the coordinator of the pro-Khomeini networks in Europe. He was also active in the promotion of pro-Iranian Islamist activities in Islamic cultural centers such as the Ahl al-Beit in Paris. As the embassy's senior translator, Gordji was present in all the negotiations in Paris concerning the French hostages in Lebanon, as well as French-Iranian relations.[30]

The field commander of the Paris network was Fuad Ali Salah, a professional terrorist who had been "groomed and trained in Iran" for this role. He is a Tunisian from a religious family who was born in Paris on May 10, 1958, and spent his childhood years there before his parents decided to return to Tunisia.[31] Salah returned to France for his education and found his way to Khomeini's entourage in Paris in 1978-79, where he was recruited.[32] In 1981-82, Salah was sent to Qom, where he attended "the very special courses . . . which provide intensive training in spiritual fundamentalism and practical terrorism."[33]

The extent of the Iranian indoctrination emerged during Fuad Salah's trial. He began his speech by saying, "In the name of *Allah* the all powerful and the destroyer of the West, accursed be all the sinful sons of Israel and Jesus." He then launched into a lengthy description of the West's historical oppression and persecution of the Third World, and especially the Muslims, that warrants retribution in the form of "horrible and barbaric death" now promised by Fuad Salah.[34]

In another court appearance on April 2, 1992, Fuad Ali Salah defiantly declared: "I am a terrorist fighter, my home is the entire world." He reiterated his commitment to the *Jihad* along the principles outlined by Abbas Mussawi. "I will continue to fight the West . . . what I have to say is that we are Muslims, and that we will exterminate each and every one of you."[35] Fuad Ali Salah receive a life sentence (He must serve 18 years before being eligible for parole).[36]

Meanwhile, Fuad Salah returned to France via Tunisia in 1983 but moved to Paris, his intended area of operations, only in 1985. By then, a marriage was arranged for him with a very religious girl from Tunisia, Fariha Korima, who received her French citizenship on October 5, 1985. As a result, Salah received a legal resident card and was thus shielded from deportations and police monitoring. At first, he "worked" as a fruit and vegetable peddler in the Paris metro (subway) system, thus thoroughly learning the system.[37]

Muhammad al-Muhajir was born in Baalbak in 1953. He is the son of Sheikh Habib Ali Ibrahim, an eminent Shi'ite theologian who concentrated on converting Sunnis to Shi'ism. He studied in Qom and in Najaf, Iraq. He was trained by Hussein Mussawi and was among the founders of the *HizbAllah* terrorist network (including suicide operations) in Lebanon. Muhammad al-Muhajir must have met Gordji in Qom, for when he arrived in Paris he was already identified as a close friend of Gordji.

Al-Muhajir's legal presence in France, and ultimately his French citizenship, were arranged through his marriage to an ex-Iranian, already a French citizen, who was working for the Iranian Embassy. For one of his operations, on July 5, 1986, al-Muhajir, purchased a BMW from a known Islamic Amal operative in West Germany, brought it to France and transferred ("sold") it to Gordji. Al-Muhajir was thus a go-between Gordji and Salah, and the Paris network and the *HizbAllah* in Lebanon.[38]

Soon after his arrival in Paris, Wahid Gordji began building the Paris network. He became very active in the promotion and organization of Islamist "religious-cultural" activities in Paris, especially in the Ahl al-Beit Center in Paris. He was also active in supporting the organizations of Iranian students in France. In 1985-86, the Paris Ahl al-Beit was among the most important centers of the Iranian community in France.[39] The Ahl al-Beit Islamic cultural center served as a meeting and recruitment place. It was a hotbed of fundamentalist proselytizing frequented by pro-Khomeini preachers and activists. One of the main organizers of the Ahl al-Beit Center was Muhammad Bakir Sayid Fadlallah, the brother of Sheikh Fadlallah, who also operated a book store that was used to conduct and coordinate communications for the *HizbAllah*.[40] During these activities, Gordji was able to spot talent and identify potential agents and operatives for the Iranian networks.

Gradually, Fuad Ali Salah became a frequent visitor to both locations associated with the network[41]. In the Center, it was possible to identify the kind of alienated youth, mainly from North Africa, who were ideal prospects for recruitment. Salah would first draw them into a fervid commitment to *Jihad* and then recruit them into active participation in networks.[42]

From the beginning, Salah was a good clandestine professional. Salah's first task in Paris was to "absorb" the military expert Muhammad al-Muhajir. In Paris, al-Muhajir first opened a book store. Soon afterwards, he "met" Fuad Ali Salah. Together they opened another store for clothing and religious cassettes. They used their book and cassette distribution and marketing efforts as cover to visit the Islamic and cultural centers in Paris and throughout France. With that, the recruitment campaign began.[43] Many of the most promising candidates were identified by Gordji, who provided their names to al-Muhajir.

In the recruitment effort, Fuad Ali Salah emerged as the central figure, the master manipulator. Salah had studied in Iran and had a perfect knowledge of Islam as well as knowledge of France, French society and conspiratorial techniques.

The first phase in his effort was to convert potential recruits into militant fundamentalists. He used three arguments to incite and interest prospects: social discrimination which led to poverty and unemployment; the growing racism of Jean-Marie Le Pen, the far-right French politician, which he claimed represented French society; and the growing Iraqi use of French-made aircraft and weapons to fight Iran. Salah would eventually entrap those most affected and influenced.

At first he asked them to safe-keep innocent, and later not-so-innocent, items in their apartments. Most became ideologically committed to the cause. Those who wavered or were frightened were intimidated by being told that they were already accomplices to violent bombings because they had unwittingly stored bombs or guns.

These sleepers were "wonderfully anonymous" and abundant.[44] The members of most of these Iranian networks remained dormant. Their members continued their normal lives and were activated only when the expert bomb makers arrived and needed lodging and transportation.

It is impossible even to estimate the number of such "dormant" networks in Paris.[45]

The recruitment effort provided the support system for the ensuing terrorist attacks in Paris. The entire bombing campaign in 1985-86 was conducted by a 10-man network, all of them Islamists recruited from diversified walks of life. They included taxi drivers, subway peddlers, university students, a restaurant owner and a perfume company manager.[46] The entire network and its fringe support system did not go beyond some 50-60 members, all of them Lebanese, Iranians, Algerians, Moroccans and Tunisians.[47] The leaders were motivated by religious fanaticism and hatred of the West, while others were coerced and manipulated by their comrades.[48]

For the initial operation, Salah's priority was to reach for an outsider. Students, especially long-term postgraduates, were used to store material because they were so different from the rest of the network's support system.[49]

Salah found his first outsider: a practicing Muslim, a Moroccan named Abdel Hamid Badaoui, who was completing his doctoral degree in mathematics. Salah appealed to Badaoui's Islamic beliefs and ultimately got him to lodge him, Salah, whenever he was in Badaoui's neighborhood. Badaoui also agreed to keep Salah's "merchandise" intended for the local Mosque.

In April 1985, Badaoui learned from Salah that one of the suitcases Salah had left behind contained explosives intended for attacks that would avenge the Iraqi Air Force's raids on Iran using French-made aircraft. At this point, Badaoui no longer dared to resist, and Salah suggested that he store the suitcase with loyal friends. On July 15, 1985, some of the explosives were distributed to a Moroccan friend of Badaoui. They would be picked up in October by Salah's messenger.[50]

Special attention was paid to the recruitment of taxi drivers, who could provide easy and non-descript means of transportation.[51] Indeed, the next recruit was Hassan Aroua, a taxi driver. Aroua came from yet another background. He was not devout and had a record of greed and a desire for quick and large sums of money. Aroua became an accomplice in October 1985 when he drove Salah and Bassam, a *HizbAllah* bomb maker, to Orly Airport to pick up the smuggled explosives and sabotage equipment.[52]

Another recruit was a Tunisian restaurant owner, Muhammad Aissa, a hard-liner who provided a safe meeting place. Aissa was a devout quiet man deeply involved in religious activities. None of his customers would later believe that he could have been involved in terrorist acts. He became part of the net by lodging Bassam. Another recruit was a Tunisian manager of a perfume company, Fethi Bourguiba, who provided lodging and storage services.[53]

Other key elements of the "sleeper" support system were providing the expert bomb planters with safe living places. Many of these support agents had family members in Lebanon and elsewhere who could be influenced to ensure the cooperation of their relatives in Paris.[54] In retrospect, Aissa and Aroua were Salah's most loyal lieutenants.[55]

The North Africans recruited by Fuad Ali Salah constituted a dormant net always in place in Paris and activated as needed. The bombing experts, Lebanese directly controlled by Tehran, would arrive and spend in Paris only the minimum time necessary.[56] In 1986, the Paris network received operational assistance from at least three experts who were sent to Paris to inspect the net and plant the bombs.[57]

In mid-1985, the first bomb expert, known only as Bassam, was infiltrated into Paris. The explosives and parts were smuggled inside printing rollers and rotary press parts sent from Lebanon for repair and maintenance in Paris. They were shipped to a phony company and Salah and Bassam had all the required papers to release them. Fathi Bourguiba provided storage for the bombs in the perfume company. It was in Bourguiba's apartment that Bassam and Salah opened the cylinders to empty the plastique explosives as well six and a half kilograms of heroin to be used to finance operations and corrupt the West at the same time. Bassam and Salah repacked the material in sealed plastic bags and Aroua drove them to Fontainebleau Forest where they buried the sacks.[58]

The net was ready by late 1985. An expert supervisor was infiltrated to Paris in early 1986.[59] He was Mohamad Salek, Rafiq-Dust's second-in-command, who arrived in Paris in January 1986, ostensibly for negotiations concerning Anis Naccache.[60]

On February 15, 1986, Fuad Ali Salah and the inspector-expert visited Badaoui and left two additional sacks of explosives and a machine-gun. Badaoui arranged with Aroua to transfer the material for safekeeping to another Moroccan named Agnaou.

The wave of bombings began. Bassam would appear in the middle of the night and remove "things" from Agnaou's apartment.[61] The first major bomb exploded in Paris on March 20, 1986, the day that Jacques Chirac was becoming the Prime

Minister of France, as mentioned earlier.[62] The network was ordered to cease operations in early April.

The network used the lull for high-level consultations and plans for deceiving the authorities. Reportedly, Fuad Ali Salah made a trip to Beirut where he met not just *HizbAllah* commanders but commanders from other extremist terrorist groups that were traditionally linked to Syria. Consequently, new militants connected with George Ibrahim Abdallah and LARF (Syrian military intelligence), arrived in Western Europe for related operations.[63] The two expert bomb makers and planters, Mahdi Biab and Yussuf Mashrif, arrived in Paris ready to participate in the anticipated escalation. Mashrif arrived from Cyprus bringing with him liquid methyl nitrate, an exceedingly potent high explosive which is extremely dangerous in its liquid form.[64]

These bomb experts were Islamists trained in Lebanon who were totally committed to the cause. They arrived in Paris a few months before the attack and melted into the crowd. They arrived in small groups, about three at a time, with excellent warning and escape plans that enabled them to flee immediately. The latest bomb planters included individuals who were well acquainted with France, having spent several years there as students. Al-Muhajir was the contact, visiting Muslim centers regularly. There was "extreme compartmentalization" among the members of the group and only the leader, Fuad Ali Salah, had full information.[65]

The first bomb in a new campaign exploded on September 4, 1986, in a Paris metro station.[66] In a Beirut communique, The Committee for Solidarity with Arab and Middle Eastern Political Prisoners (CSPPA) claimed responsibility for the attack. The group demanded the release of three terrorists jailed in France: George Ibrahim Abdallah of LARF, Anis Naccache, and Varoudjian Garabidjian.[67] Several more bombs exploded in Paris in quick succession in mid-September — at the Central Post Office (Sept. 8), City Hall (Sept. 11), a Champs Elysees pub (Sept. 14) — and at the Central Police

Headquarters on Sept. 15, the day after Chirac announced tough anti-terrorist measures. Altogether, CSPPA claimed responsibility for nine bombs in Paris in 1986. In a communique delivered in Paris, the group repeated its demand for the release of the three imprisoned terrorists.[68]

In a communique delivered in Beirut on September 14, the Committee for Solidarity with Arab and Middle Eastern Political Prisoners threatened that the French Government "will learn very soon that we will not bow to any threat of any kind." If the three terrorists were not released, "the fire will grow even bigger, spread and continue."[69] Meanwhile, after the CSPPA's City Hall bombing, another Paris bombing on September 12, 1986 was claimed by the Partisans of Justice and Freedom (PDL) based in Beirut. However, it was believed that the PDL was yet another name of the group previously identified as CSPPA and LARF.[70]

Another bomb that exploded the next day was also claimed in Beirut by the PDL.[71] The last bomb in the campaign exploded on September 17, 1986, in front of the Tati store on rue de Rennes, causing seven fatalities and 51 injuries, 16 of them severe.[72]

By now, the intensity of operations was causing strains in the Iranian network. In the middle of the bombing campaign in September 1986, Bassam needed to retrieve additional explosives from a buried stockpile. Some material was also stored with Badaoui and Agnaou. However, Agnaou panicked, shocked by the carnage he saw on TV, and refused to cooperate any longer. Fuad Ali Salah talked to him, convinced him of his righteous Islamic ways and of the importance of avenging the numerous innocent victims in Lebanon and Iran.

Badaoui was also getting scared and moved in with his uncle, leaving his apartment to Salah who promptly turned it into the network's primary bomb factory.[73] However, the leadership was apprehensive about these incidents and the network's ability to continue operating safely.

In late September 1986, after the explosion in the rue de

Rennes, the Paris network was ordered to lie low and Salah was summoned to Damascus.[74] Meanwhile, a secret coordinating meeting of several terrorist organizations was held in Nicosia, Cyprus, on September 18-19, 1986. The participants represented terrorist and clandestine groups operating in Western Europe, Japan and the Middle East. They included members of several pro-Iranian and pro-Lebanese Islamic fundamentalist organizations, the Lebanese Revolutionary Armed Factions, the Japanese Red Army, the West German Bader-Meinhof gang, the Italian Red Brigades and the French Direct Action group. The discussions centered on mapping a common war strategy against the U.S. and Israel.[75]

George Habash was one of the front leaders attending the Cyprus meeting. On September 30 and October 1, 1986, Habash met with Gen. Muhammad al-Khouly to discuss international terrorism and future operations. Consequently, on October 7, 1986, Habash was received by President Assad to discuss future operations. Part of the escalation decided upon was that "Iranian militants are now [late 1986] working with the European terrorists in Direct Action." There was also active support from Algerian intelligence for Action Directe and others through Mohand Hammami, the Algerian contact with European terrorists, whose uncle was one of the leaders of Algerian Intelligence. Hammami is a close associate of George Ibrahim Abdallah, who hired Hammami's lawyer in 1984.[76]

With this campaign in the advanced stage of preparations, Damascus and Tehran decided to integrate the experience of the Paris network in the anticipated escalation. Consequently, Fuad Ali Salah travelled to Lebanon and Damascus in October 1986 for consultations. In Beirut, Salah met with Muhammad Mehdi Diab, the supervisor of French operations who was also supervising the coordination with *HizbAllah* with the LARF terrorists in Lebanon and Western Europe. He also met Taghrid Ramadan, the chief coordinator of *HizbAllah* with "Iranian elements" concerning European operations.[77]

From the very beginning there were indications that Iran

was directly involved in the Paris bombings. In late September 1986, Salah Khalaf (Abu Iyad) explained that "the attacks in France are linked to the struggle being waged by Paris and Tehran."[78] In January 1987, Salah Khalaf further elaborated on the objectives of Iranian terrorism in France: "The key to the affair of the French hostages in Lebanon is the release of Anis Naccache. All other demands have gradually been added." Abu Iyad threatened France with the unleashing of more violence if its demands were not met. Moreover, "Iran is not asking for an end to arms sales to Iraq, for Iran, too, would like to receive French arms."

These principal objectives should not be confused with the cover names of the organizations claiming responsibility for the attacks. "The *HizbAllah*, Islamic *Jihad*, the Revolutionary Justice Organization, and the Oppressed of the Earth are all the same thing. And they are all working for Tehran," Abu-Iyad emphasized. "This edifice functions as a real party and all the different names the *HizbAllah* may take are merely covers for its operational wing."[79]

However, French security authorities concluded in the spring of 1987 that "pro-Iranian Moroccans and other Arabs" (Lebanese) were responsible for the September 1986 bombings in Paris.[80] In an immediate reaction, the Committee for Solidarity with Arab and Middle Eastern Political Prisoners renewed its threat of a summer of bombings in Paris unless Abdallah, Garbidjian and Naccache were released.[81]

It was the ideologically motivated defection of a Tunisian named Lofti (a pseudonym) that provided the identification of the Salah network and the proof that Iran was behind the Paris bombing campaigns of March and September 1986.[82] Lofti returned from Iran only in February 1987 when he decided to defect.[83] He was born in 1956 and remained a committed Khomeini-ist prior to his defection. His primary crisis was that Khomeini's Persians treated Arabs, including himself, "like dogs" and as pawns in their struggle. In Tehran, "the mullahs dream only of money and power. They want to colonize Iraq,

Syria and finally Israel," Lofti explained. During his extensive studies, Lofti had met Salah in the "universities" in Iran.[84]

Lofti told the French DST that because of his past training and credentials, Fuad Ali Salah was the most likely head of an Iranian-supported terrorist network. Lofti believed Salah was "an adherent of the Lebanese *HizbAllah.*"[85] With the help of the DST, Lofti set up an Islamist Koranic school, full of microphones, to be used to elicit confessions from the suspected participants of the Salah network.[86]

Indeed, it did not take long for the tormented Abdel Hamid Badaoui to seek spiritual advice. Confessing to Lofti, Badaoui was the first to break and admit storing explosives on Salah's orders. Agnaou broke down soon afterwards. Aroua was then identified and cooperated in the entrapment of Salah who was subsequently arrested transferring a bottle of methyl nitrate from Aroua's taxi. Aissa, Bourguiba and Muhajir were also arrested.[87] Although these arrests prevented a wave of bombings, the subsequent investigation revealed the resilience and stability of the Iranian supported terrorist network.

Hassan Aroua betrayed the existence of the cache in the woods that included 12 kilograms of plastique explosives and 25.5 liters of methyl nitrate. More than six kilograms of drugs were also found. The finding of the types of explosives used in the Paris bombings confirmed that an Iranian network was responsible for the CSPPA bombing campaign. A 7.65mm and a 11.43mm machine-pistol and several revolvers were found in the apartment of a Moroccan.[88] However, the discovery of this major cache of explosives and other terrorist sabotage equipment in the Fontainebleau Forest only served to increase awareness in Paris to the threat it faced.

The DST learned of the existence and specific locations of the cache only when Aroua volunteered the information. Though every method of search, from metal detectors to space-based sensors, was used to locate the huge cache, only the testimony of a terrorist followed by extensive manual digging by large numbers of personnel led to the ultimate discovery.[89] Thus, the discovery of the cache in the Fontainebleau Forest confirmed that it is virtually impossible to discover concealed explosives without precise intelligence and a massive effort by security forces.

Moreover, despite the major effort of the DST, uncovering the Salah network proved an intelligence failure. Wahid Gordji, the SAVAMA resident, was the real boss and organizer of Islamic terrorist networks in France and was the commanding officer of Muhammad al-Muhajir and Fuad Ali Salah. Wahid Gordji was alerted a day before the DST and the police launched their dragnet against Islamist terrorism and had ample time to fly to Switzerland and escape before being interrogated. The Lofti entrapment efforts failed to implicate the real leaders of the Islamist network. All the expert operatives — Bassam, Biab and Mashrif — were also warned and escaped.[90]

Moreover, all the hiding and storage places betrayed during the interrogation of the arrested terrorists, except for the Fontainebleau Forest cache, had been cleaned up well before the security authorities reached them.[91] The thoroughness of the advanced clean-up of the Salah network led Raymond Nart, the deputy head of the DST, to question the extent of France's previous terrorist arrests. "Since he [George Ibrahim Abdallah] was allowed to be captured," Nart concluded, "he was some sort of a support officer at the most."[92]

And there were more disturbing implications in the discovery of the Salah network. A widened investigation of Islamist circles in France pointed out that the presence of an oversight function of the sort exercised by Wahid Gordji was not limited to a single network. Gordji was identified as the SAVAMA resident in charge of sabotage operations throughout France, yet not a single dormant network was identified.[93]

Moreover, evidence emerged that new militants connected with organizations supported by Syrian military intelligence arrived in Western Europe in order to escalate sabotage operations. Their arrival was a result of contacts Fuad Ali Salah had held during a trip to Beirut where he met *HizbAllah* and Syrian-controlled terrorist commanders.[94]

Even the exposure of resupply links did not help security forces. A *HizbAllah* courier was captured in Larnaca, Cyprus, on August 18, 1986, with weapons and ammunition to be delivered to Western Europe.[95] On January 13, 1987, a Lebanese, Bashir Khudur, was arrested in Milan after flying from Beirut via Geneva with 11 kilograms of SEMTEX hidden in two picture frames and several Easter eggs. He also had 36 very sophisticated detonators disguised as the batteries of the transistor radio he was carrying. He was identified as part of the revitalization of LARF/CSPPA.[96] Even then, the security authorities were unable to break any of the remaining Islamist networks.

Meanwhile, the *HizbAllah*'s shift to the use of liquid methyl nitrate resulted in the exposure of one of its up-and-coming networks in West Germany. A back-up shipment of liquid explosives was organized via Frankfurt. The methyl nitrate was concealed in bottles of arrack. The first courier, Muhammad Ali Hammadi, was arrested on January 13, 1987, when he refused to open his liquor bottles and drink a glass. On January 26, Muhammad Ali's brother, Abbas Hammadi, was arrested in Frankfurt and led the police to additional bottles of liquid methyl nitrate. The liquid methyl nitrate captured in West Germany was identical to the explosives used by the Tunisian terrorists in their operations in Paris. Moreover, Muhammad Ali Hammadi's notebook included the names and Paris phone numbers of Salah and Bourgiba. Another name in this notebook — Wail Ramadan — also featured prominently in the notebook found on Bashir Khudur when he was arrested in Milan. Muhammad Ali Hammadi carried with him specific strike and sabotage plans and instructions for networks based in West Germany. Thus, although an Islamist network in Germany based on the Hammadi brothers was neutralized, the investigation led nowhere in the search for the intended recipients of the vast quantities of explosives almost smuggled into Western Europe.[97]

Thus, the Islamist terrorist network in Western Europe survived a major challenge virtually intact. Little wonder, therefore, that in late 1988 an indignant Wahid Gordji could claim that he was framed as part of a power struggle on Middle East policy within the French Government. He denied, of course, any connection with terrorism.[98]

CONSOLIDATING THE CURRENT TERRORIST INFRASTRUCTURE

The milestone international terrorist conference was conducted in May 1986 even as the success of the network Lofti revealed was becoming evident. The outcome of the Paris operations confirmed the approach taken in the conduct of terrorism in Western Europe. Therefore, Iran, Syria and Libya had no reason to make fundamental changes in the international terrorism infrastructure they were consolidating. Instead, they decided on major improvements and refinements of the proven system aimed at further expediting the rates, and diversifying the types, of operations these networks could undertake.

Since the mid-1980s, there has been a further centralization of command over and control of terrorist operations in Western Europe by the Iranian and Syrian governments.[99] In 1986, CSPPA turned out to be the cover for an alliance of the *HizbAllah*, LARF and ASALA which was actively supported by Iran and Syria. Of these, *HizbAllah* was the most active and lethal. Since then, *HizbAllah*, which is dominated by Iran, has become "the linchpin of the new terrorist coalition of extremists."[100] The centralization of command is evident, for example, from the fact that virtually all the *Hizballah* operatives captured, from Western Europe to Africa, have had in their possessions the telephone number of the organization's international operations center: Beirut 313-611.[101]

Syria also intensified its control over the radical Palestinians. Hafiz al-Assad is both the controller and patron of the main terrorist organizations and their leaders, whose actions are coordinated through the Palestinian Salvation Front: Abu Musa (Sa'id Musa Muragha), Ahmad Jibril, George Habash and Nayif Hawatimah. Exploiting this control, Syria consolidated a new policy of terror aimed at Israel and the United States.[102]

Still, Iran is the dominant power concerning the *HizbAllah*. "Any Syrian dialogue with the *HizbAllah* depends on Tehran," Abu Iyad pointed out.[103] The Syrian-Iranian alliance led to the formalization of a refined terrorist coalition called INTERROR. The new INTERROR treaty was signed in the Carlton Hotel in Beirut on December 20, 1988, in the wake of a large gathering of Shi'ite and Sunni religious leaders, radical terrorist leaders and intelligence officers. Syria and Iran guaranteed extensive support. The members of INTERROR declared war on the West, Israel and Saudi Arabia.[104]

Terrorist operations in Western Europe are guided through the *Majlis Shura*, the supreme organ of the *HizbAllah* in Lebanon which takes orders from Tehran and Damascus.[105] The senior commanders of the *HizbAllah* operation in Western Europe are Hussein Khalil, Muhammad Haydar Abd-al-Hammadi and Imad Mughaniyah, all veteran leaders and commanders of terrorist cells of *HizbAllah* with overseas experience. The *HizbAllah*'s power is based on the personal background and relations of the main commanders.[106]

For international operations, the *HizbAllah* maintains a close relationship with the PLO, and especially Arafat's Force 17. The coordination is maintained by the *HizbAllah*'s Imad Mughaniyah who belonged to Arafat's Force 17 in the early 1980s. Arafat and Mughaniyah still maintain close personal relations. These open lines of communications with the PLO in Tunis are so important that the Soviets intervened with the Syrians to permit this contact despite Assad's hostility toward Arafat.[107]

For example, when Muhammad Mahmed Darwish (Abu Nur), the commander of the PLO's Force 17 was captured by

Israel in 1985, he acknowledged that he took part in the smuggling of weapons to diversified terrorist groups in Western Europe, including the PLO's Force 17. According to Abu Nur, most smuggling took place from Eastern Europe, particularly East Germany, where weapons were handed over to Force 17 operatives for delivery to terrorists in Western Europe.[108]

Abu Iyad also acknowledged that the PLO has "maintained personal relations with some pro-Iranian Shi'ite leaders. They did not suddenly emerge, and we have known them for a long time. For instance, we have protected Sheikh Muhammad Hussein Fadlallah, *HizbAllah*'s spiritual guide, from the Iraqi secret services on several occasions, and he is well aware of that."[109]

In Beirut, the supreme commander-coordinator of operations in Western Europe is Col. Ahmad Akhundi of the IRGC who is a close friend and confidant of Ali Akbar Mohtashemi. Stationed in Syria since 1982, Akhundi established close relations with the Syrian intelligence service and its proteges, such as Ahmad Jibril. Ahmad Nasif is the head of foreign operations of Syrian intelligence in charge of European operations. During the Beirut fighting, Nasif tried to infiltrate *HizbAllah* terrorists onto a French hospital ship off Beirut shores, pretending they were wounded in Beirut fighting. Nasif also tried to organize a spectacular operation during the bicentennial celebration in Paris in June 1989, having the PFLP-GC activate dormant nets of ASALA in Prague, Japanese terrorists in Europe, etc. However, at the last minute the operation was called off by Tehran and Damascus.[110]

In anticipation of the escalation of the international terrorist campaign in the West, Syria enhanced the role and power of intelligence officers associated with terrorist operations. The growing influence of Syria's security organs is reflected in the rise of their key personnel, all of whom are Assad loyalists and Alawites: Ali Duba; Muhammad Nasir; Muhammad al-Khuli; Adnan Badr al-Hasan; Ali Haydar; Shafiq Fayyad; Adnan Makhluf; Ali Dib; Dib Dahir; Tawfiq Jallul; Ghazi Kan'an.[111]

General Ali Duba, the head of Syrian intelligence, shows direct and personal interest in all the overseas terrorist operations.[112]

Syria also nominated intelligence officers to key diplomatic positions. Syrian embassies are important components in the international security machine of Damascus. They are empowered to support subversion and international terrorism in various countries. The Syrian embassy also channels money to Iranian and Syrian and Palestinian sleeper agents in Germany.[113]

Similarly, Iran dispatched key diplomats prepared by Javad Mansuri to Western Europe where they were put ''in charge of the task of spreading the idea of exporting the revolution through terrorism.''[114]

Soon after the 1986 conference, Iran started actively preparing its proteges for the escalation of terrorist operations in Western Europe. Having completed several overseas operations, including the hijacking of TWA 475, with great success, Imad Mughaniyah was selected as the chief of staff of the *HizbAllah* special operations forces and its key operative for the revitalized terrorist operations.[115] Consequently, Imad Mughaniyah was in Tehran during October-December 1987 for intensive training in the Iranian special operations school north of Tehran, where the hijacking of the Kuwaiti airliner was being prepared.[116]

Since then, the *HizbAllah* operations in Western Europe have been led and coordinated by Imad Mughaniyah, Abd al-Hadi Hammadi and Muhammad Haydar. Since 1986, these three commanders have persistently inserted terrorist networks into Western Europe. The few who were captured indicated the intensity and sophistication of the operation. The Salah group was a major Iranian-*HizbAllah* terrorist network that has already been replaced.[117] Another indication of increased preparations were the frequent travels to Tehran by Sheikh Hammadi and especially Imad Mughaniyah.[118]

Two senior operatives of Abu Nidal left Lebanon in December 1989 and infiltrated into Western Europe to begin establishing new cells. In addition, new Iranian-controlled "organizations" were being created in Western Europe, such as off-shoots of ASALA, a Kurdish Amal, etc., in order to attract a wider range of the radicalized minority population.[119] Thus, an escalation in the activities of Syrian-Iranian supported terrorism against France, or Western Europe, is anticipated.[120] Indeed, it was a new group of Iranian-supported terrorists that attacked the Iraqi embassy in Paris on September 21, 1988.[121]

A most important component of the expected escalation of terrorist operations in Western Europe is the placement of new high quality commanders. The new field commanders of the Islamist terrorist operations are drawn from a small and highly professional group composed of former junior officers and NCOs of Arab armies, primarily from technical service and elite units. Many of the participating Egyptians, Syrians and Iranians underwent extensive training in the commando and special forces of their countries as well as overseas. Most of the Sunnis are dedicated members of the Muslim Brotherhood or similar radical groups, as well as radicalized Palestinians from Jordan and Lebanon. (The Arab population of the West Bank is considered highly unreliable because of its prolonged exposure to Israeli influence and because of the fear of Mossad — Israeli intelligence service — penetration.)[123]

Several operational characteristics and organizational principles were adopted since 1986 in the wake of the conferences and deliberations and on the basis of the lessons derived from the successes and failures of that year. The directives issued in the summer of 1986 include several innovations. In Europe, a separation would be maintained between centers of planning and propaganda and between operational centers. Currently, Athens is considered the primary political center in Europe because of its proximity to the Middle East. Operational centers are in Paris, London, Rome, Vienna and Madrid. Other objectives of lesser importance include Milan, Amsterdam, Nicosia and Brussels. It was highly recommended that the operatives of one center conduct their terrorist operations in a different country, even if a center already operates there. For example, the Paris center will organize terrorist strikes in England, rather than the London center, in order to reduce the ability of the local security forces to detect and pursue operatives.[124]

The long-term unified support system is based on the European Muslim communities. This population provides a sizable potential terrorist force.[125] For example, a Palestinian captain in the PLO/PLF captured on the *Achille Lauro* told his interrogators that "Within its (Italy's) borders are more than 20,000 Palestinian combatants ready to intervene!"[126] The predominance of a centralized coordinating hand, namely Iran and Syria, is clearly reflected by the fact that all the organizations, irrespective of their professed ideology and abstract objectives, always demand the release of the same prisoners in France or the West.[127] The diversity and size of the Muslim population contributes to the security of the concealed terrorist cells. For example, despite repeated terrorist attacks, it is still difficult to prove that the Shi'ite or Sunni networks are actually involved in terrorism inside France. By 1986, the primary roles of the clubs and mosques were to recruit, collect funds, set up non-operational bases, provide logistical and intelligence support, etc.[128]

Some of the centers perform major tasks. For example, the center of Iranian terrorist activities is in the former West Germany. The "cultural centers" in Hamburg and Cologne are the primary points of refuge, rearming and equipping with false documents for the Iranian terrorist network.[129] In the late 1980s, Vienna was also an important center of Iranian terrorism and the place from which the assassinations of enemies of the regime originated.[130]

The assassinations of "enemies" of the regime by special hit squads was first conducted from then West Germany. For example, Iranian SAVAMA agents assassinated Cpt. Akbar Mohammadi, the former senior pilot of Iran's top leaders, in

Hamburg in mid-January 1987. Mohammadi had defected
with Hashemi-Rafsanjani's plane to Iraq on August 19, 1986,
and from there proceeded to West Germany. He justified his
defection by claiming to be appalled by the wealth and power
accumulated by the elite while Iran was being impoverished.
Two individuals whom he had apparently not known approached
him in the street, engaged him in conversation, and then drew a
7.56mm handgun and fired at him several times from very
close range. They escaped.[131]

The streamlining of the transportation system for both
operatives and weapons significantly expedited the escalation
of terrorist operations in Western Europe. The December 1988
signing of the "action pact" cleared the way for greater cooperation between Ahmad Jibril, Abu Nidal and the *HizbAllah*. A
unified cell already existed in Italy.[132] In mid-1988, Italian
security authorities became aware of the presence of "tens of
HizbAllah members from Lebanon" in Italy.[133]

Larnaca, Cyprus, is the networks' main point of weapons
smuggling into Europe. Weapons are usually taken from
HizbAllah storage sites in the Biqaa and shipped from Sidon to
Larnaca by Syrian-controlled small cargo vessels. From Larnaca,
the cargo takes tortuous routes to avoid detection. For example, weapons loaded for Nigeria are first sent to Hamburg.
Weapons for Europe are first sent to large Persian Gulf ports,
such as Kuwait City and are attached to massive shipments.
Many of the Larnaca-based shipping companies such as Ger-
man-Oriental Co. and DSR Shipping Lines are actually fronts
for Syrian intelligence.

The magnitude of current preparations can be learned from
the late 1989 exposure of the *HizbAllah* smuggling effort in
Spain. Alissar was yet another front transport company aimed
at shielding the trafficking of terrorist material. Personnel are
shipped via two routes: (1) they fly from Larnaca to holding
bases in Eastern Europe from which they are infiltrated to the
West at the appropriate time; (2) they are smuggled by boat
into Turkey where they travel to Gaziantep and get false

documents that enable them to travel by air or rail into Western Europe.[134]

Highly sensitive equipment, weapons, drugs, funds and instructions are smuggled into Western Europe in Syrian diplomatic bags carried on board Syrian Airways on the Damascus-Athens-Frankfurt-Copenhagen route.[135]

For back-up, logistical support and services, the terrorist groups rely on local supporters or criminals in order to limit the number of foreigners involved in the conduct of the operation. Further, the key professional elements of the terrorist operations, such as operation officers, sabotage and communications experts, must be installed in Western Europe, in the general area of their intended operation, for at least a year with a credible and clean, non-diplomatic cover, so that the local security authorities will lose interest in them while the operatives get to know their area of operation. Commanders stay in the background during the strike itself. Perpetrators arrive on the scene at the last moment.[136]

The terrorist leaders who gathered in May 1986 pointed out that a careful study of past terrorist operations in Europe showed that it was impossible to prepare an operation and carry it out without the active support of at least one embassy or other diplomatic institution. The assembled leaders stated that the support of the terrorist armed struggle was the sacred obligation of the Muslim states and that they must volunteer or be made to provide such "diplomatic" services. Currently, the embassies of Syria, Libya and Iran are the most active supporters. In most cases Cuban missions act in an oversight capacity, but are not involved directly in the conduct of specific operations of Islamic and Middle Eastern groups.[137]

The leaders of Islamist terrorism looked for specific arrangements. It is imperative, they decided, that networks be organized from the beginning with fixed arrangements for constant and long-term support by specific states, insuring continuing coordination between the local networks and the diplomatic mission of the supporting state, both on-site in

Western Europe as well as in the support state's capital, where such relations can be securely maintained and orchestrated. In the case of Libya, Syria and Iran, the prospective terrorists would train and coordinate their activities with their supporting diplomats in the home capitals before moving to Western Europe.[138] Even the Fatah Revolutionary Council, which is an almost autonomous organization as far as its ability to operate, still insists on cooperating with state security services in Europe.[139]

Both Tehran and the Islamist terrorists it controls accepted the fact that securing the active support of states such as Syria justified the sacrifice of cells such as the anti-Assad Muslim Brotherhood. This was apparent when a six-member MB cell was exposed in Paris in late December 1986. Quantities of explosives and machine-pistols were found in the safe apartment as well as some 30 kilograms of explosives.[140] The six terrorists arrested (two Syrians, two Egyptians, one Jordanian and one Syrian-Lebanese living in France) were all small fry.[141]

There are strong indications that they were betrayed by Syria to create the illusion of an anti-terrorist stand by Damascus. Moreover, they were members of the Muslim Brotherhood and might have had ties with the remaining anti-Assad forces inside Syria.[142]

One reason for the suspicion was the fact the Syrian-Lebanese resident of France was apprehended by Syrian police while on a visit to Beirut and, despite his known connections with the anti-Assad Muslim Brotherhood, was permitted to go.[143]

The most important recommendation on security issues was the realization that after 15 years of operational experience in Europe, the terrorist organizations had streamlined their operations and have acquired valuable experience to the point that they are basically invulnerable to conventional surveillance — wiretaps, photography and other kinds of surveillance.[144]

It is evident that it is relatively easy and extremely inexpensive to establish a clandestine network in a West European country. When they have the support of Syria, Libya and Iran, groups such as ASALA, Islamic *Jihad*, the Fatah Revolutionary Council or the Organization for Armed Arab Struggle encounter no particular difficulty in establishing an efficient network overseas. The Middle East states support terrorism in a constant manner and have long-term oversight.

The terrorist groups proved extremely stable, some having been active for 15 years despite attempts to penetrate and break them.[145] However, there is no sure protection against well placed human sources, no defense against good spies. The most professional networks are those which are compartmentalized, organized into isolated cells so that no one has the entire picture. No one is then capable of identifying senior commanders, etc. Their presence should always be taken into account when establishing an operational net overseas.[146]

By the late 1980s, the terrorist masters were convinced that they had already completed the consolidation of a comprehensive terrorist infrastructure throughout Europe. The Muslim communities were thoroughly penetrated and subverted by the Islamists. A growing flow of emigres, especially from the *Maghrib*, insured the continued arrival of those immersed in the prevailing Islamist trends and of highly trained individuals.

The Islamist terrorist system was gearing up for the unleashing of a new wave of actions in Europe when the entire European Muslim community was subjected to two major crises that would transform its character for years to come: the Gulf War and the war in Bosnia-Herzegovina. An already traumatized community faced a profound crisis of identity because of these world events.

REJUVENATING THE *JIHAD* IN EUROPE

Islamist terrorism is returning to Western Europe with a vengeance. There has been a tremendous escalation of the

Islamist struggle against the West in Europe in the wake of the Gulf Crisis. It is being built on the frustration and agitation of the emigre communities. Large segments of these communities all over Western Europe "openly express the ambitious program of radical Islamists engaged in total war against the West."[147]

The impact of the Gulf Crisis only exacerbates and reinforces existing tensions and frustrations. On the eve of Iraq's invasion of Kuwait, Michel Debré, the former prime minister of France, pointed out that "Islam is today the number one enemy of Europe, and primarily of France." He further warned that "the hypothesis that the entire *Maghrib* will serve as a theater for a *Jihad* has become a credible hypothesis. The Islamic movement," Debre concluded, "constitutes a danger for France."[148]

The greatest potential threat is an outcome of the transformation of the Muslim emigre communities in Western Europe. Even without outside agitation, the rise of Islamic communities is a major threat to stability in Europe for the next decade. In Western Europe, Muslim communities will constitute 25% of the population by 2000. At present, Muslims constitute 7-9% of the population in England and 8-10% in France. Moreover, the Muslim emigre community, and especially the younger, European-born, generation is rapidly becoming militant Islamist. Since the mid-1980s, Iran and the *HizbAllah* have successfully conducted a massive recruitment drive among these locally-born Muslim youth. Many have received advanced terrorist training in Iran. It is a formidable threat because, by a cautious estimate, about 3%-6% of the over eight million Muslim emigres in Western Europe are actively involved in Islamist activities that border on, or are outright, subversive.[149] This means around 250,000-500,000 potential terrorists and their supporters.

The extent of the Islamist threat to Western Europe is clearly reflected in Bonn's official estimate of the growing threat of terrorism in Germany as described by Wertebach, president of the Federal Office for the Protection of the Constitution. In the spring of 1992, there were five million foreigners living in Germany, and 43,000 of them were known to be members of "extremist groups." Of these, 23,000 were considered to be "prepared for violence" but, Wertebach acknowledged, this number "could also be higher."

Most threatening were the refugees from regions already engulfed in conflict: 70,000 Tamils and Sikhs, 30,000 Afghans, 85,000 Iranians, and 70,000 Palestinians. Of the 1,700,000 Turks, 300,000 are Kurds. There were 650,000 "Yugoslavs" from all factions, and "almost two million adherents of Islam ranging from Indonesia in the Far East to Morocco in North Africa." Some 3,500 Kurds were known members of the PKK and other "extremist groups."

Ultimately, Wertebach is most worried about "state terrorist activities, above all on part of Iran."

"The Iranian intelligence service has always persecuted the opposition without mercy," Wertebach explains. In these operations the Iranians are supported by a growing Islamist population in Germany. "There is a considerable rush to Islamic fundamentalists, such as the *HizbAllah*," among the local emigre communities.[150]

Indeed, the Islamists in Western Europe have fundamental and uncompromising differences with the society in which they live. The Islamists consider democracy "the worst scourge the West inflicted on Muslim society in order to destroy it from the inside and annihilate its ancestral values," and are therefore determined to strike it at the core. For example, Salah Tamimi, a Tunisian-born activist is a student in Paris. "I am here in France to learn from the inside out the system of the West that oppresses us, to learn its science, techniques and tricks. I will then be better equipped to fight it," he concluded. "Even by violence."[151]

The religious freedoms in the West are a source of trouble. Islam is a communal way of life and the vast majority of emigrants and their European-born children live together isolated from, and hostile to, the society around them. The separation of Church and State contradicts and conflicts with the tenets of Islam, hence is a constant source of tension. The Muslim communities demand to be allowed to retain all aspects of Islam, including laws and *Urf* (a traditional Arabian law that has been absorbed into the Islamic order and legal system), some of which may be unacceptable in the West. They also seek the imposition of Islamic law, seeing it as superior to the civil law of the land that is secular, liberal, and based Judeo-Christian values. For believers, the mere acceptance of Western law means a contradiction of Islam's tenet that the *Sharia* is the world's supreme law.[152]

In early 1992, Mohand Khellil, a jurist and sociologist living in Paris, observed that despite the seeming integration into French society of the younger second generation of Muslim emigrants, "on every side there seems to be genuine agreement that the *Maghrib* immigrants are inassimilable." Furthermore, the economic situation in Europe and the oppression in North Africa ensure that they will not return home. Consequently, the Muslim communities of Western Europe are drawn together against an all-encompassing external threat: the society in which they live. The flow of largely Islamist emigrants from Algeria and Tunisia only helps swell a militant community already resistant to integration. Thus, the growing tension between Muslim communities and the liberal society will inevitably result in an Islamist outburst and even armed rebellion.[153]

Although there has been a decline in the intensity of terrorist operations since the late 1980s, the Muslim population of Europe has moved rapidly in the direction predicted by the Iranians. Feeling oppressed and rejected by the West European mainstream, the agitated communities of Muslim emigres provide ideal pools for the recruitment of terrorists and larger support networks.

The militant agitation of Algeria's FIS has proven exportable to the huge Algerian community in France. Many local imams openly identify the need to establish FIS as dominant in the Algerian diaspora. In Paris, the Islamist imams want the FIS's assistance in gaining control over the Grand Mosque. A major FIS branch was opened in Stockholm with assistance from the Libyan embassy. Unofficial cells have been opened in Algerian communities all over Western Europe[154] by emissaries sent from Algeria to propagate a return to Islam and Islamic solidarity.[155] Indeed, the huge victory of the FIS in the elections in Algeria had a major impact on the expatriate community in France. The results gave a boost to the young Islamists in their quest for dominance in the community.

A young student explained that the FIS victory heralds "the emergence of a generation that rejects a materialistic philosophy and believes that the Prophet's principles are worth as much or more than the Napoleonic Code or France's secularist laws."[156]

All this time, the Iranians have encouraged their proteges to expand autonomous networks among ethnically cohesive emigre communities. For example, in the late 1980s, the PKK was able to consolidate a network in 26 cities in Western Europe, including Berlin, Munich, Bonn, Duisburg, Hanover, Onisburg, Frankfurt, Stuttgart, Hamburg, Paris, Vienna, Stockholm and Brussels. Activities are coordinated via a center in Cologne.[157]

Tehran's analysis of the Muslim population in Europe was outlined by Annis Naccache. Many Muslims in Europe "believe that they are following the line of the Imam." These Muslims are divided into two movements, passive and active. Passive are "Islamic movements that serve as blocking agents to fight Western invasion" by defending the hub of the Muslim world from the spread of Western influence. Active are "Islamic movements that fight, inspired by the Islamic truth and Muhammadan Islam to carry a message for the whole humanity." Theirs "is the authentic Islamic struggle that recognizes the depth and essence of Islam. . . Ultimately, the goal of these movements is to bring salvation to all the oppressed in the world."[158]

Naccache explained that the Islamic struggle in Europe required the development of a new dedicated force. Because Europe's Muslims are constantly exposed to the Western way of life, Tehran "must learn from them how to combat Western thought... We can learn a great deal from the Muslims of Europe. For this reason, the West is afraid of them."

The Muslim world does not stand a chance in a frontal confrontation with the West. Therefore, unconventional methods of struggle must be developed whereby the West "is faced with Muslims who are closer to it than other Muslims."[159] Naqqash emphasized that "the West is afraid of the collective movement of the Muslims" for a good reason. [160]

In the spring of 1990, Europe's Islamists were gearing up for a marked escalation of the struggle against the West. A major conference was convened in Halluin, on the Franco-Belgian border, on May 20, 1990, in order to coordinate a common strategy for the Islamist struggle. The facilities, including a large basement crossing the border, were rented by Muhammad al-Fayadh, a Libyan intelligence official. London-based Salah Karkar, formerly of the Tunisian MTI and a veteran of the 1987 bombings against tourist facilities, was the conference chairman.

Delegations arrived from virtually all West European countries. There were also members of Moroccan, Tunisian, Egyptian, Syrian and Pakistani Islamist revolutionary organizations, as well as Libyan representatives. The conference decided on guidelines for the anti-West *Jihad*, ranging from agitating and re-Islamizing the local emigre communities to creating a "tight network of militant cells from north to south in Europe." In his speech, Karkar emphasized that only "armed action can get things moving" in the West.[161]

Thus, as the crisis in the Persian Gulf rapidly escalated later in the summer of 1990, it was anticipated that the agitated and radicalized Islamist elements of the Muslim community would rally to the cause of Saddam Hussein and embark on a terrorism campaign. Indeed, even before the invasion of Kuwait,

Baghdad had begun consolidating its terrorist capabilities in Europe with an eye to exploiting the Islamists. As described in detail in Chapter 3, the Iraqis prepared thoroughly and professionally for the conduct of this campaign. By early January 1991, Iraq believed it had completed a major terrorist infrastructure under the direct control of Baghdad in order to conduct terrorist operations in Western Europe and the United States.

A former Iraqi intelligence officer, Hussein Ali Humaydah, disclosed that for terrorist operations Baghdad recruited Iraqis and other Arabs who had lived for many years overseas and were thus familiar with living conditions there. They were trained in the Hita camp for specific terrorist missions. In addition, Iraq recruited former members of East European intelligence services to assist in preparing terrorist operations.[162]

Another direct outcome of the Gulf Crisis was the return of *al-Fatah* to active terrorism. Immediately after the invasion of Kuwait, Arafat's "striking units" in Western Europe were put on alert to attack U.S. and Israeli objectives.[163] Soon afterward, the PLO was ready to undertake "terrorist operations" in Western Europe, as well as "assassinations and bombings of civil and military targets and buildings that included well known companies and embassies, along with government facilities which the PLO had previously undertaken."[164] Several Abu Nidal terrorist assassination teams were also dispatched to Europe with Saudi diplomats as their main targets.[165] The Iraqis provided coherent terrorist priorities in Western Europe: "first Israeli targets, then Anglo-Saxon ones, and finally French ones."[166]

Egyptian intelligence warned that "Iraqi and Palestinian agents in Great Britain, the Federal Republic [of Germany], France and Italy are waiting for orders from Baghdad to carry out terrorist attacks."[167] The only thing holding these terrorists back from striking was Saddam Hussein, who ordered Arafat to keep his assets underground for the time being.[168] Indeed, a PLO official in the al-Baq'ah refugee camp in Jordan declared:

"We will expend all our efforts to challenge the Americans and British. With all that we know and possess, we will strike them. If they characterize our strikes as being 'terrorism,' so be it. We will not forsake Saddam Hussein because he represents for us at the present time the hope which America and Israel seek to abrogate."[169]

Western Europe appeared to be the main target of Iraqi terrorists. The different groups allied with Baghdad — Palestinians, Muslims, Islamists, Europeans — had their logistical and support systems in place, including arms caches and bankers. The continent was saturated with a web of sleeper networks for all organizations that were now well consolidated. Many of their members were already citizens of, and established in, their intended countries of operation. They were well organized to take care of such operational aspects as safe housing, car rentals, mail arrangements, access to weapons stockpiles, intelligence work, rear guard bases, etc.[170]

In Europe, at least, the Gulf Crisis brought many terrorist organizations that had been rivals into some form of cooperation against a common enemy. Consequently, networks were constantly evolving and the "secret alliances" expanded and consolidated. The Iraqi terrorist system was being built around well established, redundant, and secure hubs. However, the best organized and most capable Palestinian terrorist networks in Europe — these of the PFLP and the PFLP-GC — owed their primary allegiance to Syria and Iran.[171]

For example, the PFLP's West European network consisted of 50-60 expert terrorists, many of them with some 20 names and documents in several countries. This severely complicated the work of security services. In addition, the network controlled a vastly larger number of local supporters and sympathizers.[172] Both the PFLP and the FRC had excellent "sleeper" networks in Sweden and Scandinavia as a whole. Belgium, and especially Brussels, was also a center of terrorist activities, especially by PLF and PFLP-GC networks.[173] The weapons and explosives stockpiles in the Iraqi embassies would serve for the backup and resupply of the terrorist networks.[174]

The terrorist infrastructure in West Germany in the fall of 1990 reflected its central role in the Iraqi-PLO designs. Iraqi intelligence conducted thorough surveys of potential targets and provided the terrorists with plans. The Iraqis also "established specific networks, which could be used for attacks or support," with members drawn mainly from the FRC, ALF, and PFLP-GC. Meanwhile, these Palestinian terrorists already had caches of weapons and explosives in place.

Most active and organized was the PFLP, having a 20-30 terrorist strong network ready to strike. Moreover, *al-Fatah* had some 1,700 supporters in West Germany, but it was not clear how many of them were active terrorists.[175] The PFLP-GC had an excellent dormant network of 30 expert terrorists in place in former West Germany, with several clandestine support installations, including caches, in former East Germany.[176] Not to be left behind, Islamic *Jihad* of Sheikh Tamimi announced that it targeted the Frankfurt airport because of a shipment of Patriot missiles to Israel.[177]

The West German networks were very reliable because of the back-up and support provided from East Germany. Immediately after the outbreak of the Gulf Crisis, intense activities began in the Iraqi Embassy in East Berlin in preparation for the launching of terrorist operations in the West. In early September, 34 intelligence operatives registered as "technicians" arrived at the embassy. By then, large quantities of weapons and ammunition were already stored there.[178] The cultural attache, Haitam al-Ami, was the senior intelligence officer in charge of terrorist preparations and coordination with the Libyan *Amm al-Jamahiriyah* in Europe.[179]

By the time fighting broke out in the Gulf, there were about 50 Iraqi "experts" equipped with vast stockpiles of explosives and weapons in East Berlin. Moreover, they could count on, and indeed enjoyed, active assistance from former Stasi experts involved in terrorist training and support for many years.[180] There were other attempts to exploit past relations in Eastern

Europe. Several terrorists penetrated Western Europe via Czechoslovakia.[181]

Meanwhile, a sleeper network of Abu-Nidal was exposed in Portugal[182] as additional FRC hit teams were arriving from Spain.[183] In January 1991, two additional teams of Abu Nidal arrived in Spain and Portugal from the *Maghrib*, living off a large support system. Their objectives were bases used by the U.S. and the Gulf allies.[184]

Baghdad also activated dormant networks in Spain that had been originally organized by Carlos. These networks had two missions: to attack objectives in Spain and to use Spanish territory for transit to other European countries.[185] Several assassination and sabotage teams, equipped with handguns with silencers and filed off serial numbers as well as high explosives, hid in the Spanish embassy in Madrid, anticipating orders from Baghdad.[186]

Throughout the Gulf Crisis, the terrorist network in Europe remained controlled from the Middle East. Irrespective of Barazan al-Takriti's designs, Beirut was still the forward control point. Thus, despite its impressive capabilities, the *HizbAllah* remained "very discreet", although its activist commanders were in support of Mohtashemi's call for "holy alliance" with Iraq against the "American Satan." But they waited patiently for orders from Tehran. Similarly in Jordan, Islamic *Jihad* for the Liberation of Palestine under Sheikh Asa'ad Bayud al-Tamimi was spearheading the Sunni Islamist contribution to the Iraqi terrorist effort by "laundering" Iraqi intelligence, PLF, May 15, and even PFLP-GC teams on their way overseas, and activating his vast network in the *Maghrib*, Egypt and Yemen.[187]

However, as detailed in Chapter 3, when Saddam Hussein finally issued his call to launch a terrorist campaign, Iran and Syria elected to keep their terrorist networks from acting, paralyzing the Iraqi terrorist campaign.

BUDS OF THE FUTURE

The Iraqi strategic terrorist campaign was attempted only in London, and this solely because of Qaddafi's own commitment to the IRA and hatred of the British Government.

Libya has been a persistent long-term supporter of the Irish Republican Army.[188] London considers Qaddafi to be the "most dangerous" IRA supporter, having "supplied them with tons of sophisticated weapons and large quantities of SEMTEX explosive," as well as "ample funds" and other forms of assistance.[189] In the late 1980s, top IRA terrorists trained in Libya and were then clandestinely returned to Western Europe.[190] About this time, Libya provided the IRA with several SEMTEX caches and a bomb factory in London.[191]

Little wonder, therefore, that this relationship was utilized during the Gulf Crisis. London was the only place in Europe where strategic terrorism was attempted. It almost succeeded. In the fall of 1990, with Libya's support, Iraq signed an agreement with the IRA "with a view to coordinating their terrorist activities and operations against British targets."[192] This agreement was aimed entirely at satisfying Qaddafi's desire for revenge, using Saddam Hussein as a means of deflecting Western reaction. The extent of Qaddafi's cynical manipulation of Saddam Hussein can be learned from a simultaneous incident in Amman, when security personnel of Libyan Airways identified and captured an Iraqi terrorist carrying a suitcase bomb to be detonated on an American or West European aircraft. With Iran and its allies determined to paralyze Baghdad's terrorist campaign, the Libyans detained the terrorist, neutralized the bomb, and notified France.[193]

The Qaddafi-IRA deal was consummated on February 7, 1991, in the daring attack on 10 Downing Street during a meeting of the war cabinet. Three rockets were fired from a Ford Transit parked on Whitehall near the Ministry of Defense. They hit 10 Downing Street while the meeting was in session. There were no injuries, the rockets hitting some 40 feet from the building. Another bomb inside London's subway burned rather than exploded, which minimized the damage. It was a classic IRA operation based on good intelligence concerning the time of the war cabinet meeting and the ability to have both a timer and a remote control capacity for the firing mechanism. Unpredictable winds and a snow storm that affected air density were the probable reasons for the rockets missing their target.

The IRA claimed the bombing on account of "British involvement in the Gulf War."[194]

The IRA struck again on February 18, this time planting two bombs, one each in Paddington Station and Victoria Station, causing one fatality and injuring over 40. Traffic was paralyzed. Heathrow airport was also evacuated while another bomb was neutralized safely.[195]

Mu'ammar Qaddafi considers the support Libya provides to the various European terrorist movements such as the IRA, the ETA, or Yugoslavia's Muslims to be vital elements of the defense of the very existence of Libya in the forthcoming and inevitable clash with the U.S.-led Western world. Qaddafi anticipates a clash with an over-confident America that shamed Islam in the Persian Gulf. "Who would have believed that Mecca would become a protectorate, under American protection!" he declared. He believes that the only way to defend Libya against the U.S. onslaught is by a preemptive counterattack against Europe. "This is essential. The Americans attacked us with their aircraft and missiles. These were devastating and far away, and you could watch them. But the bases which the aircraft and missiles took off from were in Europe. Hence Europe must be attacked. How often have I said this? If we are capable of attacking Europe, then we must do so so, that it will refuse to have its lands used for aggression against Libya."[196]

International terrorism is the only credible instrument in the Libyan arsenal. Widespread use of terrorism against both a civilian population and military bases would be damaging.

However, growing world pressure and sanctions on the basis of Libya's support for the destruction of Pan Am Flight 103 compelled Tripoli to pretend to renounce terrorism to the point of providing London with information on the IRA. Ultimately, this information fell short of expectations.[197] Too, Qaddafi proved incapable of providing the IRA with the weapons, explosives, and funds required for sustaining their terrorist campaign against the United Kingdom.

Consequently, in the spring of 1992 the IRA shifted its affiliation to the terrorist system sponsored by Iran and Syria. This shift is apparent from documents and equipment seized in London in early August 1992 which showed "a move away from the use of the much more compact SEMTEX high explosive to the more cumbersome, but more easily smuggled, home-made version based on ordinary fertilizer." Indeed, three vans with some 13-15 tons of such explosives and various wires, electronic detonators, etc., to be used in the training of IRA bomb makers were captured in London.[198]

These new techniques and overall approach to sabotage are identical to the Iranian approach. Bombs utilizing the new technology were used in London as of early October 1992.[199] The IRA's shift in early 1993 to bombing major economic infrastructure such as the gas storage facilities in Warington is also an expression of the alignment with the terrorist strategy long advocated by Iran, Syria and their allies.

Even though there was little or no Islamist terrorism in Western Europe, the European Muslim emigre community was directly and adversely affected by the Gulf Crisis.

In the fall of 1990 there was rising hostility and frustration among the Muslims in France because of sharp cuts in the financial support for their Muslim institutions by Saudi Arabia and Kuwait. Because most of the funds had gone primarily to extremist and fundamentalist organizations, the French government had repeatedly pressured Riyadh and Kuwait to stop the funding. Now that they needed France's help, both governments agreed. As a result, Iran was able to capitalize and redirect the prevailing rage against both the Gulf States and Paris.[200]

Another indication of the growing power of the Islamists is the internationalization of *HAMAS*. In the spring of 1991, *HAMAS* was emerging as part of an international global organization based in Jordan with active cells overseas, including Western Europe (especially Germany and the United Kingdom) and the United States. "*HAMAS* has become an international organization," stated Imad al-Faluji, a *HAMAS* commander.[201]

There was a marked expansion of international activities of the Muslim Brotherhood after the Gulf War. Under the dynamic leadership of Hassan al-Turabi, the Muslim Brotherhood significantly expanded its international operations, aiming at the establishment of "a universal framework for the Islamic movement" based on an alliance of several *Ikhwan* organizations.[202]

The agitation among the North African communities in France increased in the wake of the Gulf War. Conservative Arabs were worried about the internal dynamics in the community. "France's largest Arab community, the North African community, is worried about its future after the outbreak of the war that Saddam Hussein caused by his invasion of Kuwait, and following his speeches for [Arab/internal] consumption in which he portrays the war as a holy war against the West. . . Members of the North African community fear that the war will increase the wave of hatred against them. Saddam Hussein's speeches, rebroadcast by the French media, focusing on his call for Muslims everywhere to fight a holy war, have caused the French to view the Arab community in France as terrorist and fanatics."[203]

Many emigres felt a communal shame at the extent of the Iraqi defeat and saw it as a prelude to a confrontation between the Muslim world and the West.

"The West has always declared war on us, and one has but to see with what cruelty our sister nation of Iraq was humiliated in order to realize the hatred that the West harbors for us Muslims. In Iraq, they bombed and slaughtered innocent people. Here in France and everywhere in Europe, we are reduced to slavery. Our daughters turn to prostitution; our sons are destroyed by drugs. We live in undignified conditions. That is why we are doing everything to fight the corruption and vice invading Muslim communities, here and elsewhere," explained Ali Hammoudi, an Algerian-born computer operator.[204]

Another Algerian emigre compared the process of communal humiliation and building rage to that which occurred after the Arab defeat by Israel in the Six-Day War in 1967: "I feel they [Frenchmen] are apprehensive for fear of me. I feel their anger against Saddam Hussein vented on me. Weren't the damage and humiliation we suffered from the 1967 setback enough? Why does Saddam have to make us drink the bitterness of another setback?"[205]

Indeed, as was the case in the late 1960s and early 1970s, it was after the magnitude of the defeat sank in, and because of the communal humiliation felt because of it, that the rage and frustration were transformed into a burning desire for revenge, most often expressed in the form of terrorism. Kalim Siddiqui, the founder of the Muslim Institute of London, sees in the post-Crisis shock a catalyst for a revived struggle for Islam.

"After sleeping for centuries, Islam is once again on the march. In the decades ahead, the Islamic revolution, like an irreversible torrent, will carry away and finally free peoples from colonial oppression." He is convinced that the West will adopt Islam in the wake of this process. Therefore, Siddiqui calls for "Muslim young people in all European countries to organize in order to participate in a formidable period of revolutionary change: renewal of the Islamic world."[206] Little wonder that German security authorities believe that they "will have to face the main danger after the end of the Gulf War. Then, many will certainly try to satisfy their thirst for revenge."[207]

Iran, biding its time, prepared to strike. Since the late

1980s, the Sunni Islamist support system had been organized, and networks had been established, under the guise of the International Islamic Student Federation. The establishment of this network of ostensibly "religious student movements," now reaching into Asia, Africa and Europe, had been a high priority of Turabi, and was personally handled by Mustafa Uthman Ismail.[208]

In early 1991, there was a surge in activity in the Sunni Islamist clandestine organizations, all offshoots of the Muslim Brotherhood, in Western Europe. At present, some 47 West European Sunni organizations are organized under the umbrella of the Islamic Liberation Party (*Hizb al-Takhrir al-Islami* or PLI) with headquarters near Hamburg. A PLI delegation from France visited Baghdad on January 12-14, 1991, for a terrorist conference. The PLI declared that it is committed to "use legitimate violence to destroy the enemies of Islam."

However, the PLI has Shi'ite roots, and it gravitated to the pro-Iran infrastructure. Sheikh Zallum is the titular head of PLI. The real commander of clandestine activities, especially in France and Germany, is a Palestinian named Ali Rushdi (a.k.a. Husni Nubail, Salah Turjman, "the guide with 12 identities") who has been an activist since the late 1980s after several years during which he was associated with several *Ikhwan* who were among the founders of the PLO. There are some 200 activists in France alone, all of whom are well armed. Each key activist has several passports issued in different names. The Islamists infiltrated the consular offices in Europe, especially Paris, and used them to get documentation.[209]

The PLI revival as a terrorist organization comes atop the terrorist infrastructure controlled by Syria and Iran, and serves the organizations they sponsor. This infrastructure for terrorist attacks in Europe survived the Gulf Crisis virtually intact. The Islamist and radical organizations associated with Iran and Syria thus have a vibrant system of activists and supporters that constitutes a ready base for operations. They also have large caches of weapons and explosives safely hidden all over Europe. There are booby-trapped cars stored away in several cities. A solid redundant command and control system that tightly belongs to the sponsoring states, mainly Iran, supervises these preparations. The overt control system is exercised through diplomatic channels. The covert system is exercised through student and cultural associations used by intelligence agents and operatives.

In the wake of the Gulf Crisis, the residues of the Abu-Nidal, 15 May Organization, and other pro-Iraqi networks gravitated to Ahmad Jibril for help and thus fell under Syrian-Iranian control. These networks can be used for deniable operations without involving Syria directly.[210]

Simultaneously, Iran and the *HizbAllah* markedly increased their direct involvement in, and support for, Islamist radicals and terrorists in Western Europe. In early 1991, they were promised active support from the *HizbAllah*'s Sheikh Hussein al-Mussawi during a visit to Lebanon. In a meeting with French visitors, Mussawi expressed his views on the future of France.

"You French," he told them, "may not come to know the Islamic Republic of France during your generation, but your sons and grandsons will definitely know it, *InshAllah*! For Islam is good for everyone!"

Abbas al-Mussawi emphasized that recent developments in the Middle East constituted a major factor for the escalation of such a struggle:

> By destroying Iraq and Saddam [Hussein], the West thought it would annihilate any remnant of an Islamic renaissance here and in Europe, but you will soon be singing a different tune. Everywhere, in French, German, English, and Belgian cities, soldiers of God, sincere activists, are waiting their hour of revenge in order to move into action. It will not be Saddam who will avenge us. He is an atheist who issued his appeals for a holy war only as a ruse and in order to save his regime. But let the word of

Allah resound everywhere in Europe, which has
long humiliated us and held us under its yoke.[211]

By then, Sheikh Abbas al-Mussawi's role in Iran's emerging grand design was that of a trusted emissary and coordinator who would ensure that the *HizbAllah* was ready on time to perform the allotted tasks.

The original mission-roles for the *HizbAllah* were defined in the terrorist conference in Tehran in mid-October 1991. Soon after the conference, Mussawi returned to Beirut with instructions from Tehran to activate the *HizbAllah*'s Special Operations and Security Command responsible for such activities as aircraft hijackings and bombings, as well as overseas sabotage and kidnappings. In the first phase, they were told to concentrate on launching operations in Europe.[212] Toward this end, the Command planted cells in Western Europe and prepared to launch terrorist attacks.[213]

In mid-November it became imperative to accelerate preparations. The bulk of *HizbAllah*'s Special Operations and Security Command, some 20-30 terrorists, was transferred to Iran where they were provided with new identities and documents pending activation.[214] Imad Mughaniyah is in charge of special operations such as aircraft hijackings and bombings, overseas sabotage and kidnappings. He is assisted by Abd al-Hadi Hammadi and Mustafa Badr-ad-Din, Mughaniyah's brother-in-law who had been in command of the Kuwait 17 and was released from a Kuwaiti jail in August 1990.[215]

A main objective of these *HizbAllah* cells, on the basis of the October Tehran conference and specific statements in early December, was to hit the flow of Soviet Jews to Israel by striking transit points in Europe where they are relatively vulnerable.[216] Indeed, a car bomb exploded near a bus carrying Soviet Jews in Budapest, Hungary, on December 23. The bomb was the work of "professional terrorists" and closely resembled bomb techniques characteristic of the *HizbAllah*.[217] On May 7, 1992, police in Bucharest discovered a car bomb a car bomb consisting of six kilograms of high explosives, 2,000 metal balls, and a remote control device, all hidden in a rental car. Evidence suggests that it was a *HizbAllah* operation of the type aimed at Jewish migration.[218]

In the fall of 1991, the *HizbAllah*'s Special Operations and Security Command planned to concentrate on Spain and Germany in the first phase of their operations in Western Europe. Germany is Hammadi's personal obsession because of his brothers' continued incarceration there.[219] Indeed, a detachment of *HizbAllah* commandos comprised of Hammadi loyalists entered Germany in late December or early January in order to launch terrorist strikes aimed at pressuring Bonn to release the Hammadi brothers,[220] though the *HizbAllah* denied sending a terrorist group to Germany.[221] Moreover, there were indications that Fatah Revolutionary Council terrorists "will strike at U.S. and generally Western targets in European countries" in the near future.[222]

In the summer of 1992, Tehran and Khartoum decided that special emphasis in the Islamist international movement should be put on funding and supporting al-*Jihad* groups in Western Europe and the U.S. The center for European operations is in London.[223] Egypt's Interior Minister, Maj. Gen. Muhammad Abd-al-Halim Mussa, explained that "the terrorist organization is an international organization which has its own formations and guidance offices on Egyptian and regional levels, as well as on the world level. This organization has branches in Egypt, Sudan, Tunisia, Algeria, and other places. It also has offices in Germany, Austria, England, and others."[224]

In the winter of 1991-92, the first expert terrorists of "The Islamic Tide Brigade in Europe" began arriving at their destinations. In addition to being well trained in clandestine and terrorist operations, they were specially prepared for sustained operations and the living conditions of modern Western society. Their appearance and living styles were to be totally Westernized in order to avoid attracting the attention of the local security forces.[225]

They are expert terrorists. In the fall of 1992, the graduates of the Islamist training camps in Sudan were capable of conducting sophisticated operations in the most demanding environments, both as individuals and as cadres for the export of the Islamic Revolution. In these target countries, AIM supports and sponsors "military militias to create disturbances and spread violence. It concentrates on the armed forces to benefit from their expertise in the use of arms and the ability to carry out acts of violence and assassination. Its members are also good at using secret codes, *noms de guerre* and all kinds of illegal acts, such as the expropriatation of Christian assets, theft, armed robbery, assassination, forgery of official documents, and the use of immoral methods in the implementation of tactics such as deception, lies, and misguidance."[226]

Moreover, the terrorists' operational style would further reduce the likelihood of their discovery by the Western governments.

A defector from the Egyptian *al-Jihad* Organization described how its leadership "decided to set up 'death squads' comprised of individuals able to carry out operations, 'disappear' and guarantee secrecy. These individuals would ostensibly distance themselves from the group, leading a normal daily life so that they would not cause any security trouble."

Many of the Islamic Group operatives and members trained for these missions live overseas. They arrive at the objective country to carry out an operation and return immediately to their country of origin.[227] This *modus operandi* is a direct derivative of the operational principles developed for the terrorist networks of Iran and Syria in the summer of 1986 at the Switzerland conference attended by, among others, Yussuf Nadah, then the leader of the International Muslim Brotherhood, and Sheikh Umar Abd-al-Rahman. Rahman is the Egyptian cleric who came to the United States illegally and preached radical sermons at the mosque attended by Muslims implicated in the bombing of the World Trade Center.[228]

In the summer of 1992, Tehran and Khartoum dramatically

expanded the senior control and support system for their terrorist networks that operate under diplomatic cover. This process started in late 1991, when al-Turabi took over Sudan's selection of candidates for key diplomatic positions, including ambassador posts in key Arab and European capitals.[229] By the summer of 1992, Turabi had selected loyalists who would further the cause of the Islamic Revolution.[230] These Sudanese diplomats join a comparable solid Iranian intelligence and terrorist support network comprising of the country's most senior diplomats. In effect, Khartoum adopted and is implementing the Iranian model. This perception of foreign relations and the role of embassies was developed by Javad Mansuri while a Deputy Foreign Minister.[231]

Beginning in early 1992, the Islamists' commitment to a *Jihad* against the West came to be tested in Bosnia-Herzegovina, in what was formerly Yugoslavia. A forward support and coordination center was established in the fall of 1991 in Bulgaria.[232] In early 1992, forces of the Armed Islamic Movement (AIM) assumed an expanded role in the defense of Sarajevo, and in offensive and special operations throughout Bosnia-Herzegovina. Most active are the Islamic *Jihad* forces, the elite component of the Movement's "international legion", led by 'Afghans'.[233] Tehran urged and actively supported the establishment of "volunteer forces from all over the Muslim world who would rush to help their brothers in faith in the Balkans."[234]

In Bosnia-Herzegovina, the AIM forces are organized, very disciplined, and well equipped. Their commander is Mahmud Abd-ul-Aziz, a veteran of six years of fighting in Afghanistan under Ahmad Shah Massud and other combat for "the sacred cause" in the Philippines and Kashmir, who also participated in clandestine operations in Africa for Turabi.

The "Muslim Forces" include several hundred volunteers, primarily from Iran, Algeria, Egypt, Sudan, Persian Gulf Arab states, Pakistan, Afghanistan, Syria, and Turkey. Most of them are veteran 'Afghans', most fought with the forces of

Jami'at-i-Islami and especially Ahmad Shah Massud of the Panjshir Valley in Afghanistan. As of the fall of 1992, there were 200-300 volunteer *mujahideen* in the Travnik area; 200 in the center of Bosnia; an undetermined number (in the hundreds) in Sarajevo and in eastern Bosnia-Herzegovina. They fight the Serbs and train the Bosnian forces. They also teach children the Koran and fundamentalist Islamic ways. The volunteers also train local Muslims in special operations. Meanwhile, the flow of volunteers, including Muslims from the United Kingdom, some of whom are 'Afghan' veterans, continues.[235] By early 1993, there were over 1,000 *mujahideen* from Pakistan, Iran, Sudan and Libya.[236]

In addition, Iran maintains a core of highly professional operatives, mainly Iranians from the *Pasdaran* and Lebanese from the *HizbAllah*, who provide expert training and assistance and conduct the most sensitive covert operations (intelligence and terrorism).[237] Tehran continues to provide Sarajevo with weapons and experts.[238] In early November 1992, more than 50 expert terrorists and instructors of the *HizbAllah* and the *Tawhid* (its Sunni counterpart under Sheikh Sha'ban[239]) were sent from Baalbak to Bosnia-Herzegovina to train local cadres and launch operations on their own.[240] These trainers spearhead an ongoing Iranian effort to deploy a 2,000-strong brigade of its *Al-Quds* Forces.[241] All these forces receive substantial Iranian military assistance.[242]

Indeed, since the summer of 1992, there has been a marked escalation in provocations by the Muslim forces, the goal of which is to secure military intervention by the West against the Serbs (and, to a lesser extent, the Croats). Initially, these provocations were mainly senseless attacks on their own Muslim population. The UN concluded that a special group of Bosnian Muslim forces, many of whom had served with Islamist terrorist organizations, committed a series of atrocities, including "some of the worst recent killings," against Muslim civilians in Sarajevo "as a propaganda ploy to win world sympathy and military intervention."[243] These escalated into premeditated attacks and atrocities committed against Serbian civilians trying to flee contested areas.[244] It is noteworthy that these Bosnian detachments are following exactly the principles of "the war of the weak" as outlined by the *HizbAllah*'s Ayatollah Fadlallah.

As early as in mid-August, Russian officers with the UN were apprehensive about an escalation in attacks by Muslim forces on the UN. "The greatest danger could constitute Muslim and Croat armed formations that would attempt to bloc the humanitarian corridor [from Split to Sarajevo], and in this way, provoke a large scale use of force . . . against its enemies, the Serbs," observed Maj. Mikhail Zheglov of the Russian Armed Forces assigned to the UN peacekeeping forces.[245] It would not take long for his fears to be realized in a series of attacks on the UN by Muslim forces.

The first major attack was the shooting down of an Italian G.222 transport aircraft on September 3, 1992, as it approached Sarajevo. The crash investigation concluded that Muslim forces shot down the Italian transport with two sophisticated shoulder-fired SAMs.[246] Then came the ambush of the UN relief convoy on September 8 that was carried out by a small (two- or three-man) detachment of highly trained individuals who expertly set the trap, making excellent use of the terrain and intelligence. Their tactics were virtually identical to the ambush training taught in Iran, Lebanon and Sudan. Indeed, Brig. Gen. Hussein Ali Abdul-Razek, the commander of the UN Peacekeeping Forces in Bosnia-Herzegovina, specifically accused the Bosnian Muslim forces of responsibility for the September 8 ambush.[247]

In late December 1992, Bosnian Muslim forces tried to kill the two senior UN generals in Sarajevo. Maj. Gen. Phillipe Morillon described the mortar shelling on his headquarters as a "deliberate attack" aimed at killing him and his deputy. He pointed out that the Bosnians' "firing positions were close enough to a Serbian stronghold so that the Serbs would be blamed."[248]

UN and European security officials consider these attacks to be a clear indication of a trend of intentional escalation in the anti-UN campaign waged by the Muslim militias. UN security officials in Geneva pointed out that the shooting down of the Italian transport "was in line with a growing number of Muslim actions intended to scuttle moves toward peace and to provoke outside military intervention." They added that "the Muslims have targeted United Nations troops and even other Muslims in the capital of Bosnia to throw blame on the Serbs."[249]

Even Croatia, a close ally and benefactor of Bosnia-Herzegovina, is increasingly apprehensive about the growing Islamist influence. Croatian President Franjo Tudjman has stressed the danger of the conflict in Bosnia turning into "a clash between Western countries and the Islamic world." He acknowledged that "a handful of Muslim countries" were actively supporting the Bosnian Muslims and warned that "the Muslims have been pushed to the limit. They want to continue the war at all costs in the form of a holy Islamic war," in which the Croatians feel "threatened by Muslim aspirations to create an Islamic state" in Bosnia-Herzegovina.[250]

Indeed, the Bosnian Muslims themselves threatened to use terrorism against Western targets if their demands were not met. Most reliable was the threat made in late January 1993 by Sefer Halilovic, the Commander in Chief of the Bosnian Army: "If Europe does not change its attitude, we will take steps and unleash terrorist actions on its territories. Many European capitals will be ablaze."[251]

Official Tehran examined the situation in Bosnia-Herzegovina as part of the contrast between the New World Order and the Muslims' Destiny. The situation is regarded by the Muslim world as a demonstration of the West's hostility and a precedent for taking drastic steps to reverse this course. "Islamic countries as a bloc have a unique and historic opportunity to produce the desired political changes in the global system," Tehran explains. These are fateful times that must be exploited because "such opportunities are unlikely to repeat themselves again in history." Therefore, Tehran concludes, "the Bosnia-Herzegovina tragedy and others likely to happen in the near future should act as wake-up calls for leaders in the Islamic countries and the big Islamic *Ummah* to come to their senses and accomplish their historical responsibility."[252]

Equally important is the *HizbAllah*'s threat to join the *Jihad* because "the message that the United States and Europe wish to send to the Muslims through events in Bosnia-Herzegovina" is that "a war of extermination, in its fullest sense, is being perpetrated against Muslims in an ethnic-cleansing operation to establish greater Serbia," a campaign not too different from the Zionist onslaught on Islam in the Middle East.

The *HizbAllah* concluded that "European countries, governed by (an) adventurous, anti-Islamic, extremist, chauvinist, nationalist, and ethnic mentality, intend to liquidate this Islamic pocket in Europe." The West is determined "to drive Islam from Europe, using Bosnia-Herzegovina as the model for other Muslim communities in Europe. Religious tolerance in Europe is turning into intolerance and blind fanaticism against Muslims." Therefore, the entire Muslim world must consider events in Europe as "a war against Islamic identity that is likely to spread to the Islamic world itself. Will the Muslim rulers become aware of the danger or are they still counting on Western defense of Gulf oil rigs?"[253]

This rhetorical question of the *HizbAllah* ties together the struggle of Islam in Bosnia-Herzegovina with the regional strategy of Iran and the Islamic bloc it leads. Thus, as far as the *HizbAllah* is concerned, current events in the former Yugoslavia have direct bearings on the posture of the Islamic bloc itself in the Near East. Since the *HizbAllah*'s political line is determined by Tehran, this commentary and call to arms expresses Iran's commitment and resolve.

The Islamist perception that the West, and especially the United States, is responsible for the containment of the rise of Islam increasingly shifts the focus of the most radical and

violent Islamist groups away from pressing Islamic regimes
into taking on the West to an armed struggle that is largely
waged through international terrorism. Consequently, the Islamists anticipate a cataclysmic clash with the West over the
future of Islam. In this context, the war in Bosnia-Herzegovina
is fast becoming both a catalyst and a rallying cry for the
militant Islamists. They present it as proof of the growing
danger to Islam, and as an integral part of the all-Islamic *Jihad*
against the uncompromisingly oppressive West.

In October 1992, a conference of Egypt's leading Islamists
used the events in Bosnia-Herzegovina and Somalia as precedents for the urgent need to destroy the West-dominated world
order, including the "apostate" Arab governments. They concluded that the Islamist leadership must answer to and lead
"the massive throngs thirsting for *Jihad* in the service of
Allah."[254] In Saudi Arabia, circles close to the government
described the fighting in Bosnia-Herzegovina as a "prelude to
the war between Islam and the West."[255]

In the long term, the impact of the new calls for *Jihad* on
the radicalized leftist Muslim elite is of extreme importance.
These largely European-based intellectuals are looked upon as
standard bearers by the educated, professional and relatively
liberal urban elites throughout the Arab world. Ultimately,
these elites sustain the Arab regimes and their contacts with the
West. The crisis in Bosnia-Herzegovina has revived the intellectuals' sense of Islamic identity, bringing about a profound
transformation of their political perception from leftist to Islamist. Consequently, their followers in the Middle East and
South Asia have also changed sides and quietly adopted the
Islamist cause, undermining in the process the very foundations of the regimes they serve from within. This is a significant
development, for these urban elites provide the primary cadres
of security services and the military throughout the Muslim
world.

Meanwhile, the intellectuals' new-found Islamism brings

the call for terrorism into the very heart of Western Europe. Rana Kabbani, a London-based leftist activist originally from Beirut, stresses the lingering impact of the crisis in Bosnia-Herzegovina on her own self-awareness: "We Muslims — and we now see ourselves first and foremost as Muslims in the face of increasing persecution — see a very dark future ahead of us." This rediscovery of Islam has transformed her perception of current events in the Middle East and the Muslim world as a whole. "Reading the Muslim map has become unbearably painful, and makes us clutch our Qurans ever more tightly, if only in desperation." The Muslim world has grievances against both "a West that has long colonized, manipulated and despised us, and toward our own governments, which are shamefully silent, corrupt and castrated. We have yet to earn our independence as Muslims. . ."

Thus, in the aftermath of Bosnia-Herzegovina, Rana Kabbani has lost all hope for coexistence with the West. "Muslim anger will yet set the whole world on fire, if our blood is not soon deemed as worthy of protection as our oil."[256] Having been so suddenly and profoundly disenchanted from the West they had yearned to join, these new Islamists are now ready to embark on the quest for revenge against the West that, they feel, has so failed them.

IRAN'S SECRET WARS

The growing professionalism of the Iranian terrorist system is best reflected in the relentless drive to kill Khomeini's enemies. Toward this end, in 1987 Ahmad Khomeini formed a new clandestine organization called *Service to Islam* aimed at promoting Iran's policies overseas as well as liquidating its opponents.[257] In reality, the organization was living off the SAVAMA/VEVAK networks. The placement of operatives started in early 1988. In slightly more than a year, the *Service to Islam* networks were considered operational.[258]

For example, a detachment of seven terrorists, five men and two women, crossed Spain on its way into Europe. Although the Spanish authorities identified them, they could not be arrested.[259]

Other preparations pointed to an impending escalation of terrorist acts. For example, in 1988 Iran opened a small embassy in Nicosia, Cyprus that served as a cover for secondary support of Lebanon-based operations. In early 1991, Tehran decided to significantly expand the embassy and increase its staff, communications systems and other installations associated with intelligence and terrorist activities.[260]

There were additional indications that the Iranian Government had resumed the planning of terrorist attacks in Europe with an emphasis on France and Switzerland. At first, Iranian terrorist commandos were expected to rely on the Iranian diplomatic missions.[261]

Of all the indications that the Iranian and Syrian terrorist system is ready to use the escalation of violence as a strategic instrument, most alarming is their willingness to employ nuclear terrorism, if only in the form of nuclear blackmail. In 1990, a special team of expert terrorists prepared a major operation in order to release the Abdallah brothers from French jail under the cover of a reincarnation of CSPPA. The operation called for a powerful car bomb to be driven by a suicide driver into the compound of a French nuclear power station, forcing Paris to surrender the brothers for fear of a powerful explosion. The DST was able to avert the operation at the last moment.[262]

Meanwhile, Tehran did not conceal the start of the new campaign to assassinate enemies of the regime. In mid-1989, the SAVAMA distributed a threatening pamphlet in the Iranian exile opposition communities. It served as an ultimatum for activists: "Now you, the ones who are betraying your own country and think that you can get away from the hands of the Islamic revolution of Iran and from the sharp blade of revolutionary Islam, you will be greatly disappointed. Sooner or later, you will be punished for your shameful actions." The SAVAMA pointed out that, with the cessation of hostilities with Iraq, Iran's attention would be paid to settling scores with its domestic opposition. The opposition activists were urged to return voluntarily to Iran, repent and face Islamic justice rather than face the consequences of Islamic vengeance overseas. The Tudeh (the Iranian Communist Party) broadcast the decree and emphasized its significance.[263]

Indeed, there was a corresponding escalation in violence against exiles. Four Iranian opposition leaders of the Democratic Party of Iranian Kurdistan (KDPI) were assassinated in Vienna on July 14, 1989. An Iraqi Kurd carrying an Iranian diplomatic passport was wounded. The wounded man was identified as Ja'afari Saharudi, the personal representative of Hashemi-Rafsanjani for talks with the Kurds. The assassinations were attributed to Iranian agents. Kurdish sources claimed that the Iranians asked for the meeting.[264] However, Austrian authorities believe that another Iranian diplomat was present at the meeting and that two Iranian diplomats who were involved in the assassination disappeared. Vienna issued arrest warrants for them.[265]

However, there are many unanswered questions concerning this assassination. The meeting was originally convened at Qasemlu's (then leader of the KDPI) request in order to reconcile with Tehran and redirect a combined struggle against Iraq.[266] "The meeting . . . focused on exploring ways for repentant KDP members to return to Iran and receive pardon writs," explained Mohtashemi, who should know the truth. "But the enemy . . . attacked the venue of the negotiations and murdered some people."[267]

According to the Austrian version, the meeting went bad and Bozorgyan, the Iranian official who notified the Austrian authorities of the bodies, and the other missing Iranian "official," opened fire. Saharudi was wounded by accident.[268]

The Iranians and their Kurdish allies insist that both Saddam

Hussein and the *Mujahideen ul-Khalq* were petrified by the prospects of a combined Kurdish uprising and that their agents, including the Iranian "official" who was actually working for the *Mujahideen ul-Khalq*, carried out the assassination.[269] (As discussed in Chapter 4, the latter assessment would be strongly reinforced in January 1991.) Meanwhile, official Tehran,[270] Jalal Talebani of PUK,[271] and even the PDKI, initially accused Saddam Hussein of the assassination.[272] The Iranian Embassy denied any connection with the act and condemned the attempt on the Iranian diplomat's life.[273]

A few days later, the Organization of the Strugglers of Iran claimed that a terrorist who blew himself up in a London hotel was theirs and on his way to assassinate Salman Rushdie, the Muslim writer against whom a death warrant has been issued. The terrorist, a young North African, was killed when the five pound SEMTEX bomb he was constructing exploded, killing him and destroying most of the building.[274]

In early 1990, another Iranian hit team was sent to the United Kingdom.[275] An early operation of one of these networks took place near Geneva on April 24, 1990. A two-man team shot Dr. Kazem Rajavi in the street in Coppet on Lake Geneva from close range. Another team, in a support car, blocked the road. The Iranian ambassador, Muhammad Hussein Malaek, supervised the operation. The Iranian consul general in Geneva, Karim Abadi, was directly involved in supervising the assassination and personally reported the results to Tehran by phone. In this conversation, the party in Tehran indicated that Hashemni-Rafsanjani was personally behind the assassination. Soon afterwards, the assassins left Geneva on an Air Iran flight to Tehran with diplomatic papers, with all arrangements having been made by Karim Abadi.[276] By the summer, additional Iranian teams were in position in Western Europe. However, by then the Gulf Crisis was accelerating and the Iranian terrorist network was diverted to dealing with the unfolding situation.

Once the Gulf Crisis was over, priority was again given to assassinating the enemies of the Iranian regime. These operations are controlled and decided upon by the Higher Security Council chaired by Hashemi-Rafsanjani and including Mehdi Mahdavi Karrubi and Ahmad Khomeini. All three are directly involved in the operations. Intelligence is collected by activated dormant networks, mainly in the cultural centers and other centers of the Muslim emigre communities. The actual assassinations are carried out by Iranian operatives, mainly members of *Service to Islam* organization, operating under the cover of the *al-Quds* Forces. Escape and evasion is organized by the diplomatic and official commercial entities of Iran, such as Iran Air. In March 1991, Hashemi-Rafsanjani ordered the dispatch of several assassination teams to the United Kingdom, Italy, Japan, France, Switzerland, Germany, Nigeria and Canada.[277]

The Iranian assassination detachments began working almost immediately. Iranian intelligence, under the command of Ali Salahian was responsible for feeding the teams the proper information.[278] Sheikh Tufayli had charge of the *HizbAllah* assets.[279] On April 21, 1991, Abd al-Rahman Burumand, a close ally of Shapur Bakhtiar, was stabbed to death as he returned home from a meeting with Bakhtiar. Police could not identity the perpetrators.[280]

However, it was the assassination of Shapur Bakhtiar himself on August 6, 1991, that illustrated how sophisticated the Iranian network for terrorist and covert operations had become.[281] As with previous operations, the actual operation was a combination of separate but coordinated activities by dormant networks and assets long in place and specialized assets inserted for the conduct of this specific operation.

Iranian hit teams of four men and two women arrived in France in the early summer to organize the assassination of several enemies of the regime, including Bakhtiar.[282]

Preparations for the assassination of Bakhtiar began in

early 1991. VEVAK agents in the ranks of the Iranian opposition in Paris were activated and reported back to Tehran that such an operation would be feasible. Among the VEVAK agents who made the initial inspections was 44-year-old Mrs. Fereshteh Jahanbani. She was a legitimate refugee emigre who had settled in France and operated a transport company servicing, among other places, Iran. In 1986, during a routine visit to her family in Tehran, she was arrested on trumped-up charges and agreed to serve as a VEVAK agent to get out of jail. Mrs. Jahanbani received training and was provided with secret codes, a ball-point pen with invisible ink and other spying equipment. On the VEVAK's instructions, she became an active supporter of Bakhtiar.[283]

A forward headquarters was then established in Turkey so that the operation would not be traced back to Tehran even if it failed. A Turkish merchant of Iranian descent and a VEVAK officer, Massud Ediposy, provided Iranian intelligence with office space and cover as part of his import-export company. Two VEVAK officers — Siroos Gheshgnai and Salman Timnak — arrived from Tehran and established a forward headquarters in Istanbul. Ediposy employed at least eight Turks to provide services, especially to procure diversified false Turkish documents, including several passports, that would be used by the assassination team. The VEVAK's key agent in France for this operation, Farydun Boyar Ahmadi, personally went to Istanbul to get the passports.[284]

Meanwhile, the assassination squad had to be put into place. It was this aspect of the planning that demonstrated just how important the operation was for the highest levels of Tehran. The channel selected for the insertion of the assassins was run by Mass'ud Hendi, a grand-nephew of Khomeini and a close friend and confidant of Hashemi-Rafsanjani.[285] Hendi was also a senior officer of Iranian intelligence, answering directly to Minister of Intelligence Hojjat-ol-Islam Ali Fallahian who in turn answers to Hashemi-Rafsanjani.[286]

After serving in Paris, Hendi returned to Tehran in 1986 and established a telephone company as a front for intelligence operations in France. The Iranian company developed close commercial relations with the French company Syfax. Part of their efforts included the purchase of French products and the training of Iranian experts and technicians in France. Syfax was responsible for arranging the visas for these Iranians.

In June 1991, Hendi requested visas for a few employees, which were duly granted.[287] The request for visas was initiated by Hussein Sheikhattar, an adviser to the Minister of Telecommunication.[288] Two of the "technicians" were the assassins. Because of its importance, Hendi was sent to France under the cover of a summer vacation with his family to personally supervise the operation.[289]

Meanwhile, Tehran activated its key agent in Paris concerning Shapur Bakhtiar, Farydun Boyer Ahmadi. Ahmadi had arrived in Paris in 1984 as an emigre and married within the Islamist community. In the mid-1980s, he was ordered to get close to Bakhtiar. Before long, he went to work for the Bakhtiar family and gradually became close to Shapur Bakhtiar himself. Ahmadi's claim that he was "a close friend" of Bakhtiar was far fetched. However, he knew him well enough for quite some time, and, more important, was widely known to be close to him. He had, for example, free access to Bakhtiar's home without having to make prior arrangements, and used this ability to get the assassins into the house past the French police.[290]

Once activated, Ahmadi personally went to Istanbul on July 27 to get the Turkish passports for the assassins[291] and to make final arrangements with the senior VEVAK commanders. He told them that Bakhtiar's son, who was responsible for his security, and his gardener would be gone in early August.[292]

The VEVAK operatives began arriving in Paris. There were four agents in the main detachment: two assassins and two support personnel. They arrived on July 30 with genuine

Iranian passports and visas obtained by Hendi. While in Paris, they used forged Turkish papers provided by Boyar Ahmadi.[293] Their assumed names were Ali Kaya and Musa Kocer.[294] First, an Iranian "doctor" rented an apartment, the hide-out used by the assassins. He stayed behind in a hotel near Orly, apparently ready to implement a fallback arrangement, and escaped once Bakhtiar's murder was discovered.[295] A dormant network that included several Iranians and Turks provided services, including the rental of other apartments and the providing of logistical support for the operation.[296]

The assassins were actually Ali Rad Vakili "Musa Kocer" and Muhammad Azadi "Ali Kaya."[297] Azadi is a senior official in Iranian intelligence, answering to Hashemi-Rafsanjani.[298]

After a short time in Paris to become acclimatized and to coordinate loose ends by phone with the Iranian forward base in Turkey, the time for the assassination came. It was a highly professional job. Being a frequent and known guest of Bakhtiar, Boyer Ahmadi easily led the two assassins past the tight French security. It is believed that he did not know their intent. It is not likely that there were major security failures in the protection of Bakhtiar. Azadi and Vakili then stabbed to death both Shapur Bakhtiar and his chief of staff, Furush Katibeh, after brief struggles. They used knives found in the house itself. Bakhtiar died on August 6 at 6:00 PM, but alarm was not raised until noon on August 8. By then, the assassins had begun their escape.[299]

It was at this point that problems emerged. A support agent did not arrive. Consequently, material left behind in the apartment occupied by the assassins implicated Tehran because the assassins were in constant communications with Tehran via Turkey.[300]

In order to disassociate himself from the operation, Hendi had originally planned a separate support and exfiltration system. Mrs. Anahita Mehrani, a cousin of Hendi and another dormant supporting agent living in Paris, was to provide these services. Back in the mid-1980s, both for cover and on behalf of the VEVAK, she got her husband, Johan Guir Mehrani, to open a company specializing in the export of materials to Iran, including helicopters applicable for military use. This also served as a front for the transport of agents. Mrs. Mehrani was to provide escape services for Hendi and many others. But apparently Mr. Mehrani panicked in early August. It was feared that he would betray the entire operation. Therefore, he was assassinated by the team around the time of their killing of Bakhtiar. His widow confessed to the murder, claiming irreconcilable sexual differences. More likely, the death was a punishment for his failure in the operation.[301]

As a result Hendi remained in France for a long time, quite in isolation until his arrest. At that point he implicated senior officials in Tehran in the assassination.[302] Moreover, one can assume that because they had to rush to kill Johan Guir Mehrani, Vakili and Azadi did not have time to ensure that their apartment was cleaned up, thus leaving behind important clues.

Meanwhile, Sichani Amirola Timoury, chief of security of Iran. Air at Orly, was serving as Mrs. Jahanbani's control officer and was the "mailbox" and "transmission belt" between the VEVAK in Tehran and their agent in Paris. Problems began when Timouri was activated in connection with the actual assassination. He helped Azadi and Vakili enter France on July 30. Subsequently, Timouri was to provide fallback assistance for the principals while in Paris. Hendi's instructions were "to contact (him) in the event of a problem. . ." Toward that end, Mrs. Jahanbani began working for Teimouri, providing him with communications and other services, including logistical support. Some of the calls to the VEVAK forward headquarters in Istanbul were made from her home phone. That was the way in which she was exposed.[303]

Immediately after the completion of their mission, Vakili and Azadi started their escape. Boyer Ahmadi disappeared at this point and might have been killed by the two agents.[304] A prostitute found his BMW with bloodstains and shredded clothes inside.[305] The two operatives met their contact man, an emigre from an activated dormant network, who had to drive them to a train that would take them out of France. However, he made an error and took them to Annecy instead of Nancy so they missed their train and bungled the pre-arranged exfiltration plans.

In desperation, they took a French cab from Annecy to the Swiss border. But they missed a contact man in Geneva who was to hand them new Turkish passports. Vakili was arrested on August 21st when he could not show a passport in a routine police check. He was extradited to France. Azadi succeeded in reaching safety in the Iranian embassy in Bern, and was housed in the Ambassador's residence.[306] The day after the assassination, almost 24 hours before Bakhtiar's body was found, the VEVAK department of Iranian Intelligence asked Geneva for confirmation of "the fate of an Iranian opposition figure in Europe."[307]

Once Bakhtiar's body was found, Iranian opposition leaders pointed a finger at Tehran.[308] Iran denied involvement in the Bakhtiar killing[309] and warned against using the incident to sabotage French-Iranian relations.[310] Iranian officials suggested that he committed suicide, ridden by guilt and depression.[311] Later, Tehran claimed that Hendi was recruited by French intelligence and was used for provocation.[312] Still, after first implying that the Iranian opposition was responsible for the assassinations,[313] Paris reluctantly acknowledged that Tehran was responsible for the killing of Bakhtiar and his aide.[314]

Although Iran was directly implicated in the Bakhtiar assassination, Tehran was encouraged. Following a thorough analysis and lesson learning process of recent covert operations in Western Europe, Tehran decided in a meeting of its National Security Council on December 28, 1991, which was chaired by Hashemi-Rafsanjani, to escalate the assassination campaign against enemies of the regimes.

Fallahiyan-Khuzestani (Minister of Intelligence) and Ahmad Vahidi (Commander of the *al-Quds* special terrorist squads of the IRGC) were entrusted with the implementation of these plans which would incorporate lessons learned from the Bakhtiar case.[315] VEVAK, for example, operating directly under Hashemi-Rafsanjani, now collects intelligence on potential targets for the *al-Quds* forces, ranging from enemies of the regime to objectives for sabotage. And since the autumn of 1992 the VEVAK's Western Countries Department is being rapidly expanded to include, in addition to Western Europe, North America.[316]

On September 17, 1992, an Iranian assassination team struck again, killing four senior leaders of the KDPI, including their leader, meeting at the *Mykonos* restaurant in Berlin. The assassination team, operating again under the cover of the *al-Quds* forces, was composed of two Iranian intelligence operatives and three *Hizbollahi*. The hit was highly professional and reflected the possession of excellent intelligence. The two masked assassins used a 9mm (M-63?) and a 7.65mm M-61 Scorpion machine pistol. The Iranian team included a senior hit man known only by pseudonyms (Sharif, Abu-Roman, and Khwaja), and Kazim Darabi, a Berlin-based *HizbAllah* militant who was responsible for the logistical support of the operation. The team was supported by three Lebanese Shi'ites, Fajazallah Abdu Haidar, Abbas Hussein Rhayil and Yussuf Amin. The assassin is believed to have been Ahmad Taheri, a veteran operative and terrorist, who was seen in Germany on October 23, 1992, although there is no specific evidence to connect him with the Berlin operation.[317]

The Iranian assassination campaign continues. On March 16, 1993, an Iranian hit team assassinated Muhammad Hussein Naghdi, an opposition leader, as he was driving in Rome. Two men riding a Vespa scooter suddenly appproached his car in the middle of dense traffic. One of them opened fire at close range from an Uzi submachinegun. Haghdi was hit by two well-aimed bullets — one in the face and one in the neck. He died on his way to the hospital. The killers disappeared in the traffic. The Uzi, completely clean, was later found in the trash.[318]

With so much at stake, little wonder that Iran continuously tightens its control over the Islamist international terrorist movement, ensuring that it remains an instrument of Tehran's policy. Indeed, in the summer of 1992, Ali Fallahiyan-Khuzestani, the Minister of Intelligence and Security Forces, explained that Iran has "a foreign intelligence department that collates the conspiracies hatched by world arrogance against the Islamic Revolution," and that toward this end Iran "even infiltrated the highest levels of government in some countries." He acknowledged that Iranian intelligence conducted violent covert operations all over the world, and that "those activities are on the increase every day."[319] Iran's spiritual leader, Ayatollah Ali Hussein Khamenei, acknowledged that terrorist organizations were an integral part of Iran's long arm. He warned the West against confronting Iran, pointing out that "they should know that the strength of the Islamic Republic of Iran is in the strength of faith of its *HizbAllah* forces."[320]

CHAPTER 7
ISLAMIST TERRORISM IN AMERICA (I)

America is the ultimate enemy and primary objective of Islamist international terrorism. The *HizbAllah* states that "the United States is the Great Satan and there must be no leniency in the war against it."[1] Tehran sees in the struggle against the U.S. one of the quintessentials of Khomeini's Islamic Revolution. "Any doubt about the need to struggle against the U.S. means being enslaved by the Great Satan and losing the honor and the life the Islamic Revolution has brought to this country and the whole Islamic *Ummah*," explained Hojjat ol-Islam Ali Akbar Mohtashemi.[2]

Still, until early 1993, virtually no terrorist operations took place on U.S. soil. However, this phenomenon should not be considered an indication that there is no terrorism in the U.S. On the contrary, the virtual safety enjoyed by America during the 1980s should be attributed primarily to the restraint exercised and imposed by the then-dominant states, primarily the U.S.S.R. and Cuba. Both countries were motivated by higher priorities, namely, preparations for World War III (see below) as well as the benefits and profits derived from narco-terrorism.

With diverse covert operations going on, the KGB, the GRU (Soviet Military Intelligence), and the DGI (Cuban Intelligence) were afraid of the negative ramifications that tightened security in the aftermath of a terrorist strike might have on their ability to operate in the U.S. Therefore they would not let the terrorists they controlled operate in America.

Thus, although leftist Arab terrorists have been present in the U.S., most elements have been passive and, with few exceptions in the early 1970s, did not commit acts of terrorism.

However, in the 1980s, Islamist international terrorism, controlled by Iran, Syria and Libya, assumed prominence. The masters of Islamist terrorism are more audacious and less constrained by global considerations. For them, any strike, even symbolic, at the "Great Satan" is a major achievement. With the collapse of the USSR. and Cuban inaction, the restraints they had imposed are no longer effective. Consequently, the US is no longer immune to these global developments.

Islamist international terrorism is in America for the foreseeable future.

Therefore, the situation has changed because Islamist terrorists and the states controlling them consider the U.S. to be their ultimate enemy. Moreover, the sponsoring states are willing to withstand the possible retribution terrorist strikes may bring. Little wonder that the *HizbAllah* has always emphasized that the struggle against the U.S. must take precedence over any other objective of the Islamic world: "We are moving in the direction of fighting the roots of vice and the first root of vice is America. All the endeavors to drag us into marginal action will be futile when compared with the confrontation against the United States."[3]

The states controlling the Islamist terrorist network, primarily Syria and Iran, are committed to extending their struggle into the U.S. and are willing to withstand the consequences. Therefore, in the early 1980s they began a lengthy, prudent and professional process of consolidating a stable and redundant terrorist infrastructure in America based on a myriad of dormant networks and using established methods for the insertion of experts and trigger-men. This approach is derived from, and essentially similar to, the successful terrorist build-up in Western Europe in the 1980s and incorporates many of the lessons learned from the rich operational experience accumulated there.

Two factors dominate the assessment of the chance of effective terrorist operations inside the United States:

1. The professional capabilities of the international terrorist organizations involved; and

2. The willingness of the controlling states to give the go-ahead for terrorist operations.

The conduct of sophisticated, effective and lethal terrorist operations depends on the availability of both skilled operatives and a comprehensive support infrastructure. As a rule, the support system is established in the target-country several years in advance. It collects intelligence, sets up a logistical support network and prepares the conditions for carrying out a terrorist attack. The support network then waits in a dormant state for activation by the leadership, that is, the controlling state. Then the highly skilled operatives arrive on the scene only a short time prior to the specific attacks. They activate the local support network and live off them for the duration of the terrorist operation. The presence of a support system in place is the key to the terrorist capability to strike inside the U.S.

By the early 1980s, there was already a solid, veteran and proven Shi'ite terrorist network in the U.S. based on the *Tashayu Sorkh* (Red Shi'ism) organization founded in San Jose, California, in 1965 by Mustafa Chamran Savehi.

One of the most important Iranian terrorist leaders among the "founding fathers" of the Iranian Revolution was Mustafa Chamran Savehi (1932-1981). A student in Berkeley, California, since 1957, Chamran became a revolutionary. In 1964 he took a sabbatical from his studies to receive terrorist training in Egypt. In 1965, upon his return to California, he established a guerilla/terrorist organization *Tashayu Sorkh* in order to train Iranian soldiers for the future revolutionary struggle. At first he had only five activists involved, including his brother Mahdi and an Afghan named Hossein Forqani. All of them trained with weapons in San Jose. In 1968, Chamran established the Muslim Students' Association of America which attracted large numbers of members including future Iranian leaders such as Ibrahim Yazdi.

In 1971, Chamran decided to go to Lebanon to further his pan-Islamic Shi'ite revolution. He became a devotee of Imam Musa al-Sadr who obtained for him a position as a director of a vocational school in Tyre, Lebanon. In reality, Chamran worked to build the Shi'ite Amal militia into a fighting force.

He brought into Amal two Lebanese students who had studied in the U.S.: Nabih Birri and Hussein al-Husseini. Chamran himself underwent extensive training in Palestinian terrorist camps, including specialized advanced training from Nayif Hawatimah. He was also the point man in contact with Palestinian organizations and later supervised the training of Iranian revolutionaries in Lebanon by the Palestinians. In February 1979, Chamran returned to Iran to organize the *Pasdaran* and the terrorist infrastructure. He was killed in 1981 in an air crash near the Iraqi front.[4]

Meanwhile, since the early 1970s, the Shi'ite terrorist network was also persistently building its own international cadres. This effort was one of the highest priorities of Mustafa Chamran. From Lebanon, he transformed the Muslim Students' Association he had founded in the U.S. into an international organization that would evolve into the roots of the Shi'ite international network. By the early 1970s, the Muslim Students' Association had some 700 active members, mainly Iranians and Afghans, in half-a-dozen countries.

Chamran selected trusted confidants to open additional cells, such as Kamal Kharazi and Abdul-Karim Sorush in the United Kingdom and Muhammad Gharazi in France. Their main task was to identify students with revolutionary potential and send them for guerrilla and terrorist training in Lebanon. By 1975, the Muslim Students' Association was regularly sending scores of trainees to Lebanon. After the completion of their military training, these students would return to their places of study in Western Europe and the United States and establish dormant clandestine cells.[5]

It was primarily in the U.S. that the Chamran network was cultivated from the very beginning. From the mid-1970s on,

Haj Esmail, a carpet merchant in Washington, D.C. who was a naturalized citizen, was extremely active in the black Muslim community on behalf of the Khomeini message.

In April 1980, Khalkhali ordered Haj Esmail to activate his network and assassinate Ali Akbar Tabataba'i, a former senior officer in the Shah's SAVAK. On July 22, 1980, Tabataba'i was shot by Daoud Salahuddin, a.k.a. David Belfield, a radical black Muslim and veteran of the Hanafi militant group. It was a professional operation. Several radical black Muslims, each working separately, provided the assassin with a clean hand gun, a genuine mail van and a mailman uniform's and post-action support. Salahuddin approached Tabataba'i's house as a postman delivering a package and shot him from close range when he opened the door. Daoud Salahuddin was immediately flown to New York and exfiltrated safely to Tehran via Montreal, Canada, through the services of West European radical operatives. Only some of the radical black Muslims who provided services were apprehended and convicted.[6]

QADDAFI AND LEFTIST REVOLUTIONARY TERRORISM

Since the early 1980s there has been a concentrated effort by Libya, with extensive professional help from Cuba and North Korea, to consolidate a revolutionary and terrorist infrastructure in the U.S. The system would include intelligence apparatus and logistical and operational support systems. The sponsoring states wanted this terrorist support infrastructure to be based on disgruntled elements of American society, mainly minorities. In this endeavor, Libya provided the funds and ideological profile while Cuba and the DPRK provided expertise. Consequently, virtually the entire radical and terrorist supporting apparatus in the U.S. was unified toward facilitating major terrorist operations and withstanding the reaction of the law enforcement agencies in the aftermath of such attacks.

The first practical discussions on the export of Middle Eastern terrorism into the Americas were conducted in Tripoli, Libya, in mid-June 1982, during the International Conference of the World Center for Resistance of Imperialism, Zionism, Racism, Reaction and Fascism. The Cubans exercised tight control over the other Central American and Caribbean Basin movements.[7] Cuba, Benin, Iran, Syria, and Libya established an executive committee to coordinate their struggle against the U.S. Soon afterwards, radical leaders from Costa Rica, El-Salvador and several West Indian islands arrived in Tripoli for subsequent consultations.[8] All were united in their desire to confront the U.S. on its own soil.

Two major courses of action emerged in the aftermath of these consultations in Libya. They reflected a fundamental difference in the assessment of conditions inside the U.S. The Cubans, reflecting the Soviet assessment, were committed to establishing a tightly controlled instrument of sabotage that could be used at will. The Cubans and their allies insisted that the struggle be based on a professional cadre of expert terrorists, established and trained outside the U.S. and ultimately infiltrated into the U.S. for carrying special operations. The Libyans were committed to sponsoring and fomenting a popular revolt in the U.S. through the support for, and radicalization of, various segments of the population that felt discriminated against by, and had grievances against, Washington.

In principle, both courses of action would ultimately merge into a joint operation. Once the popular revolt began, Cuba's expert revolutionary terrorists would arrive to give the revolution extra help and a quality edge over the law enforcement forces.

Meanwhile, the Cubans and Nicaraguans had already established a center of international terrorism in Nicaragua. During the 1980s it served as a shelter for wanted terrorists as well as an advanced school in the Western Hemisphere. The group of instructors included members of virtually every terrorist supporting state and organization, including Palestinians, North Koreans, Vietnamese, Czechoslovaks, Bulgarians, East Germans, Basques from the ETA, Red Brigades from Italy, Columbians from the M-19, Cubans, Iraqis, Iranians, Libyans, Irish from the IRA, Argentinian Montenegros, Uruguayan Tupamaros, West Germans, etc.[9] Yassir Arafat declared back in January 1982: "We (the PLO) have connections with all revolutionary movements throughout the world, in Salvador, Nicaragua — and I reiterate Salvador — and elsewhere in the world." He claimed that he sent pilots to Nicaragua and expert guerrilla fighters to El Salvador.[10]

By 1986, the PLO presence in Nicaragua had further expanded a nd had gained a formal base from which to launch terrorist operations in the Western hemisphere.[11] In the late 1980s, with Nicaragua going through a major internal crisis that ultimately brought down the Sandinistas, this terrorist supporting infrastructure quietly collapsed, although several individuals remained in Managua and the countryside. Even after the election of the Chamorro government in 1990, the Nicaraguan military and intelligence continued to provide some assistance to terrorists operating in America.

For Qaddafi, the confrontation with the U.S. constitutes a central tenet of Libya's grand strategy. "When we ally ourselves with revolution in Latin America, and particularly Central America, we are defending ourselves. This Satan must be clipped and we must take war to the American borders just as America is taking threats to the Gulf of Sidra and to the Tibesti Mountains," he declared.[12] However, Qaddafi's real aim was the subversion of the U.S. itself. Qaddafi threatened the U.S. with "exporting terrorism to the heart of America" that would be "capable of physical liquidation, destruction, and arson inside America."[13]

A major step in the establishment of a Libyan-supported radical alliance in the U.S. was taken in mid-April 1983 in the course of the First International Symposium on the Thought of Muammar Qaddafi, held in Tripoli. Around 1,000 "revolutionaries of various ideological shades" were brought to Tripoli to discuss the formulation of a common ideological and practical approach to accelerating and escalating the revolutionary struggle in and against the West. Special attention was paid to the U.S. delegation made up of 15 radicals representing 10 organizations, including the Afram Information Service, the Afro-Arab Foundation, the All-African Peoples Revolutionary Party, the American Indian Movement, the Black Argus, the International Indian Treaty Council, the Nation of Islam, the National Conference of Black Lawyers, the People's Association for Human Rights, and the Republic of New Afrika.[14]

On the third night of the conference, the U.S. delegation had a 45-minute audience with Qaddafi in his tent. The session was used for the evaluation of the Americans as potential allies. Qaddafi was apparently satisfied with what he saw, for on the eighth day the Americans were summoned for meetings with several Libyan senior officials.

According to a participant, the Americans were told prior to the meeting that its objective was "to determine ways and means that Libya can provide direct support to liberation fighters within the United States, as well as the mechanism through which matters could be functionally centralized, thereby averting a need for Libya to attempt to maintain separate relations with maybe 15 organizations inside a country with which they do not have diplomatic relations."[15]

The two delegates of the Nation of Islam, identified only as Larry X and Harold X, also met with Abd al-Sallam Jallud and four other senior officials to discuss cooperation with Libya. The Americans offered to launder money for Libya, but were "severely criticized" by the Libyans for not doing enough to promote "the armed struggle."[16]

Meanwhile, Libya and its allies, North Korea and Cuba, were moving quickly to establish a professional support infrastructure for the fledgling terrorist and revolutionary network in the U.S. Tripoli argued that once the reliability of the American revolutionaries was ascertained, the allies should embark on an urgent effort to complete the support infrastructure.

Libya was directly responsible for its financing. The flow of funds was to be conducted via several foreign-registered companies and individuals, not all of them Libyan. Some of these fronts had been established in the early 1980s and were now handling the more sensitive front and finance operations. Qaddafi loyalists actually founded many fronts for Libyan intelligence agencies in North America and Canada. For example, a personal friend of Qaddafi, Fadil al-Mabruk al-Dhabilah, established a company in Panama as a front for the support of operations in Central and North America.[17]

Another such company was the Manara Travel Agency, established by Mussa Hawamdah in Washington, DC, in 1980. It opened a major branch in Ontario in 1987. Manara also served as a cover for the North American branches of the Neutron International Trading Co., actually a web of Libyan-owned companies optimized for the illegal acquisition of high-tech items. In the mid-1980s, Manara would actively support covert operations in the U.S.[18]

By 1983, Qaddafi was inserting weapons and terrorists, including members of elite units of the Libyan Armed Forces, into Latin America to support both those states friendly to Libya and revolutionary organizations.[19] However, the Libyans were apprehensive about sending operatives into the U.S. itself.

The DPRK had been closely studying this task, since at least early 1983, when four small North Korean freighters escorted by several small trawlers, all fitted with a vast array of antennas and other ELINT equipment, were patrolling the Gulf of California and the shores of California and northern Mexico. Although the primary and original mission of this flotilla was to collect electronic intelligence and provide early warning in case of U.S. military intervention in Central America, the ships were well equipped to study, and possibly even conduct, insertion operations. The Korean crews were "soldiers or comman-dos" involved with Central American revolutionaries.[20]

It is noteworthy that North Korean intelligence operatives and Latin American terrorists receive advanced and special-ized training for Western Hemisphere clandestine operations in the Melli University in Iran.[21] The training courses of North Korean SPETSNAZ (special forces) include three years of English studies.[22] Moreover, the DPRK freighters used in these operations were of the same type used for the clandestine insertion of North Korean SPETSNAZ into hostile countries and for the support of international terrorist activities. One such freighter, the *Tong Gon Ae Guk-Ho*, was used to insert into the Rangoon, Burma area the detachment that attempted to assassinate the entire South Korean government on October 9, 1983, killing 17 key officials and wounding several others, including the president.[23]

Meanwhile, in accordance with the resolutions of the April 1983 conference, Qaddafi increased Libya's support for revo-lutionary movements among blacks in the U.S. Louis Farrakhan's Nation of Islam was emerging as one of the leading organizations receiving assistance from Libya.[24] The Libyans were encouraged by what, from their point of view, seemed to be initial signs of the emergence of an indigenous anti-American armed revolutionary movement.

The revolutionary movement in question was the Al-Rukn, a Chicago street gang long involved with murders, drug traf-ficking and protection rackets, whose members had converted to Islam and attached ideological connotations to their activi-ties. Moreover, the Al-Rukn sought and established close relations with the Nation of Islam — to the point that some of the Al-Rukn members were recruited into Farrakhan's security force, the Fruit of Islam.[25]

In a March 11, 1984, speech in Chicago attended by some 200 Al-Rukn members, Farrakhan declared that they "are going to play a very important part in supporting and defending the black community" in the "race war" he expected would break out in 1986. He called the Al-Rukn gang members "born warriors for true liberation, awaiting the voice of the Messiah," and told them they "were born to settle scores" with the whites.[26]

Soon afterwards, Farrakhan travelled to Libya and had a private audience with Qaddafi on May 27, 1984.[27] The leaders of Al-Rukn also travelled to Tripoli, through New York and Panama City, in search of assistance. At each stop of their trip "they met with representatives of the Libyan Government."[28]

Muammar Qaddafi delivered a televised speech at the convention of the Nation of Islam in late February 1985. Some 200 members of Al-Rukn attended the conference and cheered the militant speeches of Qaddafi and Farrakhan.[29] In his speech, Qaddafi explained that "the blacks and the red Indians are brothers-in-struggle against racism, the common enemy, the enemy of all of us." He urged the blacks in America "to struggle to establish an independent state." Qaddafi then called on the black soldiers in the U.S. military "to leave the American Army and to join your force to create black power. . . We support you in establishing an independent state and independent army; we are prepared to train and arm you. Your cause is a just one because freedom is our cause and imperialism is our common enemy."[30]

Qaddafi's entreaties were not merely idle talk. In October 1986, four members of the Al-Rukn gang were arrested in Chicago for preparing to conduct terrorist strikes on behalf of Libya, including blowing up U.S. government buildings and bringing down an airplane. A fifth escaped to Libya. An arsenal that included nearly 40 weapons, mainly small arms, but also submachine guns, a rocket launcher and anti-tank and anti-aircraft weapons was discovered in the gang's headquarters, called "the mosque." The Al-Rukn defendants were convicted in 1987 of "offering to commit bombings and assassinations on U.S. soil for Libyan payment."[31]

In 1984, Qaddafi also ordered his intelligence service to organize and train Libyan operatives for specialized terrorist operations inside the U.S. Actual preparations for their insertion took place in the summer of 1985. Toward that end, Lt. Col. Abdallah Hijazi, a military adviser to Col. Qaddafi, met with Hasan Hashim, the head of Amal's Executive Committee, in late August 1985. The meeting was particularly important because Hashim resided in the United States.[32]

In late 1985 and early 1986, Qaddafi completed the organization of suicide squads for terrorist strikes inside the U.S. Part of the dynamic that made this possible was the maturation of the first generation of Libyans who had grown up completely under Qaddafi's rule. These youths consider the Green Book (a book containing Qaddafi's thoughts) to be "their second Qoran."

"They are under the spell of a prophetic revelation and are so persuaded of its inner truth that they would commit suicide for it, for Palestine, for the Arabs, for you and me," observed a British correspondent who met them. These young terrorists, both males and females, were being trained in several barracks throughout Libya. Their self-declared objective is to "strike in America itself," and they are determined to blow up the "the Black House in Washington." According to Libyan officials, the list of applicants for "martyrdom" was far longer than anything the training system could accommodate.[33]

In early 1986, Tehran hailed these Libyan preparations and even suggested that some terrorists were already inside the U.S. "The Libyan people's committees have voiced their readiness to strike serious blows against the United States — even through the kamikaze groups they have set up in the avenues of Washington."[34] Walid Jumblatt sent a cable to Qaddafi, declaring his forces ready to join the suicide squads and "participate in strikes on U.S. interests wherever they may be."[35] In the conference of the Pan-Arab Command for Leading the Revolutionary Forces in the Arab Homeland in Tripoli in early February 1986, Ahmad Jibril delivered a statement on behalf of the six Palestinian organizations participating, saying that "The United States has declared war on the Arabs. Therefore, the Palestinian revolution believes that the war has started and that it is no longer responsible for what may happen.''[36]

A major step toward the acquisition of credible terrorist capabilities inside the U.S. was taken during the Second International Conference of the International Center for Combatting Imperialism, Zionism, Racism, Reaction and Fascism in Tripoli, Libya, in mid-March 1986. Among the over 1,000 participants comprising some 300 delegations were representatives of several West European and U.S. organizations, as well as various Central American and Caribbean organizations.[37] Special attention was paid to facilitating the escalation of the terrorist campaign in Western Europe and the U.S. Several training seminars on, and demonstrations of, weapons and explosives were conducted during the conference under strict security, especially for non-Arab and non-African delegates. These included the providing of sophisticated weapons and training to additional groups and organizations.[38]

In his opening speech, Muammar Qaddafi surveyed the current condition of the world revolutionary movement and international terrorism: ''We are more determined to continue the collective struggle and double our efforts in the fight against the fascists in Latin America — agents of imperialism and agents of the United States, the enemy of the people and the leader of international terrorism and the barbaric and savage administration which relies on nothing but the law of terrorism and the law of the jungle,'' Qaddafi declared. ''Brothers, we should stand by the people of Nicaragua against the blatant and harsh threats from the United States. We should strengthen Cuba's steadfastness in confronting U.S. imperialism. We should put our hand in the hand of our brothers, friends, and comrades, Castro and Ortega, and their comrades in Nicaragua and Cuba. We should also decide to fight alongside our comrades, the revolutionaries of Central America and Latin America, against fascism and reactionism which are supported by U.S. imperialism.''[39]

Qaddafi paid special attention to the prospect of armed struggle inside the U.S. In this speech, Qaddafi called upon "the 400,000 blacks in the U.S. Army to mutiny and leave military service. . . U.S. blacks should continue to call, covertly and openly, upon their brothers in the military institutions and the U.S. police to escape from these institutions, destroy them from inside, and smuggle their weapons out." Qaddafi also emphasized "the right of the Red Indian nation to unity and independence, and to be able to live in the land of its forefathers in the United States of America in dignity and glory. This nation, when it becomes independent and united . . . will be creating a new world of nations," he predicted.[40]

In its resolution, the Conference called for "the strengthening of revolutionary cohesiveness and the embodiment of the principle of collective struggle in confronting imperialist, Zionist, racist, reactionary, fascist terrorism," and encouraged the participants to escalate "the collective struggle for underprivileged peoples." After condemning the activities of the U.S. Navy in the Gulf of Sidra, the Conference expressed solidarity with, and promised support to, Nicaragua and Cuba:

> The conference expresses its appreciation for the steadfast stance of the Sandinista revolution in confronting the U.S. imperialist plots and declares its support and backing for the Nicaraguan people and its revolution. It also supports steadfast Cuba under the leadership of Comrade Fidel Castro in consolidating its stance against American arrogance.[41]

Special attention was then paid to the just struggle of the Red Indians against the "white invaders of North America", and that of oppressed blacks against "the policies of apartheid and racial discrimination in both American and British societies." The Conference promised help in their revolutionary struggles, namely, bringing terror to the U.S.[42]

Louis Farrakhan travelled to Libya at the head of the Nation of Islam delegation to the Second International Conference of the International Center for Combatting Imperialism, Zionism, Racism, Reaction and Fascism.[43] He was given the honor of introducing one of Qaddafi speeches.[44] In his remarks, Farrakhan explained that he and his followers "don't recognize the right of Reagan legally, morally and also according to God-given law." Discussing the Palestinian revolutionary armed struggle against Israel, Farrakhan defined his view on armed struggle. He explained that the Palestinians participating in the Conference "are not terrorists because they are struggling to undermine imperialism and racism, [and] that the pledges of the real freedom-fighters are the only ones that will bring about victory over imperialism and neo-colonialism."[45]

In late March 1986, in the wake of the U.S. clashes with Libya in the Gulf of Sidra, Tripoli urged an all out struggle against the U.S. "Let the Arab nation be transformed in its entirety into suicide squads and human bombs, missiles and aircraft to deter and resist terrorism and destroy it for good." Special emphasis was put on agitating Arabs into conducting terrorism against and in the U.S.

"O heroes of the Arab nation! Let your missiles and suicide cells chase the U.S. terrorist embassies and interests wherever they may be."[46] Muftah Muhammad Allaji quoted Qaddafi: "The Arab Nation is capable of dealing decisive blows to U.S. interests in the Arab world or anywhere else." He stressed that "the Arab nation is capable of transforming itself into suicide commandos" in order to strike at U.S. interests all over the world.[47]

Indeed, several terrorist organizations claimed operational capabilities throughout the West, as well as their readiness to strike against U.S. interests everywhere. In Damascus, Abu-Nidal announced that "all U.S. interests" are now considered "legitimate targets" for his revolutionaries. He urged all Palestinians and Arabs to unite and destroy "the imperialist presence and interests."[48] The Palestine Liberation Movement, Fatah - the Revolutionary Cells, announced that it "considers all American imperialist interests, wherever they are, as a target for our revolutionaries."[49]

The branches of the Movement of the Revolutionary Committees of Iraq in West Germany and Sweden issued a warning to the U.S. and urged all "liberation movements" to join them and "escalate their suicide operations everywhere against American imperialist interests and against their military establishment" all over the world.[50] The Arab Revolutionary Force in Turkey declared their "readiness to become fighters for freedom and . . . attack the dens of U.S. imperialism and their spies and intelligence organizations everywhere in the world."[51] The Islamic Progressive force in Turkey also issued a supporting statement, emphasizing that striking at the U.S. should be "considered as a defense of Islam everywhere."[52] The Revolutionary Force of Oxford Aerodrome, Britain, also announced their intent to become "suicide squads against America and its arrogance."[53] The Tunisian Revolutionary Force announced its commitment to carry out "inciting for the destruction of U.S. interests, wherever they might be."[54]

Although no terrorist strike followed these calls to arms, Qaddafi was delighted with the widespread reaction to his pronouncements. "*Fadayeen* operations being carried out by Arab *fadayeen* and suicide squads against imperialism and Zionism will blaze the trail to liberation and escalate the pan-Arab struggle to destroy imperialist arrogance. . . From now on let the motto of the Arab masses be: One thousand *fadayeen* and suicide operations per day."[55]

In late August 1986, two additional Lebanese groups joined the chorus of Libyan-inspired threats against the U.S.: The Movement of Arab Fadayeen — the Suicide Squads (*Harakat al-Fida'iyin al-Arab — al-Saraya al-Intihariyah*) threatened to unleash vengeance on U.S. and NATO citizens if the U.S. attacked Libya.[56] The Movement of Arab Commandos (*Harakat al-Kumandus al-Arab*) also threatened to attack U.S. and NATO personnel. The group added: "We can reach deep into the

United States, the White House, and the other NATO countries.''⁵⁷

When Libya declared its readiness to conduct terrorist
operations inside the U.S. in early 1986 there was indeed a
solid Libyan support network in place. Back in 1980, as Libyan
relations with the U.S. were rapidly deteriorating and diplomatic relations were broken, Libyan intelligence began establishing alternate methods to maintain communications with,
and control over, its assets in the U.S., most of them Libyan
students. Most important was the Peoples' Committee for
Libyan Students established in McLean, Virginia, in 1981. At
first, the Libyan clandestine activities involved mainly the
illegal acquisition of high technology items and the plotting of
assassinations of Qaddafi's enemies.⁵⁸

Financing and control were arranged through the Manara
Travel Agency in Washington. Mussa Hawamda, the Jorda-
nian-born owner and manager, was no stranger to Islamist
terrorism. Back in the early 1970s he studied for a graduate
degree in physics at San Jose State University in California,
where he became a follower of Mustafa Chamran Savehi and
was involved with his Muslim Students' Association of America.
In 1976, when he transferred to Georgetown for PhD studies,
he was already a committed Islamist revolutionary who maintained personal correspondence with Qaddafi himself. In 1980,
Hawamda opened his Manara Travel Agency on behalf of
Qaddafi with funds provided through a Lebanese, Ahmad
Murad. Muhammad Madjoub, a senior Libyan intelligence
officer, personally oversaw the Washington operations and
transferred funds to Hawamda.⁵⁹

In early 1986, the Washington, D.C., network accelerated
its activities on the basis of resolutions passed at the Tripoli
conference and the availability of Qaddafi's suicide squads
which were ready for operations inside the U.S. Salah al-Rahji
of the Peoples' Committee for Libyan Students was the on-site
commander who organized the support system for terrorist
operations. Their first task was the collection of operational

intelligence, including planning and arranging for the assassination of Oliver North in the fall of 1986 by booby-trapping his car. By then, the network had the required intelligence, but the professional assassins did not arrive.[60]

More important were the support activities for the popular revolution in the U.S. Under the supervision of Al-Rahji, several members of leftist-radical, black and Indian militant organizations received military and sabotage training. As part of other preparations for terrorism, the People's Committee for Libyan Students collected names and home addresses of over 1,000 employees of the CIA, FBI, DIA, Air Force, Army, Navy, Department of Defense, and United States Information Agency as possible terrorist targets. Al-Rahji also delivered funds to finance a series of terrorist strikes planned for early 1987.

Although nothing happened, Tripoli decided on the further expansion of the program on the basis of the April 1987 conference (see below). Thus, in June 1987, al-Rahji reported to Tripoli that his network within the Peoples' Committee was making progress in "furthering armed struggle" along with Canadian and American "secret revolutionary organizations."[61]

Hawamda, in charge of finances, arranged money laundering on a massive scale through the Manara Travel Agency. He also financed the travel of American and Canadian delegates to the 1986 and 1987 terrorist conferences in Libya, and the clandestine transport of individuals for training "in armed struggle" in Libya.

The flow of money was handled via a convoluted web of bank accounts in BCCI, its Canadian subsidiary BCC(C), and First American branches in New York and Washington. In the U.S., the money was ultimately distributed by the People's Committee for Libyan Students. In 1987, in anticipation of a marked expansion and escalation of activities, Manara opened a branch in Ontario, where funds could be retrieved directly from Libya.

The key Libyan operatives were arrested in July 1988. Al-Rahji was sentenced to five years. Hawamda jumped his $250,000 bail and vanished in Greece.[62]

During this period Libya continued to agitate every possible North American radical group. For example, some 40 Canadian and 200 U.S. activists, including several militants and members of the Nation of Islam, the American Indian Movement and the New Alliance Party, took part in the anti-U.S. Peace Conference convened in Libya on April 12-14, 1987, to commemorate the first anniversary of the U.S. bombing of Tripoli. Apparently the gathering was used for more than mere protest. A young Canadian journalist who travelled to Libya to research its clandestine activities in Canada was pushed to his death from his hotel room near Tripoli.[63]

Between January 30 and February 2, 1988, Qaddafi hosted in Libya an international conference "for the Liberation of the Red Indians' nation", attended by participants and activists from North, Central and South America.[64] "We have a base in North America" because the Indians are "time bombs inside the United States," Qaddafi explained.[65]

In the U.S., Farrakhan was reiterating his support for Qaddafi. He told the Libyan leader, "We have watched you [Qaddafi] grow, and we have grown with you."[66] This statement underlines Farrakhan's quest for eventual independence for America's blacks. "We have no hope that we can effect true reconciliation between blacks and whites in this country," he has said. "The answer ultimately is going to be separation."[67]

Meanwhile, in late March 1990, Qaddafi convened the World's People's Islamic Leadership conference in order to denounce U.S. Middle Eastern policy and declare his commitment to an uncompromising *Jihad* against the U.S. He told the group, "Faced with this serious challenge, humiliating situation and contempt toward Islamic sacred shrines, Muslims have only one choice: it is the strong confrontation and struggle against the U.S. Satan, which is manipulated by the force of evil."[68]

Qaddafi did not forget the liberation struggle of the American Indians. In June 1991, the third annual Qaddafi Prize for Human Rights was awarded to the American Indians in commemoration of 500 years of imperialist oppression and in order to help their liberation struggle.[69]

Ultimately, although the potential for radical terrorism was present in the U.S., most elements were passive and some were controlled by local forces. Isolated radical Palestinian cells have been discovered periodically in the U.S. However, their primary tasks were to channel money, provide shelter to terrorists on the run, and establish a long-lasting infrastructure. For example, seven Arabs, six of them Jordanian citizens, were arrested in Los Angeles as members of the PFLP, preparing terrorist activities.[70] Their leader, Adnan Bakhur, claimed to have been George Habbash's nephew. However, in reality, their primary conspiracy was crooked fundraising operations on behalf of the PFLP. They collected some $180 million through a embezzlement scheme involving food coupons from which they netted millions of dollars, sending most of it to the PFLP in the Middle East.[71]

Similarly, a Palestinian "mafia" operated in the U.S. in the 1980s to collect millions of dollars for terrorist organizations and to then smuggle the funds to the Middle East. Much of the money came through criminal acts, such as robbery, blackmail, embezzlement, forgery and defrauding insurance companies and the Social Security System in Florida, Texas, California, Colorado and Tennessee. Part of the money went to PLO-affiliated organizations.[72]

It is highly plausible that, should the need have arisen, this group would have assisted in sabotage or other act of terrorism. At the time of their arrest, however, they had not done so.

BACK DOOR OPERATIONS

The growth of Islam in the Caribbean began in the 1960s, centered in Trinidad and Tobago where attempts to promote regional Islamic unity through publications and radio stations, and later through the organization of training camps for Muslim youth, were made. The radicalization of the Muslim community began in the mid-1970s, with the establishment of the Islamic Dawah Movement as the dominant regional Muslim organization. The radical politicization of the Muslim community was also influenced by the black Muslim movement in the U.S. in the 1960s and 1970s.[73]

Islamist revolutionary movements were introduced in the early 1980s. Young emigrants from South Asia and Africa brought the Khomeini and Qaddafi message with them. In 1982, they were dominant in establishing the Association of Islamic Communities of the Caribbean and Latin America (AICCLA). Soon afterwards, these institutions began receiving financial assistance from Libya for the establishment of civic projects.

By 1990, a comprehensive Islamic educational social infrastructure existed throughout the Caribbean. There is a growing emphasis on spreading Islam among the Caribbean's Africans and on organizing and politicizing their communities. In addition, several scholarships for higher Islamic studies in the Near East are provided to local youth. Islamist leaders from the Near East also regularly travel to the area to proselytize in the local communities.[74]

The most promising communities were those in Trinidad and Tobago. By the late 1980s, the spread of Islam in the islands reached 60-70 conversions per week. There was a corresponding communal awareness of the importance of a "return to Islam" in all aspects of life. At the forefront of the Islamicization campaign was the Jam'aat al-Muslimeen under the charismatic leader Imam Yasin Abu Bakr who transformed the movement into a major socio-political challenge to the political and economic order on these islands, organizing several international conferences to increase awareness.[75]

Along with 200-250 followers, their wives and children, Abu Bakr established in 1984 a model Islamic commune on the western side of Port-of-Spain that recognized only "the law of Almighty *Allah*." The eight acre commune has a large mosque, a day care center, school and kitchens for the homeless. The Jamaat al-Muslimeen also maintained an armed militia who were widely perceived in Trinidad as being violent outlaws, though the group's rhetoric is highly moralistic. In 1988, the police raided the commune, seizing weapons and ammunition and arresting 34 members of the sect on charges of larceny, robbery, illegal possession of weapons, rape and murder. Abu Bakr stated then that his vigilantes were waging a war against "the menace of cocaine."[76]

These activities would not have been possible without extensive foreign assistance. Abu Bakr travelled to Libya twice and to Iran once to solicit assistance for his Islamic projects. In 1983, after a visit to Tehran, he became affiliated with Islamic *Jihad*.[77] Since then, Abu Bakr has repeatedly emphasized his close ties with Libya and has often stated that Islamist principles as defined by Qaddafi must dominate society in Trinidad and Tobago.[78]

Meanwhile, Libyan representatives travelled routinely to Trinidad and Tobago, at least until 1987. They provided financial and professional assistance for several medical and social services provided by the Jamaat al-Muslimeen. Libya financed the building of schools, clinics and mosques. At the same time, "Libyan People's Bureaus" and humanitarian facilities became centers of intelligence gathering and subversion, maintaining contact with local radicals and facilitating travel to Libya for terrorist training. The Libyans used the humanitarian aid shipments to smuggle weapons and ammunition, including those captured in Abu Bakr's commune.[79] Members of Abu Bakr's group received military training in Libya.[80] Little wonder that in early July 1990, the government denied customs approval of a shipment of medical supplies donated to Abu Bakr by Libya.[81] Prime Minister Eugenia Charles of Domenica warned that Qaddafi's growing activities in the Caribbean "may be his way of hitting at the United States."[82]

On July 28, 1990, Abu Bakr led 111 of his followers, all of them well armed (including with AK-47 and explosives provided by Libya), on an assault on the Parliament building and the TV and radio station in Port-of-Spain. They held some 40 hostages, including the prime minister and most of the cabinet. There was very little bloodshed.

In a subsequent broadcast, Abu Bakr sharply criticized the widespread corruption and poverty he blamed on the current regime and promised elections within 90 days. He claimed that Prime Minister Arthur Robinson had been overthrown by God. "God has removed him," Abu Bakr said. "No man, including me, has power. . . He gave us victory over the prime minister."

The rebels settled for a lengthy siege with their hostages at the TV station and others at the Parliament building, Red House. The next day, a rebel leader identified as Velall Abdullah claimed that Robinson had agreed to resign and hold elections within 90 days.[83]

For the next two days there were sporadic exchanges of gun fire, with little effect or and few casualties. Negotiations on the surrender of the rebels included the partial and gradual release of a few hostages. Meanwhile, Robinson negotiated an agreement with Abu Bakr according to which the government granted amnesty to the rebels and permitted their return to the commune. Although the coup failed and Abu Bakr and his followers surrendered on July 31, the hostility and desperation of the population was expressed in the widespread riots and looting that broke out once the coup was announced. Several building were set ablaze by rioters. There was scattered gunfire as looters exchanged automatic fire with police. Convoys of cars and pickup trucks were loading up with everything from looted powdered milk to refrigerators, electric stoves and television sets.[84]

The Foreign Minister, Shahadeo Basdeo, stated that there was a "direct Libyan connection" to the failed coup. Indeed, Qaddafi seemed to have tried to assist his protege. On July 29, a Libyan aircraft took off from Surinam on its way to Trinidad and Tobago and requested landing permission in Barbados, which was denied.[85] Although the government promised to release the rebels to their commune, the military ransacked the compound before the agreement was implemented. Then, on August 3rd, a mysterious fire destroyed the commune completely.[86]

Nevertheless, despite the collapse of the Islamist coup in Trinidad and Tobago, the 400,000-415,000 strong Islamic community in the Caribbean remains highly explosive and volatile, ever more vulnerable to the exploitation of their growing socio-economic misery by Libyan and Iranian Islamist agitation. The radicalization of the community is reflected in the increased number of Islamist associations, mosques and assemblies throughout the Caribbean and, increasingly, Surinam (where Muslims constitute 22% of the population).[87]

The rejuvenation of the Islamist world in the aftermath of the bombing in New York was even expressed in Trinidad. Yasin Abu Bakr, the leader of the 1990 coup attempt who had been released from jail promising not to challenge the government, threatened on March 16, 1993, to lead another "fight" against the government's "oppression" of Islam.[88]

All this time, since the early 1980s, Syria, Libya, and several Palestinian organizations under their control, have made repeated efforts to penetrate the terrorist infrastructure of Latin America as a gateway into the United States. Cuba provided vital services in establishing connections and *bona fides* (references). For example, in May 1983 Columbia's M-19 disclosed that its members and commanders were being trained in Libya, Cuba and the U.S.S.R.[89] In November 1985, Rozemberg Pavon (a.k.a. Commandante Uno) of the M-19 returned to Columbia from Libya with 100 Palestinian expert-terrorists in order to launch the "final offensive."[90]

As local terrorist organizations, primarily the M-19, were developing closer relations with drug lords, so were the Arab terrorists. Soon, they were using the same routes of infiltration into the U.S. as the drug lords. Just how close these relations were was exposed when Emilio Checa Kuri, a Lebanese accused of being linked with international drug trafficking and international terrorism, was arrested in Mexico in the summer of 1988. Checa Kuri was affiliated with pro-Syrian terrorist groups. Once released on bail, he and his two sons escaped from Mexico with Lebanese diplomatic passports and ultimately received asylum in Libya.[91]

Meanwhile, the involvement of Syria, Iran and their clients in the drug trade has also turned into a primary instrument for bringing international terrorism closer to the U.S. itself. While the Syrians were interested in the immense financial gains in the drug trade, Iran and the *HizbAllah* also had ideological motives and *fatwa*s were issued accordingly by the Shi'ite leadership.[92] "We are making these drugs for the Devil; the Devil is America, Jews, et al. We cannot kill them with guns so we kill them with drugs," the *HizbAllah* explained.[93]

The most important development in the expansion of terrorism into the U.S. was the "crack-for-terrorist" deal reached between Damascus and the Colombian drug cartel. Syria had long been eager to meet the growing need in Western Europe for cocaine. However, it proved virtually impossible to grow coca plants in Lebanon. Therefore, there emerged a need to import coca "base" and the appropriate know-how to produce "American style" crack.

Enter Talal Daizum, a drug dealer and smuggler from Kamid, and the major protege of General Mustafa Tlass who was, with his wife, personally involved in a very significant way in drug trafficking. Daizum is known for his widespread and intimate contacts with smuggling networks in Western Europe and the U.S., running through Cyprus and Turkey. His loyalty and effectiveness has been proven several times when Syrian intelligence used his couriers to carry drugs and terrorist material all the way into the U.S. At Tlass's request Daizum investigated the possibility of acquiring cocaine for Syria.[94]

During 1987-88, several high level messengers shuttled between Lebanon, Cyprus and Columbia. Major progress toward an arrangement was made in a series of meetings in Larnaca between a senior family member of the Pablo Escobar Colombian Medellin drug cartel and a senior member of the Keyrouz family, a Lebanese clan very close to the Syrian intelligence and military leadership, long associated with the Syrian drug trade. In 1989, Escobar met Rais' Assad (Rifa't Assad's son) and senior Syrian military and intelligence officials in Larnaca to discuss the expansion of their cooperation.[95]

The essence of the agreement reached was that the cartel would help Syria in its Lebanon-based cocaine activities in return for Syria supplying the Cartel with terrorist expertise and equipment so that they could take on the local governments (and even the U.S. should it intervene).[96] Indeed, the export to the Middle East of commercial quantities of coca base began in 1989-1990. Local labs located in Lebanon's Shouf mountains began producing usable cocaine and exported it to Western Europe soon afterwards.[97]

As a direct result of Escobar's visit to Larnaca, a "factory" for crack was set up in the Biqaa in January 1990 using raw materials provided from Columbia (and elsewhere in Latin America), initially to satisfy the growing demand in Western Europe and the Far East.[98] Ultimately, it took a good part of the drug infrastructure away from the reach of U.S. forces.

Soon afterwards, a few Basque expert terrorists from the ETA were sent from the Talbaya and al-Marj camps in the Biqaa and are now known to be teaching terrorists in Latin America.[99]

The Medellin Cartel was quick to put into action what it learned from the Syrians. On November 27, 1989, an Avianca Boeing 727 exploded in mid-air five minutes after taking off from the Bogota, Columbia, airport, killing 101 passengers and six crew members.[100] Investigation disclosed that a Middle Eastern-style bomb made of SEMTEX was planted by the Medellin Cartel, and that the detonator was similar to the one used to blow up Pan-Am Flight 103.[101]

Since early 1992, there has been an increase in the quantities of weapons sent to Columbia. The first major shipment took place in mid-February. A Greek-registered ship, the *El-Kiran*, collected some $20 million worth of weapons and explosives in Varna (Bulgaria), Tripoli (Libya) and somewhere in Central America. The *El-Kiran* had started its journey in Thailand where it collected a shipment of drugs for Bulgaria. By the time it reached Columbia, the *El-Kiran* carried some 900 AK-47s, several Galil assault rifles, 40 crates with RPG-7 grenade launchers, large quantities of ammunition for these weapons, and high explosives. These weapons were safely delivered to units of the ELN (the Army of National Liberation) and FARC (the Revolutionary Armed Forces of Columbia).[102] Since then, large quantities of weapons have been purchased in Eastern Europe by Syrian and Iranian buyers on behalf of Columbian terrorists. Additional shipments have reached Columbia since April 1992.

Meanwhile, the governments of Iran and Syria are actively engaged in economic warfare against the U.S. through the production and dissemination of high quality counterfeit dollar bills, primarily $100 bills. The objectives of this campaign are twofold: (1) to alleviate the dire financial shortages of both countries; and (2) to destabilize the U.S. economy. The actual smuggling of the counterfeit bills and their distribution in the U.S. (and elsewhere) are carried out by the terrorist networks already in place controlled by both states.

Majid Anaraki, an Iranian *Hizbollahi* who lived for several years in southern California, described America as "a collection of casinos, supermarkets and whore-houses linked together by endless highways passing through nowhere," all dominated and motivated by the lust for money. "Those people

in the West will put their own mothers on auction for profit,"
explained Behzad Nabavi, then Iran's Minister of Heavy In-
dustries. Khomeini himself pointed out that the Western preoccupation with the quest for money makes "prostitution a
community's way of life."[103] Thus, the possibility of being able
"to bring harm to the U.S. economy" through large-scale
counterfeit operations was extremely appealing to Tehran.[104]

Iran and its allies produce and distribute the counterfeit
U.S. banknotes in three qualities, ranging from extremely high
quality to medium and low. Even the low quality bills are quite
good. The high quality $100 bank notes are used directly
against the U.S. banking system. These bills are printed in the
Iranian official mint in Tehran, using equipment and know-
how purchased from the U.S. during the days of the Shah.
Israeli officials have affirmed, through their own intelligence,
that these dollars are being printed on "high-tech, state-owned
presses with paper acquired only by governments." The plates
used for the $100 bills are virtually perfect. They are used for
all the counterfeits. The ink is almost always of extremely high
quality. The specialized ink is mixed in the laboratories of the
national mint in Tehran by chemists who had studied in the
U.S.[105]

The initial distribution and dissemination of the counterfeit
money is centrally controlled by the highest levels of the Syrian
Government. The actual handling of counterfeit currency is
conducted by Military Intelligence from Lebanon. The most
important Lebanon-based networks smuggling the notes have
evolved from the heroin and cocaine smuggling networks
already in place. These networks operate under the tight control of, direct supervision by, and extensive assistance from
Syrian Military Intelligence. Senior officers take direct part in
the shipment of the counterfeit bills from Lebanon.[106]

One of the major players in the distribution of the high-
quality counterfeit bills is the Keyrouz clan of Diral-Ahmar,
notorious as major drug dealers and personal proteges of the
Syrian military and intelligence elite. Recently, two members

of the Keyrouz clan, Hanna and Georges (Giryes), offered to sell $100,000 in high-quality $100 bills for a lump sum of $50,000.[107] The involvement of the Keyrouz clan is of crucial significance because the heads of the clan were among the Lebanese mediators responsible for the first contacts between Syria and the Medellin Cartel. The clan now capitalizes on its contacts with international drug cartels to assist in the distribution and laundering of large-sums of high-quality counterfeit money, especially in Latin America and the U.S.

A significant portion of the counterfeit dollar bills is being distributed on behalf of Iran by *HizbAllah* networks as part of their smuggling and logistical efforts. The *HizbAllah* uses well-established networks with proven records.[108]

Tehran and Damascus are very prudent in their distribution of their high-quality counterfeit bills. They started cautiously, and then, over the course of the first 24 months of distribution, gradually expanded the circle of financial institutions and banks exposed to large quantities of the currency, to allay suspicion on the part of the institutions. The high-quality bills first emerged in the Middle East, where they were tested on local branches of foreign banks. Only when it was clear that the counterfeits were not noticed was the distribution expanded into Western Europe, primarily France, again to both local and foreign banks. When Tehran and Damascus were convinced that their high-quality counterfeit dollars passed the scrutiny of sophisticated banks they began large scale dissemination in the U.S. and Canada.

The *HizbAllah* is responsible for the distribution of the counterfeit $100 bills in the U.S. and Canada on behalf of Iranian Intelligence. Large quantities of counterfeit money are smuggled into these countries along the routes controlled by Syria and Iran and used previously for the smuggling of weapons, explosives, drugs and operatives.

The chiefs of the IRGC Intelligence and the VEVAK are convinced that their modes and avenues of entry into the U.S. are safe, and thus can sustain a greater volume of shipments.[109]

Meanwhile, since the mid-1980s there has been a consolidation and expansion of Peruvian narcoterrorism, conducted mainly by the *Sendero Luminoso* (Shining Path or SL; full name *Partido Comunista del Peru por el Sendero Luminoso del Pensamiento de Jose Carlos Mariategui*/Communist Party of Peru on the Shining Path of the Thought of Jose Carlos Mariategui), a quasi-Maoist terrorist organization under the absolute leadership and ideological guidance of Abimael Guzman (a.k.a. Presidente Gonzalo), in cooperation with international terrorists, especially the Abu Nidal Organization.

Most important was the contribution of the Abu Nidal Organization to the Sendero urban operations because they could not have taken place without the massive infusion of terrorist knowledge from veteran international terrorist organizations. Indeed, in early 1988, the Abu-Nidal Organization began helping the Shining Path consolidate its urban operations, and provided training in advanced techniques, such as sophisticated sabotage. Atif Abu-Bakr, Abu-Nidal's ex-deputy, explained: "In 1989, for example, he (Abu-Nidal) made more than $4 million in Peru. Cocaine money, to be sure."[110] The Abu Nidal touch was immediately apparent. The *Sendero Luminoso*'s urban assassination techniques and tactics are virtually identical to those used by Palestinians and the West European terrorists trained by them.

The Abu Nidal Organization was also involved in terrorist operations in Peru. A senior Abu-Nidal operative, Hussein Bouzidi (a.k.a. Ali Muhammad, Ali Issa Habatami), and two aids, an Algerian named Ahmad Assad Muhammad (a.k.a. Salam Abd al-Aziyah) and a Lebanese named Abd al-Rahman (a.k.a. Muathsim, who travelled with an Egyptian passport), were arrested in Lima in the summer of 1988 following a bombing attempt on the U.S. Embassy. In April 1990, they were released after an intense campaign by the local PLO office and supporters and allowed to remain in country. Then, on 24 July 1990, there was an assassination attempt on Yaacov

Hasson Ichab, the executive director of human relations for the Jewish community in Peru. The evidence collected, and the examination of the method, tactics and weapons used suggested that the attack was carried out by "a Shining Path death squad" with the "participation of a clandestine cell of the radical Palestinian Abu Nidal group." Indeed, when arrested back in July 1988, Bouzidi had had a hit list in his possession that included Hasson's name.[111]

Urban operations have become so important to the Shining Path strategy that, in 1989/1990, Guzman divided the *Sendero Luminoso* into two equal branches: the Revolutionary Movement of the People's Defense responsible for all terrorist activities in urban areas, and the veteran Revolutionary Front of the People's Defense that is responsible for all activities in rural areas.[112] The SL terrorist campaign in Lima and other towns in connection with the 1990 elections, while straining the organization's assets to the point of internal strife, and while being ultimately incapable of preventing the elections, did expose a redundant, solid and fairly well organized urban infrastructure with a growth potential given the allocation of the right assets.[113]

This infrastructure was revitalized on behalf of Arab causes in connection with the Gulf Crisis. In mid-January 1991, the SL led anti-U.S. pro-Saddam Hussein demonstrations. In the following months there were several bombing attacks on U.S. diplomatic facilities, but no specific perpetrator among Peru's several urban Communist terrorist movements emerged. On the basis of bomb technologies and techniques, SL operatives are believed to be responsible for some of these bombings.

However, it is in the coca-growing valleys called "liberated areas" by the *Sendero Luminoso* that the interests of international terrorists[114] such as the Abu Nidal Organization really lie. In Islamist international terrorism, sophisticated and spectacular operations are conducted by expert terrorists and key controllers who infiltrate the target country for the execution of specific operations. If needed, they also smuggle in the specialized equipment they might require. In the mid-1980s, in the aftermath of the U.S. bombing of Libya, there was apprehension among the terrorist states of massive U.S. retaliation that they might be found to be directly involved in terrorism inside the U.S. Therefore, they assisted their protege-terrorists in an effort to establish access routes for men and equipment into the U.S. through channels other than the normal diplomatic ones. Of these, Peru became a favorite of such organizations as Abu Nidal's.

Thus, for the Abu Nidal Organization, the "liberated areas" in Peru constitute safe havens with proven means of illegal transportation of men and equipment into the U.S. In 1991, there was a marked expansion of SL involvement in support for drug trafficking by guiding Columbian and local planes to isolated jungle strips.[115] Peruvian security authorities recently exposed a network of mobile high-powered beacons used to guide planes to sites of choice.[116] This was in addition to sophisticated radio and electronic equipment acquired in the late 1980s and used to expedite the safe trafficking and monitoring of hostile communications.[117] Indeed, the SL seems to be well acquainted with the comprehensive network of electronic detection systems operated by the U.S. and allied forces in South and Central America.[118]

Moreover, ideologically at least, even the *Sendero Luminoso* has a commitment to terrorism in the U.S. because it is a member of the International Revolutionary Movement, a union of 19 radical-Maoist revolutionary organizations that includes the U.S. Revolutionary Communist Party. The IRM's charter calls for mutual assistance in the pursuit of world revolution and, with the SL's increasing funds and power, Guzman might be tempted to assist the American revolutionaries.[119] Guzman's arrest has changed nothing. His replacements are even more committed to international terrorism and solidarity.

The arrangements between the Middle Eastern terrorist organizations and the Latin American drug lords are crucial factors in the insertion of expert terrorists into the U.S. because the drug lords control some of the most proven infiltration routes and have the required funds. The cooperation between the terrorist states in the Middle East, their proteges, and the drug lords of Latin America is bound to expand further.

As proven by the accumulated experience of terrorist operations in Western Europe, a comprehensive and professional support system composed of predominantly dormant Islamist cells is crucial for the success of sustained and sophisticated terrorist operations. The Hispanic and Korean graduates of the Melli University in Iran, long since ordered to establish dormant networks in the south and west of the U.S. (see chapter 3), would serve as an interface between the two network-systems. However, it is the rapidly growing Islamist community in the U.S. itself that provides international terrorism with this all-important infrastructure and support system.

THE RISE OF THE ISLAMIST NETWORK

Although Qaddafi has repeatedly tried to foment a revolution among the Blacks and Indians in America, when it came to actual operations Libyan intelligence trusted only clandestine Libyan networks and, when needed, mercenaries hired to commit specific crimes. In sharp contrast, the Iranians and their allies have been firm believers in consolidating a genuine widespread popular belief in their ideology that would in turn result in the emergence of a solid and committed support infrastructure. Such an approach proved its effectiveness in the wave of Islamist terrorist attacks in Western Europe during the 1980s. By 1986, Iran and Syria had become the dominant states controlling international terror-ism and this had direct ramifications concerning the conduct of terrorism inside the U.S.

Early warnings for this major development were in abundance. At a Maronite conference in Montreal in mid-July 1985, Lebanese Christian leaders warned that Islamic extremist groups based in Lebanon were extending their terrorist operations to North America. Western nations "have to understand the danger is for them as well," said Chakar Abu-Sleiman, the head of the Lebanese delegation. "The fallout has already reached Europe and is knocking at the door of North America," he warned.[120]

Indeed, in early 1986 there was a sharp increase in specific threats to conduct terrorism inside the U.S. For example, the Islamic *Jihad* threatened to "deal painful blows to Americans in the heart of the United States."[121] Ibrahim al-Amin declared that the *HizbAllah* "will fight America everywhere in the region and the world. For America is . . . the foremost enemy of all the Muslims of the world."[122]

During the fall of 1986 official Tehran was in a combative mood. Prime Minister Hussein Musavi explained that "U.S. imperialism, having suffered irreparable blows from Iran, intends eventually to disgrace the Islamic Revolution. . . Any action by the United States against our country will increase the anti-U.S. feelings in Iran and throughout the region."[123] When CSSPA repeated its demands for the release of three terrorists held in Paris, it extended its threat to the U.S. The CSPPA threatened to have "an appointment" with President Reagan in "his own country."[124] A written communique was distributed in Beirut:

> We will meet soon in your formidable United States. We will get acquainted with your cities and skyscrapers, and with your Statue of Liberty. We will not wait for your invitation. The streets of America will know us shortly.[125]

Similarly, in a press conference in Damascus, George Habbash blasted U.S. policy in the Middle East and threatened Washington: "As long as President Reagan continues to deal with the subject (Middle East) in this manner, I regret to say that the phenomenon of terrorism will continue, although some of these operations, in the opinion of the PFLP, do not serve the Palestinian question."[126]

Iran and its allies continued to present and acknowledge international terrorist strikes as an integral component of Tehran's global and regional strategy. For example, in a July 1987 communique from Tehran, the Kuwaiti *HizbAllah* warned both the U.S. and Kuwait against the consequences of the reflagging of Kuwaiti tankers, some of which had been attacked by Iran during the Iran-Iraq War. "The U.S. Administration should bear in mind that the Islamic Revolution is a fact which has firmly taken root around the globe and that its shoots are prepared for martyrdom anywhere in the world. . . . The *HizbAllah* is preparing itself throughout the world in order to deal blows to U.S. interests and to the strategic positions of this foremost enemy of Muslims. . . This time, Muslim fighters will attack the heart of criminal U.S. positions in Washington and New York, so that the whole world will see how Reagan and the United States, these two paper tigers, will collapse under the horrific blows dealt by Muslims."[127] In Beirut, a caller on behalf of the Mustafa Chamran Troops of the Islamic *Jihad* repeated the same warning.[128]

In early 1980, Mehdi Hashemi launched operations inside America with the objectives of "creating cores among local Islamic associations responsible for defending Iran's views (interests) . . . and even creating socio-economic disturbances if those countries should become too dangerous." Tehran was fully aware that "there can be no reasonable question of seeking the creation of an Islamic republic" in the U.S. and Canada, and, therefore, the primary objectives of the Islamist networks included, first, "discovering, overseeing and eliminating Khomeini's Iranian enemies," and, then, if possible, transferring the confrontation with the Great Satan to its own backyard.[129]

One of these early Iranian networks was first activated in December 1983. A group of Lebanese and Iranians *Hizbollahi*

almost succeeded in burning down a rented theater filled with
some 500 anti-Khomeini Iranians in Seattle, Washington. The
HizbAllah's plan called for trapping and locking the attendants
inside the burning hall and causing such heavy casualties that
the anti-Khomeini opposition would be afraid to gather and
protest against Iran for a long time to come. Unusually, this
operation was the result of a local initiative. The SAVAMA
and *HizbAllah* had agents in the ranks of the anti-Khomeini
Iranians, who, once they had learned about the plans for the
rally, decided to demonstrate the long reach of the Islamic
Revolution in a dramatic way. With active preparations well
underway, the conspirators were stopped at the last minute by
the FBI only because one of them boasted about the impending
operation.[130]

The early presence of *HizbAllah* and Iranian assets in the
U.S. was reflected in the escalation of the anti-U.S. rhetoric
and especially the threats of retribution. A caller speaking for
Islamic *Jihad* in Beirut announced that the organization would
strike very shortly at "key American targets in the Middle
East" in reprisal for U.S. policy in Lebanon. "We now have
more sophisticated methods than booby trapped cars and lor-
ries," he said.[131]

The Islamic *Jihad* Organization warned that "a hard blow
will be struck very soon against the American devil and his
allies," and signaled President Reagan, pointing out that its
militants were ready to attack "American interests and the
American Navy wherever they are."[132] Sheikh Sa'id Sha'ban
also warned the U.S. that "it will soon witness operations
against it on its soil" and emphasized that "no one can stop the
Islamic tide, which has started to upset the White House."[133]

Even official Damascus joined the campaign of threats.
The Syrian *Ba'ath* Party issued a warning in conjunction with
the 1985 TWA hijacking. Damascus warned that "President
Reagan should have realized from the very beginning that
terrorism is a two-edged weapon and that the United States,

which has begun exercising terrorism as an official policy, would have to pay a high price, because people and national liberation movements in the world cannot possibly give in to blackmail and threats, especially when their freedom and national rights are at stake.''[134]

Indeed, by the mid-1980s, the Iranian-sponsored Islamist network in the U.S. and Canada had markedly expanded and become better organized. The Islamist infrastructure already included all the components of a mature terrorist support system. These included safe houses in major cities, weapons, ammunition, money, systems to provide medical and legal aid, false identity papers and intelligence for the operatives. The network was also large in scale and spanned the United States. The primary objectives of this sleeper support network were to assist sabotage operations and the assassination of key figures, mainly on behalf of Iran but also in support of Libya. Altogether, the emphasis was on establishing long-term capabilities that could be activated on short notice.[135]

More than 100 well-trained Shi'ite terrorists were already deployed in the U.S. in late 1985. Virtually all of them had entered the U.S. via Mexico. They were concealed and shielded primarily within the population of students from Muslim countries which, in the mid-1980s, was estimated to be some 60,000 strong.[136] Tehran also made an effort to improve the terrorist skills of the members of the sleeper networks. Several Iranian "students" in the U.S., all sustained by scholarships from Tehran, were ordered to return to Iran on a periodic basis in order to receive military training. After returning to the U.S., these "students" resumed their studies and largely stayed out of major clandestine activities, waiting, as sleeper agents, for activation.[137]

In Tehran, the U.S.-Canadian operation was under the command of Ayatollah Muhammad Nassiri. He is an Iraqi-born Shi'ite who was trained in Lebanon in the 1970s and belonged to a radicalized group of *al-Fatah* that took part in the terrorist operations of Black September (a PLO special forces group responsible for countless terrorist operations in the 1970s) and its offspring. The Palestinian group Nassiri belonged to had special relations with Soviet and East European trainers. Nassiri also enjoyed the special trust of Ayatollah Khomeini because of his close relationship with Khomeini's dead son, Mustafa. Between 1984 and 1986, Nassiri visited the U.S. and Canada at least half-a-dozen times, staying two to three months at a time. He traveled all over both countries, addressing Islamic student organizations (including Egyptians, Saudis, North Africans, Iranians, Afghans, South East Asians and Black Muslims). His primary mission was to organize and supervise the Islamic *Jihad* and *HizbAllah* cells in the U.S. and Canada. Some of the networks organized by Nassiri are intended to become the skeleton of Islamic Revolutionary movements in the participants' home countries.[138]

Sheikh Majdeddin Mahalati, the brother of Hojat-ol-Islam Fazl-Allah Mahalati who, until his death in 1985, had been in charge of Iran's terrorist training system, also made a special inspection tour in the U.S. in the summer of 1985 on behalf of Khomeini.[139] This inspection trip indicated serious deliberations in Tehran about a possible activation of their U.S. networks.

Indeed, Islamist sources in Beirut disclosed in the summer of 1986 that "plans have been drawn up" in Tehran to strike at U.S. interests in the Middle East, Europe, and the U.S. itself. They added that these terrorist operations, to be conducted in the name of the *HizbAllah* or Islamic *Jihad*, "will be directed against sensitive centers considered to be highly unlikely targets and will involve an element of surprise." The Islamist sources attribute the delay in the implementation of Tehran's plans to "a wait-and-see attitude on the part of these groups after receiving information that the United States may lead a direct retaliatory campaign against them."[140]

By 1986-87, Tehran had analyzed the initial lessons of the accumulated experience of Islamist clandestine and terrorist activities in Western Europe. Iranians officials and experts also conducted numerous consultations with allies, both in the context of several major terrorist conferences and in smaller gatherings of senior leaders, primarily in Europe. This process of lesson learning and strategy formulation is described in great detail in Chapters 2, 5 and 6 above.

One of the most important lessons derived from the clandestine and terrorist activities in Western Europe was the recognition of the crucial importance of a long term presence and a locally-based support infrastructure. Tehran concluded that it was virtually impossible to sustain, let alone run, effective terrorist and intelligence networks without a solid support infrastructure on-site.

Furthermore, Iran by now already had the first cadres of Islamist expert terrorists, mainly Arab *Hizbollahi*, qualified and ready for operations in the most demanding theaters, including the U.S. All of them were graduates of the comprehensive terrorist training systems in Iran and Syria.

Therefore, the Islamist terrorist masters decided, and not without reason, that their urgent priority should be the establishment of a solid and redundant support infrastructure. The emphasis should be on the organization and consolidation of a comprehensive web of support networks that would be able to withstand any police action after major strikes. The experts in Tehran were convinced that such a support system can be safe and secure only if it rises from within a radicalized and activist Islamist community. Therefore, Iran and its allies embarked on a twin-track program to further improve their terrorist capabilities in the U.S. and Canada:

1. Gradually but quickly transform the Muslim community in the U.S., pushing it toward greater radicalization and commitment to Islamist activism that can then be exploited and manipulated to support international terrorism.

2. Prepare numerous cadres of super-expert terrorists who are not merely excellent as operatives but are capable of

sustaining operations in the U.S. under the most adverse social conditions.

For the next few years, Tehran would concentrate on acquiring these capabilities. As will be seen below, the consolidation of the support system was such a high priority that Tehran and Damascus decided on a conscientious avoidance of exposing and utilizing their rapidly improving and expanding terrorist network in the U.S. to support or facilitate terrorist operations, even at the price of inaction or even failures.

Tehran embarked on a campaign of agitation and manipulation of the Muslim communities in the United States and Canada. The Iranian analysis of the dynamics of Muslim communities in the West, based on their experience in Western Europe, is that once a community embarks on a path of greater awareness and communal activism, activities that by themselves are innocent and legitimate, a minority within this community is propelled even further to become an activist Islamist community. Subsequently, with proper agitation and organization provided by the Iranian-controlled *mullah*s and *ulama*, some of these activist Islamists can be convinced, recruited and trained to either assist Islamist terrorists as part of the support system or even to commit acts of terrorism themselves. Thus, the main Iranian objective was to begin the transformation of the Islamist segments of the community into greater activism, in order to, in turn, effect the radicalization of a relatively few extremists on the fringes to the point of willingly and actively supporting and assisting the Islamist terrorists.

By the time Iranians embarked on this campaign in 1986, there were already good indications of the susceptibility of parts of the Muslim community to Islamist agitation. There was evidence of the availability of Islamist cadres that might be influenced and manipulated. Indeed, for the initial penetration into the U.S. Muslim communities, the Iranians first relied on the activist Palestinian Islamist community.

Young members of the Islamic Council of Palestine had begun organizing in the U.S. back in the mid-1970s, joining the

World Islamic Organizations in America. By the late 1970s, several young Islamists joined the League of Arab Muslim Youth. Some became members of its executive committee. Substantive Islamist politicization began around 1980 and the Islamic Federation for Palestine was formed and consolidated in 1982-83. The first major Islamist seminar was held in Raleigh, North Carolina in the spring of 1983. It was soon followed by a seminar in Athens, Ohio, in the summer of 1984. Both seminars attracted militant Islamists committed to the "Palestinian Resistance Movement" and its "centrality in the comprehensive struggle" against the West.[141]

The Iranians and Syrians consulted with some of the Palestinian Islamist leaders and concluded that there was a manpower pool in America that could be transformed into a cohesive support system. On the basis of the experience in Western Europe in penetrating and subverting the Muslim communities from within through the use of religious leaders and activists, Tehran identified the need for a similar process in the U.S. as the number one priority.

Afghanistan would be Tehran's primary avenue into the Muslim community in the U.S. and Canada. The Iranians would rely on a mix of Afghan Islamists, Iranians masquerading as Afghans, and Arab 'Afghans' for smuggling into the U.S. and Canada Sunni *mullah*s and *ulama* and expert terrorists in order to transform and agitate the local communities, introduce the spirit of *Jihad*, and, ultimately, establish and manage networks. In the U.S. and Canada, these operatives would be absorbed and sheltered by the existing Islamist networks checked and solidified by Ayatollah Nassiri.

By then, largely due to the work of Abbas Zamani, Iran's ambassador to Pakistan, Afghan-Iranian cooperation in fighting the *Jihad* had been expanded into the integration of Afghan *mujahideen* into the fold of Islamic *Jihad* and *HizbAllah* networks in the U.S. and Canada. Because of widespread support for the Afghan resistance, *mujahideen* were accepted and supported in Western countries in places their Iranian counter-parts could not reach. Therefore, Afghans became the key to the establishment of new terrorist networks.

Ostensibly, Afghan "refugees and emigres" who resettled in the U.S. and Canada organized and assumed command over new cells and networks of the *HizbAllah* under the guise of solidarity committees with the *Jihad* in Afghanistan. Thus, even as Iran's involvement in and support for international terrorism became known, the *Hizbollahhi* were still able to travel to the West through Pakistan, using the makeshift travel documents of the Afghan refugees and resistance fighters.

Back in 1983, the cooperation between the Afghans and the Iranians reached new heights when Abbas Zamani became the Iranian ambassador to Islamabad. As Abu-Sharief, Zamani was involved in overseas operations for *al-Fath*, Black September, and other Palestinian organizations during the 1970s. He was one of the first and most ardent advocates of exporting the Islamic Revolution. Toward that end he supervised PLO support for the organization of the *Pasdaran*. All this time Zamanai was a senior KGB operative. He would be quietly recalled in 1986 after his role in Afghan-Pakistani Islamist terrorism was exposed. But while in Islamabad, Zamani coordinated the transfer of funds, weapons and trainees between Iran and the camps in Pakistan.[142]

In 1984, on the instructions of Mirhashem, Zamani approached the Afghan resistance leader Gulbaddin Hekmatyar and asked for his help. The Iranians wanted to use some of the Afghan *mujahideen* with combat experience in both Afghanistan and the Iraqi front as instructors for the terrorist brigade (see Chapter 2). They also wanted to deploy some of the Iranian terrorists in the ranks of *Hizb-i Islami* and *JundAllah* so that they could acquire combat experience in irregular warfare and as urban guerrillas. Hekmatyar agreed to both requests and their implementation started within a short time. Soon afterwards, Afghans volunteered, and in some cases were invited, to join *HizbAllah* and the Iranian subunits. Since their experience and expertise were invaluable to the Iranians, and their commitment to Islam was beyond reproach, they were accepted even though they were Sunni.[143]

At first, Tehran and Hekmatyar reached an agreement on Iranian assistance to establish an Islamic Republic in Afghanistan. In return, Iranian intelligence operatives and terrorists would be included in the *Hizb-i Islami* missions in Arab and Muslim countries and especially the Persian Gulf countries.[144] These countries are "the first tier" priorities of the Iranian terrorist brigade.[145]

Concurrently, since mid-1985, Iran was increasing its specialized terrorist training program for foreigners prepared for high-risk operations overseas. Among the first to receive this training was a group of Afghan *mujahideen* in the Mashhad area who were transferred to a camp in the Quchan district and given intensive terrorist and clandestine training under the command of Mohammad Ali Kolahduz. Some of these Afghans were prepared for terrorist operations in the U.S.[146]

In late June or early July 1987, following the success of their initial arrangements, Gulbaddin Hekmatyar signed an agreement with Iran whereby Tehran would increase its help to his *Hizb-i-Islami* group, and in return Iranians would be infiltrated into the West, especially the United States and Canada, using documents provided by the *Hizb-i-Islami*. In view of the close relations that Pakistan's ISI had with Gulbaddin Hekmatyar and the tight control they exercised over him and his forces, it is inconceivable that such strategic arrangements could have been reached without Islamabad's blessing and approval, let alone intimate knowledge.[147]

A measure of the concurrent growing extremism and radicalism of the Islamist community in the U.S., which constitutes the primary source of the support network for Middle Eastern terrorist operatives, can be found in the agitation activities in the community. The call for *Jihad* and the resurrection of the

Islamic struggle was repeatedly expressed by the local Islamists. Some of the Islamic internal publications in the U.S. even reiterated the themes of the armed struggle advocated in Europe and the Middle East.

For example, the August 22, 1986, issue of *The Bulletin of The Islamic Center* in Washington D.C. — *Under Siege* — was devoted to the validity of *Jihad* as an Islamic obligation of all the Believers. The study explained that the U.S. is considered a *Kufr* (infidel, heretic) and a "crusading imperialist" state. The bulletin emphasizes that "in order for Muslims to put an end to the existence of the illegitimate Zionist state, Muslims have to cancel all the puppet regimes in their own countries." The American Muslims are urged to actively join a world-wide *Jihad*, including in the U.S. itself. "*Jihad* is the only way to restore the honor of Muslim peoples and bring about a Muslim revolution. . . All Muslims should move and take up arms to shake the earth under the feet of the *Kuffar*."[148]

The mid-1980s also saw a growing intensity of Islamist activity in the U.S. that can be gauged from the diversity and frequency of Islamist publications, mainly in Middle Eastern languages as well as in English. Several Islamic conferences and gatherings were taking place. Most important was the seminar of the Islamic Conference for Palestine held in Plainfield, Indiana, in the summer of 1987. The bulk of the conference was devoted to questions of Islamist activism in the U.S. itself and especially universities. The conference studied "the role of the mosques and students with respect to the Palestine issue" and "the Islamic movement and the challenges of the Palestine issue."[149] Other large scale conferences took place in Houston, Texas, with 6,000 participants,[150] and Oklahoma City, Oklahoma, where 4,000 youth were urged "to adhere to their faith in words and deeds because it is the only true way to salvation."[151]

By themselves, these legal and legitimate gatherings reflect an overall increase in the Islamic awareness of the American Muslim community. However, in retrospect, they have been exploited in order to expedite the subversion of the radicalized extremist fringe minority. The subversive Islamist elements have utilized these legal and legitimate religious gatherings for agitation, recruitment and cover for their own clandestine meetings. This pattern of activities on the fringe and under the shadow of legitimate Islamic activities is identical to the practices of the Iranian-controlled terrorist networks in Western Europe. Considering the rapidly growing U.S. Muslim community, the actual number of recruits and supporters reached through this method appears to be quite large.

Moreover, there was also a growing number of Islamist gatherings and conferences at which many of the North American organizations represented were actually fronts formally affiliated with Iranian and Syrian controlled organizations in the Middle East and Europe. Messages and communiques from known radical Islamist leaders have been read at many of these conferences. It is not by accident that veteran Islamist organizations, including Chamran's Muslim Students' Association of the U.S. and Canada, have been revived and are recognized by the highest authorities in Tehran.

For example, in June 1988, Ayatollah Jannati sent a special message to the 20th annual meeting of the Muslim Students' Association of the U.S. and Canada in which he urged "efforts by Muslim students in America and Canada to fight the agents of corruption, to implement divine commands, and to deliver the message of Islam and the Iranian revolution to the people of these two nations."[152]

Financial support for organizations and individuals is channelled through various Islamic charities, some of which, like the Mostazafan Foundation in New York, acknowledge their relationship with both the Iranian Government and local Islamist organizations such as the Muslim Students' Association of the U.S. and Canada.[153]

All this time, during the late 1980s, Tehran continued to consolidate and expand its terrorist infrastructure in the U.S. As a result, in early 1989, the Iranian network in the U.S. was the most solid and dangerous of all local terrorist networks. Tehran was able to establish in the U.S. the combination of expert terrorists and Islamist zealots that had proved to be so lethal in Western Europe.

A comprehensive support infrastructure manned by dedicated individuals had already been functioning for several years. Small networks of Iranian operatives and terrorists, with their own stockpiles of weapons and explosives, were already deployed in the U.S., hidden mainly within the 30,000-strong Iranian emigre student community, more than half of them "sympathetic" to the cause of Khomeini.

Although the membership in the Muslim Students' Association was in the thousands, only less than 1,000 of them were active militants that Tehran could really rely on to conduct or support terrorism. However, because of their education and positions, these dedicated few constituted an impressive talent pool for such operations.[154] In addition, several tens of expert IRGC operatives and terrorists were already clandestinely deployed inside the U.S., ever ready to strike if ordered to. A few hundred militant Iranian students in the U.S., funded by Iranian scholarships, were expected to actively assist them or directly participate in such terrorist operations. Organized support for the entire Iranian network was conducted via the Islamic Society of North America and the Mostazafan Foundation. For routine activities, The Islamic Society was the primary instrument of communication with Tehran, while the Mostazafan Foundation was the main channel for providing the funds.[155]

CHAPTER 8

ISLAMIST TERRORISM IN AMERICA (II)

GEARING UP FOR ACTION

By the mid-1980s, Tehran was confident enough of the ability of its terrorist networks in the U.S. to begin operations on a limited scale but only for high priority causes. This confidence was based on the reports from Ayatollah Muhammad Nassiri and Sheikh Majdeddin Mahalati. Tehran could rely on the over 100 *Hizbollahi* who were organized in sleeper networks and securely concealed inside the Muslim student population. Meanwhile, Tehran was also coming under extreme pressure from its closest allies and terrorist partners, Libya and Syria, to use its impressive terrorist system to strike in the U.S. Moreover, in 1986 the U.S.S.R. and Cuba relaxed the restraints they had imposed on terrorist operations in the U.S. Nevertheless, the cautious and prudent terrorist masters in Tehran were reluctant to act haphazardly.

This is not to say that the Iranians were inactive. On the contrary, they were using existing networks to spy in support of the Iranian war effort against Iraq. For example, on September 1, 1987, a senior *HizbAllah* operative, Muhammad Harafdini, was arrested in New York with blueprints and drawings of components of F-111 strike aircraft and several missiles. A cache of spare parts and other blueprints were found in his apartment. He had worked for over a year for a defense contractor in order to obtain this data. Harafdini turned out to have been the head of an Iranian network that had been switched from preparing for sabotage operations to technological espionage for Iran.

Ironically, the collapse of the network was accidental. Another member of the network, Yassir Hamas, who had been arrested for credit card fraud, broke down while being questioned by the police and brought about the collapse of the network.[2]

However, it was a botched Libyan operation that finally convinced Tehran that it must accelerate its preparations for the activation of the Islamist terrorist networks in the U.S. and Canada. In April 1987, there were strong indications of impending terrorist attacks against casinos in Atlantic City to commemorate the anniversary of the U.S. bombing of Libya. Two expert terrorists arrived in the U.S. from the Middle East. They activated a dormant network in New York and were expected to move on to Mexico after the operation.[3] Apparently, they noticed the enhanced readiness of the law enforcement forces, cancelled the operation, and escaped safely from the U.S.

Nevertheless, preparations for terrorist strikes in the U.S. accelerated. In the fall of 1987, Iran was actively preparing suicide attacks in the U.S. and France to be conducted in the name of *Islamic Jihad*. Toward this end, the Iranian Embassy in Beirut brought over several IRGC recruiters to select the most suitable candidates for these operations from among *HizbAllah* volunteers.[4]

Concurrently, there had been a marked increase in the activities of the Syrian-Iranian support system in Lebanon since the summer of 1987. These active preparations were presented as part of Iran's support for the Palestinian armed struggle which, Tehran now argued, must include the escalation of the terrorist struggle against the U.S.: "The interests of Zionists and the Americans must come under attack throughout the world. The United States, which is a supporter of the occupiers of Palestine, and the Zionists themselves, must lose their sense of security throughout the world. The world must become a graveyard for the Americans and the Israelis."[5]

Meanwhile, the Iranians and the Syrians began testing the waters in the U.S. itself. Because these trial operations had to be deniable, Iranian and Syrian intelligence agencies started with the insertion of terrorist detachments that, if exposed, could not be associated with the Islamist networks. In principle and concept, these initial operations in the U.S. were identical to the highly successful employment of George Ibrahim Abdallah and the LARF in Western Europe in the early 1980s, as discussed in Chapter 5.

One of the earliest bombing operations was sponsored by the Syrian Socialist National Party (SSNP), an arm of Syrian intelligence and the KGB. Members of the SSNP trained for terrorist assignments in Western Europe via George Habbash's PFLP and Haddad's PFLP-SOG, which employed Carlos as senior trainer.[6] They also cooperated with foreign international terrorist organizations such as the JRA (for the significance of which see below)[7] and provided cover for the Syrian-controlled program for suicide terrorists.[8]

The planned operation was thwarted by chance on October 23, 1987, in Richford, Vermont, on the Canadian border. A Lebanese national living in Canada, Walid Kabbani, brought a backpack filled with components of a bomb powerful enough to blow up a small building into the United States at the Vermont-Canada border. Two operatives living undercover in Burlington, Vermont, who were "locally respected" merchants, Georges Younan and Walid Mourad, were to pick up the backpack and, in all likelihood, transfer it to other members of the network.

The operation was uncovered mainly because the van in which the two were waiting to pick up the pack was illegally parked. When the local police chief approached them they behaved in a suspicious manner, probably because of their nervousness, and the operation was discovered.[9] They were arrested, but no other member of the sleeper network was exposed.

In order to increase the likelihood of success, Damascus and Tehran decided to use specially inserted foreign experts. Thus in early 1988, the PFLP arranged for a Japanese Red Army (JRA) expert terrorist to infiltrate the U.S. Since early

1980s, the JRA has had a suicide corps in Lebanon "fighting together with the PFLP" all over the world.[10] One of them, Yu Kikumura, a.k.a. Abu-Shams, trained in the Biqaa, was dispatched for this mission. Although the planned operation was ostensibly to be on behalf of Libya, it was actually an action by the new system of international terrorism dominated by Iran and Syria. Indeed, a simultaneous JRA bombing in Naples, Italy, also attributed to Qaddafi, was claimed by the Organization of *Jihad* Brigades, an Islamist organization affiliated with the *HizbAllah*.[11]

Yu Kikumura started his trip on February 23, 1988, in Western Europe. He travelled through several European countries, exchanging passports and sending money to the U.S. from several banks. He finally received a visa to enter the U.S. in Paris on the 29th, using a false Japanese passport. He arrived at Kennedy Airport on March 8. He rented a small apartment in Manhattan, bought a second hand car in the Bronx, a 1980 Mazda, and gave many indications of his intention to stay in the New York area.

In reality, he soon embarked on a trip of over 7,000 miles across 17 states, during which he purchased and collected components for his bombs. Kikumura was arrested by accident on the New Jersey Turnpike on April 12, 1988, on his way back to New York. His car was full of sophisticated antipersonnel bombs disguised as fire extinguishers and made from off-the-shelf equipment he had bought and collected on his trip. He planned to detonate these bombs in mid-Manhattan on or around April 15, 1988, the second anniversary of the U.S. bombing of Libya.[12]

Kikumura's was a highly professional operation that demonstrated the terrorists' extensive knowledge of the situation in the U.S. Kikumura was provided with full details on where and how to purchase all the components needed for his bombs in a manner that would not attract the attention of law enforcement agencies. Indeed, he almost accomplished his mission successfully, for the New Jersey state trooper who arrested him approached him "more on intuition than anything else."[13]

The close relationship and cooperation between the JRA and the SSNP suggests that the two foiled operations (Vermont and Manhattan) might have been merely components of a larger effort by Syria and Iran to conduct terrorism and sabotage in the U.S. Possibly Kikumura was dispatched as a fall-back after the capture of the SSNP couriers in Vermont. Both options pointed to the network's organizational flexibility and the redundancy of assets inside the U.S. They also provided the terrorist-controlling states with valuable lessons that would be implemented in future operations.

In the late 1980s, Iran was the undisputed leader of international terrorism in the United States and Canada. Its Islamist terrorist infrastructure was by far the most comprehensive and capable in the world.

By the end of the decade, Iran and the U.S. were, in effect, involved in a very intense, yet secret, war in the Persian Gulf and Lebanon, where Syria was actively involved.[14] The Lebanese chapter of this war would culminate in the mid-air explosion of Pan-Am Flight #103 over Locherbie, Scotland, in late December 1988. Thus, Tehran and Damascus were ready to cross the threshold and order the conduct of major terrorist operations on U.S. soil. However, the Iranian and Syrian decision in principle to carry out terrorism in the U.S. should not be confused with the prudence and patience with which both countries would examine, test and carefully study every aspect and facet of their new terrorist campaign.

The emerging Iranian-Syrian long-term terrorist strategy for operations in America was for a three-phase strategy based on a gradual escalation of terrorist strikes that would test the extent and effectiveness of the reaction of American law enforcement authorities. The three phases of the Iranian-Syrian long-term terrorist strategy were as follows:

1. Use of local expendable assets to carry out operations while creating problems for the local security forces;

2. Quality attacks by operatives already on-site, living off

of and gaining operational support from the locally-based dormant networks; and

3. Spectacular strikes, including suicide attacks, by specially placed expert terrorists in order to demonstrate the global reach of the Iran-led Muslim Bloc and to avenge the Muslim world.

Furthermore, in order to further reduce the risk to the terrorist infrastructure already in the U.S. and Canada, a separate terrorist system was to be introduced with each and every phase, thus further complicating the ability of the law enforcement agencies to identify a pattern.

The three main components of the tested and proven Islamist terrorist system are:

1. the Iranian-*HizbAllah* predominantly Shi'ite network;

2. the on-site elite operatives network based on various types of 'Afghans'; and

3. the predominantly Sunni Islamist network living among the Islamist community in the U.S. and employing local assets, who were considered expendable.

In early 1993, virtually all the components of the Iranian-controlled system have been tested and proven in both the first and second phases, so that the Islamist terrorist system is essentially ready for the escalation into the third phase of the terrorist struggle, that of spectacular strikes.

THE IRANIAN-HIZBALLAH NETWORK

Pro-Iranian terrorists struck on March 10, 1989, in San Diego, California. A pipe-bomb exploded in the van of Sharon Lee Rogers, the wife of the captain of the U.S.S. Vincennes, the American Navy ship that had shot down an Iranian Airbus plane on July 3, 1988. The van was completely destroyed, but Mrs. Rogers was not hurt.[15] The bomb was found to have been a simple pipe-bomb that, if expertly placed, would have been able to create a secondary explosion that would probably have killed anyone in the van.[16] However, although secondary fire erupted, it did not have the desired effect because the initial charge was not properly placed.[17] The bomb did have an intriguing fuse that was activated by the heat from the exhaust pipe.[18]

This type of bomb would have been easily manufactured with common, low-quality ingredients available to the local Iranians.[19] Additionally, its creators would have been considered expendable if arrested by American law enforcement agencies — although in fact none were actually captured.

This incident, because it could be linked directly to Iran, marked the crossing of a threshold in Iranian-sponsored terrorism in the U.S.[20] Tehran carried out the attack on Mrs. Rogers for revenge. The mere fact that law enforcement agencies still know virtually nothing about the perpetrators testifies to the excellent quality of the Iranian network.

The attack on Mrs. Rogers epitomizes the Iranian approach to terrorism in the U.S. and Canada. For Tehran, terrorism is a primary instrument of state policy. The leaders of Iran consider their control over such organizations as the *HizbAllah* a real strategic asset. Although Tehran understood by 1986 that for the international Islamic Revolution to succeed it must be truly global in scope, it was not until the Iran-Iraq War was over that Iran was able to complete the deployment of a professional and sophisticated network aimed at political subversion and armed terror.

This network, tightly controlled by Hashemi-Rafsanjani, Ali Fallahiyan, and Muhsin Reza'i, remains at Tehran's disposal for whatever objective it chooses, at any time or place it decides to act. The Iranians dictate the character of their terrorists' operations. The pattern of these operations is sophisticated and characteristic of modern intelligence services. Uncomplicated attacks are carried out by local Islamists. They also gather the intelligence required for a complicated operation, which will be executed by professionals who arrive from abroad.[21]

Once it was decided that Iran would deliver a revenge

attack on Mrs. Rogers in the U.S., Tehran markedly accelerated the consolidation and expansion of its terrorist infrastructure in the U.S. Indeed, by early 1989, the Iranian network in
the U.S. was the most solid and dangerous of all local terrorist
networks. The desirable ratio of local Islamists and dormant
expert terrorists had been achieved. A comprehensive support
infrastructure manned by dedicated individuals was functioning. From among the 30,000 Iranian student population, Iran
could count on some 1,000 militants to conduct terrorism.[22] In
addition, several dozens of expert terrorists were clandestinely
deployed and ready to strike inside America. A few hundred of
the militant Iranian students in the U.S. were organized to
assist them or participate in such terrorist operations. A network of legal societies and foundations insured the flow of
funds from, and safe communications with, Tehran.[23]

Tehran then established forward supervision over these
networks and future operations. Two key associates and disciples of Javad Mansuri were posted to key diplomatic posts
from which they could expedite and support terrorism in the
U.S.: Muhammad Sadri is in the Iranian Embassy in Cuba and
Sayyid Ali Mussavi is in the embassy in Canada.[24] Moreover,
Kamal Kharrazi, Iran's permanent representative to the UN in
New York, is one of the founders of the IRGC.[25] This diplomatic support was markedly reinforced in the summer of 1992
with the posting of Ali Ahmad Sahlul, a hand-picked Turabi
loyalist, as ambassador to Canada to supervise U.S. operations.[26]

As the terrorist infrastructure and support system were
being readied in mid-1989, Iranian leaders began raising the
level of their calls for use of terrorism and threats to the U.S.
President Hashemi-Rafsanjani urged the widespread killing of
Americans, rather than Israelis, because "the Americans are
scattered around the world, they are everywhere."[27] Sayyid
Hassan Nasrallah declared the *HizbAllah's* commitment to
"satisfy our Imam's desire by announcing the beginning of a
real war against the United States."[28] Ayatollah Khamenei, in

his first major speech after Khomeini's death, observed: "Our enemies, including the criminal U.S., do not understand [anything] but the language of power, and nothing will prevent them from continuing their plots."[29]

Ali Akbar Mohtashemi emphasized that Iran and its allies already had the capabilities to strike at the U.S. "Throughout the world there are many *HizbAllah* cells that [have] been established by the Imam's holy breath, and they carry the banner of death to the superpower and global arrogance." He claimed that there were thousands of volunteers for martyrdom ready for attacks on and in America. Mohtashemi emphasized that Khomeini "always had an attacking-offensive attitude toward the U.S."[30]

Similarly, Mussavi-Kho'iniha, in a major sermon in the 1989 Ashura (the holiest day of Shi'ite Islam, a day of mourning and major ideological discussions, declarations, etc.) at Khomeini's tomb, emphasized the centrality of the struggle against the U.S. to Iranian doctrine, as a key element of the legacy of Ayatollah Khomeini, and the enduring source of legitimacy of the Tehran regime.

"The Imam's Islamic Revolution was for the purpose of establishing an Islamic state. There is no doubt that one of the valuable legacies of this revolution has been the profound and extensively world-wide confrontation with the global arrogance, especially the United States. . . If an authority in contemporary history has managed to mobilize for a revolution an Ummah — not the Iranian nation, but the Islamic Ummah throughout the world — against the arrogance, it has been the authority of the Islamic revolution of Iran, which, thanks be to Allah, still continues today."[31]

In late 1989, Iran was improving its international terrorist capabilities in anticipation of the imminent escalation of the Islamist struggle throughout the world. In October, Mohtashemi led a major delegation inspecting garrisons and training facilities of *HizbAllah* and Islamist Resistance forces in eastern Lebanon.

In a concluding speech, he outlined the Islamists' objectives: "We must remove the roots of America and Israel from our countries. We must strike them in their very home because it is our legal mission," Mohtashemi exclaimed. "Our *Jihad* will continue until the oppressed people rule themselves all over the world." He expected the escalation of Islamist terrorist struggle throughout the world and especially inside the U.S. Toward that end, Mohtashami explained, "the *HizbAllah* now has nuclei in Islamic and non-Islamic countries, even in the heart of America, instilling fear in the ranks of the enemies of Islam." The highly committed and trained *Hizbollahhi* in Lebanon are the Islamist revolution's main weapon. "With this weapon we can accomplish great achievements in the future," concluded Hojjat ol-Eslam Ali Akbar Mohtashami.[32]

Official Tehran was also advocating a continued struggle against the U.S. as a key part of Iran's policy and strategy. "In addition to the fact that the nations of the world regard the Islamic revolution as a pattern to follow, the *HizbAllah Ummah* of Iran has proven that in the struggle against arrogance it is able to take praiseworthy steps... The West, and especially world-devouring America, should know that the brave Iranian nation will continue the Imam's path to annihilate arrogance from the world under the leadership of Ayatollah Khamenei."[33]

In December 1989, the *HizbAllah* issued a statement reiterating their commitment to the anti-U.S. policy. "We are America's arch enemies. We view Washington's arrogant policy as one of self-interests, seeking to exploit peoples and intervene in their internal affairs... We confront this policy forcefully and firmly."[34]

The escalation in the terrorist struggle anticipated by Tehran was ultimately put on hold because of the overall dynamics in the Middle East. In the spring of 1990, as the Middle East was rapidly progressing toward the Gulf Crisis, Tehran accelerated its pronouncements that irrespective of its position vis-a-vis Iraq, there would be no let down in the struggle against the U.S., including terrorism on U.S. soil. Hojjat ol-Islam Ali

Akbar Mohtashemi, then the head of Defense and Islamic Revolutionary Guard Corps Committee in the Majlis, declared: "We have potentially big power in other countries. In the Muslim states and even in Europe and the U.S. our resources are the Muslims who are with the Islamic Revolution. Our enemies are panicked at our power abroad and at the presence of the Islamic Revolution in other lands."[35]

As the crisis was unfolding, Tehran reiterated that "Imam Khomeini, may his soul be sanctified, the pioneer of the worldwide Islamic revolution, deemed the struggle against the United States the most fundamental objective of the Islamic Revolution since the inception of the Islamic Movement." Tehran defined its relations with the U.S. as "a feud between the greatest enemy of Islam, which tramples on the honor of Muslims and all the oppressed nations in bondage, on the one hand, and the Islamic Revolution, which is a manifestation of the pure Muhammadan-style Islam, on the other."[36]

Ayatollah Khamenei explained that the U.S.-Iranian enmity was fundamental in nature and constituted the very core of Iran's policy and grand strategy. He anticipated that with the deterioration of the global situation, "all the oppressed nations of the world will stand by the Iranian nation and join their anti-U.S. struggle."[37]

Mohtashemi renewed his call for action. "The only possible relationship Iran can have with the United States is to attack U.S. interests around the world. . . The struggle against the United States and its illegitimate child Israel is a part of the Imam's political line and Iranian diplomacy must be based on this struggle, as well as holy war against oppression, and not compromise."[38] He stressed that in the case of attempts to reduce tension and crisis with the U.S., "the people and *HizbAllah* and revolutionary forces will not allow such a thing."[39]

Within the context of the Iranian-Iraqi agreement on launching a terrorist campaign at the time of the Gulf Crisis, Tehran insisted on virtual total control over the operations in the U.S.

and Canada. Indeed, during the fall of 1990 there were active preparations inside the U.S. by several organizations sponsored by Iran and Syria, including the *HizbAllah*, for the launching of "a wave of terrorist strikes" once the war with Iraq ended.[40] However, in early 1991, Tehran decided to disengage from the joint terrorist campaign and concentrate instead on furthering Iran's own interests. Consequently, terrorist strikes inside the U.S. by assets controlled by Tehran and Damascus were called off. Then, in March 1991, once the Gulf Crisis appeared to be over, Hashemi-Rafsanjani ordered the dispatch of several assassination teams to the West and a few elite teams to Canada.[41] These terrorist teams could also be used in the U.S.

Meanwhile, Iran continued to concentrate on the consolidation of the Islamist radical block it was leading, as well as the establishment of a New Islamic World Order. By now, the primary lesson Tehran had learned from the Gulf Crisis was that any furthering of its strategic interests would inevitably include a confrontation with the U.S. It was imperative to seize the initiative. In a conference with terrorist leaders convened to formulate a global strategy after the Gulf Crisis, Ayatollah Khamenei explained that "America's presence in the region has brought about a long-term threat to her, which will destroy America. The presence of the Americans in this region will cost them considerably more than their presence in Lebanon did."[42]

Sharply criticizing the U.S. policy in the Middle East, especially in the wake of the Gulf Crisis, Sheikh Fadlallah alluded to the *HizbAllah's* ability to operate inside the U.S. "We continue to ask those whom we influence not to harm America's internal security," he explained, suggesting the U.S. had better change its policy soon. "Isolation is not possible and whoever believes in the estrangement of the Arabs and Islamic world from the West is deluded and not realistic."[43]

The centrality of the uncompromising struggle against the

U.S. was reaffirmed in the Tehran Terrorist Conference on October 18-22, 1991, where over 400 delegates from 45-60 countries deliberated the strategy for the global *Jihad* against Pax-Americana that would be characterized by international terrorism.[44] (For details see Chapter 3.) Muhsin Reza'i summed up the expectations and designs of the Conference participants. "The Muslims' fury and hatred will burn the heart of Washington some day and America will be responsible for its repercussions," he predicted.[45]

Two delegations from the U.S. took part in that conference in Tehran. The first delegation was headed by Muhammad al-Asi, the Sunni Friday prayer leader of the Washington Mosque. He compared the differences between the conferences in Tehran and Madrid (the Middle East Peace Conference) to the difference "between justice and injustice."[46] Al-Asi vowed to do everything so that "American statesmen come to their senses and grasp the fact that the United States' security is in no way linked to the illegitimate existence of the terrorist Zionist regime on Palestinian soil."[47] The second delegation was headed by Abd-ul-Alim Mussa, the Shi'ite Friday prayer leader of the Mustazafeen (Oppressed) Mosque in Washington that is associated with Tehran. He urged "the annihilation of the illegitimate Zionist entity and the funnelling of all possible support for the intifadah in Palestine."[48]

In the winter of 1991-92, Tehran decided that the time was ripe to revive the terrorist assault on the U.S.. However, the ever-prudent terrorist masters in Tehran and Damascus were apprehensive about the tight security measures implemented in the U.S., and the entire West, during the Gulf Crisis in anticipation of the Iraqi terrorist offensive. They decided to conduct a major test run in order to better read Washington's reaction to "the *Jihad* crossing the Atlantic," according to a knowledgeable Iranian.[49] Argentina was selected as the site of the test run in America. The Israeli Embassy would be the target.

The selection was not accidental. Argentina has long been

a favorite entry point into the Western Hemisphere for both Syria and Iran. There is a large community of Lebanese-Syrian emigrants in Argentina with relatives in the Middle East and direct intimate contacts with their homelands. The community includes a large following of the Lebanese Shi'ite leadership, who are thus available for support to the *HizbAllah*.[50] The community was reinforced in the early 1980s with the insertion of numerous operatives prepared for long-term penetrations and the consolidation of local Islamist networks. Among them were "Muslims from Argentina" as well as "refugees" from many Arab and Muslim countries including Iran, Lebanon, Turkey, Iraq, Pakistan, Syria, and Egypt who either stayed in Argentina or used it as an entry point for their ultimate destinations in the U.S. and Canada.[51]

One of these refugees is Muhsin Rabbani (b. 1954), a Shi'ite from Tehran who arrived in Buenos Aires back in 1983. He now admits that he was sent to convert Argentines to Islam. He is the leader of the small but fiercely dedicated Islamist network in Buenos Aires called the Muslim Brotherhood of Argentina. The group includes 10 Argentines who had converted to Islam. One of them stated that he was "one of the members of the group who [has] taken upon himself the goal of destroying the State of Israel."

Rabbani runs the al-Tawhid Mosque. The group is loyal to Khomeini's message, and maintains a virtual clandestine routine. Its first major public action was the al-Quds Day march in March 1992 that ended in front of the Iranian Embassy. In his speech, the Iranian cultural attache praised Khalid al-Istambuli (Sadat's assassin) "as a symbol" for the Argentinian group.[52]

Moreover, the very top of the Argentinian political establishment is riddled with Syrian emigres who maintain very close contacts with their homeland. Many of them exploit their close relations with the Middle East for 'private ventures.' Of importance is the Yoma ring implicated in 1991 in widespread drug trafficking and money laundering in Argentina.

The ring was led by Amira Yoma, whose older sister,

Zulema, was then married to Carlos Menem, the president of Argentina. Yoma's husband, Ibrahim al-Ibrahim, played a crucial role in bringing the drugs and laundered money into Argentina. A former colonel in the Syrian military, he was appointed by President Menem to be in charge of customs at the international airport of Ezeiza. Yoma's younger brother, Karim Yoma, was a former low-level Syrian diplomat who was nominated by President Menem to be undersecretary of foreign affairs in the Argentine Government. In that capacity he used to bring large quantities of cash into Argentina.[53]

A friend and business partner of the Yoma ring was a Syrian drug and arms smuggler called Munzer (Mundhir) al-Kassar. He provided the Lebanese drugs the ring was smuggling from Europe, mainly Spain, to Argentina. The Yomas arranged for Munzer al-Kassar to receive a residency permit in Argentina and then an Argentine passport.[54] By then, the two al-Kassar brothers, Munzer and Ghasam, were also deeply involved in supporting terrorist operations on behalf of Syria. The al-Kassar brothers are friends and "business" associates of Rifa't Assad. In the fall of 1990, they were exposed as the primary weapons and explosives traffickers of the PLF and the PFLP-SC from Eastern Europe to Spain. The al-Kassar brothers had been first identified in 1987, and, having been warned, became dormant. In the fall of 1990 they were reactivated to support the new terrorist effort.[55]

In the winter of 1991-92, when Tehran and Damascus decided to proceed with a major operation, they activated a contingency plan prepared for the Gulf Crisis. Back then, explosives and specialized equipment such as fuses and detonators were smuggled into Argentina by the al-Kassar network, utilizing their expeditious entry into Argentina via the Ezeiza airport. Additional equipment, especially the new electronic remote control detonators, just introduced into operational use by the *HizbAllah*, were smuggled into Buenos Aires in early 1992.[56] Indeed, the Argentine security services believe that a Brazilian of Arab descent and a former Argentine military man who had travelled repeatedly to the Middle East since 1990 and were also involved in Gulf War-related preparations were involved in the Buenos Aires terrorist operation.[57]

The final preparations for the operation began in mid-March 1992. Argentine security sources would later conclude that the operation "must have been planned abroad with the aid of local planners who provided logistical support."[58] Israeli experts concluded that the operation was carried out "by *HizbAllah* terrorists who were assisted by the Iranian Embassy."[59] A German Red Army Faction explosives expert, Andrea Martina Klump, may have assisted in the construction of the bomb. She arrived in Uruguay only a few days before the explosion, and thus could have provided the expertise needed by the local *Islamic Jihad* cell.[60]

By now, an intelligence gathering and advance preparations operation was already well underway. Four Pakistanis, known by the names Muhammad Azam, Muhammad Nawaz, Muhammad Nawaz Chadhary, and Azhar Igbal, provided these services. They bought and maintained an apartment overlooking the Israeli Embassy from which they studied the building, and from which the remote-controlled detonator would be activated. They also purchased at above-price the Ford Fairlane used for the bomb. One of the Pakistanis rode a motorcycle just across the Embassy grounds at a high speed a few minutes before the car bomb was blown up, providing a last minute check of the operation's site.[61]

The car bomb itself was built in accordance with the proven principles of a shaped charge used by the Iranian and Syrian controlled terrorists since the bombings in Beirut. The bomb was made of over 100 kilograms of high explosives, with a 55-60 kilogram charge of hexogene reinforced by other solid plastique elements to enhance blast and fragmentation, as well as fats or wax to ensure the contours of the shaped charge. The charge was formed to have the explosion "unencased and directed." It was activated by an electronic detonator; possibly a back-up timer was also installed.[62]

On March 17, 1992, in the early afternoon, a Ford Fairlane, driven by a white male, parked just in front of the Israeli Embassy at 916 Arojjo Street in central Buenos Aires. Witnesses remembered that the driver stayed in the car, a fact that reduced the alertness of the local guards and policemen. Nobody remembered seeing him leave the car. Then, shortly after 2:30 PM local time, a huge explosion shook Buenos Aires, causing the collapse of the four-story building and spreading shrapnel and debris over a radius of 500 yards. A smoke cloud hung above the city.[63] The explosion caused 30 deaths and 252 injuries.[64]

The driver may have had to stay in the car 'till the last minute. However, searches in the explosion site showed no evidence of a suicide driver. In all likelihood he was able to escape and disappeared into Buenos Aires. Indeed, the first *Islamic Jihad* communique on the explosion at the Israeli Embassy identified the perpetrator, Abu-Yassir, as an Argentine convert.[65] The bomb was activated by remote control from the apartment building just across the street, overlooking the Israeli Embassy building.[66]

In Buenos Aires, *Islamic Jihad* claimed responsibility for the explosion that destroyed the Israeli Embassy. The operation was named after "The Martyr Child Hussein," Mussawi's son.[67] In Beirut, *Islamic Jihad* denied involvement.[68] In Tehran, Ayatollah Ali Akbar Meshkini hailed the success of the terrorists as "a source of pride to an entire nation" and announced that "there will be more" operations of the same kind.[69]

Sheikh Hussein al-Mussawi of Islamic Amal insisted that while "the *HizbAllah* is not responsible for the bombing of the Israeli Embassy in Buenos Aires, . . . the *Islamic Jihad* Organization . . . had carried out the operation, [and] might have had its own justifiable reasons for doing it.'"[70] Sheikh Nasrallah also denied the *HizbAllah's* involvement or that it had anything to do with *Islamic Jihad.*[71] Even though evidence gathered in the explosion site proved that Iran was involved in the Buenos Aires bombing,[72] Tehran denied any involvement in the operation and rejected accusations that the Iranian Embassy was involved.[73]

Meanwhile, as the preparations for the test run in Buenos Aires were already well under way, Tehran was beginning to feel a sense of urgency, a dire need to escalate the struggle against the U.S. Back in February, Tehran reiterated its view that the U.S. constituted the greatest threat to the revival of Islam and Iran. Delivering a Friday Sermon in Tehran, Ayatollah Fadlallah stressed that "world arrogance, especially American, continues to confront the Islamic revolution and pan-Islamism/all-Islamism all over the world, because it considers this movement to be against its interests."[74]

Tehran's perception was reinforced and reaffirmed during Secretary Baker's visit to ex-Soviet Central Asia where he warned the local government against close relations with Iran. Tehran considered Baker's remarks to be "a declaration of war against [Islam], a blatant effort to interfere in the Islamic countries' internal affairs and one which should be answered with a strong slap in the face by the Islamic nations. How each nation solves its problems and deals with its enemies is something which concerns the nations and their cultures. And this is a terrifying thought for the United States and its henchmen."[75] There was more than a veiled threat of use of international terrorism in the Iranian statement.

Following the killing in Lebanon of the terrorist Sheikh Abbas Mussawi by Israel on February 16, 1992, the *HizbAllah* increased its pressure on Tehran to embark on a major revenge operation. The date of the long-planned operation in Buenos Aires may have been changed to fit the need for a symbolic revenge.[76] However, it would not be until early March that a future terrorist campaign was discussed in Tehran with Sheikh Hassan Nasrallah, the newly elected secretary general of the *HizbAllah*.

In Tehran, Nasrallah stressed the importance of "armed *Jihad*" as the only viable form of struggle.[77] On March 2, Nasrallah held lengthy meetings with Maj. Gen. Vahidi, the commander of al-Quds Forces, senior Pasdaran officers, and several senior officials. "To us, the United States is always the Great Satan for whose destruction we will strive," Nasrallah told the meeting.[78]

The next day, March 3, Nasrallah met with both Hashemi-Rafsanjani and Khamenei to discuss the escalation of the *HizbAllah's* struggle.[79] That day, in meetings with Iranian leaders, Nasrallah was shown "a new plan for the escalation of the armed struggle, not just against Israel, but also against the United States." In the meeting, Nasrallah was urged by the followers of the Imam's line, mainly Ahmad Khomeini and Mohtashemi, to "turn the world into hell for the U.S., Israel and the West."[80] Apparently, he was shown a version of the long-term *Jihad* strategy agreed upon in the fall of 1991. Preparations for the escalation began immediately.

Despite the success of the test run in Buenos Aires, there remained the lingering question of the real capability of Iran's own operatives and terrorists to operate and survive in the United States. The assassination teams sent to Canada back in March 1991[81] continued to remain safely concealed either in Canada or the U.S. One of these teams would be activated as a demonstration and examination of the ability of Iranian assets to operate in the U.S.

The Iranians struck between 8:45 and 9:00 PM on March 26, 1992, in Franklin Lakes, New Jersey. A professional killer approached Mrs. Parivash Rafizadeh near her home and shot her twice in the abdomen from close range (5-6 ft). The hit was professional. A clean .45-semiautomatic was used. It was found discarded near where the getaway car had been parked. The killers disappeared without a trace. Mrs. Rafizadeh's husband and his brother had been senior officers in the Shah's SAVAK.[82] Even without Tehran's claiming credit for the assassination, it was abundantly clear to all that Iran's long hand had struck in the United States. The hitmen's safety confirmed the effectiveness and professionalism of the U.S.-based networks Tehran so urgently needed.

The assassination of Mrs. Rafizadeh took place on the eve of the greatest public demonstrations of the strength and self-confidence of the supporters of the Imam's Line in the U.S. and Canada. March 27, 1992, was declared by Tehran the International Day of Quds and the Believers were urged to publicly demonstrate their commitment to the Islamic Cause.[83] In the U.S. and Canada, the events were organized by the Muslim Student Association in U.S. & Canada — MSA (PSG), the Tawhid Association, the Islamic Educational Development League, and the Malaysian Islamic Society of North America (MISNA). Conferences were held in St. Louis, Michigan, and Washington D.C. Most important were the public demonstrations held in Washington, Ann Arbor and Dearborn, Michigan, as well as Montreal and Toronto in Canada. In Washington, hundreds of demonstrators paraded, shouting Quranic verses and *HizbAllah* slogans in Arabic, carrying *HizbAllah* banners, Islamic slogans, and pictures of Ayatollah Khomeini, Sheikh Abbas Mussawi, and other Iranian and *HizbAllah* leaders.[84]

Tehran could not, and did not, miss the significance of this show of force in the center of Washington. The preparations for implementing the anti-U.S. struggle strategy were accelerated. Indeed, in late May 1992, Sheikh Nasrallah anticipated an imminent escalation in the *HizbAllah's* struggle for the spirit of Islam. He considered all the recent developments in Lebanon, primarily the attempts to confiscate weapons and installations from the various militias, to be parts of a conspiracy against Islam controlled by the U.S. He vowed that the struggle against the U.S. and Israel would continue and even escalate.[85]

Now additional components of the vast and comprehensive Islamist terrorist network would be tested in action.

THE 'AFGHAN'S STRIKE

In the morning of January 25, 1993, a lone gunman carrying an AK-47 assault rifle calmly walked down the line of cars jammed near the entrance to the CIA headquarters in Langley, Virginia, and methodically shot several of the Agency's employees, killing two and wounding three more. He then entered a brown van and vanished.[86] The killer was soon identified as Mir Amail Kansi, a 28-year-old Pakistani.[87] What was initially interpreted as the irrational action of an individual, perhaps a disgruntled employee, was in reality the test run of the Islamists' 'Afghan' network.

Mir Amail Kansi was an Iranian long-term plant, an illegal agent infiltrated into the U.S. for operations in the Washington area and activated for the CIA killings. His background points to a clear pattern of identification, recruitment and training by the Iranian intelligence. Since the mid-1980s, the Kansi Pushtun tribe of Pakistan's Baluchistan province was involved in weapons and good transfers in and out of central Afghanistan, ostensibly in cooperation with the Pakistani ISI, but which in reality brought them into close cooperation with Iranian intelligence and Shi'ite mujahideen organizations.[88]

Since the late 1980s, and primarily in the last 18-24 months, these lines of communications have been reversed on behalf of Iran. They are increasingly used for the shipment of weapons and heroin from southern Afghanistan to Quetta and Karachi (both in Pakistan), from where they are smuggled to the West as part of the support system for the new Sunni Islamist International.[89] All of these provide an excellent manpower pool for audacious sabotage and terrorist operations. Indeed, by late 1992, there were some 1,200 'Afghans' in Pakistan who were involved in smuggling drugs from Pakistan to Europe and the United States to finance the Islamist networks in the destination countries.[90]

Mir Aimal Kansi most likely came to the attention of

SAVAMA when he was studying in Quetta College between 1983 and 1986. By then he had impeccable credentials.[91] Small changes in the life of Mir Aimal Kansi by the mid-1980s now suggest an initial approach and recruitment by a Baluchi cut-out. While in Quetta College, he was a member of the Pushtun Student Association.[92] Then he suddenly switched to the Baluchi Student Association.[93] For Kansi, this was a highly irregular move considering that he was a member of a noble Pushtun family with public social standing.[94]

In 1987, Mir Aimal Kansi began studying for his MA in English Literature in Baluchistan University, Quetta. English studies are considered the most expedient way to gain admission to and scholarships for advanced degree studies programs in the U.S. By now, he was overtly involved in Baluchi politics and participated in several publicized protests against the persecution of Baluchis by the Pakistani Government. In retrospect, this activism seems to have been designed to prepare him for his placement in the U.S., for he cited fear of persecution because of his activities on the Baluchi cause as the reason for his request for asylum in the U.S. on March 3, 1991.[95]

Mir Aimal Kansi must have been recruited by the SAVAMA when he studied at Baluchistan University in 1987-88. By now, he was increasingly involved in the Kansis' convoluted dealings with the ISI, the Shi'ite mujahideen and Iranian intelligence. It is highly likely that the actual approach by the SAVAMA and his ensuing recruitment were conducted by Iranian intelligence operatives who travelled clandestinely from the Hazarajat in central Afghanistan with the mujahideen. Iranian and *Hizbollahi* officials frequented the Quetta-Hazarajat route and thus came to know Mir Aimal Kansi. It would have been very easy for the Iranians to approach Mir Aimal Kansi while on one of these trips.[96]

In 1988, the circumstances of Mir Aimal Kansi's life made him an ideal candidate for placement as an illegal. His mother had died in 1982, and in 1988 his father was dying of cancer. By family tradition, he was the primary candidate for carrying out the required blood revenge for the 1984 assassination of his uncle Malik Gul Hasan Kansi, which was widely attributed to the CIA. There emerged an artificial tension with his half-brothers, possibly a cover for a lengthy disengagement from the family in Quetta, an otherwise unusual step in the close knit Kansi tribe.[97]

Mir Aimal Kansi was a key member of the strong-arm squad sent by an Iranian-associated Baluchi cell to intimidate American guest faculty in Quetta to the point where they had to leave town. In embarking on this operation, the cell adopted the *HizbAllah* view that the most dangerous subversive/intelligence presence of the U.S. is under the guise of academic activities because such activities contaminate young minds. Kansi and the small group burst into the university shouting "Death to America! Death to the CIA!" and attacked guest faculty. Kansi was the one responsible for drawing weapons and shooting into the air or, should the need arise, at any Americans who refused to flee. As it was, he only fired in the air.[98]

Since the incident involved direct contact with Iranian and *HizbAllah* operatives, only the most trusted local terrorists were fully initiated into this type of operations. The mere fact that Mir Aimal Kansi participated in a central way in these provocations in February 1989 testifies that he was already fully trusted by Iran.[99]

In 1989, Mir Aimal Kansi made an unusual trip to Germany. He stayed there for only a month.[100] This trip might have been a cover for a classic back door movement to Iran of highly sensitive cases. Since 1985, numerous Iranian agents/terrorists used this route to reach Iran. They would enter West Germany legally and then make an undocumented trip to Berlin. After crossing into East Berlin by subway, they would board a flight to Damascus and go on to Tehran without any need for travel documents. They would return to the West in the same manner.

Islamic cultural institutions in West Germany provided

bogus alibis for some of the more important agents/terrorists. Mir Aimal Kansi could have travelled to Syria and Iran in the same way, possibly in order to receive advanced training in preparation for U.S. operations. Indeed, Kansi openly declared his intent to emigrate to the U.S. for the first time soon after his return from Germany.[101]

While in the U.S., Kansi's behavior strongly suggests preparations for clandestine and terrorist activities. Despite his scholarly credentials, he sought employment with a courier company that serviced the CIA.[102] He gradually accumulated weapons. He also prepared a getaway plan which he executed perfectly after his action ourside the CIA, reaching Quetta, Pakistan, safely. After a week with his family, he disappeared again.[103]

Taken together, the background of the close association of the Kansi tribe with Iranian intelligence, coupled with the peculiarities of Mir Aimal Kansi, strongly suggest that he was an Iranian agent/terrorist and, therefore, that the Langley killings were an act of Iranian state-sponsored terrorism.

Concurrent developments in Iran testify to the importance of the CIA killings for Tehran. During the mid- and late 1980s, IRGC Brig. Gen. Qaani was the commander of the Eighth (Imam) Corps and in this capacity responsible for intelligence and sabotage operations in Pakistan via the Shi'ite mujahideen of Afghanistan. The IRGC was responsible for recruitment and training of Afghans and Pakistanis in Iran and for having their organization develop into networks.

With the militarization of the IRGC and the increase in Iranian terrorist operations in and via South Asia, Tehran decided to establish a dedicated organization for the support of subversion and terrorism. Consequently the Fourth Partisan Corps was established in 1992. It was detached from, but still remained connected with, the Eighth (Imam) Corps. Both Corps are under the command of Qaani. The main bases of the Fourth Partisan Corps are in Tayebad, Zahedan, Zabol and Birjand, near the border with Afghanistan and Pakistan. Qaani is now responsible for command and support of the Islamist terrorist infrastructure in Afghanistan, Pakistan, Kashmir, and India. He is also responsible for extending Iranian operations into Central Asia via Afghanistan.[104]

The four bases of the Fourth Partisan Corps were put on a higher state of readiness, and local units were reinforced, in the late fall of 1992. These forces could be used to assist Kansi in evading Pakistani authorities. According to ISI, Tehran notified Islamabad that it would assist in the search for Kansi provided that Tehran was convinced that he had committed a crime.[105]

Moreover, Mir Aimal Kansi was not the only Iranian agent being prepared in Pakistan in the late 1980s for placement as a long-term illegal in the United States. Another Iranian agent was exposed in the fall of 1989 in the course of a series of operations against Saudi aircraft originating in Pakistan, most likely in connection with Iran's Hajj wars.

The operation in question was a hijacking attempt. An Iranian called Ali Reza was detained in Karachi on September 25, 1989, on suspicion of trying to hijack a Saudi airliner. He had arrived in Karachi from Iran only in February 1989. Since then, he had been learning English in UNHCR schools while preparing to emigrate to the U.S.[106] In reality, Ali Reza was a long-term illegal plant prepared by the Iranian intelligence to be infiltrated into the U.S., possibly as an Afghan or Iranian political refugee. Apparently he was activated by the VEVAK ahead of time and sent to hijack the Saudi Arabian airliner as revenge for the execution of 16 Kuwaities in Saudi Arabia.[107] It is still not clear why Tehran decided to sacrifice a major intelligence operation that was so far highly successful for a hasty, unprofessional hijacking attempt. It was the opinion of the Pakistani security authorities at the time that the VEVAK had already had so many agents in preparation or in place that they could afford to sacrifice Ali Reza.

In the fall of 1991, Tehran anticipated the resumption of clandestine operations in the U.S. Reflecting the progress in the operatives' training and placement programs, the Iranians openly urged Arab and South Asians to join the *Jihad*. For example, Ayatollah Abdolkarim Musavi Ardebili called on Muslim zealots to attack U.S. objectives throughout the world. "Kuwaitis, Iraqis, Pakistanis, and Iranians should set up resistance cells and endanger their [Americans'] interests wherever they are," he told a gathering of students in Tehran. He stated that it was a "religious duty" for all Muslims to deprive Americans of security as they stripped Muslims of security."[108]

The Kansi case is the culmination of a lengthy process Tehran embarked on in the mid-1980s. The Iranian-Afghan mujahideen connection has been instrumental in Tehran's concentrated effort to recruit, train and sustain an indigenous cadre of operatives and terrorists in the U.S. Iran's attention was focused on the U.S. Black Muslim community because of the strong influence of Daoud Salahuddin and Qaddafi's claims of success in building terrorist cadres in the U.S. In the mid-1980s, under Khomeini's supervision, Tehran decided on a recruitment drive among blacks in the U.S. As a result of this long-term Iranian program, there is a sizeable cadre of highly motivated American terrorists in Pakistan.

Back in 1985, Iran established within the foreign ministry's export of the revolution section a department headed by a Pakistani mullah to provide clandestine assistance to hard-to-reach Islamist communities and especially "U.S. Blacks." The funds would come from the Martyrs' Foundation and be distributed via legal charities.[109] Daoud Salahuddin has been personally involved in the recruitment of Black Muslims in the U.S. for the Iranian terrorist network, as well as in the training of terrorists in Iran for operations in the U.S.[110] He was also an instructor in hand-to-hand combat and assassination techniques at an IRGC school near Tehran.[111]

Initial recruitment came from among the veteran Muslim radicals of the 1960s and 1970s and their younger followers, who were incited by romanticization of the Iranian revolution and/or the *Jihad* in Afghanistan. Special attention was paid to disgruntled and highly experienced Vietnam veterans. Some of these Americans even converted to Shi'ism. Most of them were trained in Pakistan and Iran. Since the mid-1980s, many have fought in Afghanistan and in Beirut, where some of them were formally associated with the *HizbAllah*. The organized infiltration of a select few of these American *hizbollahhi* and mujahideen back into the U.S. began around 1987-1988, once Tehran and Damascus were convinced that their infrastructure of support networks was capable of sustaining the required operations.[112]

Meanwhile, when the novelty, zeal and hope of the Iranian Revolution began to subside, Tehran shifted to recruitment among Blacks in American prisons. Because of the operation's missionary aspects, that is, converting the recruits to Shi'ism, it began under Khomeini's supervision. In early 1986, Iran began approaching and ultimately recruiting prisoners who were still incarcerated. Iranian-supported front organizations made contact with disgruntled Black Muslim prisoners in all the major prisons in the U.S.

Shi'ite charities established small communes in various cities, including Washington, D.C., ostensibly for prisoners' rehabilitation, where recruitment is finalized. After brainwashing, the ex-prisoners swear allegiance to the Ayatollah Khomeini and volunteer for *Jihad*. They are then sent to Pakistan for training with the Islamist mujahideen and the ISI. The more promising are identified and sent for additional training in Pakistan, Lebanon and Iran. Although several such ex-prisoner recruits finished terrorist training in Pakistan in 1988-1989, they were kept there and apparently only a few have already been infiltrated back into the U.S.[113] The black Muslim candidates for terrorism in the U.S. are now drawn from these cadres.

In 1992, AIM began preparations in Pakistan for the escalation of terrorist operations in the U.S. and Canada. These preparations are conducted under the cover of *Jamaat-*

ul-Furqa, ostensibly an organization led by Sheikh Mubarak Ali Shah Jilani, a Pakistani Kashmiri living in Lahore. Jamaat-ul-Furqa is really an ISI-controlled organization. Since mid-1992, ISI Brigadier Imtiaz has been responsible for "training Black Muslims from the U.S.A. and Canada through the Jamaat-ul-Furqa for terrorist operations in North America and West Europe."

Sheikh Jilani himself is directly involved in the recruitment and indoctrination of American Black Muslims in Pakistan. However, for the actual preparations, "Jilani, with the help of the ISI and the Pakistan IB, runs a training center near Lahore where Sudanese instructors carry out their task." Jilani and Imtiaz have no operational responsibility in the U.S.,[114] for this rests with Sheikh Umar Abd-al-Rahman in New York.

There are indications that some of the graduates of these Pakistani-Iranian training programs have already begun initial operations in the U.S. One example is the Fuqra "Islamic fundamentalist sect" in the Colorado Springs, Colorado, area, the leader of which was committed to the "plight of African-Americans". Some members of Fuqra are known to have originated in Pakistan and continue to maintain ties with Pakistan. Both in 1989 and 1992, police discovered explosives, bombs, guns including automatic rifles, and military manuals in their compound. In 1992, two Fuqra members, James Donald Williams (39) and Edward Ivan McGhee (37), were accused of stealing money from the state's worker's compensation fund in order to finance their operations.[115]

Ultimately, these operatives and terrorists will provide quality capabilities to the larger and more comprehensive Islamist networks in the United States and Canada, the ones based in the Muslim emigre communities.

THE NEW ISLAMIST INTERNATIONAL
IN AMERICA

In the late 1980s, Islamists in the U.S. recognized the use of propaganda in furthering their views. For example, in the U.S., "the Islamic Council of Palestine plans in the future, *InshAllah*, to expand its concerns and efforts to include an important aspect of the life of Muslims in general, and Palestinians in particular, on the American continent. The council has in mind an educational program for the new generations, whose future we regard with great hope, because great responsibilities will be placed on their shoulders to serve their beliefs and their issues."[116]

The growing Islamist activism in the U.S. was reflected in the conference of the Islamic Committee for Palestine that took place in Chicago in late December 1989. The theme of the conference was "Palestine, Intifada and the Horizons of the Islamic Renaissance." The main guest speakers were some 20 leaders of militant trends in Islam throughout the Middle East and South Asia. They discussed the role of the Islamic ummah (nation) in the struggle "to find a light in this darkness," that is, the West and especially American society, and emerging trends in "Islamic strategy for confrontation" with the West.[117] The conference chairman, Sami ar-Rayan, discussed the impact of the intifada on the U.S. Islamist community. "It [the intifada] should not be erroneously understood as a separate and unique event," he explained,. "It is part and parcel of Islamic reawakening and renaissance that is fast becoming a world-wide phenomenon."[118]

Probably the most important visitor was Sheikh Abdul Azziz Odah (Abd-al-Aziz Awdah). He was one of the prominent militant leaders of *Islamic Jihad* in the Gaza Strip since 1981 until his deportation by Israel for terrorist activities. Since then, he was active in coordinating Islamist terrorist operations with Iran, the *HizbAllah* and such Palestinian

terrorist leaders as Ahmad Jibril and Abu-Mussa.[119] In the
Chicago Conference, Sheikh Odah/Awdah discussed the urgent need to destroy Israel as the starting point for a *Jihad*
against the West. Israel, he explained, is "the evil Zionist
multifaceted dagger in the heart of Muslim lands. The hideous
instrument of tyranny is a problem for all Muslims. This
dagger serves as the front line of confrontation between Islam
and the ideological, social, political, cultural and economic
aspects of the non-Islamic West." Sheikh Odah/Awdah equated
the "struggle" between the West and Islam to "a confrontation between evil and falsehood and . . . truth and justice."[120]

By then, the HAMAS had already begun expanding its
cooperation with the Muslim Brotherhood cells in the U.S.,
using them as back-up safe installations for Middle East operation, as well as a source of funds and printed material. Many of
the key HAMAS documents are printed in the U.S. before
being smuggled into Israel and the West Bank and Gaza.[121]
Abu-Omar, an Arab-American, arrived in Israel in late 1989
and rebuilt the HAMAS after the arrest of Sheikh Yasin,
including the selection and recruitment of Amad al-Faluji as
the HAMAS commander in the Gaza Strip. The operation was
financed by the U.S. Ikhwan. He fled Israel in 1990.[122] Other
HAMAS leaders, activists and terrorists arrested in Israel in
early 1991 were in constant contact and acted in full coordination with extremist Muslim elements in Jordan, the U.S. and
Great Britain.[123] The HAMAS was opening additional branches
in the U.S., and Western Europe, mainly Germany and the
United Kingdom.

Since early 1990, Islamists escalated their threats to the
U.S. In a Beirut communique, *Islamic Jihad* Movement —
Bayt al-Maqdis — warned that "every U.S. citizen who
resides inside or outside the Islamic countries will be considered a target for attack and revenge," unless the U.S. Senate
retracted its recognition of Jerusalem as Israel's capital.[124] In
mid-May, Sheikh Sayyid Barakah, one of the leaders of *Is-*

lamic Jihad Movement in Palestine, "appealed to all free men and Mujahideen in Palestine and the Arab and Muslim world to pursue Americans everywhere and to kill them in punishment for their killing of our people in Palestine and elsewhere."[125] The Islamic Liberation Front even claimed in Amman to have caused the explosion at the Arco chemical factory near Houston, Texas on July 5, 1990. It claimed that one of its units "operating in the United States last week exploded a factory in Texas that supplies chemical weapons to the American Army."[126]

The Gulf Crisis jolted the Sunni Islamist movement in the U.S. and pushed some of its activists into action. The Ikhwan and the HAMAS assumed a harsh anti-U.S. policy as the Gulf Crisis was unfolding. The HAMAS explained that because of its general policy, aggravated by the deployment of forces to the Arabian peninsula, "all the Arab peoples not only harbor resentment and hatred but also disgust" toward the U.S. and that it is difficult to compare the extent of the Arab "hostility toward the United States, this head of a snake and the great Satan." Not one of the Arab leaders, irrespective of their deeds, "[is] capable of eradicating hatred toward the United States from our masses' hearts."[127] The HAMAS decreed that "America [is] the seat of evil in our world." The struggle with the U.S. is the essence of the *Jihad* for the very existence of Islam.[128] Rashid al-Ghanushi declared that "Today the fight against America is a priority for Islam and Muslims."[129]

The threats to conduct Islamist terrorist attacks in the U.S. increased markedly as the Gulf Crisis escalated. On October 5, 1990, Sheikh As'aad Bayyud al-Tamimi stated in Amman that by sending forces to Saudi Arabia, "Bush and Thatcher have revived in the Muslims the spirit of *Jihad* and martyrdom." He then decreed that "if war breaks out against Iraq, we will fight a comprehensive war and ruthlessly transfer the battle to the heart of America and Europe." He stated that *Islamic Jihad* already "has the forces to carry out" such strikes "within Europe and America."[130]

These were not idle threats. A delegation of senior Islamist leaders associated with the extremist militant trend of the Muslim Brotherhood, including Yunis al-Tamimi, Sheikh Tamimi's son, and Muhammad Qutb, the brother of Sayyid Qutb, the chief ideologue of the militant Muslim Brotherhood, visited the U.S. in the summer of 1990. They were the leading speakers at the convention of the Islamic Society of North America held in New Jersey between August 31 and September 3, 1990, where they exhorted the audience to follow the tenets of the Islamist trend as the only hope for Islam in the 1990s.[131]

A more important conference, the Third General Conference of the HAMAS, was held in Kansas City, Missouri, in late 1990 with a declared objective of tightening and intensifying cooperation with the Islamist movement in the U.S. Several senior HAMAS commanders, including Sheikh Jamil Hammami, Dr. Mahmud al-Azhar and Dr. Khalil Kawkah attended. The Conference was held under the banner: "Palestine is Islamic from the sea to the river."[132]

The U.S. support activities for the HAMAS continued to expand. The back-up command center was organized in the U.S. The U.S. is also a major source of funds and publications for the Islamists' public activities known as the "preaching branch" of HAMAS. The U.S. branch of the HAMAS also intervenes directly on policy formulation issues.[133]

The Islamic Association for Palestine organizes conferences to mobilize support for the Islamists in the territories, and publishes periodicals that support the HAMAS: The Monitor in English and *Al-Zaituna* (Olive Tree) in Arabic. Umar Yahya, the president of The Islamic Association for Palestine told *Al-Zaituna* that the organization's goal is to bestow upon the young Americans of Palestinian descent the notion that "our problem is a Muslim problem."[134]

Meanwhile, the militant branch of the Muslim Brotherhood and the *Islamic Jihad* continue their activities in the U.S.

On December 21-26, 1991, they organized a major conference in Phoenix, Arizona, via the Muslim Youth League and The Islamic Committee for Palestine. The conference was attended by key leaders of the Islamist terrorist organizations. Egyptian sources pointed out that Phoenix "was chosen as the venue because it is out of the way and would not attract attention." Indeed, the conference served as a cover for consultations between the Islamist terrorist leaders and their commanders in the U.S. The leaders also encouraged their militant followers to patiently endure their trials and tribulations in the U.S. and await the order to strike.[135]

The extent of the role played by the U.S. support system for HAMAS was revealed in the January 25, 1993, arrest in Israel of two Arab-Americans, Mohammed Abdel-Hamid Salah, a.k.a. Abu-Ahmed (40) and Muhammad Joma Hilmi Jarad a.k.a. Abu-Anas (37), both from Chicago, Illinois.[136]

In July-August 1992, Mohammed Abdel-Hamid Salah arrived in London for meetings with Muhammad Qassem Rashid Maaruf Suwalha (31), a senior HAMAS military commander who fled to the UK where he now runs an advance headquarters for HAMAS. Abu-Ahmed received in London detailed instructions for the Izz al-Din Qassin Squads (the special forces of HAMAS) in the Hebron area. He then went to Israel and met with local HAMAS commanders, including Salah Muhammad Suleiman Auri, the Squads' commander. He gave them $48,000 in cash to buy weapons on the black market for deniable special operations that would begin in the fall. Salah then made an inspection tour through the Gaza Strip and returned to London to provide a detailed report to Suwalha and his aides.[137]

Both Salah and Jarad arrived in Israel in mid-January 1993 to help rebuild the HAMAS leadership and command structure in the wake of the December 1992 mass arrests and deportations. By the time of their arrests, they had already distributed over $200,000 out of $650,000 deposited in their bank account. They also carried with them detailed instructions on the steps to be taken and people to be activated and promoted.[138]

Salah's visit was the more important. He flew to Israel via London where he met with senior Islamist officials and received detailed instructions on rebuilding HAMAS. In Israel and the territories he met with several key commanders, especially of the military arm and the Izz al-Din Qassin Squads that had gone underground. He activated replacements for the deportees. He also discussed with the HAMAS commanders the possibility of organizing suicide operations. All this time, Salah collected detailed reports on the military activities of the HAMAS and the general situation for reports back to the leadership in the U.S. and the UK.[139]

In his interrogation in Israel, Salah named 10 people in the U.S. whom he identified as "HAMAS leaders." He described a complete organization in the U.S. and the UK that is supporting and backing the HAMAS in the Middle East. Salah claimed that several charities in the U.S. serve as cover and instrument for channelling funds to the HAMAS. (This assertion was disputed by officials of some of these charities who acknowledged funding humanitarian projects in the territories.) Salah identified the United Association for Studies and Research in Springfield, Virginia, as a cover for the political command of the HAMAS in the U.S., and identified Ahmed Youssef, a.k.a. Abu-Ahmed, as the HAMAS leader in the U.S. Mr. Youssef denied these allegations.[140] Salah identified Mousa Abu-Marzuk, a.k.a. Abu-Omar, of Arlington, Virginia, as the HAMAS political chief in the U.S., whose "clandestine title is chief of the political bureau."[141]

The Gulf Crisis was a milestone in the radicalization of the American Islamist community. It was the most important catalyst in the Islamists' shift toward active participation in terrorism. This transformation was directly associated with the arrival of Sheikh Dr. Umar Abd-al-Rahman in New York.

Sheikh Dr. Umar Abd-al-Rahman, formally the leader of the Islamic Group (Al-Jama'a al-Islamiyah), was behind the growing militancy of the *Islamic Jihad* devotees in the late 1980s. First arrested during the 1981 purges after Sadat's assassination, he resumed his urging for armed *Jihad* against "apostasy" until his arrest, with more than 20 followers, in a gun battle in Egypt in April 1989.[142] After Abd-al-Rahman's arrest, the unrest continued with members of *Islamic Jihad* in Cairo demonstrating and clashing with police[143] and again on Id al-Idha, a major Islamic holy day, demanding the Sheikh's release.[144] Meanwhile, the *HizbAllah* in Lebanon accused Egypt of torturing Sheikh Abd-al-Rahman and his followers in prison.[145] The Egyptian Islamists accused Cairo of "a government plan in the war against the Islamic trend" and reported mass arrests and torture.[146] Sheikh Abd-al-Rahman and about two dozen followers were arrested again on August 12 following riots against places of entertainment in a clear violation of their release conditions.[147] A day later, the Sheikh was released into house arrest after serving a total of little more than four months in jail.[148]

Sheikh Umar Abd-al-Rahman believes that confrontation with the Egyptian government is inevitable because he flatly challenges the Islamic legitimacy and authority of the government's religious bodies, especially the awaqf ministry, and even the Muslim Brotherhood for their participation in political life. Sheikh Abd-al-Rahman readily admits that he is "a terrorist and extremist in the cause of Allah and His Prophet's tradition."[149] Rahman's late deputy, Dr. 'Ala' Muhyi-al-Din, stressed that Al-*Jihad* "will not retreat from defending honor which is holy, nor from opposing immorality and forbidden actions, regardless of the sacrifices which that will cost us."[150]

During the Gulf Crisis, Egyptian Islamists were at the forefront of support for Saddam Hussein. Their most notable leader, Umar Abd-al-Rahman, expressed his support for Saddam Hussein and embarked on an agitation campaign in Sudan, Pakistan and ultimately Iraq.[151] He then continued from Iraq to the U.S., by way of Pakistan and Sudan, for agitation in the local community and to prepare for an Islamist Revolution in Egypt. Several ideologists of *Islamic Jihad* considered the Gulf Crisis the best opportunity to implement the tenets of their all-Islamic Revolution because the Iraqis were willing to support, further and facilitate all acts of terrorism, including assassinations.[152]

With the growing importance of militant Islamist activism in the U.S. and the emerging need to be able to conduct terrorist operations there, the international Islamist movement decided to nominate a senior spiritual authority — that is a supreme commander — for the U.S. Sheikh Umar Abd-al-Rahman, the spiritual guide of the most radical branch of *Islamic Jihad* in Egypt,[153] arrived in the U.S. in May 1990 and established an Islamist center in the Faruq Majid Mosque in Brooklyn, New York.[154] His followers in Egypt expect him to organize an anti-U.S. Islamist revolution from his place of exile. On the basis of proven precedent, the Jihadists see in Abd-al-Rahman's absence from Egypt a sign of an escalating revolutionary process:

> Has Umar Abd-al-Rahman become a new Khomeini living in a voluntary exile and leading the revolution in Egypt through cassette tapes and the collection of contributions for the revolutionaries?[155]

Abd-al-Rahman's importance continued to grow with the evolution of Turabi's PIO. In late 1991, Turabi established a supreme council for the PIO, and the main leaders of the movement were Dr. Umar Abd-al-Rahman (Egypt), Hasan al-Turabi (Sudan), Rachid Ghanouchi (Tunisia), and Abbas Madani (Algeria, jailed).

Rachid Ghannouchi, exiled in London, and Umar Abd-al-Rahman, living in or near New York, were nominated senior members of the leadership entrusted to act as the senior representatives overseas. These leaders order their cells to commit specific terrorist attacks in accordance with a master plan and agreed upon priorities and strategy.[156] Indeed, while in Sudan, Abd-al-Rahman was one of three Islamist leaders who "personally selected" candidates for extensive terrorist and clandestine training, including psychological and Islamic tempering and conditioning so that they could sustain clandestine operations under conditions of "materialistic Western slavery" without losing their identity and Islamist zeal. These graduates would serve as new commanders of the Islamist *Jihad* in the West.[157]

In the summer of 1992, Turabi and Abd-al-Rahman met in New York to further coordinate the activities in the U.S., including the possibility of launching terrorist operations. Soon afterwards, Abd-al-Rahman intensified his fundraising in the U.S. and Canada for Islamist causes, then smuggled the money back to Egypt via Faysal Islamic Bank.[158]

In the fall of 1992, Turabi decided to further escalate operations in the U.S. Of the some $100 million allocated by Tehran as the initial budget for Turabi's Islamic Popular Arab Congress (*Al-Mu'tamar al-Arabi al-Shabi al-Islami*), a major portion is earmarked as an investment in the U.S. for the consolidation of networks and the establishment of a center for publication and communication with groups everywhere through faxes and phones.[159] These activities will be conducted through the establishment of a world-wide education and proselytization network under the cover of the Washington-based World Institute of Islamic Thought.[160]

Meanwhile, Sheikh Umar Abd-al-Rahman continues to live and preach in New York and around the country. He announced that he would return to an Islamist Egypt ruled by "Islamic Government based on the Shari'ah. The primary principle of the Shari'ah is that 'only Allah rules.'"[161]

Egypt Interior Minister, Maj. Gen. Muhammad Abd-al-Halim Mussa, warned that "Umar Abd-al-Rahman . . . is residing in the United States as a Khomeini awaiting return to take power in Egypt."[162] In the meantime, Abd-al-Rahman sends cassettes of sermons calling for Islamic Revolution in Egypt from his residence in Jersey City, New Jersey. He also signed the *fatwa* permitting the recent attacks on tourists in Egypt.[163]

From New York, Abd-al-Rahman endorsed Islamist terrorism and decreed that in attacking tourists, the *Islamic Jihad* "was merely doing its duty of forbidding what is sinful."[164] He denied involvement in an organized conspiracy, arguing that his was "not an organization of *Jihad* or repudiation. We are Islamic Groups."[165] However, a 'close disciple' of Abd-al-Rahman operating underground in Egypt, has not only acknowledged the Islamic Group's participation in, and responsibility for, attacks on tourists, but reaffirmed that there is constant contact with Abd-al-Rahman. "Telephone contact between us and Sheikh Abd-al-Rahman takes place daily and lasts for hours. The Islamic Group does not formulate any opinion on any matter without going back to him."[166] The June 1992 assassination of Dr. Faraj Fudah (an Egyptian writer and intellectual) is an example of the power and influence exercised by Abd-al-Rahman. From his exile in New York, Dr. Umar Abd-al-Rahman issued the *fatwa* sanctioning and ordering the assassination. The *Islamic Jihad*'s adherence to leaders so far apart "means the organization maintains a strong, accurate, and well organized communications network at home (Egypt) and abroad."[167]

Thus, Sheikh Umar Abd-al-Rahman's continued relations with Islamist terrorism in Egypt is indicative of his real position in the global terrorist establishment. In the U.S., Abd-al-Raham is considered by all the Egyptian Islamist factions as their supreme spiritual leader, thus further confirming that their ostensibly spontaneous actions are actually parts of a master plan.[168]

Indeed, captured Egyptian terrorists admitted that "Iran backed them financially to commit terrorist actions inside Egypt." They identified Umar Abd-al-Rahman as their supreme leader, who is also responsible for their operations.[169] The current escalation in terrorist operations, at least in Egypt, is the work of "an international front [that] has been formed to spread terrorism . . . which is financed by Iran" and has major facilities in Sudan. Under the leadership of Hasan al-Turabi, "the front is holding regular meetings in Sudan and is being financed, guided and armed by Iran."[170] In that front, Abd-al-Rahman was identified as the one who "planned terrorist operations worldwide."

Meanwhile, with the further consolidation of the PIO and AIM, Sheikh Umar Abd-al-Rahman, still in New York, was named a senior member of the supreme leadership, entrusted to act as the Islamists' senior representative in North America. Abd-al-Rahman is authorized to task the local cells to commit specific terrorist attacks in accordance with a master plan and agreed-upon priorities and strategy that are determined in Khartoum and Tehran.[172] Sheikh Abd-al-Rahman is also authorized to issue *fatwas* permitting suicide operations in North America, thus significantly simplifying the Islamists' ability to conduct terrorism in the U.S. Indeed, at present, Sheikh al-Turabi and Sheikh Abd-al-Rahman are "the most prominent" leaders of the Islamist international, the latter because of his control of U.S. operations.[173]

In early December 1992, there were indications of impending major events in Islamist international terrorism. Abd-al-Rahman summoned two of his closest aides from Egypt for urgent consultations in New York, ostensibly in connection with the judicial hearings that were scheduled to be held to consider his deportation from the U.S. In reality, they met to discuss and coordinate terrorist strikes in the Middle East and the West.

They charted the transfer of "talent" from Sudan, Afghanistan, and Lebanon to their ultimate objectives. In retrospect, it is noteworthy that about that time, Egyptian police discovered "an explosives factory and explosives and incendiary charges" in a house of one of Abd-al-Rahman's followers. The instructions arrived from overseas. On the matter of his deportation, Abd-al-Rahman was notified that fall-back headquarters were already set up in London and Khartoum for him.[174] Nevertheless, Abd al-Rahman applied for political asylum in the U.S., citing fear of retribution from Egypt in case he was deported.[175] Meanwhile, his followers are making plans for him to move to either Syria or Iran if he is deported.[176]

Sheikh Abd-al-Rahman's association with the Masjid al-Salam mosque in Jersey City, New Jersey, serves as a good example of the kind of transformation and manipulation a Muslim community undergoes at the hands of a dedicated Islamist religious leadership. Jersey City also serves as a precedent for other Muslim communities in the U.S. currently under the influence of Islamist leadership. Sheikh Abd-al-Rahman did not choose the Jersey City community by accident. It was chosen, in part, because, since the mid 1980s, many of the 300 members of the Masjid al-Salam community have been involved in Islamist and Palestinian causes, including the support of terrorism.

Until the mid 1980s, the dominant figure in the community was Egyptian-born Sultan Ibrahim Al-Gawli, a rich businessman, a PLO agent, a gold smuggler, and the patron of the community. He was the local "fixer." He loaned everybody money, arranged forged driver licenses for the illegal emigrants, arranged marriage licenses and certificates for those who needed them, thus buying the trust and support of everybody, especially the young Egyptians. Al-Gawli was also considered the "patron of the Muslim Brotherhood" in New Jersey. He was arrested in 1985 trying to smuggle weapons, including six handguns with silencers, 150 pounds of explosives, 100 fuses, remote control detonators, and additional equipment on behalf of the PLO for use as a bomb in a major public place in Israel and for the Ikhwan in Egypt who were going to use it to assassinate President Mubarak.[177]

The life of the small community revolved around the Masjid al-Salam. The young impoverished Egyptians, some of them illegal immigrants, constituted the most vibrant element of the community. They were made hostile and bitter by the hardships of immigrant life and got used to breaking the law to get by. They were drawn into the fold of the mosque as a friendly shelter against a hostile and alien world. Under such conditions they were extremely susceptible to the Islamist message and especially the militant advocacy for revenge against the sources of the Believers' plight and misery. Indeed they are flooded with Islamist material, both written and recorded, that also serves as their main contact with the Egypt they left behind. Given the right manipulation, these youth would embark on an avenging *Jihad*.

The assassination of Rabbi Meir Kahane in New York on November 5, 1990,[178] demonstrated that such militant Islamist radicalism exists in the U.S. and that some believers are ready to strike. Irrespective of whether Al-Sayyid Abdulazziz Nossair, the accused murderer, acted alone, as the official position states, or, as now seems highly likely, on behalf of an Islamist terrorist network,[179] the assassination itself is indicative of the general terrorist phenomena and climate. (Al-Sayyid Abdulazziz Nossair was acquitted of the murder charges but convicted on related assault and gun violations charges.)

Egyptian-born Al-Sayyid Abdulazziz Nossair is a typical radicalized Islamist operating within, albeit on the fringes of, U.S. Islamist communities. These individuals are pushed into extremism and radicalism that fills them with hate to such a degree that they are willing to commit violence and court martyrdom. The growing circulation of their inflammatory material reflects their increasing numbers. At least one Islamist group that maintained some contacts with other radical Islamist groups in the U.S. and abroad, including the Muslim Brotherhood and militant Islamist groups in Egypt, was associated with the Masjid al-Salam mosque in New Jersey.

Al-Sayyid Abdulazziz Nossair attended a New Jersey Islamic Center but was never a regular. Instead he prayed at home and with Islamist friends. Nossair carefully prepared for his violent course. He had several weapons, quantities of ammunition and poison, material about militant Islamist groups in Egypt, and lists of prominent Jews stored in his house. He was helped by fellow worshippers in the purchase of his weapons.[180]

Nossair is a relative of Sultan Ibrahim Al-Gawli who was released from jail on October 6, 1990, and returned to Jersey City.[181] Moreover, in late November 1990, the FBI arrested in New Jersey a Kuwaiti-born Islamist, Jamal Muhammad Warrayat, for making credible threats to assassinate President Bush and other senior officials.[182]

Sheikh Umar Abd-al-Rahman began preaching in the Masjid al-Salam mosque in Jersey City, New Jersey, in May 1990, just about the time Al-Sayyid Abdulazziz Nossair was beginning to prepare for the killing of Rabbi Kahane. While Nossair was influenced by the sermons, he was already in an advanced stage of preparation for his violent course. It is not clear if Abd-al-Rahman gave Nossair a formal *fatwa* prior to his killing of Kahane; he might only have blessed him. To be sure, stepping into the New Jersey mosque, Sheikh Abd-al-Rahman took an Islamist community already radicalized to the point of generating a terrorist, and over the next two years transformed it into a hub of Islamist militancy. His sermons at these mosques have become the source of his preaching to the rest of the Muslim world.[183]

The transformation of the Islamist communities in New Jersey and Brooklyn since the fall of 1990 because of Sheikh Umar Abd-al-Rahman, emerges as a textbook case of Islamist network building and consolidation. Sheikh Umar Abd-al-Rahman spent his first year or so in the U.S. consolidating his immediate position and establishing secure lines of communication with his support base overseas. He was also involved in the organization of the Khartoum-based Islamist international, the incitement of his followers in Egypt, and arranging the transmission of inflammatory cassettes and other material.

The accumulation of problems with logistical and financial arrangements and the traffic of 'Afghans' and other experts back into the U.S. culminated in the March 1991 killing in Brooklyn of Mustafa Shalabi, Abd-al-Rahman's first patron in the U.S.[184] During this period funds began to flow to al-Rahman from Iran via Germany.[185] A new support team, in which Ibrahim A. Elgabrowny (al-Jabaruni) played a central role, was organized. Several Egyptians who appear to have been veteran Islamist terrorists, both long-term submarines in the U.S. and new arrivals from the Middle East, made their way to New Jersey and melted into the sprawling community of Islamist youth around the mosques.[186] Meanwhile, attracted by the Sheikh's sermons and the community's dynamics, numerous local Islamists gravitated to his inner circle. Consequently, by mid-1991, Sheikh Abd-al-Rahman had established a group of devotees fiercely loyal to him who would kill and be killed in the name of the *Jihad* he preaches, exactly the same way he had galvanized his devotees and loyalists in Egypt.

The period between October 1991 and March 1992 was crucial for the escalation of Islamist terrorism in the U.S. As described above, there were several phases during which Tehran and its allies formulated their long-term terrorist strategy, starting and culminating with conferences in Tehran. Moreover, the command structure of the Armed Islamist Movement, the Sunni terrorist international, was being consolidated in Khartoum. Having been named the U.S.-based leader, Sheikh Abd-al-Rahman, with his network of devotees, began consolidating their own command and control mechanism, as well as a support and logistics infrastructure.[187]

The bulk of these preparations were completed in the summer of 1992 by the time Abd-al-Rahman had held discussions with Turabi. They studied closely the strength of the Islamist community in the U.S., examining its ability to withstand a massive anti-Islamic assault and its ability to withstand a major terrorist operation.[188]

Meanwhile, between March and December 1992, the Islamist terrorist network conducted actual preparations for a major terrorist strike at the heart of the Great Satan. Initially, the bulk of the work was done clandestinely by expert terrorists, both in New York and overseas, who conducted a survey of potential targets. Specific planning such as bomb design followed. The specific plans were completed in Tehran by the experts. It is highly likely that some experts were even sent to New York during the summer and fall to personally inspect the potential targets in order to better design and calculate the type and size of the needed bombs. They took advantage of the main lesson learned from the Kikumura operation, namely, that one can get everything in the U.S. A major sabotage operation can be carried out with little or no need for smuggling tremendous amounts of explosives, especially the telltale plastiques.

The network's professionals took care of several seemingly mundane logistical issues such as the safe transfer of funds from overseas. They also prepared getaway plans, including obtaining foreign passports. The loyal Nicaraguans provided those. Ibrahim A. Elgabrowny (42 years old), was one of the senior professionals of the network's support system. In 1991 he arranged for Islamic supporters to attend the Nossair trial, as well as for transportation and bodyguards for the defense. He is also the president of the executive board of the mosque used by Abd-al-Rahman.[189] Elgabrowny was the support man between the elusive and shadowy professionals and the local expendables. Authorities would find in Elgabrowny's apartment five Nicaraguan passports, including one for the incarcerated Nossair. The authorities also found there a 9 mm pistol, 150 rounds of ammunition and two stun guns.[190]

Most important was the identification, recruitment, and manipulation of the expendables, the local zealots who would actually carry out the operation and be sacrificed in the process. The preparation of expendables is a lengthy process, for it requires thorough psychological tempering and conditioning. The primary candidates are desperate drifters within the Islamist community who are yearning for revenge, overcommitted to the cause in principle. They must be susceptible to the influence of the spiritual leaders such as Sheikh Abd-al-Rahman. Their loyalty must be unquestionable, preferably reinforced through blood ties. In addition, the recruiters search for people with usable skills who can be manipulated into shielding the real experts.

The search narrowed in the fall, as reflected in the emergence of financial arrangements. Numerous new bank accounts were opened, some jointly by the expendables, for their immediate use. Money was wired from Germany, a classic point of transfer from Iran, to New Jersey. The accounts remained relatively small, totalling between $50,000 and $100,000 at any given time. Two deposits of $5,500 and $2,500 were wired in late 1992 and were withdrawn a month later. At least $8,000 were deposited in a joint account held by Mohammed Salameh, Nidal A. Ayyad and other unknown partners on the eve of the operation.[191]

Mohammed A. Salameh (26) from Jersey City was the classic expendable. He is the son of a Jordanian military officer who escaped in 1967 from Biddiya to Zarka, Jordan.[192] He grew up amid the intense hatred toward the West prevailing in the Islamist Palestinian community of northern Jordan after Black September (when the Jordanian forces slaughtered radical Palestinians, suppressing the PLO's "state within a state"). Many of the area's youth were recruited in 1986-87 by Khalil al-Wazir (Abu-Jihad) for *Islamic Jihad*, with the help of the Jordanian Muslim Brotherhood. Some were even sent for training in Afghanistan.[193] Salameh could have been identified and recruited at that time. He arrived in the U.S. on February 17, 1988, on a Jordanian passport with a six months visa and the real intention to remain in the U.S. indefinitely. He had lived as an illegal alien since then.[194]

Upon his arrival in the U.S., Salameh made contact with his distant cousin, Ibrahim A. Elgabrowny. Elgabrowny assisted Salameh in getting documents, including a drivers license, using his own apartment as Salameh's address. He also brought Salameh to the El Salam mosque in New Jersey, exposing him to Abd-al-Rahman. He was also introduced to another mutual cousin, Al-Sayyid Abdulazziz Nossair. Salameh settled into the life of an illegal alien, living in a small apartment with three roommates (two women and one man). He remained devoutly religious, isolated and remote from the society around him. His sole social life centered around the Masjid al-Salam mosque. Meanwhile, Salameh became very close to Nossair. He faithfully attended his trial and visited him in jail. It is thus highly likely that Salameh was strongly influenced by Nossair's beliefs and commitment to the *Islamic Jihad*. Moreover, Salameh had become a devoted and active follower of Sheikh Abd-al-Rahman.[195]

By the fall of 1992, Salameh was completely trapped in the Islamist web, wholly captivated by the call to *Jihad*, and isolated from and hostile to the American society around him. His trustworthiness and commitment were repeatedly demonstrated. Moreover, as a cousin of Elgabrowny, Salameh could be trusted to shield his associates. He was thus ripe for recruitment for a glorious act of *Jihad*.

The terrorist leaders now needed a "bomb maker," another expendable, to shield the real experts by diverting the law enforcement investigators away from the principals in the aftermath of the terrorist strike. Nidal A. Ayyad is a young (25 year old) chemical engineer living in Maplewood, New Jersey, recently married and expecting his first child. Born in Kuwait of Palestinian descent, he is the main provider for an extended family he brought to the U.S. once he received his U.S. citizenship.

Ayyad was frustrated, in need of money, and thus an ideal "professional expendable." Moreover, Ayyad is a devout Islamist who has attended the New Jersey mosque since the early 1990s. Ayyad knew Salameh for about a year, befriended him and was eager to help. Their friendship might not have been spontaneous and Salameh might have targeted and entrapped Ayyad. By the end of 1992, Ayyad was committed. He had joint bank accounts with Salameh. He went with him to lease the van used in the planned attack. He provided the know-how in mixing the chemicals to make the explosives.[196] To ensure his incrimination, Salameh repeatedly called Ayyad from the storage company site where the chemicals used for making the bomb were stored.[197]

In late November 1992, the terrorist leaders in the U.S. were confident that they could launch a major terrorist strike in the middle of New York. It was time for the presentation of their project to the terrorist masters from Tehran and Khartoum. Indeed, in early December 1992, there were indications of impending major events in Islamist international terrorism. Abd-al-Rahman summoned two of his closest aides from Egypt for urgent consultations in New York.[198] In addition to overall strategic discussions concerning Islamist terrorism, these aides had both the knowledge and the authority to inspect the proposed plans and carry an authoritative detailed report back to Tehran and Khartoum.

One of the last pre-strike checks took place in late January. On January 22, a caller to the U.S. Embassy in Algeria, speaking in the name of the PFLP, threatened a bombing in New York City within 48 hours unless Palestinian deportees were returned to Israel. A second call came on the 24th, extending the deadline to January 26.[199] The PFLP would later deny any connection with the bombing.[200] The motive behind these calls was to create a provocation that would tell the terrorist masters what kind of precautions and defensive measures the American authorities might be taking if they knew that a skyscraper was going to be hit. Moreover, two false warnings were likely to influence the law enforcement authorities not to take any subsequent warning seriously. Should there be a leak from the forthcoming operation, the reaction would most likely be muted.

In early February 1993, Tehran seems to have conducted a last-minute study of the challenge. As described in Chapter 4, the entire issue of conducting terrorist operations in the U.S.

and Canada was studied during the terrorist conference in Tehran, and guidelines for future operations were issued.[201] It is highly likely that the very small select group of senior Iranian and *HizbAllah* commanders who held separate discussions concerning future terrorist operations also studied and reexamined the impending operation in New York. Such a last minute oversight is characteristic of the ever-prudent and professional Tehran.

During January and February 1993, the actual preparations for and by the expendables accelerated. Safe storage was organized. The explosive was easy to make from readily acquired chemicals. The three main chemicals were nitric and sulfuric acid, and urea, which is common in fertilizers. Hundreds of pounds of industrial chemicals that could be used to make a bomb, including nitric acid and sulphuric acid, ingredients in nitroglycerine, were purchased and stored at a storage site, A Space Station, in New Jersey. The 1,000 pounds of chemicals used for the actual bomb cost only $400. Explosives made from the chemicals found could have left the traces of nitrates found after the World Trade Center bombing.[202]

Several items that can be used for timers and detonators were purchased. Among them were small metal alarm clocks that may have been used as timers for the bomb. Three such clocks were found in the New Jersey apartment of one of the bombing suspects.[203] Moreover, tools and parts were found at an apartment Salameh used which, a police expert said, constituted evidence of a "bomb maker."[204]

The final approval for the operation was received, most likely from Tehran, perhaps via Khartoum, only a few days prior to the actual operation. As the spiritual leader, Sheikh Abd-al-Rahman must have given his blessing to the operation, promising eternal life to all involved. Within the organizational framework of the Islamist international, Abd-al-Rahman "inspired" the bombing, and may have issued a formal *fatwa* concerning the personal fate of the participants. Only Tehran could issue the final order.[205] The professional terrorists began their preparations. Indeed, many Arab men visited the Salameh apartment, especially at night. Neighbors later reported much nighttime activity. Boxes were taken in and out. Several young Egyptians who lived in nearby apartments suddenly left for Egypt during the week of the explosion.[206]

The time was ripe to expose the "expendables." Salameh and Ayyad rented the Rayder Ford Econoline van used to plant the bomb.[207] The explosives were mixed from the nitric and sulfuric acid and the urea. The 1,000 pound bomb was made on the eve of the operation. The explosive was fashioned in the form of a thick paste which was loaded into cardboard boxes and then piled in the truck. The main explosive charge was ignited with several smaller nitroglycerine bombs, which in turn were activated by simple blasting caps. These were most likely stolen. A lot of expertise was needed in rigging the bomb and insuring near-simultaneous detonations. Bottles of compressed hydrogen gas were placed on top of the explosive to create a destructive fireball when detonated. In order to insure an enhanced blast, the half-a-dozen or so cardboard boxes containing the bomb had to be specially organized and the nitro and caps precisely placed.[208] While Salameh might have been capable of mixing the chemicals, it would take an expert to place the nitro and caps. Moreover, the combination of explosives and compressed gases is a classic Iran-style bomb, used from Beirut to Kuwait to Paris.

The van-bomb was then driven and placed in the exact location. A second car, most likely a cab, was used to drive away the van driver and any other terrorists involved.[209] Indeed, a 33-year-old Egyptian immigrant, Mahmud Abu-Halima (or Abouhalima), who worked as a cab driver in Jersey City and Brooklyn, is believed to have provided these transportation services. Abouhalima attended the El-Salam mosque and was a friend of Salameh.[210]

The bomb that exploded on February 26, 1993, at 12:18 P.M., in the B-2 level of the underground parking garage of the World Trade Center paralyzed the emergency systems of the entire complex. The blast ripped a 180-by-12-foot hole in a wall above an underground train station, creating a 200-by-100-foot crater in the garage below the center's Vista Hotel. The Vista Hotel's first floor was gutted, and the building suffered severe structural damage. Smoke reached up as high as the 96th floor in the 110-story twin towers.

Six workers were killed and over 1,000 injured, mostly from smoke inhalation.[211] The bomb was well placed because it knocked out the entire communications and fire control systems for the buildings, broke five of eight electrical feeder cables and caused a flood that drowned the backup generators meant to handle any emergency.[212]

Only an expert would know where to place such a bomb, how much explosives to use, and how to direct the blast-and-heat wave to cause maximum damage. Indeed, the logic behind the explosion, that of using the structure of the building to echo and reinforce the blast-and-heat wave, is characteristic of the bomb-making techniques taught in Iran. The same approach to designing and placing bombs was repeatedly used by *HizbAllah*-affiliated operations in Beirut and Buenos Aires.

Meanwhile, Tehran demonstrated for the entire Muslim world that it was actually responsible for the New York bombing. This was done in a unique indirect manner that speaks volumes in the conspiratorial environment of the Middle East. On February 26, the main Friday Sermon in Tehran was delivered by Iran's spiritual leader, Ayatollah Khamenei. A major portion, repeated around 8:30 AM (EST) by Iran's international media for the entire Muslim world, was devoted to the plight of the Muslims of Bosnia and Iran's position.

Khamenei started by acknowledging the inability of Iran and other Muslim communities to send enough volunteers and military assistance to Bosnia. "We regret that we cannot defend that nation. We regret the Muslim youth cannot reach there for defense because the roads are blocked," he said. Khamenei attributed this sorry situation to an intentional anti-

Muslim campaign of the West, led by the U.S.

However, he emphasized, these constraints should not prevent Iran and the Muslim world from actively assisting the Bosnian Muslims. "We must protect them as much as we can. And I don't mean financial or material help, though that may also be necessary. We must give them all [types of] political support, we must endeavor [to do it]!" Khamenei exclaimed. This assistance, he said, must ensure that the West stop its assault on the Bosnian Muslims, as well as be punished for their current plight.[213]

Immediately after the explosion, there were numerous calls claiming responsibility, many of them in the name of warring factions in the former Yugoslavia. In the first reports soon after the explosion, these claims were given prominence in the American media. The "Serbian Liberation Front" was singled out, even though there was no previous knowledge of this group and its statement differed from all known patterns of Serbian rhetoric.[214] Even the authorities paid special attention to the Balkan motive. "That is that the Bosnians, the Serbians, Croatians, the Muslims, all these conflicts in the area might lead you to the conclusion that because they're meeting in New York there might be some connection with the explosion there," FBI director William Sessions explained.[215] These reports reverberated throughout the Muslim World immediately.

Thus, the importance of the Khamenei sermon is that about four hours before the explosion in New York, claimed in the name of Serbian Muslim plight, it provided a very explicit warning that the Bosnian cause was about to hit world attention. For the Muslim world, this chain of events constitutes a recognition of Iran's responsibility for delivering the terrorist strike at the heart of America.

Meanwhile, Salameh continued to follow his instructions. Because he had reported the van stolen, he approached the rental agency and insisted on having his $400 deposit returned. He continued to press for the return, even as the media hinted that identifiable parts of the van were recovered. Salameh was arrested as he came to pick up the deposit.[216] Traces of nitrate were found on the rental paper.[217] That Salameh was arrested so quickly was "a case of dumb luck."[218]

However, Salameh's entire behavior in the aftermath of the explosion clearly indicates that ultimately it was only a question of time before he was identified and caught. "He is either dumb or some kind of martyr," remarked one senior law enforcement official.[219]

Salameh is a martyr. An illegal alien, he lived in complete anonymity, beyond the routine reach of the law. Had he not reported the van stolen, the van would have been written off as one of many vehicles stolen or lost on a daily basis. Moreover, he could have even reported the van stolen to the Ryder Company, foregone the deposit, and still disppeared into anonymity. Salameh did not live at the address given. Because he was an illegal alien there were no traceable records of his life in the U.S.

Still, he insisted on getting back his deposit, even registering the van as stolen with the police and attracting undue attention to himself. This is a form of behavior most unbecoming a veteran of more than four years of living as an illegal alien. Salameh is not stupid. He was following his instructions to the letter. His true role was to be captured so that the Islamists could transform his trial into a politicized show trial demonstrating the American conspiracies against Islam.

Things went badly for the other conspirators. Ayyad's business card was found in Salameh's possession. Elgabrowny could have avoided exposure and arrest by simply denying any knowledge of Salameh but, he took a punch at the police who came to question him and was arrested. His association with the others would emerge only subsequently.

By now, the expert terrorists, the "masterminds," had long gone. Most likely, they safely escaped to the Middle East. An investigator believed that the terrorist masters "left him

[Salameh] behind as a signature. Maybe it was their game plan all along to leave him behind." With this in mind, the plan to attract attention to Salameh "worked perfectly," for the expert terrorists got away.[220]

Abouhalima suddenly left New York on March 6, two days after the arrest of Salameh. Using his German passport, he flew to Pakistan, the site of the headquarters of Sheikh Abd-al-Rahman's Islamic Group, via South Africa and Germany. One or two accomplices probably also flew out with him. They seem to have used false passports. The three made last minute ticket purchases just to get out of North America.

Abouhalima was the driver of the cab that escorted the van and evacuated whoever was in the van. An 'Afghan', he was one of the principals, the on-site professional leader activated for the operation, who also provided direct support services to the expert terrorists who arrived from overseas. Capturing him became urgent because he was able to identify accomplices. From Pakistan, Abouhalima continued to Egypt where he was arrested.[221]

It did not take long for the magnitude of the operation to become clear to the investigators. Traces of nitrate were immediately found in the World Trade Center, providing the first concrete evidence of a bomb. Police Commissioner Raymond Kelly confirmed that it was a bomb, on the basis of "the magnitude of the explosion, the fact that a significant amount of heat was generated, and the fact that traces of nitrate were found."[222] Gilmore Childers, Assistant U.S. Attorney, characterized the bombing as "the single most destructive act of terrorism on American soil."[223] James Fox of the FBI acknowledged that investigators now believe that the bombing was carried out by "a large, well-known terrorist group, a group that knows what it's doing."[224] Investigators pointed out that there was evidence that Salameh had been recruited by a terrorist group, most likely Iranian-sponsored.[225] Salameh was "part of a conspiracy," investigators said.[226]

ONLY THE BEGINNING

The Muslim World was stunned but not surprised by the explosion in New York. It was clear that a new era in the relations between the U.S. and the Muslim world has begun. "*Allah* knows, but it seems that the American magic is beginning to turn on its master. Regardless of who was behind the recent explosion in New York's World Trade Center, the explosion rang down the curtain on an era of security and stability enjoyed by the United States over the past 50 years," the Islamists announced.[227]

Mainstream Arabs agree, pointing out that "fundamentalism . . . moved the battle to the very heart of what it calls 'the Great Satan.' " They warn that as a result of the U.S. policy in the Middle East, defined as "declaration of confrontation" with Islam, "confrontation with the fundamentalist trends will escalate in the Arab world," and may even spread to the rest of the world.[228] Conservative Arabs tried to distance themselves from the Islamist trend, arguing that the New York bombing must have been part of "an organized malicious campaign" against Islam.[229]

That the indirect Iranian claim of responsibility was not lost on the militant Islamists was made clear on February 28, when Imad al Alami, one of the ardent Sunni leaders of the HAMAS and its representative in Iran stated that in view of "recent developments," the Sunni Islamists now recognize that "there is an identical view in the strategic outlook" between Shi'ite Iran and the Sunni Islamists. He explained that the HAMAS reached this conclusion because "there were forms of assistance from the Iranian people to help the steadfastness of the Palestinian people in the occupied territories" which exceeded by far mere financial and material assistance, and were, instead, in the "Islamic dimension."[230]

On March 6, once Salameh was arrested, Tehran began a propaganda blitz about the New York bombing. The overriding theme was that the blaming of Muslims, Islamists and even

Iran for the bombing was all a part of a conspiracy aimed at inciting the West to embark on an anti-Islamic Crusade. Tehran warned that the U.S. efforts "to attribute the New York explosions to Muslims have met strong reactions from Islamist groups."[231]

Tehran was becoming increasingly combative and defiant, arguing that "if support for Palestine and the oppressed Palestinians was terrorism, Iran was proud of it."[232] Tehran argued for "serious revision" in the policy supporting the export of the revolution in order to further strengthen the commitment to the Islamists. It warned that "showing any leniency and flexibility ... would be misinterpreted by the enemy and would further embolden it to pursue its illegitimate objective." It concluded that "this fresh U.S. propaganda aggression should be confronted by further underlining the Islamic-revolutionary stands."[233] The HAMAS reiterated the Iranian line that the accusation of Islamist involvement in the bombing was the beginning of a U.S.-Israeli conspiracy against Islam, and vowed to resist steadfastly.[234]

Starting March 10, Tehran suddenly shifted its emphasis to defiance and taking the initiative. In a well publicized sermon, Ali Akbar Nateq-Nouri, the Speaker of the Majlis, called the U.S. accusations about Iranian involvement with terrorism "psychological warfare with specific political aims." He called for stern counter-measures. "The resistant nation of Iran does not fear a psychological war and will march toward sacred goals of the Islamic system with greater unity and solidarity," he said. "Experience has shown that the more pressure exerted by enemies on us, the stronger our people become." Over two thirds of the Majlis members issued a statement urging an immediate escalation of the struggle against the U.S., to peak on al-Quds (Jerusalem) Day, March 19.

"We deeply believe that obliteration of Israel and the downfall of world arrogance headed by the United States are possible. The United States is trying in vain to take advantage of every incident against Islam and Muslims," the Majlis statement said.[235]

Defining the U.S. as "the world's most dangerous state sponsor of terrorism," Tehran outlined its own anti-terrorist policy. Iran did not condemn the New York bombing but stressed that it was morally and politically wrong to rejoice over the killing of innocent people by bombs in Western countries. Tehran reiterated its enduring support for the export of the Islamic revolution. "Just as we support the liberation struggle of the people around the world, we are not prepared to support terroristic and deviant actions or even express pleasure about them." Iran then reiterated the validity of the *fatwa* urging the killing of Salman Rushdie to stress that at times violence can be in accordance with the objectives of Islam.[236]

Islamist terrorist leaders echoed the Iranian call for *Jihad*. Most important was a March 11 speech by Sheikh Asa'ad Bayud al-Tamimi, the leader of the Tehran-sponsored *Islamic Jihad* — Bayt al-Maqdis, a.k.a. *HizbAllah*-Palestine, who had been intimately involved in preparing for Islamist terrorism in the U.S. during the Gulf crisis. He connected the Western "hate" for Muslims in the aftermath of the New York bombings and the forthcoming commemoration of al-Quds Day through *Jihad*. "There is fury, fury everywhere . . . I call on the West to understand this — that Islam is escalating and cannot be resisted," he declared. "An oppressed person will hit his enemy in any place," he explained. "I pray that Allah may tear apart America just as the Soviet Union was torn apart because it leads injustice in the world," he added.[237]

Ultimately, while Iran, Syria, Sudan and their allies control the most effective international terrorist networks in the United States, the extent of their ability to sustain operations and strike repeatedly largely depends on the Islamist communities within which they seek shelter. Thus, irrespective of whether Al-Sayyid Abdulazziz Nossair, Amail Kansi, or Muhammad Salameh acted alone, or whether they were members of a subversive group, the fact remains that they were involved in a violent crime motivated by radical Islamist beliefs. These very acts of terrorism testify to the existence of a vibrant Islamist communal structure in the U.S. identical to that of numerous Islamic communities in Western Europe that have been harboring, supporting, and recruiting Islamist terrorists, both individuals and networks. Now that the masters of Islamist international terrorism have given the order to strike, there should be no doubt that the bombing in the World Trade Center was, indeed, only the beginning.

CONCLUSION

The bombing of the World Trade Center in New York City
was a global and historic milestone, not only because it
brought the reality of Islamist terrorism, already present in
the U.S., to the forefront of public attention but because it
propelled the international Islamist community across its
own Rubicon.

The terrorist bomb demonstrated that it was now permis-
sible and possible to strike at the heart of America. In essence,
the primary legacy of the bombing will prove, unfortunately, to
have been the encouragement it gave like-minded individuals
and organizations. Indeed, French experts believe that the New
York bombing amounts to "the beginning of a 'war' between
radical Islam and the United States."[1]

Therefore, the bombing of the World Trade Center must be
considered as a strategic operation, and should to be examined
in the context of ongoing developments in the entire Islamic
movement, its internal dynamics and its policy vis-a-vis the
West, especially the United States.

Controlled by the terrorist states, the Islamists have prepared for a long time for this era. From their point of view, the
strike in New York is but a milestone in a long term historical
process that will not be decided by any single event. Abd al-
Muhsin Fadlallah, a cousin of the spiritual leader of the
HizbAllah Ayatollah Muhammad Hussein Fadlallah, summed
up the approach of Iran and the Islamists to the struggle
against the U.S.: "People who believe in God and see things in
the long term, they will win. People who think only of the next
hour, of their immediate surroundings, they will not win."[2]

Fully aware of the magnitude and complexity of the obstacles ahead, the Islamists have embarked on a deliberate and
protracted process of preparing for, and waging, their kind of

war against the West, and especially the U.S. International terrorism is the Islamists' most effective weapon. Toward this end, highly professional terrorist cells and networks are already in place in the United States, Canada, Western Europe and elsewhere, ready for such an escalation. As instruments of state policy, the Islamist terrorist networks await orders from Tehran, Damascus and Khartoum before launching their operations.

For the Islamists — both states and movements — there is no ambiguity to the profoundness of their struggle against the United States, or to its ultimate objective. Theirs is a fateful struggle. Radical Islam is determined to win virtually at all cost and through the employment of all available means. As the *HizbAllah* stated unequivocally, "The United States is the Great Satan and there must be no leniency in the war against it."[3] Hojjat-ol Islam Ali Akbar Mohtashemi argues that the mere waging of the relentless *Jihad* is in itself the essence of the Islamists' spirit. "Any doubt about the need to struggle against the U.S. means being enslaved by the Great Satan and losing the honor and the life [that] the Islamic Revolution has brought to this country [Iran] and the whole Islamic *ummah*," he declared.[4]

Since 1991, Islamist leaders have been convinced that there are unique circumstances and opportunities in the world today to warrant the escalation of their struggle. Ahmad Khomeini underlined the fatefulness of the inevitable *Jihad* with the U.S.: "After the fall of Marxism, Islam replaced it, and as long as Islam exists, U.S. hostility exists, and as long as U.S. hostility exists, the struggle exists."[5]

The Islamist leaders are most encouraged by the rise of Islam, by the accelerating and expanding spread of Islam all over the world, by the widespread return to traditionalism throughout the Muslim world, and by the growing popular shift from leftist theories to revolutionary Islam as the primary mode of Third World ideological expression. Therefore, they argue, Islam must achieve results NOW. Hence, their fateful

struggle with the West is both imminent and inevitable. Tehran
has a very clear perception of the world situation and the
challenges facing Islam. It is convinced that the immediate
future presents both grave threats and unique opportunities for
Muslims.

> A great tempest has overtaken Islam. Nations are
> trying to find their 'Islamic identity' and are counting
> the minutes until they hoist its flag. They are
> anticipating the day when Islamic rule's glorious
> banner will fly over their countries. . . Today the
> Islamic nations feel the need to revive the lost
> grandeur of Islam and the Muslims. This is a human
> feeling which the world should understand. The
> world should conform to Islam's new conditions
> and should know that there is little it can do to alter
> the situation to harm Islam and that whatever it
> does will only harm itself.[6]

The Islamists are convinced that the leaders of the West
have already realized the gravity and magnitude of the Islamist
challenge. Consequently, they believe, the U.S. is leading the
West on a campaign to contain and enslave the Muslim world.
It is this onslaught from the West, explains Ayatollah Fadlallah,
that drives the Islamists to escalate their anti-Western *Jihad*.
"The Westerners — Americans and Europeans — plan to
involve the Muslims in various issues. . . The West has com-
piled this plan to upset the Muslims' equilibrium and tranquil-
ity and prevent solidarity and unity among Muslims so that
Muslims will not become a power and will be unable to take
their own affairs and rule into their own hands."[7]

In view of the gravity of the danger, Fadlallah explains,
Western policies constitute "the declaration of a war against
Islam, which has brought freedom and justice to the world.
This is an act against dynamic Islam, which has risen against
world arrogance. The West is trying to distract this Islam from
its positions and to involve it in problems so that Islam will not

become a power threatening the interests of world arrogance. "But the Muslims can rise to confront this plot by better understanding their problems and by adopting deliberate stances."

Fadlallah believes that the key to the triumph of Islam lies in seizing the initiative and embarking on the most effective form of war against the West. The Islamists, he argues, "can use their strength in the best way possible to concentrate their efforts against America's great aggressiveness, which today targets the world of Islam. It is under these conditions that we can advance."[8]

Tehran is convinced that a cataclysmic confrontation with the U.S. is inevitable, if only because Washington is determined to block the rise of Islam. "No matter how we look at it, the solution [to the America's problems] would be linked with the defeat of Iran as an important and potential regional and world power." The struggle with Iran, Tehran believes, is a key to the U.S. ability to impose its will on the new post-Cold War world. "Iran is a repository of a very deep form of Islam, which makes it an indicator of the future world order." Thus, the only solution and viable option is a *Jihad*. Tehran must therefore ensure that "the wave of Islamism is boosted abroad as one of the pillars of our national security."[9]

By embarking on, and leading, the *Jihad* against the United States, Tehran has established itself as the undisputed supreme leader of the Islamists. The examples set by Tehran have already rejuvenated and changed the Muslim world. Sayyid Shaykh Hassan Nasrallah, the Secretary General of the *HizbAllah*, stresses the importance of Iranian influence on the rise and militancy of the Islamist movements. "The Islamic Revolution awakened Muslims and endowed them with prestige, which is evident in Muslim nations' strong presence on the scene of *Jihad* and struggle against Western-affiliated regimes. By its support of the oppressed nations against tyranny and oppression, Islamic Iran has affirmed its loyalty to the oppressed.''[10] Now these Islamists rally behind Iran, eager and ready to support and implement its call for a fateful *Jihad* against, and in, America.

The explosion at the World Trade Center in New York came immediately after these statements had been made, and should thus be considered an integral part of the Islamists' formulation of the new phase of their resolute *Jihad* against the United States. Tehran now presents the bombing as a strategic strike that challenges the viability of the Clinton Administration, and its domestic and foreign policies alike.

The explosion occurred in the earliest days of the Clinton Administration, causing a tremendous economic disaster exactly at the time when the Administration is trying to revitalize the U.S. economy. (Damage estimates have been in the range of a little more or a little less than $1 billion.) ''In such difficult circumstances, the explosion has intensified [American] insecurity and has made it obvious that the economy is exceptionally vulnerable. The explosion in the World Trade Center will have an adverse effect on Clinton's plans to rein in [sic] the economy.'' Tehran stresses that the New York explosion, just like the Los Angeles riots, should be viewed as expressions of despair and the general deterioration of the U.S.[11]

Tehran argues further that the mere association of Iran with the explosion in New York is part of an American conspiracy to shift attention from the collapse of its posture and position in the Middle East, and to find an excuse for striking at Iran in order to prevent the rise of Islam as a dominant force.

Tehran is resolved never to be reconciled with U.S. policy. ''Iran does not have to conform to the demands of the new world order. It does not desire liberal Western democracy.''

In this view, Washington will try to blame Iran for its failures in the Middle East and use the bombing in New York as a pretext by which to attack Iran. ''The explosion at New York's World Trade Center can provide the cure for all the woes mentioned above,'' Tehran declares.[12]

Therefore, Tehran concludes, the bombing in New York is

merely the beginning of a violent eruption in the United States. "It is quite likely that any unrest in the future will stem from the erroneous and arrogant policies of the United States at home and abroad. The United States should refrain from its domineering tyrannization of nations and its belligerent interference in the various parts of the world." The introduction of the international element is significant, for it leads Tehran to a polemic on who has the right, and is likely, to take revenge.

Tehran has no doubt that the Islamists are the chosen instrument. "According to the divine traditions, tyranny never goes unpunished in the world. The arrogant U.S. policies are entirely comprised of tyranny and aggression. Even though initially tyranny inflicts anguish on the oppressed, ultimately, divine wrath gives the devout persons the upper hand and they annihilate the tyrant."[13]

Tehran also leaves no doubt that it is spearheading the Islamist drive against the U.S.: Iran "exposes and impedes U.S. and Western policies in the world. The West and the United States have always felt the need to inflict a decisive and shattering blow to Iran."

According to Tehran, recent strike at the very heart of the Great Satan merely provides an excuse for Washington to go after Iran. The source of the enmity, Tehran states, is in objective reasons, namely, Iran's regional and global policies. Therefore, as the threat to Iran increases, resolute and drastic counter-measures, such as strategic terrorist strikes, must be implemented. "The threat against the national security of the Islamic Republic of Iran has become more serious. We should not give any pretext to the enemy. Officials are the ones who should speak on the issue and no direct comments should be made." In other words, Tehran should do what is right against the U.S., but keep quiet about it.[14]

Ayatollah Fadlallah described the New York bombing as being essentially a conspiracy against the Islamists aimed at instigating and justifying an all out assault on Islam. His rationale for this assertion is of crucial significance because in making it he confirms that the bombing of the World Trade Center was in fact an act of state controlled terrorism.

Fadlallah ridicules the accusations leveled against the Islamists arrested in New York because, he claims, Islamists in the United States have no interest in striking out against the U.S. government. "Islamists don't benefit anything from it because Islamists living in the United States have freedom of movement. The United States, which fights the freedom of peoples in the Third World through regimes linked to it, grants freedom to these people when they emigrate to the United States." Therefore, it is the oppressed outside the United States who may have enough grievances, and in these grievances the reasons, to deliver such a powerful strike at America.

Indeed, Fadlallah anticipates an Islamist revolution at the heart of the Arab world. The process only gains strength from American pressures on, and hostility toward, the Arabs, creating favorable circumstances for the Islamist triumph.[15] Therefore, the cycle of violence between the Unitted States and the Arab or Muslim world is bound to expedite the triumphant Islamist revolt. The bombing in New York serves as a powerful instigator for such a cycle of violence, one desired by the Islamists.

Indeed, on the eve of *Al-Quds* Day, March 19, 1993, Iran's spiritual leader, Ayatollah Khamenei, called on "dear people and all Muslim nations to hold the international *Quds* Day ceremonies this year more warmly and enthusiastically than in previous years." In view of the unfolding situation in the Middle East, "the Palestinian strugglers . . . need worldwide support," Khamenei explained. The events of *Al-Quds* Day, to be followed by a worldwide Islamist surge, will constitute "a popular manifestation for the resolute rejection of imperialistic and collaborationist plans."[16]

Large numbers of Iranians and foreign volunteers poured into the streets of Tehran to commemorate *Al-Quds* Day. The entire Iranian leadership was present at the ceremonies. A government statement reaffirmed the commitment to the continuation of *Jihad* operations against "Islam's foremost foes," namely, the United States, "the occupiers of *al-Quds*," and the "Serb butchers." Tehran urged the Muslim youth around the world to form "resistance cells," i.e. terrorist networks, against the enemies of Islam, and promised all possible help.[17]

In Beirut, the *HizbAllah* conducted a massive *al-Quds* Day rally in which the Iranian strategy was further elucidated by Shaykh Nasrallah. "The choice is resistance, the choice is continuing the *Jihad*. We will continue our resistance until the whole [Muslim] nation rises and we will present more martyrs from among our leaders, clerics and warriors," he declared, alluding to the resumption of suicide terrorist operations.[18]

The Tehran-led Islamists are convinced that they are on the verge of a marked escalation in their fateful *Jihad* against the United States and the West. The bombing of the World Trade Center was a strategic strike in this *Jihad*, aimed at demonstrating the Islamists' reach and announcing the opening of a new escalatory phase in their war against America.

The bombing in New York was merely a prelude to a new terrorist campaign in which America is the target.

NOTES

CHAPTER 1
RADICAL ISLAM AGAINST THE US

1. Abd al-Qadir as-Sufi ad-Darqawi, *Jihad — A Ground Plan*, London, Diwan Press, 1978

2. Ayatollah Muhammad Baqir al-Sadr, *The Source of Power in the Islamic Government/State*, Tehran, 1980, p. 37

3. Menashri D., *Iran in Revolution*, Tel-Aviv, Ha-Kibutz Ha-Meuhad, 1988, p. 94

4. Dietl W., *Holy War*, New York, Macmillan, 1984, p. 281; Muttam J., *Arms and Insecurity in the Persian Gulf*, New Delhi, Radiant, 1984, p. 158; Bani-Sadr Abdol-Hassan, *The Fundamental Principles and Percepts of Islamic Government*, Lexington KT, Mazda, 1981, p. 71

5. Laffin J., *Holy War: Islam Fights*, London, Grafton Books, 1988, pp. 13-14

6. Q. in Algar Hamid (ed. & tr.), *Islam and Revolution: Writings and Declarations of Imam Khomeyni*, London, KPI, 1981, pp. 286-287

7. Malik Brigadier S.M., *The Quranic Concept of War*, n.p., 1979

8. Motahari Sheikh Mortaza, *Islamic Movements in the Last One Hundred Years*, Tehran, 1979, p. 83

9. Laurent A. and Basbous A., *Secret Wars in Lebanon*, Paris, Gallimard, 1987, p. 227

10. Sablier E., *Valeurs Actuelles*, 6 April 1987

11. Taheri Amir, *Holy Terror*, London, Huchinson, 1987, pp. 88-89

12. de Morais C.B., *Semanario*, 10 May 1986

13. Taheri, op.cit. (Holy Terror), p. 89

14. NuriZadeh Dr. Ali, *Al-Dustur*, 12 February 1990

15. Gorouh-e Yazandegan, *Letre Persane*, No. 46, June 1986; Sablier R., *Valeurs Actuelles*, 1 April 1985; Dietl, op.cit., pp. 163-164; Taheri, op.cit., (Holy Terror), p. 72

16. Mihail R., *Le Figaro*, 18 April 1990; Taheri, op.cit. (Holy Terror), p. 166; Taheri Amir, *The Spirit of Allah*, Bethesda MD, Adler & Adler, 1986, p. 221; Gorouh-e Yazandegan, *Letre Persane*, No. 46, June 1986; Raffy S., *Le Nouvel Observateur*, 28 March - 3 April 1986; Sablier R., *Valeurs Actuelles*, 1 April 1985; Qallab Salih, *al-Sharq al-Awsat*, 5 February 1989; *Al-Majallah*, 5-11 November 1983; Adams N., *Reader's Digest*, September 1990

17. Laurent and Basbous, op.cit., p. 237; Sobhani Sohrab, *The Pragmatic Entente: Israeli-Iranian Relations, 1948-1988*, New York NY, Prager, 1989, p. 106; Dietl, op.cit., p. 163

18. Sablier R., *Valeurs Actuelles*, 1 April 1985

19. Norton A.R., *New Outlook*, January 1984

20. Taheri, op.cit., (Holy Terror), pp. 70-71; Delafon G., *Beirut: The Soldiers of Islam*, Paris, Stock, 1989, p. 72; Segev S., *The Iranian Tiangle*, Tel Aviv, Ma'ariv, 1981, p. 67; Segev S., *The Iranian Connection*, Jerusalem, Domino, 1989, p. 113; Raffy S., *Le Nouvel Observateur*, 28 March - 3 April 1986; Qallab Salih, *al-Sharq al-Awsat*, 5 February 1989

21. Radio Tehran, 20 February 1979; Segev, op.cit. (Iranian Triangle), p. 68; Segev, op.cit. (Iranian Connection), p. 111; Delafon, op.cit., p. 73

22. Kifner J., *New York Times*, 7 May 1979

23. *Keyhan*, 5 July 1984

24. *Washington Star*, 20 January 1979

25. Q. in McForan D., *The World Held Hostage*, New York NY, St.Martin's, 1986, p. 66; Souresrafil Behruz, *Khomeyni and Israel*, England, I Researchers, 1988, p. 44

26. Jaber Hala, *The Sunday Correspondent*, 26 November 1989

27. Sablier E., *Valeurs Actuelles*, 6 April 1987; Bonomo J., *Le Figaro Magazine*, 11 January 1986; Dunn M., *Defense and Foreign Affairs*, August 1985; Taheri, op.cit. (Holy Terror), p. 89

28. *Jamahiriya Mail*, 6 March 1982; *Conservative Digest*, February 1984; Essack Karrim, *The Mathaba International*, Dar es-Salaam, Thakers, 1987, p. 2; Sicker Martin, *The Making of a Pariah State*, New York NY, Praeger, 1987, p. 120; Spaulding W.H., *Political Warfare*, No. 18, Fall 1991

29. *Report on the General Congress of the World Center for Resistence of Imperialism, Zionism, Racism, and Reaction*, prepared for the Central Committee of the New Jewel Movement, Grenada; Q. in *Grenada Documents: An Overview and a Selection*, Washington D.C., The Department of State and the Department of Defense, September 1984, pp. 34-1 - 34-5

30. *Al-Fajr Al-Jadid*, 1 September 1982

31. Haselkorn A., The Radical Etente: Revolutionary Anti-Imperialism in the 1980s, in *State Terrorism and the International System*, Proceedings of The International Security Council's Conference in Tel Aviv, Israel, 26-28 January 1986, pp. 51-68

32. Bonomo J., *Le Figaro Magazine*, 11 January 1986

33. Taheri, op.cit. (Holy Terror), p. 92 & 95

34. Simpson J., *Behind Iranian Lines*, London, Fontana, 1988, p. 226

35. Taheri, op.cit. (Holy Terror), p. 92; Material provided by Iranian and Palestinian sources

36. JANA, 30 March 1983; Tehran International Service, 1 April 1983

37. Wolf J., *New York City Tribune*, 31 October 1984

38. Free Voice of Iran, 2 March 1982; Bulloch J., *Daily Telegraph*, 24 May 1982; Sicker M., *The Bear and the Lion*, New York NY, Prager, 1988, p. 123

39. de Morais C.B., *Semanario*, 10 May 1986; *Keyhan*, 6 February 1986

40. *Hurriyet*, 13 April 1982

41. Bulloch J., *Daily Telegraph*, 24 May 1982
42. Sablier R., *Valeurs Actuelles*, 1 April 1985; Bonomo J., *Le Figaro Magazine*, 11 January 1986
43. Taheri, op.cit. (Holy Terror), pp. 96-97; Selhami Muhammad, *Jeune Afrique*, 25 January 1984; Dunn M., *Defense and Foreign Affairs*, August 1985; Bonomo J., *Le Figaro Magazine*, 11 January 1986
44. Taheri, op.cit. (Holy Terror), pp. 98-99
45. Taheri, op.cit. (Holy Terror), pp. 96-97; Dunn M., *Defense and Foreign Affairs*, August 1985; Bonomo J., *Le Figaro Magazine*, 11 January 1986
46. Selhami Muhammad, *Jeune Afrique*, 25 January 1984; Bonomo J., *Le Figaro Magazine*, 11 January 1986
47. Bonomo J., *Le Figaro Magazine*, 11 January 1986
48. Jacquard R., *The Secret Dossiers of Terrorism*, Paris, Albin Michel, 1985, pp. 93-95
49. Jacquard, op.cit. (Terrorism), pp. 93-95
50. *Keyhan*, 30 October 1986; Voice of the Liberation of Iran, 1 March 1986; *Keyhan*, 6 February 1986; Jacquard, op.cit. (Terrorism), p. 100; Dunn M., *Defense and Foreign Affairs*, August 1985; Taheri, op.cit. (Holy Terror), pp. 96-97; Bonomo J., *Le Figaro Magazine*, 11 January 1986
51. Dunn M., *Defense and Foreign Affairs*, August 1985
52. Jacquard, op.cit. (Terrorism), p. 95
53. Taheri, op.cit. (Holy Terror), pp. 96-97; Delafon, op.cit., p. 176; Dunn M., *Defense and Foreign Affairs*, August 1985; Bonomo J., *Le Figaro Magazine*, 11 January 1986; Material provided by Iranian sources
54. *Keyhan*, 8 August 1985
55. *Keyhan*, 8 August 1985
56. *Al-Bayan*, 23 July 1983; *Al-Anba'*, 13 August 1985
57. *Keyhan*, 8 August 1985
58. Domenach J-M, *Le Monde*, 15 June 1984
59. NuriZadeh Dr. Ali, *Al-Dustur*, 6 November 1989
60. Brynen R., *Sanctuary and Survival: The PLO in Lebanon*, Boulder Co, Westview, 1990, pp. 143-153
61. *The Daily Telegraph*, 6 June 1980; Laffin J., *The PLO Connection*, London, Corgi Books, 1982, pp. 102-103
62. Delafon, op.cit., pp. 57-58
63. Shapira S., *The Jerusalem Quaterly*, Spring 1988
64. Laurent and Basbous, op.cit., p. 239
65. Delafon, op.cit., p. 58
66. Shapira S., *The Jerusalem Quaterly*, Spring 1988; Delafon, op.cit., p. 83
67. Jarry E., *Le Monde*, 9 September 1982; Voice of Palestine from San'a, 17 September 1982; Hawatimah Nayif to *Al-Khalij*, 4 October 1982; Voice of the Arab Homeland, 5 October 1982; Sablier E., *Politique International*, April 1984

68. AFP, 12 September 1982; Voice of Lebanon, 7 September 1982; Radio Monte Carlo, 7 September 1982; WAKH, 4 September 1982; Radio Monte Carlo, 1 September 1982

69. Sablier E., *Politique International*, April 1984

70. IRNA, 7 November 1982; Radio Damascus, 9 November 1982

71. Damascus Televison, 9 November 1982

72. IRNA, 7 November 1982

73. Laurent and Basbous, op.cit., p. 241; Delafon, op.cit., p. 82 74. Taheri, op.cit. (Holy Terror), pp. 120-121

75. Sablier E., *Politique International*, April 1984

76. NuriZadeh Dr. Ali, *Al-Dustur*, 6 November 1989

77. Bulloch J., *The Independent*, 26 April 1988

78. Ya'ari E., *Wall Street Journal*, 16 August 1989

79. Bulloch J., *The Independent*, 26 April 1988

80. *Mardi Matin*, 25 February 1986; Moruzzi J.-F., *Le Quotidien*, 27 February 1986; *Le Figaro*, 7 March 1986

81. Radio Free Lebanon, 21 November 1982; Radio Free Lebanon, 23 November 1982; Delafon, op.cit., pp. 83-86; Laurent and Basbous, op.cit., pp. 246-247

82. *Al-Nahar*, 27 November 1982

83. *L'Orient le Jour*, 25 November 1982

84. Voice of Lebanon, 10 December 1982; Voice of Lebanon, 17 March 1983; Radio Free Lebanon, 18 March 1983; Beylau P., *Le Point*, 11 May 1987

85. *Al-Watan al-'Arabi*, 11 December 1987

86. Beylau P., *Le Point*, 11 May 1987

87. Laurent and Basbous, op.cit., pp. 241-242; Delafon, op.cit., p. 87; Raviv H.A., *Bamahane*, 16 August 1989

88. *Al-Watan al-'Arabi*, 11 December 1987

89. *Liberation*, 19 March 1985

90. Raviv H.A., *Bamahane*, 16 August 1989

91. Taheri, op.cit. (Holy Terror), p. 126

92. Newman B. (with Rogan B.), 'The Covenant', New York NY, Crown, 1989, pp. 220-221; Moss R., *Daily Telegraph*, 5 January 1981

93. Jacquard, op.cit. (Terrorism), pp. 97 & 99; Selhami Mohamad, *Jeune Afrique*, 25 January 1984

94. Delafon, op.cit., p. 45; Laurent and Basbous, op.cit., p. 253

95. Laurent and Basbous, op.cit., pp. 254-255; Sablier R., *Valeurs Actuelles*, 1 April 1985

96. Laurent and Basbous, op.cit., pp. 254-255

97. Voice of Lebanon, 29 September 1984

98. Voice of Lebanon, 26 March 1983

99. Voice of Lebanon, 6 April 1983

100. Voice of Lebanon, 12 April 1983

101. Radio Free Lebanon, 15 April 1983

102. Voice of Lebanon, 19 April 1983
103. Radio Free Lebanon, 27 April 1983; Radio Monte Carlo, 27 April, 1983
104. Damascus Domestic Service, 12 April 1983; Syrian Television, 12 April 1983
105. Damascus Domestic Service, 14 April 1983
106. Voice of the PLO from Baghdad, 20 April 1983
107. Laurent and Basbous, op.cit., pp. 254-255
108. Taheri, op.cit. (Holy Terror), p. 126
109. Beirut Domestic Service, 19 April 1983; Delafon, op.cit., pp. 48-49
110. Martin D.C. and Walcott J., *Best Laid Plans*, New York NY, Harper & Row, 1988, p. 105
111. *Liberation*, 19 March 1985
112. Laurent and Basbous, op.cit., pp. 254-255
113. Newman, op.cit., p. 182
114. ibid, pp. 220-221
115. Voice of Lebanon, 18 April 1983; Beirut Domestic Service; 18 April 1983; Radio Free Lebanon, 18 April 1983; AFP, 19 April 1983; Pintak L., *Beirut Outtakes*, Lexington MA, Lexington Books, 1988, p. 102
116. Wright R., *Sacred Rage*, New York NY, Linden Press / Simon and Shuster, 1985, p. 16
117. Radio Free Lebanon, 18 April 1983; AFP, 18 April 1983; *New York Times*, 19 April 1983; Delafon, op.cit., p. 49 118. Beylau P., *Le Point*, 11 May 1987
119. *New York Times*, 19 April 1983
120. Laurent and Basbous, op.cit., p. 255
121. Dobson C. & Payne R., *War Without End*, London, Haarp, 1986, p. 37
122. Radio Damascus, 20 September 1983
123. *Al-Ra'i al-'Amm*, 20 September 1983; KUNA, 20 September 1983
124. *Resalat*, 20 July 1987
125. Delafon, op.cit., pp. 59-60; Selhami Muhammad, *Jeune Afrique*, 25 January 1984
126. Taheri, op.cit. (Holy Terror), p. 126; *Jerusalem Post*, 27 October 1983
127. Delafon, op.cit., pp. 59-60; Dobson & Payne, op.cit., pp. 37-38
128. *Le Monde*, 6-7 November 1983
129. *Jerusalem Post*, 27 October 1983
130. Radio Free Lebanon, 28 October 1983
131. Jacquard, op.cit. (Terrorism), pp. 120-121; Delafon, op.cit., pp. 59-60; *Al-Watan Al-'Arabi*, No. 409, 14-20 December 1984
132. Dobson & Payne, op.cit., p. 37; Wright R., *In the Name of God*, New York NY, Simon & Schuster, 1989, p. 122; Taheri, op.cit. (Holy Terror), p. 126
133. Voice of Lebanon, 26 October 1983
134. Wright, op.cit. (In the Name of God), p. 122
135. Delafon, op.cit., p. 51
136. Jacquard, op.cit. (Terrorism), p. 94

137. Jacquard, op.cit. (Terrorism), pp. 120-121
138. Voice of Lebanon, 26 October 1983
139. Pean P., *The Threat*, Paris, Fayard, 1987, p. 121
140. Delafon, op.cit., p. 57
141. Voice of Lebanon, 23 October 1983
142. Jacquard, op.cit. (Terrorism), p. 120
143. *Le Nouvel Observateur*, 30 October 1983; *Le Monde*, 6-7 November 1983; Delafon, op.cit., pp. 59-60
144. Wright, op.cit. (Sacred Rage), p. 87; Material provided by Iranian sources
145. *Le Nouvel Observateur*, 30 October 1983; Radio Free Lebanon, 30 October 1983
146. Delafon, op.cit., pp. 59-60
147. Voice of Lebanon, 2 January 1984
148. Delafon, op.cit., pp. 59-60
149. Laurent and Basbous, op.cit., p. 254; Delafon, op.cit., p. 60
150. Zaray O., *Ha'aretz*, 26 October 1983
151. Zaray O., *Ha'aretz*, 23 October 1983
152. Zaray O., *Ha'aretz*, 26 October 1983
153. *Al-Watan Al-'Arabi*, 14-20 December 1984; Laurent and Basbous, op.cit., p. 254; Delafon, op.cit., p. 60
154. Jacquard, op.cit. (Terrorism), p. 94
155. Doron A., *Ma'ariv*, 20 December 1991; Thomas G., *Journey into Madness*, New York, Bantam, 1989
156. Beirut Domestic Service, 23 October 1983; Damascus Domestic Service, 23 October 1983; AFP, 23 October 1983; Delafon, op.cit., p. 51; Jacquard, op.cit. (Terrorism), p. 94; Thomas, op.cit., p. 27
157. Delafon, op.cit., p. 57
158. Wright, op.cit. (Sacred Rage), p. 70
159. AFP, 23 October 1983; AP, 23 October 1983; Beirut Domestic Service, 23 October 1983
160. AFP, 24 October 1983
161. *Tishrin*, 24 October 1983; SANA, 24 October 1983
162. AFP, 24 October 1983
163. Kauffmann J.-P., *Le Matin*, 28 October 1983; Durand-Souffland J.M., *Le Monde*, 2 November 1983
164. Voice of Lebanon, 28 October 1983
165. IRNA, 15 November 1983
166. Radio Free Lebanon, 19 November 1983
167. IRNA, 28 November 1983; Voice of Lebanon, 26 November 1983; Voice of Lebanon, 25 November 1983
168. Beirut Domestic Service, 25 November 1983
169. Voice of Lebanon, 26 November 1983; Voice of Lebanon, 30 November 1983; Voice of Lebanon, 24 December 1983
170. Radio Free Lebanon, 29 November 1983

171. IRNA, 29 November 1983
172. Tehran International, 4 December 1983
173. Delafon, op.cit., pp. 85-87
174. Tehran Domestic Service, 13 February 1984
175. IDF Radio, 4 November 1983; Voice of Lebanon, 4 November 1983
176. Voice of Arab Lebanon, 4 November 1983; AFP, 4 November 1983
177. *Al-Watan Al-'Arabi*, 14-20 December 1984
178. al-Jasim Ghazi, *Al-Watan*, 6 June 1985
179. *Al-Watan Al-'Arabi*, 14-20 December 1984 180. Wright R., *Sunday Times*, 4 November 1984
181. Voice of Lebanon, 25 November 1983; Voice of Lebanon, 30 November 1983
182. *Liberation*, 19 March 1985
183. *Monday Morning*, 31 October 1983
184. *Liberation*, 19 March 1985
185. Al-Shira Malaf, *The Islamic Movement in Lebanon (Al-Harakat al-Islamiyya fi Lubnan)* , Beirut, Dar Sannin, 1984, pp. 146-148
186. *Liberation*, 19 March 1985
187. Al-Shira, op.cit., p. 148
188. Malih S.A., *Monday Morning*, 15-21 October 1984
189. *Al-Nahar Al-'Arabi wa al-Duwali*, 20-26 August 1984 190. Malih S.A., *Monday Morning*, 15-21 October 1984
191. Al-Shira, op.cit., pp. 145-146
192. Malih S.A., *Monday Morning*, 15-21 October 1984
193. Al-Shira, op.cit., pp. 161-162
194. ibid, pp. 226-227
195. ibid, p. 263
196. Sablier R., *Valeurs Actuelles*, 1 April 1985
197. Beylau P., *Le Point*, 11 May 1987
198. Sablier E., *Politique International*, April 1984
199. Harif Y., *Ma'ariv*, 25 April 1986
200. *Al-Nahar*, 29 December 1983
201. Laffin, op.cit. (Holy War), pp. 225-226
202. *Al-Watan Al-'Arabi*, 14-20 December 1984
203. Fadlallah Ayatollah Muhammad Hussein, *Al-'Ahd*, 2 January 1988
204. *The Times*, 16 January 1985; Greenfield R.H., *Sunday Telegraph*, 7 July 1985; Grolig E., *Kurier*, 29 June 1985
205. *The Times*, 16 January 1985
206. *Creation of an Independent Brigade for Carrying out Unconventional Warfare in Enemy Territory*, Minutes of a Top Secret meeting in Tehran on 26 May 1984; *The Times*, 16 January 1985; Ginzburg H.Y., *Ha'aretz*, 11 March 1985; *Die Welt*, 25 March 1985; Greenfield R.H., *Sunday Telegraph*, 7 July 1985; Grolig E., *Kurier*, 29 June 1985
207. Grolig E., *Kurier*, 29 June 1985

208. Greenfield R.H., *Sunday Telegraph*, 7 July 1985

209. *Creation of an Independent Brigade for Carrying out Unconventional Warfare in Enemy Territory*, Minutes of a Top Secret meeting in Tehran on 26 May 1984; *The Times*, 16 January 1985; Ginzburg H.Y., *Ha'aretz*, 11 March 1985; *Die Welt*, 25 March 1985; Greenfield R.H., *Sunday Telegraph*, 7 July 1985

210. Greenfield R.H., *Sunday Telegraph*, 7 July 1985

211. *Al-Watan al-'Arabi*, 11 December 1987

212. *Creation of an Independent Brigade for Carrying out Unconventional Warfare in Enemy Territory*, Minutes of a Top Secret meeting in Tehran on 26 May 1984; Grolig E., *Kurier*, 29 June 1985; *The Times*, 16 January 1985

213. *Pourquoi Pas?*, 3 July 1985

214. *Pourquoi Pas?*, 3 July 1985; Selhami Muhammad, *Jeune Afrique*, 25 January 1984

215. Selhami Muhammad, *Jeune Afrique*, 25 January 1984

216. *Pourquoi Pas?*, 3 July 1985

217. *Liberation*, 19 March 1985

218. Tripoli Voice of Greater Arab Homeland, 2 March 1984

219. Tripoli Voice of Greater Arab Homeland, 12 March 1984

220. JANA, 14 August 1985

221. *Al-Watan Al-'Arabi*, 14-20 December 1984

Chapter 2

THE NEW SYSTEM OF INTERNATIONAL TERRORISM

1. Delafon G., *Beirut: The Soldiers of Islam*, Paris, Stock, 1989, p. 164

2. Fisk R., *The Times*, 18 June 1985

3. The International Headquarters of the *HizbAllah*, *Open Letter Addressed by the HizbAllah to the Opressed/Downtrodden in Lebanon and in the World*, Tehran, 16 February 1985

4. Tripoli Domestic Service, 28 March 1985

5. Tripoli Domestic Service, 31 March 1985

6. *Al-Safir*, 21 March 1985

7. Fisk R., *The Times*, 18 June 1985

8. Radio Nejat-e Iran, 4 July 1985; Free Voice of Iran, 27 July 1985

9. Free Voice of Iran, 12 August 1985

10. Radio Nejat-e Iran, 24 August 1985

11. Free Voice of Iran, 22 August 1985

12. Material provided by KhAD defectors with the Afghan resistance in the Herat area.

13. *Early Warning*, April 1986

14. Raufer X., *Political Warfare*, No. 19, November 1991; Jacquard R., Ponteaux J.-M., Reverier J.-L., *Le Point*, 21 September 1991; Jacquard

R., Ponteaux J.-M., Reverier J.-L., *Le Point*, 6 July 1991; Raufer X., *L'Express*, 5 July 1991; Raufer X., *L'Express*, 1 November 1990; Pontaut J.-M. & Reverier J.-L., *Le Point*, 27 August 1990; Material provided by Libyan, French and African sources

15. Essack Karrim, *The Mathaba International*, Dar es-Salaam, Thakers, 1987, p. 2; Spaulding W.H., *Political Warfare*, No. 18, Fall 1991

16. Libyan Television Service, 2 February 1986

17. Tripoli Voice of Greater Arab Homeland, 4 February 1986

18. AFP, 3 February 1986

19. Tripoli Voice of Greater Arab Homeland, 4 February 1986

20. *Political Communique Issued on 18 March by the Second International Conference of the International Center for Combatting Imperialism, Zionism, Racism, Reaction and Fascism*, Tripoli Voice of Greater Arab Homeland, 18 March 1986

21. Taheri Amir, *Jeune Afrique*, 7 May 1986; *Ma'ariv*, 4 April 1986

22. *Ma'ariv*, 4 April 1986

23. Padhatsur R., *Ha'aretz*, 9 July 1986; Segal D., *Soldier of Fortune*, August 1986; Eldar A., *Ha'aretz*, 21 May 1986; Lesieur J., *Le Point*, 10 February 1986; Kol Yisrael, 14 January 1986; Kol Yisrael, 16 January 1986

24. Ma'oz M., *Asad: The Sphinx of Damascus*, New York NY, Weidenfeld & Nicolson, 1988, p. 173

25. Zaq M., *Ma'ariv*, 22 September 1986

26. *Al-Thawara*, 9 July 1986; Damascus Domestic Service, 9 July 1986

27. *Tishrin*, 29 September 1986; Damascus Domestic Service, 29 September 1986

28. Damascus Domestic Service, 9 July 1986

29. Abdullah Aslam, *Arabia*, May 1986

30. Tehran Domestic Service, 14 November 1986

31. Fadlallah Ayatollah Muhammad Hussayn, *Middle East Insight*, July-October 1986

32. Statement of the Central Committee of the Popular Front for the Liberation of Palestine — General Command as read on Al-Quds Palestine Arab Radio, 7 February 1990

33. Bulloch J., *The Independent*, 22 June 1988

34. Birand Mehmet Ali, *Milliyet*, 23 March 1991

35. NuriZadeh Dr. Ali, *Al-Dustur*, 16 October 1989

36. Taheri Amir, *Jeune Afrique*, 7 May 1986

37. Taheri Amir, *Jeune Afrique*, 7 May 1986

38. Radio Tehran, 8 February 1987

39. Taheri Amir, *Jeune Afrique*, 7 May 1986

40. *Al-Ahd*, 12 February 1988

41. *Ettela'at*, 20 August 1985

42. *Liberation*, 19 March 1985

43. Taheri Amir, *Jeune Afrique*, 7 May 1986

44. The International Headquarters of the *HizbAllah*, *Open Letter Addressed by the HizbAllah to the Opressed/Downtrodden in Lebanon and in the World*, Tehran, 16 February 1985
45. Delafon, op.cit., p. 90
46. Nasrallah Sayyid Hassan on Tehran Domestic Service, 13 February 1984
47. Hamadah Ali, *Al-Nahar al-'Arabi wa al-Duwali*, 18-24 March 1985
48. *La Revue du Liban*, 27 July - 3 August 1985; al-Mussawi Sheikh Hussein to *Al-Nahar al-'Arabi wa al-Duwali*, 10-16 June 1985
49. Judiyah Imad, *Al-Ittihad*, 7 June 1985
50. *Inquiry*, April 1987
51. Kabbarah Ruba, *Al-Majallah*, 15-21 July 1987
52. *Al-'Ahd*, 30 December 1988
53. *Jumhuri-ye-Eslami*, 25 March 1989
54. *Keyhan*, 9 December 1989
55. Tehran Domestic Service, 12 August 1989
56. IRNA, 28 December 1989
57. *Jomhuri-ye Eslami*, 20 August 1987; AFP, 21 August 1987
58. Tehran Domestic Service, 14 November 1989
59. Zughyab Shibril, *Al-Hawadith*, 13 February 1987
60. IRNA, 27 February 1990
61. *Keyhan*, 25 September 1986
62. Tehran Domestic Service, 16 April 1987
63. Zughyab Shibril, *Al-Hawadith*, 13 February 1987
64. *Al-Nahar*, 10 August 1986
65. Asi Thurayya, *Al-Hawadith*, 10 July 1987
66. IRNA, 27 June 1987
67. IRNA, 19 January 1988
68. *Al-'Ahd*, 21 April 1988
69. Voice of the Oppressed, 3 December 1989
70. Abd-al-'Azim Sulayman, *Al-Musawwar*, 20 October 1989
71. al-Muhajir Sheikh Ja'far, *Al-Safir*, 22 January 1988
72. Jawdiyah Imad, *Al-Ittihad Al-Usbu'i*, 2 July 1987
73. Yaghi Subhi Mundhir, *Al-Nahar al-'Arabi wa al-Duwali*, 9-15 February 1987
74. *Kayhan International*, 3 March 1985
75. *La Revue du Liban*, 27 July - 3 August 1985
76. *Nehzat*, 18 July 1985
77. Kabbarah Ruba, *Al-Majallah*, 1-7 October 1986
78. *La Revue du Liban*, 27 July - 3 August 1985
79. *Keyhan*, 27 July 1986
80. Q. in Delafon, op.cit., pp. 100-101
81. Nader George, *Middle East Insight*, June-July 1985
82. *Tercuman*, 28 December 1988

83. *Al-Mukharrar*, 2 April 1988; *Ha'Aretz*, 4 April 1988; Sharon D., *Davar*, 6 May 1988

84. *Al-'Ahd*, 4 March 1988

85. Fadlallah Sheikh Muhammad Hussayn, *Al-'Ahd*, 11 March 1988 86. *Al-Qabas*, 15 June 1988

87. *Elevtherotipia*, 26 June 1988

88. *Al-Shira'*, 8 August 1988

89. Arshadi Samir, *Kayhan al-'Arabi*, 4 November 1989

90. *Resalat*, 22 November 1989

91. Voice of the Oppressed, 25 October 1989

92. Jaber Hala, *The Sunday Correspondent*, 26 November 1989

93. JANA, 21 March 1990; JANA, 20 March 1990; JANA, 19 March 1990

94. Tripoli Domestic Service, 19 March 1990

95. Tripoli Television Service, 20 March 1990

96. JANA, 21 March 1990; JANA, 20 March 1990; JANA, 19 March 1990

97. JANA, 20 March 1990

98. Tripoli Television Service, 20 March 1990

99. JANA, 20 March 1990

100. Tripoli Television Service, 20 March 1990

101. Tripoli Television Service, 20 March 1990

102. Tripoli Television Service, 20 March 1990

103. *Keyhan Hava'i*, 7 March 1990

104. *Jomhuri-ye Eslami*, 27 January 1990

105. *Jomhuri-ye Eslami*, 27 January 1990

106. Beirut Voice of National Resistance, 23 February 1990

107. AFP, 23 February 1990

108. Tehran International Service, 4 May 1990

109. *Abrar*, 24 May 1990

110. *Keyhan Hava'i*, 7 March 1990

111. Zaq M., *Ma'ariv*, 22 September 1986

112. Peroncel-Hugoz J.-P. as cited in *Keyhan*, 18 September 1986

113. de Morais C.B., *Semanario*, 10 May 1986

114. de Morais C.B., *Semanario*, 10 May 1986

115. al-Husayni Sharif, *Al-Shira*, 15 March 1986; *Al-Watan al-'Arabi*, 11 December 1987; Delafon, op.cit., p. 152

116. Tehran Domestic Service, 6 September 1989

117. Voice of the Liberation of Iran, 18 April 1986

118. Gueyras J., *Le Monde*, 25 October 1986

119. de Morais C.B., *Semanario*, 10 May 1986

120. Peroncel-Hugoz J.-P. as cited in *Keyhan*, 18 September 1986

121. Gueyras J., *Le Monde*, 25 October 1986; Sablier E., *Valeurs Actuelles*, 6 April 1987

122. Ozeskici Oktay, *Hurriyet*, 11 November 1986; *Bulvar*, 17 November 1986; Pazarci Emin, *Bulvar*, 10 December 1986; *Cumhuriyet*, 24 February 1987

123. *Hurriyet*, 25 November 1986
124. IRNA, 18 March 1987
125. *Marmara*, 25 November 1986; *Bulvar*, 16 November 1986
126. Gueyras J., *Le Monde*, 25 October 1986
127. Pean P., *The Threat*, Paris, Fayard, 1987, p. 262; Delafon, op.cit., p. 175
128. *The Iranian Revolution as Seen by World Muslims*, The Culture Office of Iran's Istanbul Consulate General, 1987; Q. in Yetkin Cetin & Corlu Murat, *Milliyet*, 7 June 1989
129. Al-Matrafi Khalid, *Al-Madinah*, 11 June 1990
130. NuriZadeh Dr. Ali, *Al-Dustur*, 12 February 1990
131. *Keyhan*, 6 October 1988; Heller Y., *Le Monde*, 8 October 1988; Bulloch J., *The Independent*, 1 October 1988; *NLA Quarterly*, Autumn 1988; Material provided by Iranian sources in Europe
132. *Al-Tadamun*, 1 May 1989
133. NuriZadeh Dr. Ali, *Al-Dustur*, 16 October 1989
134. *Al-Dustur*, 22 January 1990; *Ha'aretz*, 24 January 1990
135. Grange S., *Defense & Armament Heracles*, November 1989
136. *Tehran Times*, 27 July 1989
137. Arshadi Samir, *Kayhan al-'Arabi*, 4 November 1989
138. NuriZadeh Dr. Ali, *Al-Dustur*, 11 June 1990
139. Voice of the Oppressed, 7 June 1989
140. Al-Matrafi Khalid, *Al-Madinah*, 11 June 1990; *NLA Quarterly*, Autumn 1988; Material provided by Iranian sources in Europe
141. Tehran Domestic Service, 6 September 1989
142. Sablier R., *Valeurs Actuelles*, 1 April 1985
143. NuriZadeh Dr. Ali, *Al-Dustur*, 6 November 1989; NuriZadeh Dr. Ali, *Al-Dustur*, 11 September 1989
144. *Al-Watan al-'Arabi*, 11 December 1987
145. Muhammad Jalah, *Al-Majallah*, 20 April 1988
146. Bayram Ibrahim, *Al-Ittihad Al-Usbu'i*, 4 December 1986
147. Delafon, op.cit., p. 20
148. Coskun Ender, *Hurriyet*, 17 November 1986; Sabah G., *Ha'aretz*, 12 October 1989
149. Coskun Ender, *Hurriyet*, 17 November 1986
150. Nafadi Basimah, *Al-Ittihad Al-Usbu'i*, 26 February 1987
151. Voice of Lebanon, 15 May 1988; Hussayn al-Mussawi to *Nouveau Magazine*, 23 July 1988
152. Muhammad Jalah, *Al-Majallah*, 20 April 1988
153. Radio Free Lebanon, 22 March 1986; Radio Free Lebanon, 9 September 1986; Coskun Ender, *Hurriyet*, 17 November 1986; Coskun Ender, *Hurriyet*, 18 November 1986; Voice of Lebanon, 1 March 1987; *Al-Watan al-'Arabi*, 11 December 1987; *Nokta*, 12 March 1989; Raviv H.A., *Bamahane*, 16 August 1989; Delafon, op.cit., pp. 152-153
154. Coskun Ender, *Hurriyet*, 18 November 1986; *Nokta*, 12 March 1989

155. Radio Monte Carlo, 14 December 1987
156. Delafon, op.cit., p. 175; Ya'ari E., *Wall Street Journal*, 16 August 1989
157. Jacobsen D. with Astor G., *Hostage: My Nightmare in Beirut*, New York NY, Donald I. Fine, 1991, p. 290
158. Delafon, op.cit., p. 175
159. Morrot B., *Le Figaro*, 4 December 1989; Mahnaimy U., *Yediot Aharonot*, 24 June 1988; Bulloch J., *The Independent*, 26 April 1988
160. Morrot B., *Le Figaro*, 4 December 1989; *Al-Nahar Al-'Arabi wa Al-Duwali*, 16 January 1989; Bulloch J., *The Independent*, 22 June 1988
161. Ya'ari E., *Wall Street Journal*, 16 August 1989
162. Gabay Sh., *Ma'ariv*, 11 August 1989
163. Mahnaimy U., *Yediot Aharonot*, 24 June 1988
164. Delafon, op.cit., p. 175
165. Radio Najat-e Iran, 7 October 1985
166. de Morais C.B., *Semanario*, 10 May 1986; Sablier E., *Valeurs Actuelles*, 6 April 1987
167. Radio Najat-e Iran, 7 October 1985; Material provided by Afghan sources
168. *Marmara*, 3 November 1986
169. *NLA Quarterly*, Autumn 1988; Material provided by Iranian sources in Europe
170. Bazoft Farzad, *The Observer*, 30 October 1988; *NLA Quarterly*, Autumn 1988; Material provided by Iranian sources in Europe
171. Tsdakah Sh., *Ha'aretz*, 7 February 1986; de Morais C.B., *Semanario*, 10 May 1986; *NLA Quarterly*, Autumn 1988; Laffin J., *Holy War: Islam Fights*, London, Grafton, 1988, pp. 83-84; Material provided by Iranian sources in Europe
172. *Al-Dustur*, 18 December 1989; *Ha'aretz*, 19 December 1989
173. *Al-Sharq Al-Awsat*, 24 April 1988; material provided by Iranian in Europe
174. *NLA Quarterly*, Autumn 1988; Material provided by Iranian sources in Europe
175. Morrot B., *Le Figaro*, 4 December 1989; Material provided by Iranian sources in Europe
176. *Cyprus Mail*, 5 May 1988
177. Haeri Safa, *The Independent*, 4 April 1988; *Ha'aretz*, 25 April 1988
178. *Tercuman*, 28 December 1988; Material provided by Iranian sources in Europe
179. *Al-Sharq Al-Awsat*, 24 April 1988; Delafon, op.cit., p. 176; Material provided by Iranian sources in Europe
180. *Tercuman*, 28 December 1988; Bazoft Farzad, *The Observer*, 21 February 1988
181. *NLA Quarterly*, Autumn 1988; Material provided by Iranian sources in Europe
182. *Al-Watan al-'Arabi*, 18 September 1987
183. Laffin, op.cit., pp. 83-84; Material provided by Iranian sources in Europe

184. *NLA Quarterly*, Autumn 1988; Material provided by Iranian sources in Europe
185. de Morais C.B., *Semanario*, 10 May 1986
186. *Keyhan*, 7 June 1990
187. Morrot B., *Le Figaro*, 4 December 1989
188. *Al-Ray'*, 27 December 1987
189. Bulloch J., *Independent*, 26 April 1988; *Al-Itihhad*, 15 January 1988
190. Voice of Lebanon, 23 January 1988
191. DPA, 21 November 1987; *Al-Itihhad*, 15 January 1988
192. Morrot B., *Le Figaro*, 4 December 1989
193. Radio Free Lebanon, 5 July 1990
194. Fisk R., *The Times*, 18 June 1985
195. Burdan D., *DST*, Paris, Robert Laffont, 1990, p. 161
196. Coskun Ender, *Hurriyet*, 18 November 1986; *Nokta*, 12 March 1989
197. Selhami Mohamad, *Jeune Afrique*, 25 January 1984
198. *Al-Ba'ath*, 5 Mat 1985; Radio Damascus, 4 May 1985
199. Damascus Television Service, 10 July 1985
200. *Liberation*, 19 March 1985
201. Alexander Y. & Sinai J., *Terrorism: The PLO Connection*, New York NY, Crane Russak, 1989, p. 56; Zarai O., *Ha'aretz*, 26 October 1986; Coskun Ender, *Hurriyet*, 19 November 1986
202. Khashanah Rashid, *Al-Watan*, 12 April 1988
203. *Al-Watan*, 9 June 1988; *Al-Watan*, 10 June 1988
204. Ben-Yishai R., *Yediot Aharonot*, 15 December 1989
205. Bulloch J., *The Independent on Sunday*, 10 June 1990
206. Raufer X., *Le Debat*, March-May 1986
207. Radio Free Lebanon, 5 May 1989; *L'Express*, 4 May 1989
208. *Al-Thawarah*, 27 October 1989; INA, 27 October 1989
209. Jacquard R., *The Secret Dossiers of Terrorism*, Paris, Albin Michel, 1985, pp. 97 & 99
210. *Ha'aretz*, 6 December 1985
211. Haselkorn A., *New York city Tribune*, 15 September 1989; Material provided by Israeli sources
212. Fisk R., *The Times*, 18 June 1985
213. Zara'i O., *Ha'aretz*, 21 June 1987
214. *Al-Majallah*, 24-30 July 1985
215. *Al-Siyasah*, 26 June 1985
216. Ryuichi Hirokawa, *Shukan Yomiuri*, 9 October 1983
217. Selhami Mohamad, *Jeune Afrique*, 25 January 1984; Voice of Lebanon, 22 August 1984; Tehran International Service, 14 June 1988
218. Ryuichi Hirokawa, *Shukan Yomiuri*, 2 October 1983; *The Japan Times*, 12 January 1984

219. *Fight Together for the Movement for Disarmament and Against Nuclear Weapons — on the Occasion of 10th Anniversary of Lydda*, A Japanese Red Army Pamphlet, 30 May 1982

CHAPTER 3

IRAN AND THE NEW MUSLIM WORLD ORDER

1. Hirel S. & Landon P., *Le Figaro*, 14 August 1990
2. *Al-Rayah al-Islamiyah*, 20 April 1990
3. Shamis G., *Monitin*, February 1991; *Hurriyet*, 31 January 1991; TANJUG, 31 January 1991; *Ukaz*, 16 October 1990; *Ha'aretz*, 8 November 1990; INA, 20 August 1990; INA, 19 August 1990; INA, 18 August 1990; Radio Tehran, 17 August 1990; Radio Tehran, 16 August 1990; IRNA, 16 August 1990; *Jomhuri-ye Islami*, 16 August 1990; *Keyhan International*, 16 August 1990; *Tehran Times*, 16 August 1990; *Ettela'at*, 16 August 1990; *Keyhan*, 16 August 1990; *Resalat*, 16 August 1990; INA, 16 August 1990; *Al-Jumhuriyah*, 16 August 1990; *Ettela'at*, 15 August 1990; *Keyhan*, 15 August 1990; *Resalat*, 15 August 1990; *Al-Riyad*, 15 September 1990; INA, 15 August 1990; IRNA, 15 August 1990; Radio Baghdad, 15 August 1990; Radio Tehran, 15 August 1990; Matar Khalil, *Al-Sharq al-Awsat*, 21 June 1990; *Ha'aretz*, 21 June 1990; *Al-Dustur*, 20 June 1990; IRNA, 18 June 1990; *Keyhan*, 14 June 1990; *Tehran Times*, 7 June 1990; *Al-Sharq al-Awsat*, 7 June 1990; Radio Tehran, 6 June 1990; IRNA, 6 June 1990
4. *Ukaz*, 16 October 1990; *Hurriyet*, 31 January 1991
5. Matar Khalil, *Al-Sharq al-Awsat*, 21 June 1990
6. Colvin M., *The Sunday Times*, 22 July 1990
7. Iran's Flag of Freedom Radio, 1 June 1990; Radio Tehran, 1 June 1990; Radio Tehran, 3 June 1990; Radio Tehran, 10 June 1990; Tehran International Service, 11 June 1990; Radio Tehran, 11 June 1990; Al-Quds Palestinian Arab Radio, 12 June 1990
8. Iran's Flag of Freedom Radio, 1 June 1990; Radio Tehran, 11 June 1990
9. Radio Tehran, 9 June 1990; Radio Tehran, 10 June 1990; Tehran International Service, 11 June 1990; Radio Tehran, 11 June 1990
10. Radio Tehran, 11 June 1990; Al-Quds Palestinian Arab Radio, 12 June 1990
11. Voice of the Oppressed, 5 June 1990
12. Voice of the Oppressed, 30 June 1990
13. *Al-Shira'*, 30 July 1990
14. ADN, 3 July 1990
15. Amr Wafa', *Al-Quds al-'Arabi*, 21 June 1990
16. Tripoli Television Service, 15 July 1990
17. JANA, 23 July 1990; Voice of the Greater Arab Homeland, 26 July 1990
18. AFP, 15 July 1990

19. Al-Quds Palestinian Arab Radio, 2 July 1990; Tehran International Service, 7 July 1990; *Al-Mujahid*, 6 July 1990

20. *HAMAS* Leaflet No. 60, 9 July 1990; Al-Quds Palestinian Arab Radio, 9 July 1990

21. Abid Tawfiq, *Al-Dustur*, 14 May 1990

22. *Al-Shira'*, 23 July 1990

23. Radio Tehran, 26 July 1990; IRNA, 26 July 1990; Tehran Television Service 25 July 1990; Radio Tehran, 25 July 1990; IRNA, 25 July 1990

24. *Jomhuri-ye Islami*, 25 July 1990

25. IRNA, 28 July 1990; AFP, 28 July 1990; IRNA, 27 July 1990; AFP, 27 July 1990; *Keyhan International*, 29 July 1990; *Ha'aretz*, 29 July 1990

26. Radio Monte Carlo, 5 August 1990; MENA, 6 August 1990; *Keyhan*, 23 August 1990; *Al-Shira'*, 10 September 1990

27. Jacquard R., *The Secret Cards of the Gulf War*, Paris, Edition'1, 1991, pp. 209-210

28. Gabay Sh., *Ma'ariv*, 16 November 1990

29. Voice of Lebanon, 11 August 1990

30. *Ha'aretz*, 12 August 1990

31. Voice of the Oppressed, 11 August 1990; IRNA, 11 August 1990

32. Eldar A., *Ha'aretz*, 8 August 1990

33. INA, 8 August 1990; INA, 11 August 1990; *Al-Jumhuriyah*, 13 August 1990; Beirut Domestic Service, 15 August 1990

34. *Al-Watan al-Arabi*, 24 August 1990

35. INA, 13 August 1990; INA, 9 August 1990; *Sawt al-Sha'b*, 4 August 1990

36. INA, 13 August 1990; *Swat al-Sha'b*, 30 August 1990; al-'Absi Ibrahim, *Al-Ahali*, 5 September 1990

37. *Arbeiderbladet*, 27 August 1990

38. *Ha'aretz*, 28 November 1990

39. *Arbeiderbladet*, 27 August 1990

40. Al-Quds Palestinian Arab Radio, 27 August 1990

41. Shahin M.M., *Jordan Times*, 3 September 1990; Chipaux F., *Le Monde*, 5 September 1990; INA, 1 September 1990; INA, 4 September 1990; Baghdad Domestic Service, 4 September 1990

42. Chipaux F., *Le Monde*, 5 September 1990

43. INA, 15 August 1990

44. Al-Quds Palestinian Arab Radio, 15 August 1990

45. INA, 30 August 1990

46. IRNA, 17 August 1990

47. *Al-Safir*, 14 August 1990

48. *Al-Liwa'*, 22 August 1990

49. Radio Tehran, 12 September 1990; IRNA, 12 September 1990; *Keyhan International*, 15 September 1990; IRNA, 15 September 1990

50. Radio Tehran, 12 September 1990; IRNA, 12 September 1990; *Jumhuri-ye Islami*, 13 September 1990; IRNA, 13 September 1990

51. *Al-Dustur*, 13 September 1990; *Al-Ra'y*, 14 September 1990; al-Shubu Faysal, *Sawt al-Sha'b*, 16 September 1990
52. IRNA, 28 September 1990
53. Voice of the Oppressed, 15 September 1990; Tehran International Service, 14 September 1990
54. AFP, 28 September 1990
55. AFP, 28 September 1990
56. IRNA, 17 August 1990
57. Inbari P., *Al Hamishmar*, 6 September 1990
58. Radio Tehran, 4 October 1990
59. Hirel S. & Landon P., *Le Figaro*, 14 August 1990
60. Jacquard R., *Le Quotidien de Paris*, 3 September 1990
61. *Al-Sharq al-Awsat*, 25 September 1990
62. Tsdakah Sh., *Ha'aretz*, 17 August 1990
63. *Al-Thawrah*, 30 December 1990; INA, 30 December 1990
64. *Al-Thawrah*, 31 December 1990
65. *Al-Jumhuriyah*, 17 December 1990
66. Shukri Faruq, AFP, 29 December 1990
67. *Al-Ray al-Sha'ab*, 29 December 1990; *Ha'aretz*, 30 December 1990
68. Darbyshire N., *Daily Telegraph*, 9 January 1991
69. Jacquard R., *Le Quotidien de Paris*, 3 September 1990
70. *Foreign Report*, 24 January 1991
71. *Ha'aretz*, 21 December 1990; *El Nacional*, 20 December 1991; Jacquard, op.cit. (Gulf War), p. 204
72. Mahanaimi U., *Yediot Aharonot*, 15 January 1991
73. Sallinger P., ABC-TV; Material provided by sources in Europe
74. Mehanaimi U., *Yediot Aharonot*, 14 September 1990
75. Gabay Sh., *Ma'ariv*, 16 November 1990; Mehanaimi U., *Yediot Aharonot*, 14 September 1990
76. Gabay Sh., *Ma'ariv*, 16 November 1990
77. Mahanaimi U., *Yediot Aharonot*, 15 January 1991; Gabay Sh., *Ma'ariv*, 16 November 1990
78. Jacquard R., *Le Quotidien de Paris*, 3 September 1990
79. Mahanaimi U., *Yediot Aharonot*, 15 January 1991; Mehanaimi U., *Yediot Aharonot*, 14 September 1990
80. Abd-al-Khaliq Lahib, *al-Jumhuriyah*, 2 November 1990
81. INA, 6 November 1990; INA, 14 November 1990
82. Jacquard R., *Le Quotidien de Paris*, 3 September 1990
83. INA, 3 October 1990; INA, 8 October 1990
84. Shamis G., *Monitin*, February 1991; *Sawt al-Kuwayt al-Duwali*, 24 November 1990; *Kayhan International*, 10 November 1990
85. IRNA, 31 December 1990; AFP, 1 January 1991
86. *Stern*, 22 November 1990
87. Voice of the Oppressed, 16 November 1990

88. *Kayhan International*, 17 November 1990; IRNA, 17 November 1990
89. *Keyhan*, 18 December 1990
90. *Kayhan International*, 22 December 1990
91. *Ha'aretz*, 14 January 1991; Mahanaimi U., *Yediot Aharonot*, 15 January 1991
92. Voice of Free Iraq, 7 January 1991
93. Radio Madrid, 30 December 1990
94. Matar Khalil, *Al-Sharq al-Awsat*, 21 June 1990
95. Jacquard R., *Le Quotidien de Paris*, 3 September 1990
96. Inbari P., *Al Hamishmar*, 4 November 1990
97. *Al-Zahirah*, 29 December 1990
98. *Al-Alam*, 28 October 1990
99. Haddad Teresa, *Sawt al-Sha'b*, 29 December 1990; Awdah Awdah, *Al-Ra'y*, 2 January 1991
100. *Sawt al-Sha'b*, 5 January 1991
101. Voice of the PLO (Baghdad) , 3 January 1991
102. Voice of the PLO (Baghdad) , 4 January 1991
103. Gabai Sh., *Ma'ariv*, 15 January 1991; *Yediot Aharonot*, 17 January 1991
104. *Washington Times*, 27 December 1990
105. AFP, 16 January 1991; *Yediot Aharonot*, 17 January 1991; *Ha'aretz*, 15 January 1991
106. *Yediot Aharonot*, 17 January 1991; Gabai Sh., *Ma'ariv*, 16 January 1991; *Ha'aretz*, 16 January 1991; *Yediot Aharonot*, 15 January 1991
107. *Washington Post*, 23 July 1991; Nir O., *Ha'aretz*, 24 July 1991; *Yediot Aharonont*, 24 July 1991
108. Tunis Domestic Service, 15 January 1991; AFP, 15 January 1991; *Yediot Aharonot*, 16 January 1991; *Yediot Aharonot*, 15 January 1991; *Ma'ariv*, 15 January 1991; *Ha'aretz*, 16 January 1991
109. Soudan F. & Marouki Manoubi, *Jeune Afrique*, 29 January 1991
110. Gabai Sh., *Ma'ariv*, 16 January 1991
111. AFP, 15 January 1991; Voice of Palestine (Algeria) , 15 January 1991; MENA, 15 January 1991; Gabai Sh., *Ma'ariv*, 16 January 1991; *Yediot Aharonot*, 16 January 1991; *Ha'aretz*, 16 January 1991; Soudan F. & Marouki Manoubi, *Jeune Afrique*, 29 January 1991; *Washington Post*, 23 July 1991; Nir O., *Ha'aretz*, 24 July 1991; Jacquard, op.cit. (Gulf War), p. 225
112. Gabai Sh., *Ma'ariv*, 16 January 1991; *Ma'ariv*, 15 January 1991
113. Darbyshire N., *Daily Telegraph*, 9 January 1991
114. *Bild*, 18 January 1991; *Yediot Aharonot*, 17 January 1991; *Al-Jumhuriyah*, 16 January 1991
115. *Sawt al-Kuwayt*, 1 February 1991
116. *Sawt al-Kuwayt al-Duwali*, 21 June 1991
117. Radio Monte Carlo, 17 April 1991
118. Rabin E., *Ha'aretz*, 15 February 1991

119. Richard J.-A., *Le Figaro*, 24 January 1991
120. *Al-Zahirah*, 17 February 1991
121. Richard J.-A., *Le Figaro*, 24 January 1991
122. Richard J.-A., *Le Figaro*, 24 January 1991
123. Jacquard, op.cit. (Gulf War), p. 216
124. *Wiener Zeitung*, 23 January 1991; *Der Standard*, 22 January 1991; Grolig P., *Kurier*, 20 January 1991; ORF-TV, 20 January 1991
125. Abu-Ghannam Nadim and Fadlallah Amal, *Monday Morning*, 21-27 January 1991
126. Kashani A., *Jomhuri-ye Islami*, 21 January 1991
127. Voice of Lebanon, 24 January 1991
128. *Al-Dustur*, 22 January 1991
129. Voice of Lebanon, 10 March 1991; *Al-Dustur*, 6 March 1991; Awdah Awdah, *Jordan Times*, 23 February 1991
130. AFP, 18 February 1991
131. *Ha'aretz*, 11 March 1991
132. Gueyras J., *Le Monde*, 1 February 1991
133. Gueyras J., *Le Monde*, 1 February 1991
134. Schoenhuber A., *Der Morgen*, 26 January 1991
135. *The Star*, 24-30 January 1991
136. IRNA, 18 March 1991; Iranian Television, 18 March 1991
137. Abd-al-Rahim Umar, *Al-Ra'y*, 21 March 1991
138. Iranian Television, 18 March 1991
139. Raufer X., *L'Express*, 22 August 1991
140. Al-Matrafi Khalid, *Al-Madinah*, 11 June 1990
141. Al-Quds Palestinian Arab Radio, 29 April 1991
142. IRNA, 18 March 1991
143. Zara'i O., *Ha'aretz*, 27 February 1991
144. IRNA, 30 March 1991
145. *Jomhuri-ye Islami*, 6 May 1991
146. *Ha'aretz*, 19 April 1991
147. IRNA, 21 May 1991
148. *Al-Fajr*, 3 June 1991
149. *Die Presse*, 25-26 May 1991
150. *Ha'aretz*, 13 June 1991; Radio Monte Carlo, 21 May 1991
151. Voice of Palestine (Algiers) , 26 May 1991; Radio Monte Carlo, 26 May 1991; Radio Damascus, 26 May 1991; *Ha'aretz*, 26 May 1991; Radio Monte Carlo, 27 May 1991; Radio Damascus, 27 May 1991; Radio Jordan, 27 May 1991; *Yediot Aharonont*, 27 May 1991; *Ha'aretz*, 27 May 1991; Radio Monte Carlo, 28 May 1991; Radio Damascus, 28 May 1991; AFP, 28 May 1991; Zara'i O., *Ha'aretz*, 3 June 1991
152. *Ha'aretz*, 29 May 1991; Zara'i O., *Ha'aretz*, 3 June 1991; Al-Quds Palestinian Arab Radio, 24 July 1991
153. *Ha'aretz*, 15 July 1991; Zara'i O., *Ha'aretz*, 8 July 1991; *Ha'aretz*, 7 July

1991; *Ha'aretz*, 5 July 1991; AFP,

5 July 1991; Radio Lebanon, 4 July 1991; AFP, 4 July 1991; Zara'i O., *Ha'aretz*, 3 July 1991; Mahanaimi U. & Shibi H., *Yediot Aharonot*, 3 July 1991; AFP, 3 July 1991; Zara'i O., *Ha'aretz*, 2 July 1991; *Ha'aretz*, 1 July 1991

154. Radio Monte Carlo, 30 August 1991; AFP, 30 August 1991

155. Zara'i O., *Ha'aretz*, 16 July 1991; Sheikh Abbas al-Mussawi to *Al-Hayah*, 18 July 1991; Abdullah al-Amin to *Al-Khalij*, 19 July 1991; AFP, 19 July 1991; Sheikh Abbas al-Mussawi to Radio Free Lebanon, 22 July 1991

156. *Ha'aretz*, 4 July 1991; Radio Monte Carlo, 4 July 1991; *Ha'aretz*, 5 July 1991

157. Rabin E. & Horowitz M., *Ha'aretz*, 24 September 1991

158. *Sawt al-Kuwayt al-Duwali*, 21 June 1991

159. *Ha'aretz*, 23 July 1991; *Al-Watan al-Arabi*, 21 July 1991

160. *Al-Majallah*, 9 October 1991

161. INA, 11 June 1991; INA, 12 June 1991; INA, 13 June 1991; INA, 14 June 1991; INA, 15 June 1991; INA, 16 June 1991; Zara'i O., *Ha'aretz*, 27 June 1991

162. Zara'i O., *Ha'aretz*, 27 June 1991

163. *Sawt al-Kuwayt al-Duwali*, 11 July 1991; INA, 13 July 1991

164. Zara'i O., *Ha'aretz*, 16 July 1991

165. JANA, 14 July 1991

166. Voice of the Greater Arab Homeland, 19 July 1991; *Al-Jamahiriyah*, 19 July 1991

167. Mansur Riyad, *Sawt al-Sha'b*, 8 July 1991

168. *Jomhuri-ye Islami*, 5 August 1991

169. *Sawt al-Kuwayt al-Duwali*, 18 August 1991

170. Voice of the Oppressed, 9 April 1991

171. Kammuni Raja', *Al-Hawadith*, 29 March 1991

172. Voice of Lebanon, 21 May 1991

173. *Al-Hayah*, 25 May 1991

174. *Al-Hayah*, 25 May 1991

175. Voice of the Oppressed, 17 May 1991

176. *Salam*, 16 July 1991

177. *Al-Hayah*, 25 May 1991

178. Radio Tehran, 5 June 1991

179. *Salam*, 17 July 1991

180. Radio Tehran, 12 July 1991

181. *Salam*, 17 July 1991

182. Radio Tehran, 12 July 1991

183. *Salam*, 17 July 1991

184. *Salam*, 18 July 1991

185. Voice of the Islamic Republic of Iran, 15 August 1991

186. IRNA, 11 August 1991

187. *Foreign Report*, 16 May 1991

188. Reuter, 19 August 1991; Radio Tehran, 19 August 1991

189. Voice of the Oppressed, 6 September 1991

190. Radio Tehran, 4 October 1991

191. IRNA, 4 October 1991; Reuter, 4 October 1991

192. Fisk R., *Ma'ariv*, 11 October 1991

193. Al-Quds Palestinian Arab Radio, 14 October 1991

194. Radio Tehran, 16 October 1991; Reuter, 16 October 1991 195. *Ha'aretz*, 18 October 1991

196. Iranian Television, 17 October 1991; Radio Tehran, 18 October 1991; Sharif Imam-Jomeh, Reuter, 19 October 1991; Radio Tehran, 19 October 1991; IRNA, 20 October 1991; Iranian Television, 20 October 1991; Iranian Television, 17 October 1991; Radio Tehran, 18 October 1991; IRNA, 21 October 1991; IRNA, 23 October 1991; Radio Tehran, 25 October 1991; IRNA, 20 October 1991; *Ha'aretz*, 18 October 1991

197. IRNA, 25 October 1991

198. Radio Monte Carlo, 20 October 1991

199. Radio Tehran, 19 October 1991

200. Radio Tehran, 18 October 1991

201. IRNA, 19 October 1991; Sharif Imam-Jomeh, Reuter, 19 October 1991; IRNA, 20 October 1991

202. Radio Tehran, 19 October 1991

203. IRNA, 20 October 1991; Reuter, 20 October 1991

204. Hussain Murshahid, *JANE's Defence Weekly*, 16 November 1991

205. IRNA, 20 October 1991; Reuter, 20 October 1991

206. Radio Tehran, 21 October 1991; IRNA, 21 October 1991; Radio Tehran, 22 October 1991; IRNA, 22 October 1991

207. Radio Tehran, 21 October 1991

208. Iranian Television, 24 October 1991

209. IRNA, 21 October 1991

210. Faruqi Anwar, AP, 21 October 1991; IRNA, 22 October 1991

211. IRNA, 20 October 1991

212. Faruqi Anwar, AP, 21 October 1991

213. IRNA, 21 October 1991

214. *Jomhuri-ye Islami*, 21 October 1991; Faruqi Anwar, AP, 21 October 1991

215. *Jomhuri-ye Islami*, 22 October 1991; IRNA, 22 October 1991

216. IRNA, 22 October 1991; Faruqi Anwar, AP, 22 October 1991; Radio Tehran, 22 October 1991

217. IRNA, 23 October 1991

218. IRNA, 25 October 1991; *Ha'aretz*, 24 October 1991

219. Radio Tehran, 22 October 1991

220. Radio Monte Carlo, 24 October 1991

221. Al-Quds Palestinian Arab Radio, 18 October 1991; *Ha'aretz*, 18 October 1991

222. Radio Monte Carlo, 19 October 1991

223. Voice of Lebanon, 21 October 1991

224. IRNA, 22 October 1991

225. *Al-Diyar*, 28 October 1991; Reuter, 28 October 1991; Faruqi Anwar, AP, 28 October 1991

226. Radio Tehran, 30 October 1991

227. Ladki Nadim, Reuter, 15 October 1991; Reuter, 30 October 1991; AP, 30 October 1991; AP, 28 October 1991; Zara'i O., *Ha'aretz*, 27 October 1991

CHAPTER 4

THE NEW ISLAMIST INTERNATIONAL

1. *Al-Wadi*, July 1982

2. al-Tilmisani Umar, *Al-Da'wa*, March 1979

3. Q. in Jansen J.J.G., Echoes of the Iranian Revolution in the Writings of Egyptian Muslims, in Menashri D. (ed.), *The Iranian Revolution and the Muslim World*, Boulder Co, Westview Press, 1990, p. 212

4. Hanafi H., *Al-Watan al-Arabi*, 29 November 1982

5. Hamudah Adil, *Bombs and Qorans: The Story of the Jihad Organization*, Cairo, Sinai al-Nashr, 1986, p. 36

6. *Al-Safir*, 28 May 1982

7. Al-Husni Al-Salami, *Al-Dustur*, 6 April 1987; Tunis Domestic Service, 27 March 1987

8. *Al-Manar*, 13 January 1992; Inbari P., *Al Hamishmar*, 17 January 1992; *Al-Watan*, 8 December 1989

9. *Al-Watan*, 8 December 1989

10. *Al-Siyasah*, 17 October 1985

11. Barazi Ma'an, *The Daily Star*, 14 November 1984

12. *Kayhan International*, 3 March 1985

13. *Al-Siyasah*, 17 October 1985

14. Tehran Domestic Service, 5 May 1985; IRNA, 4 May 1985

15. Tehran Domestic Service, 5 May 1985

16. IRNA, 6 May 1985

17. *Keyhan*, 27 July 1986

18. Heikal Muhammad, *Autumn of Fury*, New York NY, Random, 1983, pp. 214 & 256

19. Material provided by Afghan resistance sources; Van Dyk J., *In Afghanistan*, New York NY, Coward-McMann, 1983, pp. 98-101

20. Mubarak Hisham, *Rose al-Yusuf*, 24 August 1992; 'Afghans', *Al-Wasat*, 13 July 1992

21. Roy O., *Islam and Resistance in Afghanistan*, 2nd. Ed., Cambridge MA, Cambridge University Press, 1990, p. 233

22. 'Afghans', *Al-Wasat*, 13 July 1992
23. Bonner A., *Among the Afghans*, Durham NC, Duke University Press, 1987, p. 176
24. Taheri Amir, *Holy Terror*, London, Huchinson, 1987, p. 206
25. Mubarak Hisham, *Rose al-Yusuf*, 14 September 1992
26. Roy O., *The Failure of Political Islam*, Paris, Editions de Seuil, 1992, p. 151
27. Material provided by several Afghan resistance sources
28. 'Afghans', *Al-Wasat*, 13 July 1992
29. Material provided by several Afghan resistance and Pakistani sources
30. *Ha'aretz*, 26 August 1987; *Ha'aretz*, 29 September 1987
31. Hasan Tariq, *Rose al-Yusuf*, 22 July 1991
32. SUNA, 30 June 1989; Radio Omdurman, 30 June 1989; MENA, 30 June 1989; AFP, 30 June 1989; SUNA, 1 July 1989; Radio Omdurman, 1 July 1989; MENA, 1 July 1989; AFP, 1 July 1989; SUNA, 2 July 1989; Radio Omdurman, 2 July 1989; MENA, 2 July 1989; AFP, 2 July 1989
33. Hanaqah Ahmad, *Al-Anba'*, 7 April 1990
34. Husayn Tariq, *Rose al-Yusuf*, 10 February 1992; Hasan Tariq, *Rose al-Yusuf*, 22 July 1991
35. *Ettela'at*, 2 October 1990
36. *Ettela'at*, 4 October 1990
37. *Ettela'at*, 4 October 1990
38. *Ettela'at*, 2 October 1990
39. Hasan Tariq, *Rose al-Yusuf*, 22 July 1991
40. Yared M., *Jeune Afrique*, 19-25 March 1992; SUNA, 25 April 1991
41. Abu-Zahr Walid, *Al-Watan al-Arabi*, 8 May 1992; SUNA, 30 April 1991; SUNA, 29 April 1992; Radio Umdurman, 29 April 1991
42. Voice of Palestine (Algeria) , 26 April 1991, Radio Monte Carlo, 26 April 1991
43. SUNA, 25 April 1991
44. SUNA, 26 April 1991
45. Radio Umdurman, 28 April 1991
46. *Al-Ribat*, 30 April 1991
47. Yared M., *Jeune Afrique*, 19-25 March 1992 48. *Al-Watan al-Arabi*, 4 December 1992
49. *Al-Watan al-Arabi*, 4 December 1992
50. Mu'awiyah Yasin, *Al-Hayah*, 16 November 1991
51. Iranian Television, 17 October 1991; Radio Tehran, 18 October 1991; Sharif Imam-Jomeh, Reuter, 19 October 1991; Radio Tehran, 19 October 1991; IRNA, 20 October 1991; Iranian Television, 20 October 1991; IRNA, 25 October 1991
52. Yared M., *Jeune Afrique*, 19-25 March 1992
53. *Salam*, 4 February 1992

54. *Al-Watan al-Arabi*, 4 December 1992; Al-Qurashi Ahmad, *Sawt al-Kuwayt*, 17 March 1992; Basyuni Salah, *Al-Wafd*, 10 January 1992

55. *Al-Jumhuriyah*, 2 August 1992; Husayn Tariq, *Rose al-Yusuf*, 10 February 1992

56. SUNA, 15 November 1991; *Al-Inqadh al-Watani*, 3 January 1992

57. Mu'awiyah Yasin, *Al-Hayah*, 16 November 1991

58. Yared M., *Jeune Afrique*, 19-25 March 1992

59. Raio Ummdurman, 12 December 1991

60. SUNA, 12 December 1991

61. Material provided by Iranian sources; IRNA, 14 December 1991; SUNA, 12 December 1991; *Al-Khalij*, 16 January 1992; *Kayhan*, 16 January 1992

62. SUNA, 30 December 1991; SUNA, 13 December 1991; IRNA, 13 December 1991; SUNA, 14 December 1991; IRNA, 14 December 1991; SUNA, 15 December 1991; IRNA, 15 December 1991; SUNA, 16 December 1991; IRNA, 16 December 1991; SUNA, 17 December 1991; IRNA, 17 December 1991

63. SUNA, 15 December 1991; Arafah Muhammad Jamal, *Al-Sha'b*, 17 December 1991; Al-Mirghani Uthman, *Al-Sharq al-Awsat*, 18 December 1991

64. SUNA, 2 January 1992

65. Awdah Muhammad and Bakri Mahmud, *Misr al-Fatah*, 2 March 1992

66. *Nimrooz*, 7 February 1992; material provided by Iranian and Arab sources

67. *Nimrooz*, 7 February 1992; Material provided by Iranian sources

68. *Al-Wafd*, 19 January 1992; Haeri Safa, *Al-Hayah*, 13 January 1992; *Al-Wafd*, 5 January 1992

69. Husayn Tariq, *Rose al-Yusuf*, 10 February 1992

70. Mirghani Uthman, *Al-Sharq al-Awsat*, 22 February 1992

71. Mirghani Uthman, *Al-Sharq al-Awsat*, 23 March 1992

72. *Al-Watan al-Arabi*, 4 December 1992

73. Material provided by Iranian sources; Mirghani Uthman, *Al-Sharq al-Awsat*, 23 March 1992

74. Yared M., *Jeune Afrique*, 12-18 March 1992; *Al-Wasat*, 16-22 November 1992; *Al-Watan al-Arabi*, 6 November 1992

75. *Al-Watan al-Arabi*, 4 December 1992; *Al-Wasat*, 14-20 December 1992

76. *Al-Watan al-Arabi*, 6 November 1992

77. Radio Free Lebanon, 27 January 1989

78. Ya'ari E., *Wall Street Journal*, 16 August 1989; Delafon G., *Beirut: The Soldiers of Islam*, Paris, Stock, 1989, pp. 156-157

79. Yared M., *Jeune Afrique*, 12-18 March 1992; Yared M., *Jeune Afrique*, 19-25 March 1992; Yared M., *Jeune Afrique*, 10-16 September 1992; Ma'ruf Mahmud, *Al-Quds al-Arabi*, 12 October 1992; *Al-Watan al-Arabi*, 6 November 1992

80. Chikhi Lamine, *Liberte*, 15 October 1992

81. NuriZadeh Dr. Ali, *Al-Majallah*, 8 December 1992
82. *Ha'aretz*, 9 December 1992; al-Shubashi Sharif, *Al-Ahram*, 8 December 1992
83. Muhanna Majdi, *Al-Wafd*, 3 December 1992
84. Abbas Samayah, MENA, 13 December 1992; *Al-Watan al-Arabi*, 22 January 1993
85. Amanullah, *The Frontier Post*, 2 December 1992
86. *Ha'aretz*, 9 December 1992; al-Shubashi Sharif, *Al-Ahram*, 8 December 1992; *Al-Watan al-Arabi*, 27 November 1992
87. Rizq Hamdi, *Rose al-Yussuf*, 23 November 1992
88. Rizq Hamdi, *Rose al-Yussuf*, 23 November 1992
89. Radio Iran, 24 December 1992
90. *Al-Watan al-Arabi*, 25 December 1992; al-Sharif Yussuf, *Rose al-Yussuf*, 14 December 1992; *Al-Sharq al-Awsat*, 30 November 1992; Radio Iran, 29 November 1992; Iranian TV, 29 November 1992; Radio Iran, 30 November 1992; Iranian TV, 30 November 1992
91. *Ha'aretz*, 9 December 1992
92. *Uktubar*, 20 December 1992
93. Yared M., *Jeune Afrique*, 19-25 March 1992
94. Husayn Tariq, *Rose al-Yusuf*, 10 February 1992; Hasan Tariq, *Rose al-Yusuf*, 22 July 1991
95. Radio Monte Carlo, 8 May 1990; SUNA, 9 May 1990
96. Rizq Hamdi, *Rose al-Yusuf*, 10 August 1992
97. Al-Qurashi Ahmad, *Sawt al-Kuwayt*, 17 March 1992
98. *Al-Shira'*, 16 September 1991
99. *Al-Sudan al-Hadith*, 16 November 1991
100. Atwan Abd-al-Bari, *Al-Quds al-Arabi*, 9 January 1992 101. SUNA, 16 December 1991
102. *Al-Diyar*, 3 February 1992; *Al-Wafd*, 6 February 1992
103. Al-Qurashi Ahmad, *Sawt al-Kuwayt*, 17 March 1992; Ben-Yishai R., *Yediot Aharonot*, 10 April 1992
104. *Ma'ariv*, 21 January 1992
105. Husayn Tariq, *Rose al-Yusuf*, 10 February 1992
106. Husayn Tariq, *Rose al-Yusuf*, 10 February 1992; Al-Ahram Press Agency, 17 December 1992; *Al-Wafd*, 15 December 1991; *Al-Wafd*, 4 December 1991; *Al-Sharq*, 19 August 1991; *El-Watan*, 25 November 1992
107. *Al-Shira'*, 11 November 1991; Voice of the Mountain, 29 October 1991; AFP, 28 October 1991; AP, 28 October 1991
108. *Al-Wafd*, 3 November 1991; *Akhbar al-Jumhuriyah*, 9 November 1991; MENA, 9 November 1991
109. *Rose al-Yusuf*, 22 June 1992
110. *Al-Wafd*, 3 November 1991; *Akhbar al-Jumhuriyah*, 9 November 1991; MENA, 9 November 1991
111. *Al-Wafd*, 3 November 1991

112. *Al-Wafd*, 4 December 1991

113. *Al-Wafd*, 19 January 1992; Haeri Safa, *Al-Hayah*, 13 January 1992; *Al-Wafd*, 5 January 1992; Sharaf-al-Din Ahmad, *Al-Sudan al-Hadith*, 19 November 1991

114. *Al-Jumhuriyah*, 23 May 1992

115. Sharaf-al-Din Ahmad, *Al-Sudan al-Hadith*, 19 November 1991; *Al-Diyar*, 3 February 1992; *Al-Wafd*, 6 February 1992

116. SUNA, 22 November 1991; SUNA, 20 November 1991

117. Abu-Hasabu Muhammad, *Al-Hayah*, 27 February 1992

118. Husayn Tariq, *Rose al-Yusuf*, 10 February 1992; *El-Chourouq*, 4 September 1992; Radio Tunis, 4 September 1992

119. *Al-Wafd*, 20 January 1993; *Al-Watan al-Arabi*, 4 December 1992; *Al-Watan al-Arabi*, 27 November 1992; Abd-al-Sattar Abd-al-Nabi and Hilmi Majdi, *Al-Wafd*, 24 November 1992; *Le Journal*, 29 December 1992; Reuters, 29 December 1992

120. *Al-Watan al-Arabi*, 9 October 1992; *Al-Watan al-Arabi*, 6 November 1992; Abd-al-Sattar Abd-al-Nabi and Hilmi Majdi, *Al-Wafd*, 24 November 1992

121. Peri S., *Yediot Aharonot*, 14 December 1992

122. Sa'dah Ibrahim, *Akhbar al-Yawm*, 14 November 1992

123. Abbas Samayah, MENA, 13 December 1992; *Al-Watan al-Arabi*, 22 January 1993

124. Al-Ahram Press Agency, 17 December 1992

125. *Jomhuri-ye Islami*, 5 December 1992

126. *Al-Ahrar*, 2 November 1992

127. *Al-Akhbar*, 2 September 1992; MENA, 2 September 1992; MENA, 27 August 1992

128. *Ha'aretz*, 9 December 1992; *Al-Ahram*, 8 December 1992

129. *Al-Safir*, 21 July 1992

130. *Uktubar*, 20 December 1992

131. Abd al-Salam Faraj, *The Absent Percept*, Cairo, 1981 as cited in *Al-Ahrar*, 14 December 1981 & *Al-Ahram* 14 December 1981; Q. in Sivan E., *Radical Islam: Medival Theology and Modern Politics*, New Haven CT, Yale University Press, 1985, p. 20

132. Vatikiotis P.J., *Islam and the State*, London, Croom Helm, 1987, pp. 131-132

133. *Inquiry*, September 1985

134. Chaliand G., *Terrorism*, London, Saki Books, 1987, p. 120

135. Idris Muhammad al-Sa'id, *Al-Khalij*, 27 August 1989; Effendi Abdel Wahab, *Inqury*, February 1988

136. Bar-Yossef A., *Ma'ariv*, 22 September 1988

137. IRNA, 30 March 1991

138. *Al-Quwat al-Musallahah*, 27 August 1992

139. *Al-Wasat*, 14-20 December 1992

140. SUNA, 30 December 1991; AFP, 30 December 1991
141. Atwan Abd-al-Bari, *Al-Quds al-Arabi*, 9 January 1992
142. *Al-Wasat*, 14-20 December 1992
143. Mubarak Hisham, *Rose al-Yusuf*, 14 September 1992
144. *Al-Sharq al-Awsat*, 20 November 1992
145. *Al-Watan al-Arabi*, 19 February 1993; Rabin E., *Ha'aretz*, 18 February 1993; *Al-Watan al-Arabi*, 12 February 1993; Material provided by Iranian sources
146. *Al-Watan al-Arabi*, 19 February 1993; Rabin E., *Ha'aretz*, 18 February 1993; *Al-Watan al-Arabi*, 12 February 1993; Material provided by Iranian sources
147. *Al-Watan al-Arabi*, 19 February 1993; Rabin E., *Ha'aretz*, 18 February 1993; *Al-Watan al-Arabi*, 12 February 1993; Material provided by Iranian sources
148. *Al-Watan al-Arabi*, 19 February 1993; Rabin E., *Ha'aretz*, 18 February 1993; *Al-Watan al-Arabi*, 12 February 1993; Material provided by Iranian sources
149. Material provided by Iranian and Lebanese sources
150. *Al-Sharq al-Awsat*, 30 November 1992
151. *Resalat*, 14 December 1992
152. Roy, op.cit., (Political Islam)
153. ibid.

CHAPTER 5

IN WESTERN EUROPE (I)

1. Sablier E., *Valeurs Actuelles*, 6 April 1987
2. Darsh Dr. S.M., *Muslims in Europe*, London, Ta-Ha, 1980
3. Hammud Ibrahim, *Our Path*, Tehran, 1984
4. *Daily Star*, 28 September 1984; *Al-Liwa*, 27 September 1984
5. Lesieur J., *Le Point*, 10 February 1986
6. Smolowe J., *Time*, 20 October 1986
7. Raufer X., *Le Debat*, March-May 1986
8. Pontaut J-M, *Le Point*, 21-27 June 1985
9. Erhel C., *Liberation* 6-7 September 1986
10. Schmitt J. et.al., *Le Point*, 4 February 1985
11. Raufer X., *Le Debat*, March-May 1986
12. *Al-Watan Al-'Arabi*, 25-31 January 1985
13. *Al-Wahdah*, 13 January 1986; MAP, 14 January 1986
14. Ploquin F., *L'Evenement du Jeudi*, 26 July 1990
15. Buob J., Haeri S. & Raufer X., *L'Express*, 10 April 1987
16. *Al-Sharq Al-Awsat*, 27 November 1989; al-Tunisi, *Al-Sharq Al-Awsat*, 27 November 1989
17. Buob J. & Haeri Safa, *L'Express*, 13 July 1984; Buob J., Haeri Safa & Raufer X., *L'Express*, 10 April 1987

18. Jacquard, op.cit., p. 292
19. *Al-'Alam*, 19 April 1986; NuriZadeh Dr. Ali, *Al-Dustur*, 12 February 1990
20. Jacquard R., *The Secret Dossiers of Terrorism*, Paris, Albin Michel, 1985, pp. 76-84; Roland M., *National Hebo*, 5 July 1985
21. *Africa Confidential*, No. 9, 25 April 1984
22. *Al-Watan Al-'Arabi*, 3-9 February 1984; *Africa Confidential*, No. 9, 25 April 1984
23. Bulloch J., *Daily Telegraph*, 14 May 1984
24. Tariq Abi, *Al-Inqadh*, No. 8, April 1984
25. *Pourquoi Pas?*, 3 July 1985
26. Buob J., Haeri S. & Raufer X., *L'Express*, 10 April 1987
27. Buob J., Haeri S. & Raufer X., *L'Express*, 10 April 1987
28. *Pourquoi Pas?*, 3 July 1985
29. Sablier R., *Valeurs Actuelles*, 1 April 1985
30. *Avanti*, 18 January 1985
31. *Pourquoi Pas?*, 3 July 1985
32. *Pourquoi Pas?*, 3 July 1985
33. *Al-Bayadir Al-Siyasi*, 28 September 1985
34. Sablier E., *Valeurs Actuelles*, 6 April 1987
35. *Pourquoi Pas?*, 3 July 1985
36. *Le Quotidien de Paris*, 21 August 1989; KUNA, 21 August 1989
37. *Al-'Alam*, 19 April 1986; *Europeo*, 10 January 1987
38. *Al-Watan Al-'Arabi*, 25-31 January 1985
39. Sablier E., *Valeurs Actuelles*, 6 April 1987
40. *Al-Watan Al-'Arabi*, 25-31 January 1985
41. Jacquard, op.cit. (Terrorism), pp. 79-81; Roland M., *National Hebo*, 5 July 1985
42. Pontaut J-M, *Le Point*, 21-27 June 1985
43. Jacquard, op.cit. (Terrorism), pp. 79-81; Roland M., *National Hebo*, 5 July 1985; *Nokta*, 12 March 1989
44. *National Hebdo*, 20-26 March 1986
45. Laroche J.A., *National Hebdo*, 27 February - 5 March 1986
46. *Pourquoi Pas?*, 3 July 1985
47. *Al-'Alam*, 19 April 1986; Laroche J.A., *National Hebdo*, 27 February - 5 March 1986
48. Buob J. & Haeri Safa, *L'Express*, 13 July 1984
49. *Al-'Alam*, 19 April 1986
50. Laroche J.A., *National Hebdo*, 27 February - 5 March 1986
51. Bonomo J., *Le Figaro Magazine*, 11 January 1986
52. *Al-'Alam*, 19 April 1986
53. *Europeo*, 10 January 1987; *Al-'Alam*, 19 April 1986; Buob J. & Haeri Safa, *L'Express*, 13 July 1984
54. Buob J. & Haeri Safa, *L'Express*, 13 July 1984

55. *Al-Watan Al-'Arabi*, 25-31 January 1985; Buob J. & Haeri Safa, *L'Express*, 13 July 1984
56. Buob J. & Haeri Safa, *L'Express*, 13 July 1984
57. Wright R., *Sunday Times*, 4 November 1984
58. Bonomo J., *Le Figaro Magazine*, 11 January 1986
59. *Kurier*, 1 September 1983
60. Grolig E., *Kurier*, 21 June 1985; *Al-'Alam*, 19 April 1986
61. Grolig E., *Kurier*, 29 June 1985
62. *Wiener Zeitung*, 24 June 1986
63. *A Tarde*, 26 December 1984; *O Diabo*, 1 January 1985
64. Leven J.-F., *L'Express*, 6-12 February 1987
65. *A Tarde*, 29 March 1985
66. Leven J.-F., *L'Express*, 6-12 February 1987
67. Mossin B.A., *Arbeiderbladet*, 24 February 1987 68. Ellegaard L., *Berlingske Aften*, 11-17 April 1986
69. Bernert P., *VSD*, 8 January 1986; Bonomo J., *Le Figaro Magazine*, 11 January 1986
70. Bernert P., *VSD*, 8 January 1986; Bonomo J., *Le Figaro Magazine*, 11 January 1986
71. Andreoli M., *Panorama*, 14 February 1988; *La Republica*, 22 December 1987; *Avanti*, 18 January 1985
72. *Al-Sharq Al-Awsat*, 27 November 1989; AP, 25 November 1989; al-Tunisi, *Al-Sharq Al-Awsat*, 27 November 1989
73. AP, 25 November 1989
74. Qazzi Munir, *Al-Watan Al-'Arabi*, 8 December 1989
75. Reix J.-C., *Le Figaro*, 8 December 1989
76. Qazzi Munir, *Al-Watan Al-'Arabi*, 8 December 1989
77. Reix J.-C., *Le Figaro*, 8 December 1989
78. Qazzi Munir, *Al-Watan Al-'Arabi*, 8 December 1989
79. Qazzi Munir, *Al-Watan Al-'Arabi*, 8 December 1989; Reix J.-C., *Le Figaro*, 8 December 1989
80. Khan A., Lesieur J. & Rousselle F., *Le Point*, 17 February 1986
81. Al-Husni Al-Salami, *Al-Dustur*, 6 April 1987; Tunis Domestic Service, 27 March 1987
82. Oberle T., *Le Figaro*, 28 June 1990
83. Morrot B., *Le Figaro*, 4 December 1989
84. Sablier E., *Valeurs Actuelles*, 6 April 1987; Material provided by Iranian and Arab sources in Europe
85. Sablier E., *Valeurs Actuelles*, 6 April 1987
86. Laroche J.A., *National Hebdo*, 27 February - 5 March 1986
87. Zarai O., *Ha'Aretz*, 24 June 1986; Zarai O., *Ha'Aretz*, 23 September 1986
88. Zarai O., *Ha'Aretz*, 23 September 1986; Zarai O., *Ha'Aretz*, 24 June 1986; Material provided by Israeli sources and sources in Europe
89. Dietl W., *Holy War*, New York NY, Macmillan, 1984, p. 333

90. *Le Point*, 13 August 1984
91. Rodriguez N., *O Diabo*, 2 July 1985
92. *Al-Dustur*, 6 August 1984; *Arab Times*, 13 October 1984; *Al-Siyasah*, 12 October 1984
93. *Al-Dustur*, 6 August 1984; *Arab Times*, 13 October 1984; *Al-Siyasah*, 12 October 1984
94. *O Agon*, 3 October 1984
95. *Arab Times*, 13 October 1984; *Al-Siyasah*, 12 October 1984
96. *Al-Dustur*, 6 August 1984
97. ANSA, 27 November 1984; ANSA, 28 November 1984
98. *Al-Watan Al-'Arabi*, 14-20 December 1984
99. AFP, 28 November 1984
100.*Al-Nahar*, 15 December 1984
101.Mathiopoulos D., *To Vima*, 5 December 1984
102.Mathiopoulos D., *To Vima*, 5 December 1984 103. AFP, 3 December 1984
104.*Al-Watan Al-'Arabi*, 25-31 January 1985 105. Bhatia S., *Observer*, 3 February 1985
106.Burdan D., *DST*, Paris, Robert Laffont, 1990, pp. 94-95; Pean P., *The Threat*, Paris, Fayard, 1987, p. 133
107.Bernert P., *VSD*, 8 January 1986
108.Zarai O., *Ha'Aretz*, 24 June 1986
109.Bernert P., *VSD*, 8 January 1986
110.*Al-Watan Al-'Arabi*, 25-31 January 1985
111.Laffin J., *Holy War: Islam Fights*, London, Grafton Books, 1988, pp. 171-172
112.Pontaut J-M, *Le Point*, 21-27 June 1985
113.Bulloch J., *Independent*, 26 April 1988
114.Taheri Amir, *Holy Terror*, London, Huchinson, 1987, p. 106
115.Bernert P., *VSD*, 8 January 1986
116.*Al-Bayadir Al-Siyasi*, 28 September 1985
117.Bernert P., *VSD*, 8 January 1986
118.*Pourquoi Pas?*, 3 July 1985
119.*Al-Watan Al-'Arabi*, 25-31 January 1985
120.*Pourquoi Pas?*, 3 July 1985
121.Roland M., *National Hebo*, 5 July 1985
122.Bernert P., *VSD*, 8 January 1986
123.*Al-Watan Al-'Arabi*, 25-31 January 1985
124.*Pourquoi Pas?*, 3 July 1985
125.Selhami Muhammad, *Jeune Afrique*, 25 January 1984; Bernert P., *VSD*, 8 January 1986
126.*Pourquoi Pas?*, 3 July 1985
127.*Al-Watan Al-'Arabi*, 25-31 January 1985
128.Bernert P., *VSD*, 8 January 1986

129. Zarai O., *Ha'aretz*, 24 June 1986; *Ha'aretz*, 30 September 1986; *Pourquoi Pas?*, 3 July 1985; Material provided by Israeli sources, Iranian and Arab sources in Europe

130. Raufer X., *Le Debat*, March-May 1986

131. Gayatte G., *Valeurs Actuelles*, 7 April 1986

132. Burdan, op.cit., p. 89

133. Raufer X., *Le Debat*, March-May 1986

134. *Keyhan*, 8 August 1985

135. AFP, 27 December 1985; AP, 27 December 1985; *Ha'aretz*, 29 December 1985

136. *Ha'aretz*, 15 December 1987; *Ha'aretz*, 6 February 1987

137. JANA, 29 December 1985

138. *The Sunday Times*, 5 January 1986

139. Laurent E., *Le Figaro*, 4 January 1986

140. Evans M., *Daily Express*, 10 December 1985

141. Radio Monte Carlo, 17 January 1986

142. Cunha J.R., *O Jornal*, 3-10 January 1986; Barakat Daud to *Kurier*, 3 January 1986

143. *Al-Siyasah*, 3 January 1986

144. Al-Sa'id Sana', *Akhbar Al-Yawm*, 7 December 1985

145. *Ha'aretz*, 15 December 1987

146. Sablier E., *Valeurs Actuelles*, 6 April 1987

147. Laurent E., *Le Figaro*, 4 January 1986

148. Raufer X., *Le Debat*, March-May 1986

149. Laurent E., *Le Figaro*, 4 January 1986

150. *Ha'aretz*, 15 December 1987; Raufer X., *Le Debat*, March-May 1986; *Ha'aretz*, 6 February 1987

151. *The Sunday Times*, 5 January 1986

152. Laurent E., *Le Figaro*, 4 January 1986; Sciubba R., *Avanti!*, 31 December 1985

153. Fisk R., *The Times*, 28 January 1986; *The Sunday Times*, 5 January 1986

154. *The Sunday Times*, 5 January 1986

155. *L'Unita*, 9 January 1986

156. *Ha'aretz*, 3 January 1986

157. Sciubba R., *Avanti!*, 31 December 1985; *The Sunday Times*, 5 January 1986

158. *Ha'aretz*, 3 January 1986

159. Sciubba R., *Avanti!*, 31 December 1985; *The Sunday Times*, 5 January 1986

160. Raufer X., *Le Debat*, March-May 1986; Sciubba R., *Avanti!*, 31 December 1985

161. Sciubba R., *Avanti!*, 31 December 1985

162. Bernert P., *VSD*, 8 January 1986

163. Material provided by European sources

164. *Profil*, January 1986; KUNA, 8 January 1986

165. *Al-Wahdah*, 13 January 1986; MAP, 14 January 1986; *Ha'aretz*, 14 January 1986

166. *Al-Siyasah*, 16 January 1986

167. *Ha'aretz*, 30 September 1986; Material provided by Israeli sources, Iranian and Arab sources in Europe

168. Raufer X., *Le Debat*, March-May 1986; Bernert P., *VSD*, 8 January 1986

169. Makinsky M., *Defense National*, December 1986

170. Khan A., Lesieur J. & Rousselle F., *Le Point*, 17 February 1986; Laroche J.A., *National Hebdo*, 27 February - 5 March 1986; Gayatte G., *Valeurs Actuelles*, 7 April 1986

171. Makinsky M., *Defense National*, December 1986; Lesieur J., *Le Point*, 10 February 1986

172. Khan A., Lesieur J. & Rousselle F., *Le Point*, 17 February 1986

173. Laroche J.A., *National Hebdo*, 27 February - 5 March 1986

174. Derogy J. & Carmel H., *Top-Secret Israel*, Paris, Robert Laffont, 1989, pp. 121-122

175. Derogy & Carmel, op.cit., pp. 121-122

176. McGirk T., *Sunday Times*, 20 April 1986; *Der Spiegel*, 12 May 1986; *Yorkshire Post*, 25 October 1986; Insight, *The Sunday Times*, 26 October 1986; Derogy & Carmel, op.cit., pp. 121-122

177. Derogy & Carmel, op.cit., p. 122; Dagan D., *Ha'aretz*, 23 April 1986; Dagan D., *Ha'aretz*, 25 April 1986; *Der Spiegel*, 12 May 1986; Tendler S., *The Times*, 25 October 1986

178. Derogy & Carmel, op.cit., p. 122

179. Insight, *The Sunday Times*, 26 October 1986; Derogy & Carmel, op.cit., p. 122

180. *The Times*, 16 October 1986; Murtagh P., *Guardian*, 16 October 1986; Derogy & Carmel, op.cit., p. 123

181. Tendler S., *The Times*, 25 October 1986; Insight, *The Sunday Times*, 26 October 1986; *Ma'ariv*, 17 October 1986; Derogy & Carmel, op.cit., p. 123; Burdan, op.cit., p. 161

182. *Ha'aretz*, 14 October 1986; *The Times*, 16 October 1986; Murtagh P., *Guardian*, 16 October 1986; Tendler S., *The Times*, 25 October 1986; Insight, *The Sunday Times*, 26 October 1986; Derogy & Carmel, op.cit., p. 124

183. *Der Spiegel*, 12 May 1986

184. *Frankfurter Allgemeine*, 22 August 1990; *Frankfurter Allgemeine*, 24 August 1990; Die Welt, 30 August 1990; Reuth R.G., *Frankfurter Allgemeine*, 4 September 1990; *Die Welt*, 10 September 1990; ADN, 8 November 1990

185. *Der Spiegel*, 12 May 1986; *Ha'aretz*, 1 August 1986; Tendler S., *The Times*, 25 October 1986; *Yorkshire Post*, 25 October 1986; Insight, *The Sunday Times*, 26 October 1986

186. AFP, 26 November 1986
187. Derogy & Carmel, op.cit., p. 122; Blundy D. & Lycett A., *Qaddafi and the Libyan Revolution*, Boston MA, Little Brown, 1987, pp. 4-5; Norton-Taylor R., *The Guardian*, 16 April 1986; *Der Spiegel*, 12 May 1986; Tendler S., *The Times*, 25 October 1986; Hersh S., *New York Times Magazine*, 22 February 1987
188. Dagan D., *Ha'aretz*, 23 April 1986; Tendler S., *The Times*, 25 October 1986; Davis B.L., *Qaddafi, Terorism, and the Origins of the US Attack on Libya*, New York, NY, Praeger, 1990, p. 117
189. *Die Welt*, 30 August 1990; *Die Welt*, 31 August 1990; Reuth R.G., *Frankfurter Allgemeine*, 4 September 1990
190. *Bild am Sonntag*, 4 May 1986
191. ADN, 8 November 1990
192. Insight, *The Sunday Times*, 26 October 1986
193. Henry I., *Daily Telegraph*, 7 October 1986; *The Times*, 16 October 1986; *The Times*, 25 October 1986; Insight, *The Sunday Times*, 26 October 1986; Derogy & Carmel, op.cit., pp. 119-120 & 126-127
194. Tsdakah Sh., *Ha'aretz*, 18 April 1986; Insight, *The Sunday Times*, 26 October 1986; *The Times*, 25 October 1986; Derogy & Carmel, op.cit., pp. 119-120 & 126-127
195. Henry I., *Daily Telegraph*, 7 October 1986; *The Times*, 16 October 1986; Murtagh P., *Guardian*, 16 October 1986; *The Times*, 25 October 1986; Insight, *The Sunday Times*, 26 October 1986; Zarai O., *Ha'aretz*, 26 October 1986; Derogy & Carmel, op.cit., pp. 119-120 & 126-127
196. Tsdaka Sh., *Ha'aretz*, 24 October 1986; *Yorkshire Post*, 25 October 1986; Tendler S., *The Times*, 25 October 1986
197. Q. in *The Times*, 25 October 1986
198. Radio Monte Carlo, 7 October 1986
199. Harif Y., *Ma'ariv*, 25 April 1986
200. *Al-Ittihad*, 7 December 1986; KUNA, 7 December 1986; Derogy & Carmel, op.cit., pp. 126-127
201. Al-Ahmar Abdallah, *Al-Ba'ath*, 16 November 1986 202. Derogy & Carmel, op.cit., pp. 126-127
203. Radio Free Lebanon, 19 October 1986
204. Henry I., *Daily Telegraph*, 22 October 1986
205. *Bild*, 18 November 1986
206. *Frankfurter Allgemeine Zeitung*, 17 March 1988

CHAPTER 6

IN WESTERN EUROPE (II)

1. Raffy S., *Le Nouvel Observateur*, 28 March - 3 April 1986 2. Pontaut J.-M., *Le Point*, 15 June 1987
3. Burdan D., *DST*, Paris, Robert Laffont, 1990, p. 272

4. Makinsky M., *Defense National*, December 1986
5. *Le Monde*, 12 April 1986; Makinsky M., *Defense National*, December 1986
6. Harif Y., *Ma'ariv*, 25 April 1986
7. *Mardi Matin*, 25 February 1986; Moruzzi J.-F., *Le Quotidien*, 27 February 1986; *Le Figaro*, 7 March 1986; Bulloch J., *Independent*, 26 April 1988; Burdan, op.cit., pp. 257-259
8. AFP, 26 February 1986
9. Raffy S., *Le Nouvel Observateur*, 28 March - 3 April 1986
10. Burdan, op.cit., pp. 310-312
11. Burdan, op.cit., pp. 310-312
12. Sablier E., *Valeurs Actuelles*, 6 April 1987
13. Raffy S., *Le Nouvel Observateur*, 28 March - 3 April 1986
14. Burdan, op.cit., p. 280
15. Voice of the Mountain, 21 March 1986; Plenel E., *Le Monde*, 7/8 September 1986
16. *Le Monde*, 17 September 1987
17. Burdan, op.cit., p. 281
18. Raffy S., *Le Nouvel Observateur*, 28 March - 3 April 1986; *Le Monde*, 17 September 1987; Grange S., *Defense & Armament Heracles*, November 1989
19. Voice of Lebanon, 24 March 1986; *Al-Nahar*, 24 March 1986
20. Radio Free Lebanon, 23 March 1986; *Al-Mustaqbal*, 23 March 1986
21. Plenel E., *Le Monde*, 7/8 September 1986
22. *Liberacion*, 23 July 1987; Toker Y., *Ha'aretz*, 24 July 1987
23. Zaki Faysal, *Al-Thawara*, 30 September 1986
24. Plenel E., *Le Monde*, 7/8 September 1986
25. Laroche J.A., *National Hebdo*, 27 February - 5 March 1986
26. Beylau P., *Le Point*, 15 June 1987
27. *Al-Watan al-Arabi*, 27 November 1992
28. Beylau P., *Le Point*, 15 June 1987
29. AFP, 3 April 1992
30. Kaidi Hamza, *Jeune Afrique*, 30 November 1988; Pontaut J.-M., *Le Point*, 15 June 1987; Beylau P., *Le Point*, 15 June 1987; Raffy S., *Le Nouvel Observateur*, 12-18 June 1987; Peri S., *Yediot Aharonot*, 20 July 1987; Pean P., *The Threat*, Paris, Fayard, 1987, pp. 289-290
31. Pontaut J.-M., *Le Point*, 15 June 1987
32. Darcourt P. and Morrot P., *Le Figaro*, 28-29 October 1989
33. Pontaut J.-M., *Le Point*, 15 June 1987
34. Greilsamer L., *Le Monde*, 12 February 1990
35. AFP, 3 April 1992
36. AFP, 14 April 1992
37. Pontaut J.-M., *Le Point*, 15 June 1987
38. Pontaut J.-M., *Le Point*, 15 June 1987; *Le Nouvel Observateur*, 3-10

April 1987; Sablier E., *Valeurs Actuelles*, 6 April 1987; *Le Nouvel Observateur*, 12-18 June 1987; Darcourt P. and Morrot P., *Le Figaro*, 28-29 October 1989; Raffy S., *Le Nouvel Observateur*, 12-18 June 1987; Pean, op.cit., p. 244

39. Pean, op.cit., pp. 289-290
40. Chambaz J., *Le Quotidien de Paris*, 5 June 1987; Pean, op.cit., p. 278
41. Pontaut J.-M., *Le Point*, 15 June 1987
42. Chambaz J., *Le Quotidien de Paris*, 5 June 1987
43. Pontaut J.-M., *Le Point*, 15 June 1987; Darcourt P. and Morrot P., *Le Figaro*, 28-29 October 1989
44. Lesieur J., *Le Point*, 1 June 1987
45. Chambaz J., *Le Quotidien de Paris*, 5 June 1987
46. Pontaut J.-M., *Le Point*, 15 June 1987
47. Chambaz J., *Le Quotidien de Paris*, 5 June 1987
48. Pontaut J.-M., *Le Point*, 15 June 1987
49. Lesieur J., *Le Point*, 1 June 1987
50. Pontaut J.-M., *Le Point*, 15 June 1987
51. Lesieur J., *Le Point*, 1 June 1987
52. Pontaut J.-M., *Le Point*, 15 June 1987
53. Pontaut J.-M., *Le Point*, 15 June 1987; Pean, op.cit., pp. 244-245
54. Lesieur J., *Le Point*, 1 June 1987
55. Darcourt P. and Morrot P., *Le Figaro*, 28-29 October 1989
56. Darcourt P. and Morrot P., *Le Figaro*, 28-29 October 1989
57. Pontaut J.-M., *Le Point*, 15 June 1987
58. Pontaut J.-M., *Le Point*, 15 June 1987
59. Pontaut J.-M., *Le Point*, 15 June 1987
60. Raffy S., *Le Nouvel Observateur*, 28 March - 3 April 1986
61. Pontaut J.-M., *Le Point*, 15 June 1987
62. Raffy S., *Le Nouvel Observateur*, 28 March - 3 April 1986; *Le Monde*, 17 September 1987; Darcourt P. and Morrot P., *Le Figaro*, 28-29 October 1989
63. Lesieur J., *Le Point*, 1 June 1987; Ploquin F., *L'Evenement du Jeudi*, 11-17 June 1987
64. Pontaut J.-M., *Le Point*, 15 June 1987
65. Lesieur J., *Le Point*, 1 June 1987
66. Paris Domestic Service, 4 September 1986; AFP, 4 September 1986
67. AFP, 5 September 1986; *Al-Nahar*, 5 September 1986; Paris Domestic Service, 5 September 1986
68. AFP, 15 September 1986; AFP, 14 September 1986; Luxemburg Domestic Service, 14 September 1986; Paris Domestic Service, 14 September 1986; AFP, 11 September 1986; *Ha'aretz*, 16 September 1986; Toker Y., *Ha'aretz*, 17 September 1986; Burdan, op.cit., pp. 282-283, & 297
69. AFP, 14 September 1986

70. Marion G., *Le Monde*, 14-15 September 1986
71. *Le Monde*, 16 September 1986
72. AFP, 17 September 1986; *Ha'aretz*, 18 September 1986; Pean, op.cit., p. 7; Burdan, op.cit., pp. 301-302
73. Pontaut J.-M., *Le Point*, 15 June 1987; *Le Monde*, 17 September 1987; Darcourt P. and Morrot P., *Le Figaro*, 28-29 October 1989
74. Pontaut J.-M., *Le Point*, 15 June 1987; Ploquin F., *L'Evenement du Jeudi*, 11-17 June 1987
75. *Al-Ittihad*, 17 October 1986
76. Bourget J.-M., *Paris Match*, 10 October 1986
77. Pean, op.cit., p. 246; Pontaut J.-M., *Le Point*, 15 June 1987
78. *Le Monde*, 27 September 1986; Makinsky M., *Defense National*, December 1986
79. Chemali A., *Le Matin*, 29 January 1987; *Keyhan*, 12 February 1987
80. AFP, 19 May 1987
81. AFP, 25 May 1987
82. Ploquin F., *L'Evenement du Jeudi*, 11-17 June 1987
83. *Le Monde*, 17 September 1987
84. Ploquin F., *L'Evenement du Jeudi*, 11-17 June 1987
85. Ploquin F., *L'Evenement du Jeudi*, 11-17 June 1987; Pean, op.cit., p. 240
86. Pean, op.cit., pp. 240-243
87. Pontaut J.-M., *Le Point*, 15 June 1987; Raffy S., *Le Nouvel Observateur*, 12-18 June 1987; Darcourt P. and Morrot P., *Le Figaro*, 28-29 October 1989
88. Pontaut J.-M., *Le Point*, 15 June 1987; Chambaz J., *Le Quotidien de Paris*, 5 June 1987; Raffy S., *Le Nouvel Observateur*, 12-18 June 1987; Ploquin F., *L'Evenement du Jeudi*, 11-17 June 1987; *Le Monde*, 17 September 1987; Darcourt P. and Morrot P., *Le Figaro*, 28-29 October 1989
89. Lesieur J., *Le Point*, 1 June 1987
90. Chambaz J., *Le Quotidien de Paris*, 5 June 1987; Pontaut J.-M., *Le Point*, 15 June 1987; Raffy S., *Le Nouvel Observateur*, 12-18 June 1987; Ploquin F., *L'Evenement du Jeudi*, 11-17 June 1987
91. Lesieur J., *Le Point*, 1 June 1987
92. Pean, op.cit., p. 240
93. Pontaut J.-M., *Le Point*, 15 June 1987
94. Lesieur J., *Le Point*, 1 June 1987
95. *I Simerini*, 20 August 1986
96. ORF, 13 January 1987; ANSA, 14 January 1987
97. Pean, op.cit., pp. 251-252; Pontaut J.-M., *Le Point*, 15 June 1987; Sablier E., *Valeurs Actuelles*, 6 April 1987; *Ha'aretz*, 18 January 1987; Darcourt P. and Morrot P., *Le Figaro*, 28-29 October 1989
98. Kaidi Hamza, *Jeune Afrique*, 30 November 1988

99. Harif Y., *Ma'ariv*, 25 April 1986; Grange S., *Defense & Armament Heracles*, November 1989; Jacquard R., *Le Quotidien de Paris*, 27-28 January 1990

100. Grange S., *Defense & Armament Heracles*, November 1989

101. Jacquard R., *Le Quotidien de Paris*, 27-28 January 1990

102. Harif Y., *Ma'ariv*, 25 April 1986

103. Chemali A., *Le Matin*, 29 January 1987; *Keyhan*, 12 February 1987

104. Olimpio G., *Corriere Della Sera*, 18 December 1989

105. Morrot B., *Le Figaro*, 4 December 1989; Pontaut J.-M., *Le Point*, 15 June 1987

106. Jacquard R., *Le Quotidien de Paris*, 27-28 January 1990; Grange S., *Defense & Armament Heracles*, November 1989; Lesieur J., *Le Point*, 1 June 1987

107. Grange S., *Defense & Armament Heracles*, November 1989; Bulloch J., *Independent*, 26 April 1988

108. Yudelovich G., *Ma'ariv*, 17 October 1986

109. Chemali A., *Le Matin*, 29 January 1987; *Keyhan*, 12 February 1987

110. Jacquard R., *Le Quotidien de Paris*, 27-28 January 1990

111. *Al-Dustur*, 5 March 1990

112. Jacquard R., *Le Quotidien de Paris*, 27-28 January 1990

113. *Al-Dustur*, 5 March 1990

114. NuriZadeh Dr. Ali, *Al-Dustur*, 12 February 1990; Hughes J., *Christian Science Monitor*, 25 May 1990

115. Morrot B., *Le Figaro*, 4 December 1989

116. Bulloch J., *Independent*, 26 April 1988

117. Jacquard R., *Le Quotidien de Paris*, 27-28 January 1990

118. Morrot B., *Le Figaro*, 4 December 1989

119. Olimpio G., *Corriere Della Sera*, 18 December 1989

120. Jacquard R., *Le Quotidien de Paris*, 27-28 January 1990

121. INA, 21 September 1988

122. Zarai O., *Ha'aretz*, 24 June 1986; *Ha'aretz*, 30 September 1986; Material provided by Israeli sources and sources in Europe

123. Khan A., Lesieur J. & Rousselle F., *Le Point*, 17 February 1986

124. Raufer X., *Le Debat*, March-May 1986; Bernert P., *VSD*, 8 January 1986; Material provided by Israeli sources and sources in Europe

125. Olimpio G., *Corriere Della Sera*, 18 December 1989

126. Bernert P., *VSD*, 8 January 1986

127. Makinsky M., *Defense National*, December 1986

128. Gayatte G., *Valeurs Actuelles*, 7 April 1986

129. Khan A., Lesieur J. & Rousselle F., *Le Point*, 17 February 1986

130. *Ha'aretz*, 10 August 1989

131. *Keyhan*, 22 January 1987; *Ha'aretz*, 18 January 1987

132. Olimpio G., *Corriere Della Sera*, 18 December 1989

133. *Ha'aretz*, 6 July 1988

134. Olimpio G., *Corriere Della Sera*, 18 December 1989
135. Zehavi E., *Ha'aretz*, 3 May 1989
136. *Ha'aretz*, 30 September 1986; Material provided by Israeli sources and sources in Europe
137. Zarai O., *Ha'Aretz*, 24 June 1986; *Ha'aretz*, 30 September 1986; Material provided by Israeli sources, Iranian and Arab sources in Europe
138. Zarai O., *Ha'Aretz*, 24 June 1986; *Ha'aretz*, 30 September 1986; Material provided by Israeli sources, Iranian and Arab sources in Europe
139. Raufer X., *Le Debat*, March-May 1986
140. AFP, 20 December 1986
141. *Le Monde*, 23 December 1986; Gauffre J-P, *L'Express*, 9 January 1987
142. *Le Monde*, 23 December 1986
143. Gauffre J-P, *L'Express*, 9 January 1987
144. Material provided by Israeli sources, Iranian and Arab sources in Europe
145. Raufer X., *Le Debat*, March-May 1986
146. Raufer X., *Le Debat*, March-May 1986; Material provided by Israeli sources, Iranian and Arab sources in Europe
147. Aziz Phillipe, *Le Point*, 27 May 1991
148. *Ha'aretz*, 27 June 1990
149. Aziz Phillipe, *Le Point*, 27 May 1991
150. *Frankfurter Allgemeine*, 21 May 1992
151. Aziz Phillipe, *Le Point*, 27 May 1991
152. Vatikiotis P.J., in *Ha'aretz*, 9 July 1992; Simmons M., *New York Times*, 11 January 1993; Drozdiak W., *Washington Post*, 21 May 1992; Duponchelle V., *L'Actualite*, 5-6, October 1991
153. Khellil Mohand, *The Integration of Maghrib Emigres in France*, Paris, Editions Presses Universitaires de France, 1991; Mabrouk Malika, *Jeune Afrique*, 26 February 1992
154. Malaurie G., *L'Express*, 9 February 1990
155. Aziz Ph., *Le Point*, 30 April 1990
156. Bernard P. & Tincq H., *Le Monde*, 29 December 1991
157. Sardan Tolga, *Milliyet*, 23 May 1991
158. *Salam*, 17 November 1991
159. *Salam*, 17 November 1991
160. *Salam*, 18 November 1991
161. Aziz Phillipe, *Le Point*, 27 May 1991
162. MENA, 2 December 1990
163. Mehanaimi U., *Yediot Aharonot*, 14 September 1990
164. *Al-Watan al-Arabi*, 24 August 1990
165. Gertz B., *Washington Times*, 24 September 1990
166. Jacquard R., *Le Quotidien de Paris*, 3 September 1990
167. DPA, 29 September 1990
168. Mehanaimi U., *Yediot Aharonot*, 14 September 1990
169. *Al-Watan al-Arabi*, 24 August 1990

170. Richard J.-A., *Le Figaro*, 24 January 1991
171. Richard J.-A., *Le Figaro*, 24 January 1991
172. Raufer X. to Villemoes L., *Berlingske Weekend*, 1 March 1991
173. Richard J.-A., *Le Figaro*, 24 January 1991
174. *Ha'aretz*, 14 January 1991
175. Scherer P., *Die Welt*, 4 February 1991
176. Jacquard R., *The Secret Cards of the Gulf War*, Paris, Edition'1, 1991, p. 212
177. *Frankfurter Allgemeine*, 22 February 1991
178. DPA, 14 September 1990; ADN, 15 September 1990; Dagan D., *Ha'aretz*, 17 September 1990
179. Jacquard, op.cit. (Gulf War), p. 216
180. Scherer P., *Die Welt*, 4 February 1991; Richard J.-A., *Le Figaro*, 24 January 1991; Jacquard, op.cit. (Gulf War), p. 212
181. *Zemedelske Noviny*, 14 September 1990; *News India*, 8 February 1991
182. *O Diabo*, 14 August 1990
183. *O Jornal*, 21-27 September 1990; *Publico*, 14 September 1990; *O Jornal*, 14-20 September 1990; AFP, 14 September 1990
184. Miguez A., *La Vanguardia*, 20 January 1991
185. Rueda F., *Tiempo*, 27 August 1990
186. *Ha'aretz*, 25 April 1991
187. Richard J.-A., *Le Figaro*, 24 January 1991
188. *The Sunday Times*, 1 April 1990; *The Economist*, 31 March 1990
189. Montalbano W.D., *Los Angeles Times*, 13 January 1989
190. Shamis G., *The Nation*, 6 January 1989
191. *Ha'aretz*, 22 December 1988; Adams J., *The Sunday Times*, 22 January 1989
192. *Al-Ittihad*, 29 September 1990; MENA, 29 September 1990
193. Pean P. & Soudan F., *Jeune Afrique*, 12-18 November 1992
194. Press Association, 7 February 1991; Reuter, 7 February 1991; Press Association, 8 February 1991; Reuter, 8 February 1991; *The Times*, 8 February 1991; *Independent*, 8 February 1991; *Guardian*, 8 February 1991; *The Daily Express*, 8 February 1991; *Ha'aretz*, 8 February 1991; *Ma'ariv*, 8 February 1991; *The Times*, 9 February 1991; *The Daily Express*, 9 February 1991
195. Press Association, 18 February 1991; *The Times*, 19 February 1991; *The Independent*, 19 February 1991; Ben-Vered A, *Ha'aretz*, 19 February 1991
196. Voice of the Greater Arab Homeland, 19 October 1991
197. Colvin M., *The Sunday Times*, 10 May 1992
198. Rose D., *The Observer*, 23 August 1992
199. Tendler S. & Ford R., *The Times*, 13 October 1992; Sharrok D. & Murray A., *Guardian*, 13 October 1992; Tendler S., *The Times*, 12 October 1992; Leppard D. & Rufford N., *The Sunday Times*, 11 October 1992; Mallie E.

& rose D., *Observer*, 11 October 1992; Mullin J. & Campbell D., *Guardian*, 8 October 1992

200. Handworker H., *Ha'aretz*, 4 September 1990
201. Reuter, 11 April 1991; *Ha'aretz*, 11 April 1991
202. Hasan Tariq, *Rose al-Yusuf*, 22 July 1991
203. *Al-Majallah*, 13 February 1991
204. Aziz Phillipe, *Le Point*, 27 May 1991
205. *Al-Majallah*, 13 February 1991
206. Aziz Phillipe, *Le Point*, 27 May 1991
207. *Die Welt*, 1 March 1991
208. *Al-Wafd*, 4 December 1991
209. Aziz Phillipe, *Le Point*, 27 May 1991
210. Pundak R., *Ha'aretz*, 25 October 1991
211. Q. in Aziz Phillipe, *Le Point*, 27 May 1991
212. Ladki Nadim, Reuter, 15 October 1991; Zara'i O., *Ha'aretz*, 27 October 1991; AP, 28 October 1991; Reuter, 30 October 1991; AP, 30 October 1991
213. Colvin M., *The Sunday Times*, 8 December 1991
214. Taheri A., *Al-Sharq al-Awsat*, 21 November 1991
215. Ladki Nadim, Reuter, 15 October 1991; Reuter, 30 October 1991; AP, 30 October 1991; AP, 28 October 1991; Zara'i O., *Ha'aretz*, 27 October 1991
216. Colvin M., *The Sunday Times*, 8 December 1991; Radio Tehran, 18 October 1991
217. Radio Budapest, 23 December 1991; MTI, 23 December 1991; AP, 23 December 1991; Reuters, 23 December 1991; MTI, 25 December 1991; Radio Budapest, 26 December 1991; Haller S., *Magyar Namzet*, 21 January 1992
218. Rosen I. & Avraham L., *Ma'ariv*, 10 May 1992; *Tineretul Liber*, 7 May 1992
219. Ladki Nadim, Reuter, 15 October 1991; Reuter, 30 October 1991; AP, 30 October 1991; AP, 28 October 1991; Zara'i O., *Ha'aretz*, 27 October 1991
220. *Berliner Zeitung*, 11 January 1992; ADN, 11 January 1992
221. `Voice of the Oppressed, 13 January 1992
222. Poliviou T., *O Agon*, 8 March 1992
223. Mubarak Hisham, *Rose al-Yusuf*, 14 September 1992
224. Al-Ahram Press Agency, 23 December 1992; *Al-Ahram*, 24 December 1992
225. *Al-Wafd*, 4 December 1991; *Al-Wafd*, 3 November 1991; Husayn Tariq, *Rose al-Yusuf*, 10 February 1992; *Al-Wafd*, 15 December 1991; *Rose al-Yusuf*, 22 June 1992
226. *Al-Wasat*, 14-20 December 1992
227. *Rose al-Yusuf*, 27 July 1992

228. Zarai O., *Ha'Aretz*, 24 June 1986; Zarai O., *Ha'Aretz*, 23 September 1986
229. *Al-Sharq al-Awsat*, 7 November 1991; *Al-Sharq al-Awsat*, 2 November 1991
230. *Al-Watan al-Arabi*, 16 October 1992
231. NuriZadeh Dr. Ali, *Al-Dustur*, 12 February 1990
232. *Al-Wafd*, 4 December 1991
233. Yared M., *Jeune Afrique*, 12-18 March 1992; Yared M., *Jeune Afrique*, 19-25 March 1992; Yared M., *Jeune Afrique*, 10-16 September 1992
234. *Jomhuri-ye Islami*, 9 August 1992
235. Yared M., *Jeune Afrique*, 10-16 September 1992; *Globus*, 14 October 1992; Taha As'ad, *Al-Hayah*, 30 October 1992; *Al-Sharq Al-Awsat*, 22 October 1992; *France Soire*, 11 August 1992; *Newsweek*, 5 October 1992; Harden B., *Washington Post*, 27 August 1992; Englberg S., *New York Times*, 23 August 1992; Hedges C., *New York Times*, 5 December 1992; TANJUG, 28 September 1992; TANJUG, 26 February 1993
236. *Le Figaro*, 18 January 1993
237. Kruschelnycky A., *The European*, 28-31 January 1993; Material provided by Iranian sources
238. Englberg S., *New York Times*, 23 August 1992
239. *Al-Siyasah*, 17 October 1985; *Kayhan International*, 3 March 1985
240. *Ha'aretz*, 10 November 1992
241. Mijalkovski M., *Vojska*, 11 February 1993; Material provided by Iranian sources
242. *France Soire*, 11 August 1992; Kruschelnycky A., *The European*, 28-31 January 1993; Radio Zagreb, 10 September 1992; Gordon M.R., *New York Times*, 10 September 1992; *Washington Post*, 10 September 1992
243. Doyle L., *The Independent*, 22 August 1992; Strobel W., *Washington Times*, 23 August 1992; ABC World News Tonight, 31 August 1992; *New York Times*, 22 June 1992
244. Cohen R., *New York Times*, 18 September 1992
245. Zheglov Maj. M., *Krasnaya Zvezda*, 19 August 1992
246. Binyon M. & Phillips J., *The Times*, 5 September 1992; Harden B., *Washington Post*, 17 September 1992
247. *Washington Times*, 10 September 1992; *Washington Post*, 10 September 1992
248. Burns J.F., *New York Times*, 26 December 1992
249. Binyon M. & Phillips J., *The Times*, 5 September 1992
250. *Le Figaro*, 18 January 1993
251. Relea F., *El Pais*, 27 January 1993
252. Mowlana Hamid, *Kayhan International*, 23 August 1992; IRNA, 23 August 1992
253. Voice of the Oppressed, 16 September 1992
254. al-Hadidi Mu'taz, *Al-Sha'b*, 13 October 1992
255. *The Middle East*, October 1992

256. Kabbani Rana, *Africa Events*, September 1992
257. Al-Matrafi Khalid, *Al-Madinah*, 11 June 1990
258. Material provided by Iranian sources
259. EFE, 9 March 1989; *Ha'aretz*, 10 March 1989
260. Ben-Yishai R., *Yediot Aharonot*, 26 April 1991
261. DPA, 11 June 1991
262. Ovsiyenko Sergey & Rafayenko Nikolay, *Rossiyskiye Vesti*, 14 July 1992
263. Voice of Iran Toilers, 9 November 1989
264. AFP, 14 July 1989; IRNA, 17 July 1989; AFP, 17 July 1989; Danninger S., *Der Standard*, 17 July 1989
265. Tehran Domestic Service, 19 July 1989
266. Radio Tehran, 14 July 1989; *Tehran Times*, 16 July 1989 267. IRNA, 15 July 1989
268. Material provided by Iranian sources in Europe
269. Material provided by Iranian and Kurdish sources
270. IRNA, 17 July 1989
271. AFP, 17 July 1989
272. IRNA, 19 July 1989
273. IRNA, 17 July 1989
274. Darbyshire N., *Daily Telegraph*, 5 August 1989
275. *The Independent*, 12 April 1990; *Ha'aretz*, 13 April 1990
276. Anderson J. & Van Attah D., *Washington Post*, 10 June 1990; Hughes J., *Christian Science Monitor*, 25 May 1990; Anderson J. & Van Attah D., *Washington Post*, 21 May 1990
277. Raufer X., *L'Express*, 22 August 1991; *Ha'aretz*, 9 August 1991; Press Association, 23 July 1991; Press Association, 18 July 1991; AP, 17 July 1991; Reuter 17 July 1991
278. Pontaut J.-M., *Le Point*, 7 September 1991
279. *Ha'aretz*, 21 August 1991
280. AFP, 21 April 1991; Handworker H., *Ha'aretz*, 22 April 1991; Reuter, 8 August 1991; Pontaut J.-M. & Reverier J.-L., *Le Point*, 31 August 1991
281. Raufer X., *L'Express*, 22 August 1991
282. France-Inter Radio, 8 August 1991; *Ha'aretz*, 9 August 1991
283. Ponteau J.-M., *Le Point*, 5 October 1991; Tourancheau P., *Liberation*, 4 October 1991; *Ha'aretz*, 29 September 1991
284. Ponteau J.-M., *Le Point*, 5 October 1991; *International Herald Tribune*, 6 September 1991
285. Pontaut J.-M., *Le Point*, 21 September 1991; Tourancheau P., *Liberation*, 4 October 1991
286. AFP, 23 September 1991
287. Pontaut J.-M., *Le Point*, 21 September 1991
288. AFP, 22 October 1991; Ponteau J.-M., *Le Point*, 5 October 1991
289. Pontaut J.-M., *Le Point*, 21 September 1991
290. Lombard M.-A., *Le Figaro*, 4 October 1991; Pontaut J.-M., *Le Point*, 7

September 1991; *Liberation*, 21 August 1991; Handworker H., *Ha'aretz*, 11 August 1991

291. Ponteaut J.-M., *Le Point*, 5 October 1991

292. Raufer X., *L'Express*, 29 August 1991

293. Pontaut J.-M., *Le Point*, 21 September 1991; Lombard M.-A., *Le Figaro*, 4 October 1991

294. AFP, 13 August 1991

295. Tourancheau P., *Liberation*, 4 October 1991

296. Pontaut J.-M., *Le Point*, 7 September 1991; Reuter, 19 September 1991

297. Raufer X., *L'Express*, 22 August 1991; AFP, 23 September 1991

298. Handworker H., *Ha'aretz*, 2 September 1991

299. AFP, 9 August 1991; Reuter, 8 August 1991; *Liberation*, 22 August 1991; Raufer X., *L'Express*, 22 August 1991; *Liberation*, 21 August 1991; Handworker H., *Ha'aretz*, 18 August 1991; Renard J., *Le Quotidien de Paris*, 17-18 August 1991; Handworker H., *Ha'aretz*, 11 August 1991; *Ha'aretz*, 9 August 1991; Handworker H., *Ha'aretz*, 2 September 1991

300. Pontaut J.-M. & Reverier J.-L., *Le Point*, 31 August 1991

301. *Le Point*, 5 October 1991

302. *Ha'aretz*, 22 September 1991: Radio Paris, 20 September 1991

303. Tourancheau P., *Liberation*, 4 October 1991; Lombard M.-A., *Le Figaro*, 4 October 1991; Ponteaut J.-M., *Le Point*, 5 October 1991

304. Handworker H., *Ha'aretz*, 18 August 1991

305. AFP, 13 August 1991

306. Pontaut J.-M. & Reverier J.-L., *Le Point*, 31 August 1991; *Le Figaro*, 4 September 1991; Handworker H., *Ha'aretz*, 2 September 1991; *Le Figaro*, 2 September 1991; Reuter, 19 September 1991; AFP, 13 August 1991; *Ha'aretz*, 13 August 1991; AFP, 12 August 1991; Handworker H., *Ha'aretz*, 22 August 1991; AFP, 21 August 1991; Handworker H., *Ha'aretz*, 28 August 1991; AFP, 27 August 1991

307. Raufer X., *L'Express*, 29 August 1991; Handworker H., *Ha'aretz*, 2 September 1991

308. AFP, 8 August 1991; AP, 8 August 1991; Reuter, 8 August 1991

309. IRNA, 9 August 1991; AFP, 9 August 1991; IRIB TV, 12 August 1991

310. *Kayhan International*, 11 August 1991; *Tehran Times*, 11 August 1991; IRNA, 11 August 1991; Mamedi J., *Jahan-ye Islam*, 10 August 1991

311. *Ettela'at*, 11 August 1991; IRNA, 11 August 1991

312. Reuter, 22 September 1991; *Ha'aretz*, 24 September 1991

313. *Le Monde*, 14 August 1991; Handworker H., *Ha'aretz*, 15 August 1991

314. Morrot B., *Le Figaro*, 3 September 1991; Ponteaut J.-M., *Le Point*, 5 October 1991

315. *Al-Jumhuriyah*, 4 January 1992; INA, 4 January 1992

316. *Al-Watan al-Arabi*, 27 November 1992

317. Hufelschulte J., *Focus*, 18 January 1993; Dietl W., *Terrorismus Extremismus Organisierte Kriminalitat*, January 1993; Raufer X.,

L'Express, 18 December 1992; Kinzer S., *New York Times*, 19 September 1992; Voice of Iranian Kordestan, 21 September 1992; IRNA, 20 September 1992; Voice of Iranian Kordestan, 18 September 1992

318. AP, March 16, 1993; Reuters, March 16, 1993
319. Iranian TV, 30 August 1992
320. Radio Tehran, 13 July 1992

CHAPTER 7

ISLAMIST TERRORISM IN AMERICA (I)

1. *Al-'Ahd*, 4 March 1988
2. IRNA, 18 July 1990
3. The International Headquarters of the *HizbAllah, Open Letter Addressed by the HizbAllah to the Opressed/Downtrodden in Lebanon and in the World*, Tehran, 16 February 1985
4. Taheri Amir, *Holy Terror*, London, Huchinson, 1987, pp. 69-70; Dietl W., *Holy War*, New York, Macmillan, 1984, p. 164; Delafon G., *Beirut: The Soldiers of Islam*, Paris, Stock, 1989, pp. 72-73
5. Taheri, op.cit., (Holy Terror), pp. 69-70
6. Taheri, op.cit. (Holy Terror), pp. 87-88; Kupperman R. and Kamen J., *Final Warning*, New York NY, Doubleday, 1989, p. 47
7. Report on the General Congress of the World Center for Resistence of Imperialism, Zionism, Racism, and Reaction, prepared for the Central Committee of the NJM, Grenada; Q. in *Grenada Documents: An Overview and a Selection*, Washington D.C., The Department of State and the Department of Defense, September 1984, pp. 34-1 - 34-5
8. *Focus on Libya*, March 1984; Sicker M., *The Making of a Pariah State*, New York NY, Praeger, 1987, p. 120
9. Moore J.N., *The Secret War in Central America*, Frederick MD, FIBS-UPA, 1987, p. 151
10. *Background Paper: Nicaragua's Military Build-Up and Support for Central American Subversion*, Washington D.C., the Department of State and the Department of Defense, 18 July 1984
11. Blumenkrantz Z., *Ha'aretz*, 18 June 1986
12. Tripoli Voice of Greater Arab Homeland, 1 September 1983
13. Tripoli Domestic Service, 11 June 1984
14. *Early Warning*, September 1983
15. *Early Warning*, September 1983
16. Agres T., *Washington Times*, 4 June 1985
17. Tariq Abi, *Al-Inqadh*, No. 8, April 1984
18. Kinsella W., *Ma'ariv*, 25 August 1989; Adams J.R., *Forward*, 20 December 1991
19. *Daily Telegraph*, 30 April 1983; *Manchester Guardian*, 23 April 1983; AP, 23 April 1983; Reuter, 4 April 1983; AP, 4 April 1983; Tripoli

Domestic Service, 11 June 1984

20. *Information Digest*, 22 June 1984; Seper J., *Arizona Republic*, 7 June 1984; Seper J., *Arizona Republic*, 6 June 1984; *San-Diego Tribune*, 6 June 1984; Seper J., *Arizona Republic*, 5 June 1984

21. Laffin J., *Holy War: Islam Fights*, London, Grafton, 1988, pp. 83-84

22. Golits A., *Krasnaya Zvezda*, 30 August 1990

23. Bermudez J.S. Jr., *North Korean Special Forces*, London, JANE's, 1988, pp. 98-101; Bermudez J.S. Jr., *Terrorism: The North Korean Connection*, New York NY, Crane Russak, 1990, pp. 139-142

24. Foxman A. & Boland M., *Washington Times*, 19 August 1992; Kinsella W., *Wall Street Journal*, 13 December 1991; *Focus on Libya*, March 1988; *Information Digest*, 22 June 1984

25. Foxman A. & Boland M., *Washington Times*, 19 August 1992; Merriner J. & Casey J., *Chicago Sun Times*, 30 December 1987; *Insight*, 11 November 1985

26. *Information Digest*, 22 June 1984; *Insight*, 11 November 1985; *Focus on Libya*, March 1988

27. *Information Digest*, 22 June 1984

28. *Focus on Libya*, March 1988

29. *Chicago Sun-Times*, 25 February 1985; *Focus on Libya*, March 1988

30. Tripoli Domestic Service, 25 February 1985

31. *Ma'ariv*, 3 November 1986; Possley M., *Chicago Tribune*, 7 November 1986; Drell A., *Chicago Sun Times*, 30 December 1987; *Focus on Libya*, March 1988; O'Connor M., *Chicago Times*, 27 May 1992; Foxman A. & Boland M., *Washington Times*, 19 August 1992

32. Voice of Lebanon, 31 August 1985

33. Hirst D., *The Guardian*, 20 January 1986; *Washington Times*, 21 January 1986

34. Tehran International Service, 7 January 1986; Tabriz International Service, 7 January 1986

35. Voice of the Mountain, 27 March 1986

36. Radio Monte Carlo, 6 February 1986

37. Taheri Amir, *Jeune Afrique*, 7 May 1986; *Ma'ariv*, 4 April 1986

38. *Early Warning*, April 1986

39. Tripoli Voice of Greater Arab Homeland, 17 March 1986

40. Tripoli Voice of Greater Arab Homeland, 17 March 1986

41. Political Communique issued on 18 March by the Second International Conference of the International Center for Combatting Imperialism, Zionism, Racism, Reaction and Fascism, as read on Tripoli Voice of Greater Arab Homeland, 18 March 1986

42. Political Communique issued on 18 March by the Second International Conference of the International Center for Combatting Imperialism, Zionism, Racism, Reaction and Fascism, as read on Tripoli Voice of Greater Arab Homeland, 18 March 1986

43. Tripoli Domestic Service, 17 March 1986; Foxman A. & Boland M., *Washington Times*, 19 August 1992
44. Tripoli Domestic Service, 17 March 1986
45. JANA, 17 March 1986
46. Voice of the Greater Arab Homeland, 26 March 1986
47. AFP, 25 March 1986
48. AFP, 25 March 1986
49. JANA, 26 March 1986
50. JANA, 26 March 1986
51. Voice of the Greater Arab Homeland, 26 March 1986
52. Voice of the Greater Arab Homeland, 26 March 1986
53. Voice of the Greater Arab Homeland, 27 March 1986
54. Voice of the Greater Arab Homeland, 28 March 1986
55. Voice of the Greater Arab Homeland, 28 March 1986
56. Radio Free Lebanon, 29 August 1986
57. Voice of Lebanon, 30 August 1986
58. Kinsella W., *Ma'ariv*, 25 August 1989; Agres T., *Washington Times*, 4 June 1985; Adams J.R., *Forward*, 20 December 1991
59. Kinsella W., *Ma'ariv*, 25 August 1989; Murphy C. & Evans S., *Washington Post*, 22 July 1988; Adams J.R., *Forward*, 20 December 1991
60. Kinsella W., *Ma'ariv*, 25 August 1989; Adams J.R., *Forward*, 20 December 1991
61. Kinsella W., *Ma'ariv*, 25 August 1989; Adams J.R., *Forward*, 20 December 1991
62. Kinsella W., *Ma'ariv*, 25 August 1989; Adams J.R., *Forward*, 20 December 1991
63. Adams J.R., *Forward*, 20 December 1991; Kinsella W., *Ma'ariv*, 25 August 1989
64. JANA, 26 January 1988; Voice of the Greater Arab Homeland, 3 February 1988
65. Libyan Television, 30 January 1988
66. *The Final Call*, 11 September 1989
67. *Washington Times*, 27 February 1990
68. Tripoli Television Service, 27 March 1990
69. JANA, 8 June 1991
70. Landau B., *Ha'aretz*, 28 January 1987
71. Ganor A., *Ha'aretz*, 5 March 1987
72. *Ha'Aretz*, 29 May 1989
73. Quick Abdullah Hakim, *Africa Events*, February 1990
74. Quick Abdullah Hakim, *Africa Events*, February 1990; Turner K., AP, 28 July 1990; Bailby E., *Jeune Afrique*, 6-12 August 1992
75. Quick Abdullah Hakim, *Africa Events*, February 1990
76. AP, 28 July 1990; Fraser T., AP, 30 July 1990; French H., *New York Times*, 31 July 1990; *Ha'aretz*, 31 July 1990

77. AP, 30 July 1990; Primorac M., *Libya's Terrorism in the Americas*, Washington D.C., CIASF, 1990, p. 2

78. AP, 28 July 1990

79. French H., *New York Times*, 31 July 1990; Primorac, op.cit., pp. 2-3

80. AP, 29 July 1990

81. AP, 28 July 1990

82. *Defense and Foreign Affairs Weekly*, 16-22 January 1989

83. AP, 28 July 1990; CANA, 28 July 1990; EFE, 28 July 1990; AFP, 28 July 1990; AP, 29 July 1990; CANA, 29 July 1990; EFE, 29 July 1990; AFP, 29 July 1990; AP, 30 July 1990; CANA, 30 July 1990; EFE, 30 July 1990; AFP, 30 July 1990; AP, 31 July 1990; CANA, 31 July 1990; EFE, 31 July 1990; AFP, 31 July 1990; AP, 1 August 1990; CANA, 1 August 1990; EFE, 1 August 1990; AFP, 1 August 1990

84. AP, 28 July 1990; CANA, 28 July 1990; EFE, 28 July 1990; AFP, 28 July 1990; AP, 29 July 1990; CANA, 29 July 1990; EFE, 29 July 1990; AFP, 29 July 1990; AP, 30 July 1990; CANA, 30 July 1990; EFE, 30 July 1990; AFP, 30 July 1990; AP, 31 July 1990; CANA, 31 July 1990; EFE, 31 July 1990; AFP, 31 July 1990; AP, 1 August 1990; CANA, 1 August 1990; EFE, 1 August 1990; AFP, 1 August 1990

85. CANA, 31 July 1990; CANA 30 July 1990

86. CANA, 3 August 1990

87. Bailby E., *Jeune Afrique*, 6-12 August 1992

88. AP, 16 March 1993

89. Radu M. and Tismaneanu V., *Latin American Revolutionaries*, Washington D.C., Pergamon-Brassey's, 1990, pp. 172-173

90. *Ha'aretz*, 21 November 1985

91. J. Jesus Rangel M., *Excelsior*, 15 August 1988

92. *Le Point*, 11 September 1989

93. Q. in *Soldier of Fortune*, May 1988

94. Fishman A., *Hadashot*, 10 May 1991; Moniquet C., *L'Express*, 8 May 1987; material provided by Israeli and Lebanese sources

95. Ehrenfeld R., *Narco-Terrorism*, New York NY, Basic, 1990, p.59; CNN, 7 November 1989; Knox C. (pseud.), *Soldier of Fortune*, May 1988; material provided by Israeli and Lebanese sources

96. Material provided by Israeli sources

97. Fishman A., *Hadashot*, 10 May 1991

98. *Al-Shira'*, 5 February 1990

99. Material provided by Israeli sources

100. Radio Cadena Nacional, 27 November 1989; EFE, 27 November 1989

101. DPA, 16 February 1990; *El-Tiempo*, 16 February 1990

102. Rubio M., *El Tiempo*, 28 May 1992

103. Taheri, op.cit., (Holy Terror), p. 195

104. *Nimrooz*, 12 June 1992

105. *Yediot Aharonot*, 5 February 1992; *Le Figaro*, 30-31 May 1992; *Nimrooz*, 12 June 1992; *Kayhan International*, 21 June 1992; ITIM, 2 October 1992

106. Material provided by Lebanese sources

107. Material provided by Lebanese sources

108. *Yediot Aharonot*, 5 February 1992; NBC Nightly News, 27 February 1992; *U.S. News & World Report*, 30 March 1992; *Le Figaro*, 30-31 May 1992; *Nimrooz*, 12 June 1992; *Kayhan International*, 21 June 1992; ITIM, 2 October 1992; Material provided by Iranian and Lebanese

109. *Yediot Aharonot*, 5 February 1992; *Le Figaro*, 30-31 May 1992; *Nimrooz*, 12 June 1992; *Kayhan International*, 21 June 1992; ITIM, 2 October 1992; Material provided by Lebanese sources

110. *L'Evenement du Jeudi*, 26 July 1990

111. *Expresso*, 26 July 1990; *Ha'aretz*, 26 July 1990; *Ha'aretz*, 7 February 1989; Primorac, op.cit., p. 5

112. *El Comercio*, 8 June 1990; *Caretas*, 10 April 1990; Gustavo Gorriti to *Expresso*, 11 & 12 October 1990

113. *La Republica*, 18 July 1990; *Caretas*, 10 April 1990

114. Tarazona-Sevillano Gabriela with Reuter J.B., *Sendero Luminoso and the Threat of Narcoterrorism*, New York NY, Praeger, 1990

115. *Caretas*, 30 September 1991

116. *El Comercio*, 29 June 1991

117. *Expresso*, 14 December 1989; *Expresso*, 15 December 1989; *El Comercio*, 28 June 1990

118. Gorriti G., *Caretas*, 23 March 1992

119. *El Diario Internacional*, March 1991; *Caretas*, 15 April 1991

120. *The Citizen*, 19 July 1985

121. Radio Monte Carlo, 13 January 1986

122. *Kayhan*, 9 February 1986

123. Tehran Domestic Service, 29 October 1986

124. AFP, 18 September 1986

125. *Al-Nahar*, 18 September 1986

126. Radio Monte Carlo, 4 October 1986

127. Tehran Domestic Service, 11 July 1987

128. Radio Free Lebanon, 17 July 1987; *Al-Nahar*, 17 July 1987

129. Yazandegan Gorouh-e, *Letre Persane*, June 1986

130. Kupperman and Kamen, op.cit., pp. 47-48; Duffy B. et.al., *US News & World Report*, 6 March 1989

132. AFP, 8 September 1984

133. AFP, 4 November 1984

134. *Al-Nahar*, 14 January 1985

135. Zaruf Muhammad, *Al-Thawrah*, 23 July 1985 133. Agres T., *Washington Times*, 4 June 1985

136. Anderson J. & Van Atta D., *Washington Post*, 17 January 1986

137. Agres T., *Washington Times*, 4 June 1985
138. Taheri, op.cit. (Holy Terror), pp. 108-109; *Early Warning*, November 1987; Material provided by Iranian sources in the Europe
139. Anderson J. & Van Atta D., *Washington Post*, 17 January 1986; Material provided by Iranian sources in the Europe
140. *Al-Qabas*, 26 September 1986
141. Uriyan Dr. Sami, *Al-Sharq al-Awsat*, 17 December 1989
142. Taheri, op.cit. (Holy Terror), pp. 166-167; *Early Warning*, November 1987; Muttam J., *Arms and Insecurity in the Persian Gulf*, New Delhi, Radiant, 1984, p. 158; Segev S., *The Iranian Connection*, Jerusalem, Domino, 1989, p. 122; The Material provided by Iranian sources in Europe and Afghan resistance sources
143. Material provided by Afghan resistance, Pakistani, and Iranian sources
144. Lashkul V., *Izvestiya*, 1 June 1987; Material provided by Afghan sources
145. *Creation of an Independent Brigade for Carrying out Unconventional Warfare in Enemy Teritory*, Minutes of a Top Secret meeting in Tehran on 26 May 1984
146. Radio Najat-e Iran, 7 October 1985; Material provided by Afghan sources
147. Material provided by Iranian and Afghan resistance sources; Taheri, op.cit. (Holy Terror), pp. 166-167; *Early Warning*, November 1987
148. *The Bulletin of The Islamic Center — Under Siege*, Washington D.C., 22 August 1986
149. Uriyan Dr. Sami, *Al-Sharq al-Awsat*, 17 December 1989
150. *Huston Post*, 22 December 1986
151. SPA, 25 December 1987
152. *Ettela'at*, 8 June 1988
153. Foundation documents; Gertz B., *Washington Times*, 9 March 1989
154. Duffy B. et.al., *US News & World Report*, 6 March 1989
155. Gertz B., *Washington Times*, 9 March 1989

CHAPTER 8

ISLAMIST TERRORISM IN AMERICA (II)

1. Taheri Amir, *Holy Terror*, London, Huchinson, 1987, pp. 108-109; Agres T., *Washington Times*, 4 June 1985; Anderson J. & Van Atta D., *Washington Post*, 17 January 1986; *Early Warning*, November 1987; Material provided by Iranian sources in the Europe
2. Shamir Sh., *Ha'aretz*, 3 September 1987
3. Shamir Sh., *Ha'aretz*, 21 April 1987
4. IDF Radio, 13 October 1987; Material provided by Israeli sources
5. Rohani Sayyid Hamid, *Keyhan*, 30 January 1988
6. Bourget J.-M., *Paris Match*, 10 October 1986; Burdan D., *DST*, Paris, Robert Laffont, 1990, pp. 88-90
7. Fusako Shigenobu, *Ryudo*, October 1982

8. Damascus Television Service, 10 July 1985; *Liberation*, 19 March 1985
9. *New York Times*, 28 January 1988; *Wall Street Journal*, 11 February 1988; *New York Times*, 18 May 1988; *Los Angeles Times*, 18 May 1988; Kupperman R. and Kamen J., *Final Warning*, New York NY, Doubleday, 1989, p. 10
10. Ryuichi Hirokawa, *Shukan Yomiuri*, 2 October 1983; Ryuichi Hirokawa, *Shukan Yomiuri*, 9 October 1983
11. *New York Times*, 15 April 1988; *New York Times*, 16 April 1988; *Daily Yomiuri*, 18 April 1988
12. Rudolph R., *Newark Star Ledger*, 5 February 1989; Kupperman and Kamen, op.cit., pp. 10-12 & 84; Farrell W.R., *Blood and Rage*, Lexington MA, Lexington MA, 1990, pp. 212-213
13. Kupperman and Kamen, op.cit., p. 11
14. *Newsweek*, 13 July 1992
15. Reinhold R., *New York Times*, 11 March 1989
16. Perry A., *Los Angeles Times*, 11 March 1989
17. Reinhold R., *New York Times*, 12 March 1989
18. Engelberg S., *New York Times*, 13 March 1989
19. Perry A., *Los Angeles Times*, 11 March 1989
20. Wright R., *Los Angeles Times*, 11 March 1989
21. Ben-Yishai R., *Yediot Aharonot*, 10 April 1992
22. Duffy B. et.al., *US News & World Report*, 6 March 1989
23. Gertz B., *Washington Times*, 9 March 1989
24. NuriZadeh Dr. Ali, *Al-Dustur*, 12 February 1990
25. *Al-Watan al-Arabi*, 27 November 1992
26. *Al-Watan al-Arabi*, 16 October 1992; *Al-Sharq al-Awsat*, 7 November 1991; *Al-Sharq al-Awsat*, 2 November 1991
27. Radio Tehran, 5 May 1989; IRNA, 5 May 1989
28. Voice of the Oppressed, 6 June 1989
29. IRNA, 13 June 1989; *Ha'aretz*, 14 June 1989
30. Radio Tehran, 7 August 1989; *Yediot Aharonot*, 8 August 1989
31. Tehran Domestic Service, 12 August 1989
32. *Al-'Ahd*, 27 October 1989
33. *Jomhuri-ye Eslami*, 4 November 1989
34. Tehran International Service, 16 December 1989
35. IRNA, 19 March 1990
36. *Keyhan*, 3 May 1990
37. IRNA, 31 May 1990; Radio Tehran, 4 June 1990
38. AFP, 3 June 1990
39. IRNA, 3 June 1990
40. Nir O., *Ha'aretz*, 15 January 1991
41. Raufer X., *L'Express*, 22 August 1991; *Ha'aretz*, 9 August 1991; Press Association, 23 July 1991; Press Association, 18 July 1991; AP, 17 July 1991; Reuter 17 July 1991

42. Iranian Television, 18 March 1991
43. Fadlallah Ayatollah al-Sayid Muhammad Hussayn, *Middle East Insight*, July/August 1991
44. Iranian Television, 17 October 1991; Radio Tehran, 18 October 1991; Sharif Imam-Jomeh, Reuter, 19 October 1991; Radio Tehran, 19 October 1991; IRNA, 20 October 1991; Iranian Television, 20 October 1991; Iranian Television, 17 October 1991; Radio Tehran, 18 October 1991; IRNA, 21 October 1991; IRNA, 23 October 1991; Radio Tehran, 25 October 1991; IRNA, 20 October 1991; *Ha'aretz*, 18 October 1991; IRNA, 25 October 1991
45. *Kayhan*, 21 October 1991
46. Radio Tehran, 22 October 1991
47. IRNA, 22 October 1991
48. IRNA, 20 October 1991
49. Material provided by Iranian sources in Europe
50. *Ma'ariv*, 19 March 1992
51. *Keyhan*, 8 August 1985
52. *Hadashot*, 19 March 1992
53. Strenthal S., *Insight*, 10 June 1991
54. *Clarin*, 15 January 1992; *Clarin*, 7 May 1992
55. *ABC*, 21 November 1990
56. *Clarin*, 7 May 1992; Tsdaka Sh., *Ha'aretz*, 1 May 1992; Material provided by Israeli sources
57. Noticias Argentinas, 29 March 1992
58. TELAM, 18 March 1992
59. Sadeh D., *Yediot Aharonot*, 27 March 1992
60. Figueroa J., EFE, 20 March 1992
61. *Buenos Aires Herald*, 29 March 1992
62. *Noticias Argentinas*, 6 May 1992; TELAM, 18 March 1992
63. TELAM, 18 March 1992; *Ha'aretz*, 18 March 1992; *Yediot Aharonot*, 18 March 1992
64. *Ha'aretz*, 20 March 1992
65. *Hadashot*, 19 March 1992; *Ha'aretz*, 19 March 1992
66. *Noticias Argentinas*, 6 May 1992
67. Noticias Argentinas, 18 March 1992
68. AFP, 19 March 1992
69. Iranian TV, 20 March 1992
70. Radio Free Lebanon, 30 March 1992
71. Voice of Lebanon, 31 March 1992
72. *New York Times*, 9 May 1992
73. Iranian Television, 9 May 1992
74. Radio Tehran, 14 February 1992
75. *Jomhuri-ye Islami*, 9 February 1992
76. Tsdaka Sh., *Ha'aretz*, 1 May 1992

77. Radio Tehran, 2 March 1992
78. Radio Tehran, 2 March 1992
79. Radio Tehran, 3 March 1992
80. *Al-Watan al-Arabi*, 13 March 1992; Bkhor G., *Ha'aretz*, 20 March 1992
81. Raufer X., *L'Express*, 22 August 1991; *Ha'aretz*, 9 August 1991; Press Association, 23 July 1991; Press Association, 18 July 1991; AP, 17 July 1991; Reuter 17 July 1991
82. Hanley R., *New York Times*, 28 March 1992; Hanley R., *New York Times*, 29 March 1992
83. Radio Tehran, 27 March 1992
84. International Day of *Quds* documents; personal observations
85. Voice of the Oppressed, 26 May 1992
86. *Washington Post*, 26 January 1993; *Washington Times*, 26 January 1993; *New York Times*, 26 January 1993
87. Lewis N.A., *New York Times*, 10 February 1993; Jehl D., *New York Times*, 11 February 1993
88. Rashid Ahmad & Adams J., *The Sunday Times*, 14 February 1993; Shaka Shakil & Ahbasi Ansar, *The News*, 14 February 1993
89. Ahmad Mushtaq, *Dawn*, 25 May 1988; Navik, *Hurmat*, 16-22 March 1988; Rizvi Dr. Yasin, *Hurmat*, 7-13 April 1988
90. Abbas Samayah, MENA, 13 December 1992
91. Zulfiqar Shahzada, *The Nation*, 12 February 1993
92. *Pakistan Times*, 17 February 1993
93. *Pakistan Observer*, 9 March 1993
94. *The News*, 18 February 1993
95. Shahid Saleem, *Dawn*, 12 February 1993; Zulfiqar Shahzada, *The Nation*, 12 February 1993; Ikbar Anwar, *The News*, 12 February 1993; *Nawa-i Waqt*, 12 February 1993; *The News*, 18 February 1993
96. Material provided by Afghan, Pakistani and Iranian sources
97. Zulfiqar Shahzada, *The Nation*, 12 February 1993; Zulfiqar Shahzada, *The Nation*, 15 February 1993; *The News*, 18 February 1993
98. *The News*, 18 February 1993
99. Material provided by Afghan, Pakistani and Iranian sources
100. Shahid Saleem, *Dawn*, 12 February 1993; Zulfiqar Shahzada, *The Nation*, 12 February 1993; Ikbar Anwar, *The News*, 12 February 1993; *The News*, 18 February 1993
101. *The News*, 18 February 1993
102. Rashid Ahmad & Adams J., *The Sunday Times*, 14 February 1993; Jehl D., *New York Times*, 11 February 1993; *The News*, 18 February 1993
103. Zulfiqar Shahzada, *The Nation*, 12 February 1993; Ikbar Anwar, *The News*, 12 February 1993; AFP, 12 February 1993
104. *Al-Watan al-Arabi*, 27 November 1992
105. *The News*, 16 February 1993; IRNA, 13 February 1993
106. AFP, 25 September 1989

107. Material provided by Pakistani security sources

108. *Kayhan International*, 5 October 1991

109. Radio Nejat-e Islam, 23 June 1985

110. Anderson J. & Van Atta D., *Washington Post*, 17 January 1986; Taheri, op.cit. (Holy Terror), pp. 87-88

111. Kupperman and Kamen, op.cit., p. 47

112. Robberson T., *Washington Post Magazine*, 16 December 1990; Roy O., *The Failure of Political Islam*, Paris, Editions de Seuil, 1992, pp. 146 & 151; Material provided by Iranian sources in the UK; Pakistani and Afghan resistance sources

113. *Jang*, 14 May 1986; Robberson T., *Washington Post Magazine*, 16 December 1990; Waldman P., *Wall Street Journal*, 6 January 1993; Roy O., op.cit. (Political Islam) pp. 146 & 151; Material provided by Iranian sources in the Europe; Pakistani and Afghan resistance sources

114. Kirpekar Subhash, *Times of India*, 28 October 1992; *Indian Express*, 18 January 1993; Material provided by Iranian sources in the UK; Afghan resistance sources; Indian intelligence sources

115. *Denver Post*, 1 November 1992; *Washington Times*, 18 October 1992; *Rocky Mountain News*, 16 September 1989; Finley B., *Denver Post*, 27 December 1992

116. Uriyan Dr. Sami, *Al-Sharq al-Awsat*, 17 December 1989

117. Conference Papers of the Islamic Committee for Palestine

118. *Response*, January 1990; Conference Papers of the Islamic Committee for Palestine

119. *Al-Fajr*, 23 August 1987; *Al-Fajr*, 28 August 1987; Kohen O., *Hadashot*, 13 October 1987; *Globe and Mail*, 26 October 1987

120. *Response*, January 1990; Conference Papers of the Islamic Committee for Palestine

121. *HAMAS* Documents

122. *Ha'aretz*, 9 April 1991; Israeli TV, 11 April 1991; Reuter, 11 April 1991; Ginor B., *Matara*, No. 20, 1991; *Al-Wafd*, 4 December 1991

123. Voice of Israel, 10 February 1991; Ginor B., *Matara*, No. 20, 1991; Material provided by Israeli sources

124. *Al-Nahar*, 25 April 1990; Voice of the Oppressed, 25 April 1990; Radio Monte Carlo, 24 April 1990

125. Voice of the Oppressed, 22 May 1990

126. AFP, 13 July 1990

127. Farraj Hamdi, *Al-Quds al-'Arabi*, 8 October 1990

128. Imad al-'Alami to *Filastin al-Muslimah*, December 1990

129. *Keyhan*, 18 December 1990

130. Awdah Awdah, *Al-Ra'y*, 5 October 1990

131. *Islamic Horizons*, August 1990; *Islamic Horizons*, September 1990; *Islamic Horizons*, October 1990; Conference papers of the Islamic Society of North America

132. Ginor B., *Matara*, No. 20, 1991; Israeli TV, 11 April 1991; *Ha'aretz*, 11 April 1991

133. Yaari E., *New York Times*, 27 January 1993; Miller J., *New York Times*, 17 February 1993

134. Nir O., *Ha'aretz*, 1 February 1993

135. *Al-Wafd*, 4 December 1991

136. Official Announcement of the Government of Israel, 31 January 1993

137. Official Announcement of the Government of Israel, 31 January 1993; Rabin E., *Ha'aretz*, 1 February 1993; Miller J., *New York Times*, 17 February 1993

138. Official Announcement of the Government of Israel, 31 January 1993; Rabin E., *Ha'aretz*, 1 February 1993; Hoffman D., *Washington Post*, 1 February 1993; Miller J., *New York Times*, 17 February 1993

139. Official Announcement of the Government of Israel, 31 January 1993; Rabin E., *Ha'aretz*, 1 February 1993; Hoffman D., *Washington Post*, 1 February 1993; Miller J., *New York Times*, 17 February 1993

140. Miller J., *New York Times*, 17 February 1993

141. Yaari E., *New York Times*, 27 January 1993; Miller J., *New York Times*, 17 February 1993

142. *Rose al-Yussuf*, 24 April 1989; Sheikh Dr. Umar Abd-al-Rahman interviewed by Adil al-Sanhuri, *Al-Anba'*, 13 April 1989; al-Jubayli Ahmad, *Al-Wafd*, 8 April 1989; AFP, 8 April 1989; MENA, 9 April 1989; Voice of the Oppressed, 14 April 1989; AFP, 14 April 1989; al-Jubayli Ahmad, *Al-Wafd*, 15 April 1989; Abd al-Qadir Abd al-Wahid, *Al-Ahram*, 15 April 1989; AFP, 17 April 1989; Ahmad Fikriyah and al-Jubayli Ahmad, *Al-Wafd*, 17 April 1989; AFP, 18 April 1989; al-Tarabishi Mustafa, *Al-Ahram*, 5 June 1989; Abdallah Ahmad, *Al-Sha'b*, 5 September 1989

143. Hilmi Majdi, *Al-Wafd*, 26 April 1989; Hilmi Majdi, *Al-Wafd*, 27 April 1989; MENA, 30 April 1989

144. Radio Free Lebanon, 14 July 1989; Radio Beirut, 15 July 1989; AFP, 11 July 1989

145. Voice of the Oppressed, 8 August 1989

146. *Al-Sha'b*, 8 August 1989; al-Qammash Ali, *Al-Sha'b*, 25 July 1989

147. Hilmi Majdi, *Al-Wafd*, 12 August 1989; Radio Monte Carlo, 12 August 1989

148. *Al-Wafd*, 13 August 1989; Abdallah Ahmad, *Al-Sha'b*, 5 September 1989

149. Tantawi Hisham, *Al-Watan*, 23 February 1989

150. Jabar Karam, *Rose al-Yussuf*, 5 November 1990

151. MENA, 30 October 1990; Jabar Karam, *Rose al-Yussuf*, 5 November 1990

152. Jabar Karam, *Rose al-Yussuf*, 5 November 1990

153. Tantawi Hisham, *Al-Watan*, 23 February 1989

154. *New York Times*, 16 December 1990; *Ha'aretz*, 17 December 1990

155. Jabar Karam, *Rose al-Yussuf*, 5 November 1990

156. *Al-Jumhuriyah*, 2 August 1992; Husayn Tariq, *Rose al-Yusuf*, 10 February 1992

157. *Al-Wafd*, 3 November 1991; *Akhbar al-Jumhuriyah*, 9 November 1991; MENA, 9 November 1991

158. Rizq Hamdi, *Rose al-Yusuf*, 10 August 1992

159. Al-Ahram Press Agency, 12 December 1992

160. *Al-Watan al-Arabi*, 4 December 1992

161. Al-Kinani Ahmad, *Al-Sha'b*, 4 August 1992

162. Al-Ahram Press Agency, 23 December 1992; *Al-Ahram*, 24 December 1992

163. *Al-Ahram Weekly*, 4-10 February 1993

164. Siblah Majdi, *Al-Musawwar*, 4 December 1992

165. Al-Ahram Press Agency, 23 December 1992; *Al-Ahram*, 24 December 1992

166. Abd-al-Latif Najwan, *Al-Musawwar*, 4 December 1992

167. *Rose al-Yusuf*, 22 June 1992; *Al-Ahram*, 17 June 1992

168. Hasanayn Abduh, *Al-Wafd*, 16 November 1992

169. Hasanayn Abduh, *Al-Wafd*, 21 November 1992

170. *Misr al-Fatah*, 23 November 1992

171. Hasanayn Abduh, *Al-Wafd*, 21 November 1992

172. *Al-Jumhuriyah*, 2 August 1992; Husayn Tariq, *Rose al-Yusuf*, 10 February 1992; *Al-Watan al-Arabi*, 6 November 1992; *Al-Watan al-Arabi*, 4 December 1992; *Al-Wasat*, 14-20 December 1992

173. *Al-Wasat*, 14-20 December 1992

174. *Al-Hayah*, 12 December 1992

175. *Al-Ahram Weekly*, 4-10 February 1993 176. Yunus Jamal, *Al-Wafd*, 15 February 1993

177. Manor H., *Ma'ariv*, 10 April 1992; Frank A., *Newark Star-Ledger*, 19 December 1985

178. AP, 5 November 1990

179. Shamir Sh., *Ha'aretz*, 12 November 1990; Chang D., *Daily News*, 5 March 1993

180. Kifner J., *New York Times*, 7 November 1990; *New York Post*, 7 November 1990; *New York City Tribune*, 8 November 1990; Kifner J., *New York Times*, 9 November 1990; *New York City Tribune*, 9 November 1990; Avni B., *Ha'aretz*, 9 November 1990; Hedges C., *New York Times*, 13 November 1990; *New York Times*, 21 November 1990; McKinley J.C. Jr., *New York Times*, 1 December 1990; Kifner J., *New York Times*, 11 December 1990

181. *New York City Tribune*, 8 November 1990; Hedges C., *New York Times*, 13 November 1990; Shamir Sh., *Ha'aretz*, 14 November 1990; Frank A., *Newark Star-Ledger*, 19 December 1985

182. *New York Times*, 1 December 1990

183. *New York Post*, 5 March 1993

184. Waldman P., *Wall Street Journal*, 6 January 1993; Juffe M., *New York Post*, 5 March 1993; Marzulli J. & Sheridan D., *Daily News*, 5 March 1993

185. AP, 15 March 1993; Reuters, 13 March 1993

186. Kleinfield N.R., *New York Times*, 6 March 1993

187. *Al-Jumhuriyah*, 2 August 1992; Husayn Tariq, *Rose al-Yusuf*, 10 February 1992; *Al-Watan al-Arabi*, 6 November 1992; *Al-Watan al-Arabi*, 4 December 1992; *Al-Wasat*, 14-20 December 1992

188. Rizq Hamdi, *Rose al-Yusuf*, 10 August 1992

189. Mitchell A., *New York Times*, 9 March 1993

190. Reuters, 5 March 1993; Blumenthal R., *New York Times*, 7 March 1993; McFadden R.D., *New York Times*, 6 March 1993; *New York Post*, 6 March 1993; *New York Post*, 5 March 1993

191. Blumenthal R., *New York Times*, 11 March 1993; Blumenthal R., *New York Times*, 12 March 1993; Behr P., *Washington Post*, 12 March 1993; AP, 15 March 1993; Reuters, 13 March 1993

192. Hedges C., *New York Times*, 8 March 1993

193. Zarai O., *Ha'aretz*, 31 July 1986; 'Afghans', *Al-Wasat*, 13 July 1992

194. *New York Times*, 5 March 1993; Kleinfield N.R., *New York Times*, 6 March 1993; McFadden R.D., *New York Times*, 6 March 1993; Hedges C., *New York Times*, 8 March 1993; *New York Post*, 8 March 1993

195. Kleinfield N.R., *New York Times*, 6 March 1993; Broderick D., *New York Post*, 5 March 1993; *New York Times*, 5 March 1993

196. Mitchell A., *New York Times*, 11 March 1993; *New York Times*, 14 March 1993

197. Blumenthal R., *New York Times*, 12 March 1993

198. *Al-Hayah*, 12 December 1992

199. AP, 3 March 1993; Blumenthal R., *New York Times*, 10 March 1993

200. AFP, 4 March 1993

201. *Al-Watan al-Arabi*, 19 February 1993; Rabin E., *Ha'aretz*, 18 February 1993; *Al-Watan al-Arabi*, 12 February 1993; Material provided by Iranian sources

202. Treaster J.B., *New York Times*, 11 March 1993; McFadden R.D., *New York Times*, 6 March 1993; Capeci J. & O'Shaughnessy P., *Daily News*, 7 March 1993; Blumenthal R., *New York Times*, 2 March 1993; McFadden R.D., *New York Times*, 1 March 1993; Blumenthal R., *New York Times*, 6 March 1993; Blumenthal R., *New York Times*, 3 March 1993

203. Treaster J.B., *New York Times*, 8 March 1993

204. Reuters, 5 March 1993

205. Juffe M., *New York Post*, 5 March 1993

206. Kleinfield N.R., *New York Times*, 6 March 1993

207. *New York Times*, 5 March 1993

208. Treaster J.B., *New York Times*, 11 March 1993; Tabor M.B. *New York Times*, 26 March 1993

209. AP, 3 March 1993; *Newsday*, 3 March 1993
210. AP, 13 March 1993; *Newsday*, 13 March 1993; Mitchell A., *New York Times*, 14 March 1993; *Newsday*, 14 March 1993; AP, 15 March 1993; Gibson D., *The Record*, 17 March 1993; Carley W.M., *Wall Street Journal*, 17 March 1993
211. AP, 26 February 1993; Reuters, 26 February 1993; AP, 27 February 1993; Reuters, 27 February 1993
212. Reuters, 27 February 1993; *New York Times*, 27 February 1993; Carley W.M., *Wall Street Journal*, 1 March 1993
213. Radio Tehran, 26 February 1993; IRNA, 26 February 1993; Reuters, 26 February 1993
214. AP, 26 February 1993; Reuters, 26 February 1993
215. AP, 27 February 1993
216. *New York Times*, 5 March 1993; *Daily News*, 5 March 1993; AP, 3 March 1993; *Newsday*, 3 March 1993
217. *New York Post*, 5 March 1993
218. *Time*, 15 March 1993
219. McAlary M., *Daily News*, 5 March 1993
220. *New York Post*, 6 March 1993; Capeci J. & O'Shaughnessy P., *Daily News*, 7 March 1993
221. Gibson D., *The Record*, 17 March 1993; Carley W. M., *Wall Street Journal*, 17 March 1993; Blumenthal R., *New York Times*, 18 March 1993; *New York Times*, 21 March 1993
222. AP, 27 February 1993
223. Reuters, 5 March 1993
224. Blumenthal R., *New York Times*, 10 March 1993
225. Dan U., *New York POst*, 8 March 1993; Blumenthal R., *New York Times*, 10 March 1993
226. Blumenthal R., *New York Times*, 9 March 1993
227. *Al-Quds al-Arabi*, 1 March 1993
228. Sam'an George, *Al-Hayah*, 6 March 1993
229. *Al-Sharq al-Awsat*, 6 March 1993; *Al-Fajr*, 8 March 1993
230. Reuters, 28 February 1993
231. Radio Tehran, 6 March 1993; IRNA, 6 March 1993; Iranian TV, 6 March 1993; Radio Tehran, 7 March 1993; Iranian TV, 7 March 1993; IRNA, 7 March 1993
232. *Tehran Times*, 8 March 1993; IRNA, 8 March 1993
233. *Salam*, 8 March 1993; IRNA, 8 March 1993
234. Awdah Awdah, *Al-Ra'y*, 8 March 1993
235. IRNA, 10 March 1993; Radio Tehran, 10 March 1993; Reuters, 10 March 1993
236. *Salam*, 10 March 1993
237. Reuters, 11 March 1993

CONCLUSION

1. Soudan F., *Jeune Afrique*, 11-17 March 1993
2. *The Times*, 4 March 1987
3. *Al-Ahd*, 4 March 1988
4. IRNA, 18 July 1990
5. IRNA, 20 October 1991; Reuter, 20 October 1991
6.   *Jomhuri-ye Islami*, 9 February 1992
7. *Ettela'at*, 28 January 1993
8. *Ettela'at*, 28 January 1993
9. Reza'iyan Majid, *Kayhan*, 24 January 1993
10. *Ettela'at*, 13 February 1993
11. Badamachian Asadollah, *Resalat*, 3 March 1993
12. Azizi Ahmad, *Ettela'at*, 7 March 1993
13. Badamachian Asadollah, *Resalat*, 3 March 1993
14. Azizi Ahmad, *Ettela'at*, 7 March 1993
15. Reuters, 15 March 1993; *Al-Anwar*, 16 March 1993
16. Radio Tehran, 18 March 1993; IRNA, 18 March 1993; Reuters, 18 March 1993
17. Radio Tehran, 19 March 1993; IRNA, 19 March 1993; Reuters, 19 March 1993
18. Ladki Nadim, Reuters, 19 March 1993

Inform Yourself About Your Politicians Through S.P.I. Books